S0-AIO-490

Men, Women, and Issues in American History

VOLUME I

The Dorsey Series in History

Men, Women, and Issues in American History

VOLUME I

Edited by

HOWARD H. QUINT

MILTON CANTOR
Both of the
University of Massachusetts

Revised Edition   *1980*

 The Dorsey Press
Homewood, Illinois   60430

Irwin-Dorsey Limited   Georgetown, Ontario   L7G 4B3

© THE DORSEY PRESS, 1975 and 1980

All rights reserved. No part of this publication may be
reproduced, stored in a retrieval system, or transmitted,
in any form or by any means, electronic, mechanical,
photocopying, recording, or otherwise, without the prior
written permission of the publisher.

ISBN 0-256-02311-5
Library of Congress Catalog Card No. 79–56088

Printed in the United States of America

1 2 3 4 5 6 7 8 9 0 ML 7 6 5 4 3 2 1 0

LEARNING SYSTEMS COMPANY—
a division of Richard D. Irwin, Inc.—has developed a
PROGRAMMED LEARNING AID
to accompany texts in this subject area.
Copies can be purchased through your bookstore
or by writing PLAIDS.
1818 Ridge Road, Homewood, Illinois 60430.

For our sons and daughters
—scholars all—
May they have inherited our strengths,
not our shortcomings.

Janet and David Quint

David, Elisabeth, and Daniel Cantor

Introduction

College and university undergraduates are often as interested in the characters on the stage of history as in the historical process itself. For more than anything else it is the dramatis personae who bring history alive and make it not only the record of what men and women have thought and done but, in most instances, an exciting story in itself. Many are the students unfortunately who find history uninstructive and irrelevant, but rare are these same students who do not find themselves absorbed by historical biography, particularly when it presents people as they were and not what mythologizers have made them.

The essays in these volumes seek to place individual men and women within the context of their age, and, at the same time, to explore what contributions—political, economic, social, or intellectual—they have made to their society. In attempting to understand their values and goals, it is essential to understand those forces that shaped them; namely, family traditions and background, friendships which influenced them, religious and educational attachments which had an impact, economic commitments to which they may have been devoted, the social class to which they were seamlessly wedded, the changing historical circumstances that formed the backdrop against which they played out their lives. Knowing this congeries of attitudes and events, we know the men and women themselves; and, knowing them, we throw a spotlight on the society itself and the historical period that bounded their time on earth.

Contributors to these volumes include men and women of all academic ranks, from professors emeriti to assistant professors, as well as the distinguished former director of the Folger Library. They come from private and tax-supported colleges and universities and without exception are highly respected for their work in the fields of American history and American studies. They represent a wide spectrum of viewpoints, though on the whole we should have to say that their approach is essentially in the so-called Whig tradition of historical writing that has been the dominant one in this country. In the planning stage for *Men, Women, and Issues in American History,* the editors suggested a general format for the organization of the individual essays, but the reader will quickly realize that it has not been followed in all instances. We have accepted the departures because we endorse Carl Becker's dictum that every man must be his own historian and because we believe that every historian must organize the ideas presented in the manner most satisfactory to himself or herself.

The editors wish to acknowledge here, with appreciation, the assistance given them in various ways, large and small, by their colleagues in the Department of History at the University of Massachusetts/Amherst. Equally, they want to express publicly and thus for the record their gratitude for the secretarial help of Mary Reddington, Sandra Mailho, Susan West, Barbara Einfurer, and Jane Marino.

February 1980   HOWARD H. QUINT
                                                   MILTON CANTOR

Contents

1

English Civilization
Transplanted in the New World

JOHN SMITH
JOHN WINTHROP
WILLIAM PENN

by Max Savelle
University of Washington

America was built by individual men and women. Many who first came to America were laborers, the workers who built its farms, docks, ships, and cities; others were architects, the master builders. The three greatest architects of this people—three of the most creative individual society-builders of 17th-century America—were John Smith, John Winthrop, and William Penn. Smith personified the pragmatic factor of English colonization, Winthrop the religious, and Penn the humanitarian.

* * *

Before them lay America, a continent to conquer and to occupy, a homeland yet to be created. Little did they imagine the magnitude of the task, or the historical significance of the enterprise upon which they were embarked. The three small ships, *Susan Constant, Discovery,* and *Godspeed,* sailed into the placid waters of Chesapeake Bay on April 21, 1607. In all, the colonists numbered a few more than one hundred souls, of whom 59 were "gentlemen" who were allergic to hard work.

One of the ships, probably the *Susan Constant,* carried a prisoner, a man who would one day become the leader and saviour of the colony—who would, indeed, emerge as one of the most significant leaders of that generation of English colonizers and imperialists—Captain John Smith.

1

John Smith was a member of the first generation that included Humphrey Gilbert, Walter Raleigh, Richard Hakluyt, Samuel Purchas, John Popham, Francis Drake, Thomas Smythe, Ferdinando Gorges, Edwin Sandys, Francis Bacon, and a host of others. In his philosophy of English imperialism, Smith was a disciple of Richard Hakluyt and a friend of Samuel Purchas. But as a man of action, fitting the end to the philosophy, he was his own man, a loner. Smith's impact upon Elizabethan expansion was crucial, although generally underestimated.

Smith was a man of action at the time that he mounted the stage of history in Virginia. He had narrowly escaped hanging for "insubordination" and "conspiracy" during a stopover of the fleet in the West Indies, and arrived at Jamestown still "detained" on board ship. But he came—it was discovered when the sealed instructions to the expedition from the London Company division of the Virginia Company were opened—as a member of the seven-man council that would govern the colony. The other council members were quarreling and intriguing among themselves—some of them against Smith—so the captain was not immediately admitted to full standing, despite the instructions. It was not long, however, before he came into his position and, in the second year (September 1608), he was elected president of that council, which meant, in effect, governor of the colony.

During the preceding year, Smith had already shown the pragmatic bent that made him the saviour of Virginia. He had managed to intimidate the Indians and had even succeeded in getting food from them. Now he purged the colony of its stagnation by making all the colonists, even the "gentlemen," work—with a stern order that "he who works not, eats not"—either in the production of food or in the preparation of commodities such as clapboard, cedar and cypress boards, sassafras, and other items that could be profitably shipped home to the Company. While the colonists were busy, Smith the explorer and anthropologist had also been at work. He mapped Chesapeake Bay and its tributaries as well as the distribution of the region's Indian tribes, an enterprise that resulted in the first of his famous maps, "The Map of Virgina."

John Smith returned to England, suffering from a gunpowder burn, in the fall of 1609. Thereafter, for several years, he lived in London in relative obscurity. But this was a period when he prepared his *Description of Virginia*, published (with his Map of Virginia) in 1612. These years, too, were filled with intense activity connected with the founding of the colonies in America; and we may be sure that he was moving about in the midst of it.

Smith next turned his attention to New England, and in March 1614 he commanded an expedition financed by Marmaduke Rawdon and his associates for "North Virginia." He was now instructed to search for mines of gold and copper as well as to hunt for whales—or, as a last resort, to obtain a cargo of fish or to trade with the Indians for furs. A purely speculative voyage, in the end it did not pay expenses.

Smith, meanwhile, was really thinking of more farsighted and scientific matters. While his crewmen hunted for gold they were not to find, pursued whales that would not be caught, and fished for cod that somehow failed to fill the ship's hold, Smith himself explored the coast of "North Virginia." Inspired by the French name for Canada, "New France," he now dubbed the region south of it "New England," a name that stuck. While exploring and trading for furs, he also formulated plans for a colony. This was his true love.

Once more, Smith the colonizer dominated Smith the commercial captain. His enthusiastic description of New England won the support of some members of the moribund "North Virginia Company," notably Sir Ferdinando Gorges and Sir John Popham, and he managed to scrape together enough capital for yet another expedition. Two ships, with the 17 men who actually were to found the colony, set out in the spring of 1615; the site of the colony would be chosen after the ships made landfall. Unhappily, while one ship sailed quickly to New England, the larger vessel—on which Smith was sailing—had to turn back because it was unseaworthy. Another ship was equipped and departed on June 24, 1615. But Smith's "bad hap by sea" still pursued him: he was caught by pirates, first English, who found his ship not worth capturing, then French, who also found little to take from him. While aboard the French vessel his own sailed off and returned to England.

It was while "marooned" on the French ship that Smith wrote *A Description of New England,* one of his most famous books. The French pirate—or privateer—the Sieur du Poiron, detained Smith for a number of weeks, during which time the Frenchman took several English, Portuguese, and other vessels. Smith was finally allowed to go to France on board a Portuguese caravel that Poiron had captured. Then, after a series of typically fantastic adventures, he eventually returned to England. Apparently he did not arrive penniless, because he seems to have received a share of the loot from the Portuguese caravel and financial assistance from a French lady of Rochelle (Smith, always a bachelor, was saved or dramatically assisted by high-born ladies—including Pocahontas—on an astonishing number of occasions).

John Smith still possessed a burning desire to push forward the expansion of the English empire in America. He would, however, never return to the colonies. He is properly thought of as a man of action and as a pragmatist, and his chief ambition was to build colonies but, paradoxically, his only experience with actual settlements was his relatively brief but significant career as the dominating spirit in the planting and the saving of Virginia. His really great contribution to the history of the founding of the British empire in America was intellectual. It was the contribution of a writer, a promoter, a thinker, a philosopher of imperialism.

John Smith began his career as a publicist for colonization with the publication of *A True Relation of such occurrences and accidents of noate as hath happened in Virginia . . .* , in 1608, while he was still in that colony. At least a half dozen books followed—on Indians, geography, settlements—all contributing to the literature of English colonial imperialism. His final book, *Advertisements for the unexperienced Planters of New England, or anywhere,* was published in 1631 and was a series of practical suggestions for colonizers and colonists. By this time the foundations of the English empire in America had been laid—in Virginia, in New England, and in the Caribbean area. It must have been a matter of great satisfaction to Smith, in the last year of his life, to contemplate this great event and his part in it.

For John Smith, colonizing was not to be entered upon lightly: "It is not a worke for every one to manage such an affaire, as make a discovery and plant a Colony, it requires all the best parts of art, judgment, courage, honesty, constancy, diligence, and industry, to do but neere well; some are more proper for one thing than another, and therein best to be imploied: and nothing breeds more confusion then misplacing and misimploying men in their undertakings." Yet it is a noble work; for "truly there is no pleasure comparable [to the creation of new societies] to a generous spirit; . . . to see daily new Countries, people, fashions, governments, strategems; [to] releeve the oppressed, comfort his friends, passe miseries, subdue enemies, adventure upon any feazable danger for God and his Country." But knowledge of the new land, and a realization of the problems to be faced could be acquired only by actual observation and experience. So many expeditions failed, he said, because of the imperfect knowledge and inadequate experience of the "home-bred adventurers" who started out ignorant of the nature of the land to which they were going and unprepared for the hardships and the problems they would meet.

Smith's pragmatic recommendations for the founding of colonies were based upon solid geographic descriptions, survey of the terrain and, most important of all, his two famous maps. He spent much time while in Virginia exploring and surveying Chesapeake Bay and its tributaries. Along with his *Map of Virginia* Smith published a description of the flora and the fauna of the country. He was especially interested, of course, in those products such as cedar, oak and walnut, woods for clapboards, sassafras and skins, that might profitably be exported to England, but he also displayed a sharp and curious eye for plants such as the chinquapin and animals such as the opossum that were peculiar to America.

Similarly, after exploring the coasts of New England, he published his equally famous *Map of New England,* the place-names on which, according to Smith, were designated by Prince Charles of England (later King Charles I). On this map, however, he omitted the names of the Indian tribes, since he never made any extended overland exploration of the region, and in his *Description of New England* he mentions them only briefly. As always, the geographer Smith was more interested in the merchantable products of the country—magnificent forests for masts, yards, lumber, and naval stores, furs to be had of the Indians, salt, whales, fruits, wild animals and, above all, many kinds of fish, the most important of which was cod. He hoped there were mines of copper, iron, gold and silver, but as a realist he could not promise them. "I need not despaire but that there are metals in the Country; but I am no alcumist, nor will promise more then I know. . . ." He was nothing if not a realist. "Yet when the foundation is laid . . . , and a common-wealth established, then such there may better be constrained to labour than here [in England]. But to rectifie a common-wealth with debaushed people is impossible, and no wise man would throw himselfe into such a society, that intends honestly, and knowes what he undertakes. For there is no country to pillage as the Romans found: all you expect from thence must be by labour."

Government in the New World should be in the hands of one strong man, a tough but benevolent dictator. Smith cited Cortez, Pizarro, and other great leaders; he was obviously thinking of himself, and the manner in which he had saved Virginia, as the successful colonial director and the perfect type of leader.

Smith was an integral part of the great economic expansion of England, and he knew and encouraged the economic motives of the merchants, the land speculators, and the common people who provided the brawn and sinew of the movement. But it seems clear that although he was certain, in his own mind, of the colonies' golden economic future, and although this conviction was the basis of his appeal to the merchant supporters of colonizing enterprises, his own interest in colonization was not primarily economic. Rather it was a vision of expanding the glory, might, and welfare of England and its people.

To be sure, the capitalists who funded the movement of people to the New World would, and should, Smith thought, receive a profit on their enterprises. Indeed, in one sense, colonies were commercial ventures; not only would the merchants profit but England itself would become richer and more powerful in the international balance of power. The ultimate basis of profit was commerce: for "there is nothing more inricheth a Common-wealth than much trade, nor no meanes better to increase than small [low] custome [duties] as *Holland, Genua, Ligorne,* and divers other places can well tell you; and doth most beggar those places where they take most [highest] custome [duties]. . . ."

Once the process of peopling the empty spaces of the world was started, Smith believed, those who actually went overseas would find there a better life than they knew in England. "Who can desire more content that hath small meanes," he says, "or but onely his merit to advance his fortunes, than to tread and plant that ground he hath purchased by the hazard of his life; if he have but the taste of vertue and magnanimity, what to such a minde can bee more pleasant than planting and building a foundation for his posterity, got from the rude earth by Gods blessing and his owne industry without prejudice to any; . . . what so truly su[i]tes with honour and honesty, as the discovering things unknowne, creating Townes, peopling Countries, informing the ignorant, reforming things unjust, teaching vertue [,] and gaine to our native mother Country a Kingdome to attend her, find imploiment for those that are idle, because they know not what to doe. . . ." What could be more exciting, more exhilarating than participating in, even dominating, the great events taking place in the course of westward expansion? John Smith knew what was going on; if ever there was a man with a sense of the movement of history, he was that man.

And what of the inhabitants of the countries John Smith described— the Indians—the "salvages"? Here Smith the geographer became Smith the anthropologist. To be sure, his references to Indians were skimpy in his accounts of New England. By contrast, his Virginia studies were extensive, careful, and thoroughgoing. In them, he estimated the Indian population and described their tribal divisions, government, methods of making war, clothing—if any, personal ornamentations, lodgings, agriculture, family life, hunting and fishing methods, mores, and music (made with drums, rattles, pumpkin shells, in bass, tenor, counter-tenor, meane, and treble). "These mingled with their voices sometimes 20 or 30 together, make such a terrible noise as would rather affright than delight any man." He describes their dancing, their medicine, and their religion, including child sacrifice. "But their chiefe God is the Divell. Him they call *Oke* and serve him more of feare than love."

The "salvages," he says, are strong and tough, inured to the most rigorous physical hardship, and possessing a knowledge of wood-lore that made for survival in the most desperate circumstances. But "they are inconstant in every thing, but what feare constraineth them to keepe. Craftie, timerous, quicke of apprehension, and very ingenuous. Some are of disposition fearefull, some bold, most cautelous [cautious], all Savage. Generally covetous of Copper, Beads, and such like trash. They are soon moved to anger, and so malicious, that they seldome forget an injury: they seldom steal from one another, least their conjurers [magicians] should reveale it, and so they be pursued and punished. That they are thus feared is certaine, but that any can reveale their offences by conjuration I am doubtfull."

As for Indian relations with whites, Smith was convinced that the vast culture-gap between the two peoples was unbridgeable; the Indians could never be won over by love. They were too inherently savage. They could be subjugated, however, and should be; eventually they would become a valuable labor force for the English.

Smith's descriptions constitute one of the most valuable early accounts of the Indians as they were when the white men came. But these descriptions are more: they also indicate a comprehension of the larger imperial problem of the relations of an expanding empire with native peoples.

In *The True Travels, Adventures, and Observations of Captaine John Smith* (published in 1630), he recognized that Englishmen had founded colonies in the West Indies. Thus the British empire now included three groups of colonies in America, all of which were by this time proving their value both to the motherland and to the settlers. The three, especially New England and Virginia, were interdependent, "and to those of *New England* may it not be a great comfort to have so neare a neighbour of their own Nation, that may furnish them with their spare cattell, swine, poultry, and other roots and fruits, much better than from *England*." There should never exist any envy between the two colonies, for it was always intended that they would complement each other. "Now when these shall have laid the foundations, and provided means beforehand; they may entertain all the poore artificers and laborers in *England*, and their families which are burthensome to their Parishes and Countries [counties] where they live upon almes and benevolence for want of worke.... For there is vast [waste] land enough for all the people in *England, Scotland*, and *Ireland*: and it seems God hath provided this Country [New England] for our Nation, destroying the natives by the plague...."

Smith's knowledge of the West Indies was secondhand, and he always thought of Virginia and New England as his two "children." Nonetheless, he regarded the island colonies as indispensable to the English empire.

Underlying and permeating all of John Smith's thinking about colonization in America was a concept of manifest destiny inherent in the westward spread of peoples. "For God did make the would to be inhabited with mankind, and to have his name knowne to all Nations, and from generation to generation: as the people increased they dispersed themselves into such Countries as they found most convenient. And here in *Florida, Virginia, New-England*, and *Cannada*, is more land than all the people in Christendome can manure [cultivate], and yet more to spare than all the natives of those Countries can use and culturate. And shall we keep such a cayle [hassle] for land, and at such great rents and rates [in England] when there is so much of the world uninhabited, and as much more in other places, and as good or rather better than any wee possesse, were it manured and used accordingly."

Adam and Eve began it, and Noah continued it. Many peoples contributed to the spread of humanity—Hebrews, Greeks, Romans, and others. The *"Portugals* and *Spaniards"* led the way to America. Their achievements revealed, by contrast, the "idlenesse and ingratitude" of the English, "and neglect of our duty and religion we owe our God, our King, and Countrey, and want of charity to those poore Salvages, whose Countries we challenge, use, and possesse . . . , Where we doubt not but by Gods gracious assistance, and the adventurers willing minds and speedie furtherance to so honorable an action, in after times to see our Nation enjoy a Country, not onely exceeding pleasant for habitation, but also very profitable for commerce in generall; no doubt pleasing to almightie God, honourable to our gracious Soveraigne, and commodious generally to the whole Kingdome." England had both a right and duty to colonize America as a part of God's plan for peopling the Earth.

This was written of Virginia in 1608. But it was typical of John Smith throughout his career; he might as well have been describing the young three-part empire in 1631, the last year of his life. The founding of this empire was a national enterprise: it redounded, under God, to the benefit of the Nation, the King, and the whole people. "For my part," said Smith, "I cannot chuse but grieve, that the actions of an Englishman should be inferior to any, and that the command of England should not be as great as any Monarchy that ever was since the world began, I mean not as a Tyrant to torment all Christendome, but to suppress her disturbers, and conquer her enemies."

John Smith was one of the greatest voices of Elizabethan-Jacobean imperialism. He was a pragmatist, a colony builder, a propagandist, a promoter. But he was also a statesman, with a vision of a wider, more powerful empire and of a new English people in America. His ideas were not exactly original, but he seems to have been more a nationalist than most, more a conscious imperialist, more a man of action. He seems to have caught a clearer vision than many of his contemporaries of the potential splendor promised by the new English nation in the western world. As one of the Jacobean poets wrote, of the three little ships,

> Let England knowe our willingnesse,
>   for that our work is good,
> We hope to plant a Nation,
>   where none before hath stood.

*   *   *

Somewhere on the Atlantic, on board the good ship *Arbella,* Master John Winthrop addressed his fellow-passengers thus: "Wee are a Company professing our selves fellow members of Christ, wee ought to account our selves knitt by this bond of love, and live in the experience of it . . . for the worke wee have in hand, it is by a mutuall consent through a speciall overruleing providence, . . . to seeke out a place of Cohabitation and Consorteshipp under a due forme of Government both civill and ecclesiasticall . . . for wee must Consider that wee shall be as a Citty upon a Hill, the eies of all people are uppon us. . . ." A true expression of the spirit of the settlement of Massachusetts, this remark set the tone of the history of New England for a century or more. It was quite unlike the pragmatism of Captain John Smith and introduced a new and different factor—that of religion—into the formation of the American nation.

John Winthrop was a leading stockholder in the Massachusetts Bay Company, a corporation formed by a group of merchants and landed "gentry" with Puritan convictions. The Company received its charter in March 1629. A week later Charles I dissolved Parliament, not calling it again for nearly twelve years. Political, ideological, and religious persecution was abroad in England. The Puritans were frightened—and not on the score of repression alone. Young people, including John Winthrop's own two sons, were falling into worldly, even dissolute ways. For the Puritans, English society appeared to be falling into a slough of sin. Surely it was high time to consider snatching the Puritans' families out of this miasma of moral and social degeneration into the cleaner, purer "wilderness" of America.

John Winthrop certainly considered it. As he wrote his wife Margaret in May 1629, "I am very persuaded, God will bringe some heavye Affliction upon this lande [of England], and that speedylye: but be of good Comfort. . . . If the Lord seeth it wilbe good for us, he will provide a shelter & a hidinge place for us & others. . . ." Whatever happened, he would place himself entirely under the guidance of God.

But that was not all. As the possibility grew in his mind, he systematically and carefully weighed the pros and cons. "This lande growes wearye of her Inhabitantes"; life is vile and base, children and friends are only burdens, not blessings. Living is so expensive and luxurious that it is impossible for a man to exist on honest wages or "keepe sayle with his equalls" (that is, in modern terms, "keep up with the Joneses"). By contrast, the world in America is wide open for occupation, neither crowded nor corrupted. Why should a man fight to own and wrest a living from one acre of land in England when he can have hundreds of acres there just for the taking? Finally, would it not be wise and worthy in God's eyes to lead an infant church of Puritans into the wilderness to grow and flourish there? Surely it was preferable to facing the harsh oppression and destruction of this church by the juggernaut of state and church in England. He would go: he would sell his home; he would answer God's calling; he would lead his people to America.

Now here he was, with a thousand people following him, and he had set the tone for their subsequent history, a tone of high commitment to an intensely religious, intensely idealistic migration. The colonizers paused at Salem and, after looking around for the best place to settle, went on to Shawmut Peninsula where they founded Boston. Here they began their religion-infused society, one step toward the redemption of the world.

From Boston as a hub the colonists spread out upon the land. The communities they built were modeled largely upon those in England. Each town was also a church congregation, received a patent from the General Court, and in turn parceled out land to its members. Winthrop, the Governor, remained in Boston, but the settlers carried with them into their new communities his high dedication to the purpose of founding societies based upon covenants: the bonding force of the covenants was Christian love.

The merchants of Boston and Salem built ships and began a trade that radiated outward like the spokes of a wheel. They furnished manufactured goods to the inland towns; they sent schooners out on the fishing banks and brought back fish for themselves as well as for export to Virginia and the West Indies; and they soon were exporting fish to England itself and to Spain and Portugal as well. Already, in 1630, within a year of his arrival, Winthrop had had built the 30-ton bark, *The Blessing of the Bay,* which he dispatched to trade with the Indians and to carry furs to England.

After a while Margaret and her sons joined John Winthrop in Boston, and there they made a home they came to love. Margaret died in 1647 and John married again. His new wife, Martha Caytmore, presented him with another son, but he himself died on March 26, 1649, at the age of 60. Through 20 years he had led his people in the building of the "City upon a Hill," and he had been the most important single figure in this work.

If John Smith was a man of action and ideas, John Winthrop was a man of ideas and actions. With Winthrop, ideas came first. Above all, he was a theological-political philosopher, the first and surely the most important to appear on American shores before William Penn.

As he said in his "City upon a Hill" speech, the society—the body politic—was founded upon a social compact, a "covenant" among its members that bound them in Christian love. But this society had also a covenant or compact with God who would "expect a strickt performance of the Articles contained in it [our compact with Him]." Therefore, they must build the institutions of their "City" in such a way as to make sure that the covenant with God would be faithfully carried out.

But how? The Massachusetts Bay Company was a business corporation; its voting members or "freemen" were simply stockholders in the

Company. As the colony took shape, it was discovered that only about 15 stockholders were present, eight of whom were members of the governing council. By reason of sheer necessity this small group ran the colony for the first year or two; in 1631 it called a meeting of "all the freemen of the commons" (probably all or most of the male settlers) to take an oath of allegiance to the government, to ratify the work the council had thus far done, and to authorize the council to elect the governor. All of these were done.

But these people (each was now called "freeman," in the sense of "citizen") were not all stockholders of the Company. Nor, apparently, were they all committed to the ideal of the godly commonwealth envisaged by Winthrop and his fellow Puritans. If the "mission" were to continue to conduct itself according to the "Articles" of the covenant with God, it must be kept in the hands of the godly. For this reason, therefore, when the council undertook to expand the number of freemen with full voting rights in the company—now a commonwealth—it enacted that "noe man shalbe admitted to the freedome [citizenship] of this body politicke, but such as are members of some of the churches within the lymitts of the same." Religion and government were thus brought together in a single body of religious men. Their agreement to do so was a sort of "covenant" or social compact. By this act the Massachusetts Bay Company disappeared and the Commonwealth of Massachusetts was created. Also, the religious idea and the political institution were fused into one.

Step by step the General Court of the colony became a representative body; it separated the council from the assembly, thereby transforming the original one-house general court into a two-house legislature. It also adopted the "Massachusetts Body of Liberties" to govern the entire colony. These derived in part from English common law, in part from the Bible, and in part from the measures already passed by the General Court. By the mid-1640s the political structure had taken shape. John Winthrop took part at every step in its evolution, in the formulation of the ideology that rationalized its structure, and its ongoing relationship with the ideal of the city on a hill.

In the first place, as Winthrop had said in his *Arbella* discourse, God, in his wisdom, had "soe disposed The Condicion of Mankinde, as in all times some must be rich some poore, some highe and eminent in power and dignitie; others meane and in subjeccion." It was God's will that authority be vested in men who were "highe and eminent in power and dignitie." Once given authority, the magistrates were to be trusted to rule benevolently and wisely.

Massachusetts Bay, then, was a government by the Magistrates who were elected by the representatives of the church-member freemen of the commonwealth. The people elected these officials but, once chosen, their authority was unchallengeable. In 1645 Winthrop, then deputy-governor, was accused of exceeding his authority as a magistrate and was tried by the General Court. On his acquittal, he asked permission to make a "little speech" to the people explaining the relationship, as he saw it, between the people and their governors. This "little speech" is the classic explanation of the Puritan theory of government:

> The great questions that have troubled the country are about the authority of the magistrates and the liberty of the people. It is yourselves [the people] who have called us to this office [of magistrate], and being called by you, we have our authority of God, in way of an ordinance, such as hath the image of God eminently stamped upon it. . . . The covenant between you and us is the oath you have taken of us [made us take], which is to this purpose, that we shall govern you and judge your causes by the rules of God's laws and our own, according to our best skill. . . . For the other point concerning liberty, I observe a great mistake in the country about that. There is a twofold liberty, natural (I mean as our nature is now corrupt) and civil or federal. The first is common to man with beasts and other creatures . . . it is a liberty to evil as well as to good. [The exercise of this liberty leads to evil and to the degeneration of men into wild beasts.] The other kind of liberty I call civil or federal, it may also be termed moral, in reference to the covenant between God and man, in the moral law, and the politic covenants and constitutions, amongst men themselves. . . . This liberty is maintained and exercised in a way of subjection to authority; it is of the same kind of liberty wherewith Christ hath made us free. The woman's own choice makes such a man her husband; yet being so chosen, he is her lord, and she is to be subject to him; yet in a way of liberty, not of bondage; and a true wife accounts her subjection her honor and freedom, and would not think her condition safe and free, but in her subjection to her husband's authority. . . . [Complaint, resistance to government, rebellion, are all exercises of "Natural liberty" and, therefore, evil], but if you will be satisfied to enjoy such civil and lawful liberties, such as Christ allows you, then will you quietly and cheerfully submit unto that authority which is set over you, in all the administrations of it, for your good.

Winthrop's philosophy is clear: government is the product of a compact between the people and their rulers, who administer for the people. Magistrates are elected by the people, but once in office they are responsible to God: the people must trust them and obey them. Criticism, demands for reform, the very idea of governmental accountability, are contrary to the will of God in whose name government acts. Such actions are manifestations of the rankest, rowdiest, most reprehensible democracy. Winthrop was a benevolent, godly authoritarian; he was no democrat.

Such was the benevolently authoritarian godly state of the Puritans according to their foremost New World political philosopher. But the city-on-a-hill was not happy, despite its high political idealism. Within the first five years of its founding and for at least two decades afterward, the colony was torn by religious and political dissension. As an escape-hatch for dissenters from Anglicanism in England, Massachusetts had attracted a horde of strong-minded men and women, Puritans all, who disagreed, sometimes bitterly, among themselves and with Winthrop over the question of how the city-on-a-hill was to be built and administered. These radical dissenters caused trouble. Roger Williams, for example, criticized the colony for occupying land that rightfully belonged to the Indians, for its religious requirement for citizenship, for its intolerance, and for its continuing pretense that its religion was not and should not be "separated" from Anglicanism. Mistress Ann Hutchinson and her brother-in-law Reverend John Wheelwright and their followers struck at the very marrow of Puritan divinity by preaching the heretical doctrine that the Holy Ghost dwells in every man after his salvation, and that "good works" were not necessarily a sign of salvation. Samuel Gorton questioned the doctrine of the Trinity, denounced a "hireling ministry," and even denied the existence of heaven and hell. Finally, Dr. Robert Child petitioned for a presbyterian form of government and more religious toleration. All of these dissenters, and many others, in the 1630s and 1640s, tore at the seamless fabric of the model society that John Winthrop was giving his life to establish.

Winthrop and the Puritan establishment fought back; one after another all of these troublemakers were banished from the city-on-a-hill. Winthrop and his "orthodox" Puritan colleagues were explicitly and convincedly "intolerationists," determined to maintain the purity of their Puritan society against all the malignant disciples of the Devil who had the temerity to challenge it. In other words, anything that interfered with the work of God, and threatened to overthrow it, could never be tolerated. Intolerance of dissent was completely logical if one were convinced that the dissent was a threat to God's work. The ideal of service to which Winthrop subscribed could never be permitted to be destroyed by a Roger Williams, an Anne Hutchinson, a Samuel Gorton, or a Robert Child. This had ever been the justification of intolerance; it remained the basis for intolerance in Massachusetts and in America long after Winthrop's death. It was written into the rationalization of the Puritan state, just as later it was written into the life-style of the United States. Love existed within the city, to be sure; but not the slightest toleration for such dangerous divisions and putatively destructive doctrines.

Winthrop and his dominant group of Puritans did not come to America to establish religious freedom. Far from it: they came to establish a society based upon the truth as they saw it. Anyone who challenged that truth must stay away—or enter Massachusetts Bay at his peril.

Within the colony, then, the Puritan ideal of the exclusive, tribal city upon a hill had succeeded in establishing itself, though not without trial and trouble. Winthrop might very well have congratulated himself and his co-workers upon their success. But the Puritan state was a member commonwealth in the nascent English empire of which Captain John Smith was the prophet. What were, or should be, according to the political philosophy of the Puritans, the relationships of the new state with the parent state of England? The matter had to be confronted, for in 1634 the king created the "Commission for Foreign Plantations" to supervise colonial affairs. Moreover, this commission, headed by the Puritans' old arch-enemy, Archbishop William Laud, decided to call in all colonial patents and charters.

How should they meet this challenge? The colony decided to resist the order, and by force, if necessary. Under their charter they were empowered to govern themselves as a "body politicke"; they would have to defend their possessions; otherwise, as Winthrop says, it must be their policy "to avoid or protract." Avoid and protract they did, for the next three-quarters of a century, and the policy was successful. The question arose again in 1638, and Winthrop was commissioned to write to the commission. His letter—or petition—was evasive, to be sure, in that he took no step to return the charter; but it also contained something of Winthrop's view of the nature of the empire. We humbly profess, he says, "that we are ready to yield all due obedience to our Sovereign Lord the King's Majesty, and to your Lordships under him. . . . We came under the authority of the great seal of England; we transferred our families, our estates there, and we have enlarged His Majesty's dominions. If we were to lose our patent," he continued, "we should suffer much distress; and people here will think His Majesty has cast them off, and that hereby they are freed from their allegiance and subjection, and thereupon will be ready to confederate themselves under a new government, for their necessary safety and subsistence, which will be of dangerous example unto other plantations. . . ."

The most dramatic part of the remonstrance is Winthrop's bold suggestion that if the charter were recalled, the people of Massachusetts Bay would consider themselves absolved of their allegiance to Charles I and would be compelled to seek the protection of some other government, perhaps (by implication) that of France. What, in short, he was demanding was nothing less than internal sovereignty for Massachusetts. His conception of empire, albeit dimly perceived, was a federal empire composed of internally sovereign states under the king of England. Indeed, he anticipated the thinking of most American Whigs in the imperial crisis that preceded the American Revolution.

John Winthrop had little or no such anthropological interest in the Indians as characterized the writings of John Smith and William Penn.

Like other Puritans, he thought of the Indians as being of another nation, perhaps descendants of the ten lost tribes of Israel, with customs and institutions other than those of the English. But they were "benighted" heathens, largely dominated by the Devil and, therefore, fit subjects for conversion to the Puritan form of Christianity.

Winthrop's own concern with the Indians was chiefly political and economic and revolved around such issues as occupation and ownership of the land. Some of the colonists themselves—notably Roger Williams—questioned the right of the English to take land already occupied by the Indians. This problem had arisen even before the Puritans left England and it continued, with increasing intensity, to plague the relations with the Indians in the early years of settlement. Winthrop, with his legalistic mind, was led to try to find some rationalization—some legal justification—for the Puritan occupation. His search concluded with a quasi-legal concept that served as precedent for later Euro-American empires and for their relations with native peoples: that is, the doctrine of effective occupation, or, as he called it, the doctrine of *vacuum domicilium*. As Winthrop stated: "That [land] which lies common, and hath never been replenished or subdued is free to any that possesse and improve it." Indians have a natural right to occupy and use the land, but since they have not enclosed it (fenced it in, that is) or improved it, or cultivated it in any extensive way, they cannot be said effactually to occupy it. They have not established a "civil right" (a right under international law) to it. Such being the case, the English may occupy the land to which the Indians have not established a legal title. Finally, to cap the argument that the English are doing right in occupying the unoccupied land, it is evident that God intended them to do so, since "God hath consumed the Natives with a great Plauge [plague] in those partes, soe as there be few inhabitantes left."

The Indians were an ever-present factor—an external factor, to be sure—in the life and growth of the city-on-a-hill. They were a fearsome element, and some Puritans were more conscious than Winthrop of the reality of the vast culture-gap between the two peoples. But the Puritans were most careful to do the Indians justice as they (the Puritans) understood it. Winthrop, himself convinced of the applicability of the doctrine of *vacuum domicilium*, scrupulously adhered to it. There, by and large, his interest in the Indians ended.

John Winthrop, then, is to be seen as a political philosopher, but his political philosophy was a system of thought in the service of religion. People make government on the basis of a social compact, but once the government is established, it draws its inspiration from and is responsible to God, not the people. The people must obey. The government is absolute, in a sort of benevolent absolutism. Similarly, in Winthrop's gestating philosophy of the federal English empire, God's intent for the new society comes first; practical relationships follow.

Winthrop was educated at Cambridge and was a member of the Inner Temple. The formulations of his political convictions, however, arose out of specific, *de facto* situations, and were the religiously suffused and dictated responses to them. One might call his thinking "theological politics"; i.e., political ideas cast in a religious mould. It is for this, the religious coloration of political theory, that he is most significant in our early history.

*   *   *

When on October 28, 1682, William Penn stepped ashore from the ship *Welcome* at Newcastle on the Delaware, near his new city of Philadelphia, just then a-building, he came with the intention of creating a new society. Its chief characteristics, as he envisioned it, would be Christian love, religious freedom, and the rule of justice. He planned to spend the rest of his life there.

William Penn was a Quaker. Of the Quakers and of their doctrine of the "inner light" or "inner voice" he wrote that "We believe this gift of light and grace, through Jesus Christ, to be universal; and that there is not a man or woman upon earth that hath not a sufficient measure of this light, and to whom this grace hath not appeared, to reprove their ungodly works of darkness, and to lead them that obey it to eternal salvation." Here also was a universalism which, in contrast to the exclusive tribalism of the Puritans, embraced all men everywhere. His new society would be built upon this universal principle.

But Penn was much more than a Quaker. After all, the Quakers were a tiny minority sect in England and on the continent of Europe. Penn was deeply motivated by religion in everything that he did; but to exaggerate the place of religion in his career would be to distort his life and diminish his achievement. Penn trod the boards of a much broader stage. He was a world statesman, a political thinker, and a humanitarian whose purview included the whole human race. He would expand the burgeoning British empire; but he would also extend the benefits of his new society to all who emigrated, especially from the continent of Europe but, eventually, from all over the world as well. He expected to be a leader of many peoples and, incidentally, to make a lot of money.

Penn brought with him three now-famous documents that remain important to our understanding of the history of Pennsylvania, of the continuing growth of the Empire, of the later United States, and of Penn himself. These were his charter to the vast dominion given him by his friend Charles II in payment of a debt that the sovereign owed Penn's father, the Frame of Government (constitution) he had drafted for the province, and a body of laws he had drawn up for the colony while in England.

Penn's charter was an essentially feudal document illustrative of the feudal—or personal—relationship between king and subject. It made Penn and his heirs "the true and absolute Proprietaries." But there were also several modern touches. For example, the charter required that Penn make his laws "by and with the advice, assent and approbacon of the freeman [citizens] of the said countrey, ... or of their Delegates." Here was a recognition of the modern constitutional principle of representative government. He had to promise to enforce the English navigation laws, to maintain a permanent agent or attorney in England, and to allow appeals from his courts to the king. Taxation must be by the consent of the people; the king, for his part, promised never to tax the colony except by act of Parliament! Pennsylvanians would one day appeal to this document as the fundamental and inviolable charter of their right to govern themselves. This charter to Penn, binding Pennsylvania to England as it did, is one of the clearest links in a chain of institutional relationships then being forged confirming the federal compact view of the empire.

The "Frame of Government," the constitution for Penn's new state, was a clumsy affair, almost wholly unsuitable for efficient operation in a struggling frontier society. It was built on theory, sprung from the minds of Penn, Algernon Sidney, and probably John Locke as well as James Harrington. Because of its unwieldiness, it had to be revised again and again until Penn and his people finally devised the Charter of Privileges of 1701, which remained the constitution for the colony until the American Revolution.

But the philosophy of government that William Penn wrote into it was of dramatic and eternal significance. This philosophy voiced his humanism and his faith in the capacity of men to manage their political affairs. Thus we find Penn saying, in the preface to the Frame, "When the great and wise God had made the world, of all his creatures it pleased him to choose man his deputy to rule it; and to fit him for such a charge and trust, he did not only qualify him with skill and power, but with integrity to use them justly. ..." When men turned away from the voice of the divine law within them, an external law, or government, became necessary. As the apostle Paul stated, Penn continues, "The powers that be are ordained of God. Whosoever therefore resisteth the power, resisteth the ordinance of God. ... This settles the divine right of government beyond exception, and that for two ends; first, to terrify evil-doers; secondly, to cherish those that do well."

But government is of no fixed and inflexible nature. Thus, Penn declared, again in the preface, "I do not find a model in the world, that time, place, and some singular emergences have not necessarily altered; nor is it easy to frame a civil government, that shall serve all places alike. . . . Government, like clocks, go from the motion men give them, and as governments are made and moved by men, so by them they are ruined too. Wherefore governments rather depend upon men, than men upon governments. Let men be good, and the government cannot be bad; if it be ill, they will cure it. But if men be bad, let the government be never so good, they will endeavour to warp and spoil it to their turn." Penn meant what he said. Governments were made by men and for men; and they could change or improve it whenever and however they might wish. "He who thinks it to be an end, aims at a profit—to make a trade of it—but he who thinks it to be a means, understands the true end of Government."

How different was Penn's relativistic, flexible, humanistic concept of the state from the absolute, inflexible, authoritarian commonwealth of the Puritan John Winthrop!

Nowhere, probably, is Penn's humanitarianism more clearly manifest than in the laws he drew up for Pennsylvania while in England and which were then adopted (with additions) by the assembly itself. The very first chapter of the laws provided for complete religious freedom for all but atheists. Beyond that, in a day in which England had some 200 laws carrying the death penalty, Penn's laws reduced the number to two —treason and murder. In a day, too, when prisons were noisome dens of misery, filth, and vice, Penn's laws provided a radical measure of reform that anticipated the incipient prison reform of the Enlightenment. His laws also provided for divorce, and there were many measures dealing with morality (incest, sodomy, rape, bigamy, etc.) with the severe (to the modern mind) penalty of life imprisonment for second offenses. The selling of rum to the Indians was prohibited, and provision was made for public care of the indigent poor. The practice of "due process" was required in all cases, as was jury trial; but witnesses were required only to make a solemn promise to tell the truth, thus abolishing the oath, since Quakers could take no oaths.

The code of laws of Penn's new colony was surely the most humane code in effect in the entire western world at that time. After Penn's death, it became somewhat more severe, but he had introduced into American jurisprudence a body of law that was both humane and just, based upon the principle that the severity of punishment should be proportionate to the seriousness of the offense—an ideal that American jurisprudence has been working toward, if somewhat irregularly, ever since.

Seen against the background of Restoration England, William Penn was a radical worker for human freedom; his government and laws for Pennsylvania amply demonstrate the fact. But the most precious of all freedoms, for him, was the freedom to worship God as one thought best— that is, following the dictates of the Voice within.

Penn had come to this conviction through two routes: his own persecution as a youth because of his Quakerism, and by his observation of the cruelties and absurdities of religious persecution both in England and on the Continent. He had composed one of his most famous works, *The Great Case of Liberty of Conscience* . . . , while a prisoner in Newgate jail. In the first place, he insisted, persecution for one's beliefs is futile and absurd. Moreover, it is a disruption of the good order of an otherwise peaceful state. Persecution was also anti-Christian; it was a violation of the fundamental rights of Englishmen; it was a usurpation of the authority and the prerogative of God. "Force never yet made either a good Christian, or a good subject."

So far, Penn's argument for freedom of conscience is negative, permissive, defensive. But freedom of religious belief, or of thought itself, is also positive. Freedom of worship, like freedom of thought, means freedom of expression. A Quaker, moved by the Inner Light, speaks not merely of himself, but of God. But he does not merely "suffer" God to speak: he listens to what He says, and learns thereby. Thus freedom of worship, freedom of thought, freedom of assembly, and freedom of expression are the means toward a positive forward movement of human life. Freedom thus becomes a creative force in human affairs. Men learn from one another, and any man may have the answer to a present problem. Representative government, says Penn, is based upon reason and the exercise of reason. Reason must be free to solve the problems of the state as well as of religion. Penn was no democrat. He deplored and opposed revolutionary violence. He did not go beyond the positive aspects of freedom of religion. But he was also a lifelong advocate of the doctrine of freedom of the mind, which, when carried over into secular thought, is, needless to say, the *sine qua non* of democracy.

Given Penn's unchanging conviction of the social and political necessity of freedom of religion, it was no accident that both the first chapter of his "Great Law," and the first article of the Charter of Privileges of 1701, should provide for complete freedom of worship for all persons who believe in one God. By implication, at least, this would include Buddhists, Moslems, Catholics, Indians, Africans, and even the benighted Anglicans of Penn's own native England! Office holding, however, was limited to those who accepted the divinity of Christ. To the 20th-century mind, this might appear a serious reduction of Penn's professed principles. Yet the Charter of Liberties of Pennsylvania was probably the most liberal constitution, so far as religion was concerned, in the western world. It also set a model for the later constitutions of the states that would emerge during the Revolution.

The people who came to Pennsylvania with William Penn were all Englishmen. But already scattered along the Delaware were settlements of Dutchmen, Swedes, and Finns. Within the next year or two many Germans began to come. By 1685 Penn could report that the population of his colony numbered over 8,000 people, who "are a Collection of divers Nations in Europe: As French, Dutch, Germans, Swedes, Danes, Finns, Scotch, Irish and English; and of the last equal to all the rest: . . . they live like People of One Country, which Civil Union has had a considerable influence towards the prosperity of that place."

Within another generation more non-English groups had accepted his invitation to enter into the experiment—among them Jews, Scots, Negroes, French Hugenots, and others, not to mention the native Indians. Pennsylvania was clearly the most polyglot colony in America. And out of this reality—out of Penn's own intent, indeed—was born the New World image of the "melting pot."

One of William Penn's major concerns, both humanitarian and pragmatic, were the Indians. He did not question the right of the king to give him a huge tract of land, but he also recognized that it was owned by the Indians and that, for him legally and justly to possess it, he must buy it from them. Besides this pragmatic consideration, however, he was genuinely interested in the Indians and their ways, and he was determined to avoid the abuses and misunderstandings that had led to savage warfare, mutual distrust, and bitter hatred between white and redman in colonies founded earlier. He was determined that his people and the Indians, as children of God, should live alongside each other as good neighbors, bound together by mutual respect, justice, and Christian love. When Penn sent his representatives ahead of him to lay the foundations of his colony, he strictly instructed them to respect the Indians' feelings: "Be tender of offending the Indians . . . we have their good in our eye, equal with our own interest . . . make a friendship and league with them. . . . Be grave; they love not to be smiled on."

Legend has it that soon after his arrival William Penn held a "treaty" with the Indians of the region under a great elm tree at Shackamaxon, at which the two groups pledged mutual friendship and the Indians sold Penn a tract of land along the Delaware River. The legend is almost certainly based on fact. In any case, Penn reported in 1685 that he had made seven such purchases of land. And he rejoiced in the cordial relations that existed between his people and their Indian neighbors: "so far are we from ill terms with the Natives, that we have liv'd in great friendship. . . . if any of them break our laws, they submit to be punisht by them: and to this they have tyed themselves by an obligation under their hands. We leave not the least indignity to them unrebukt, nor wrong unsatisfied. Justice gains and aws them."

William Penn, like Captain John Smith before him, had a genuine anthropological interest in the Indians. After living two years near them he wrote a clear and sympathetic description of their mores. Their language, he stated, "is lofty, yet narrow; but like the Hebrew, in signification full [Penn inclined to the belief that the Indians were descended from the lost ten tribes of Israel]; it is relatively unstructured. He described the Indians' customs with their children, as well as their marriages, houses, diet, hunting, hospitality, burials, and use of wampum. "They are great concealers of their own resentments . . . but in liberality they excel: nothing is too good for their friend . . . the most merry creatures that live, feast and dance perpetually; they never have much, nor want much . . . a little contents them. . . . Since the Europeans came into these parts they are grown great lovers of strong liquors, rum especially." Of their religion, Penn observed, "These poor people are under a dark night in things relating to religion. . . ." Yet they believe in one God and in immortality, he reported; they make sacrifices to their great god, usually the first fruits, and they express their worship in songs and dances.

Penn describes the Indians' government in great detail, and procedures at their councils: "they speak little, but fervently, and with elegance: I have never seen more natural sagacity . . . he will deserve the name of wise that outwits them in any treaty about a thing they understand." He also notes their arrangements for the maintenance of the peace and good relations between the two societies. We have agreed, he declares, that all differences shall be decided by six men on each side. The decision of this group was final. "Do not abuse them," he enjoined, "but let them have justice; and you win them: the worst is, that they are the worse for the Christians; who have propagated their vices, and yielded them tradition for ill, and not for good things. . . ."

How different was William Penn's attitude toward and understanding of the Indians from that of Captain John Smith!

William Penn was in England during the Glorious Revolution of 1688–89 and the accession of William and Mary to the English throne, and he viewed with dismay the outbreak of the War of the Palatinate that took place almost immediately afterward. These were sad years for him in any case. The colonists back in Pennsylvania were squabbling, which led him to rebuke them and to speak of himself as a "man of sorrow." Meanwhile, owing to his known friendship with the exiled James II, his enemies at court attacked his charter and succeeded in having it suspended in 1692. (He was exonerated, however, and his charter restored in 1696.)

It was during this period of unhappy retirement that Penn turned his mind to the problem of war and peace and wrote his famous *Essay Toward the Present and Future Peace of Europe*. As many political thinkers have done since then, he asked the predictable questions: Why do nations fight with each other, and how can war, an atrocity in itself, be avoided?

There are three causes of war, he reasoned: the first is the necessity of defense against an aggressor; the second is the need to recover territory seized by an enemy; the third is the imperialistic drive of one nation to take the possessions of another. War is undertaken, in the first two cases, in the name of justice; if justice can be achieved without fighting, war becomes unnecessary. In the case of an imperialistic aggression, if the combined power of the community of nations is brought to bear upon the aggressor, he can be forced to desist; justice will thus be achieved by collective action. Let there be an international diet, or parliament, therefore, to decide the justice of international causes, with a sovereignty that transcends the sovereignties of the component states and that has the power to enforce its decisions. Penn then listed the many benefits to be derived from such an international institution for the preservation of peace.

Speaking here was Penn the idealist, Penn the humanitarian, Penn the rational internationalist, but not Penn the realist. He failed to recognize, in this problem as in many others, that it was not in the nature of other men, especially statesmen, to be as humanitarian and idealistic as he was.

It was because of the international situation, apparently, that William Penn turned his thoughts to the desirability of organizing a union of the English colonies along the American seaboard. On February 8, 1697, Penn presented to the English Board of Trade a plan for a union of the North American colonies. He proposed creation of an intercolonial assembly composed of deputies from all the colonies (two from each colony); the president of this assembly would be a "commissioner" (or governor-general) appointed by the king; this assembly would meet in the most nearly central colony, presumably New York, as often as need be in time of war, and every two years in time of peace. Even though a pacifist, Penn recognized war as a fact of political life that had to be acknowledged. The business of the assembly would be "to hear and adjust all matters of complaint or difference between Province and Province" or disputes between private citizens of two different colonies, or the return of fugitives from justice. The assembly would also consider matters concerning intercolonial commerce. But it would be especially charged "to consider of ways and means to support the union and safety of these Provinces against the publick enemies" such as the French or the Spaniards. In such cases it would contrive united armed forces and decide the quotas of men and supplies to be furnished by each colony for the common defense.

The idea of an ongoing, permanent colonial assembly for peacetime purposes was apparently unprecedented. Like his plan for international peace, Penn's scheme fell on deaf or disinterested ears. But here, again, he articulated an idea that was to grow dramatically among Americans of the 18th century, one that would be re-formulated by Benjamin Franklin in 1754 and actually implemented in the Articles of Confederation and in the Constitution of the United States of 1787.

William Penn finally returned to his colony in 1699. Once more he sought a peaceful solution to the factional struggles and succeeded in formulating the Charter of Privileges of 1701, which, as has been noted, remained the colony's constitution until the Revolution. Departing for England shortly thereafter, he never returned to Pennsylvania. He knew, however, that his new society, based on his own humanitarianism, was a success.

*   *   *

Captain John Smith, Master John Winthrop, and Friend William Penn, so different from one another, nonetheless had certain basic characteristics in common: each was an outstanding empire-builder driven by the forces of his time to found new societies and to expand the bounds of the British empire in America. Each was a man of ideas who had the stature and the power to carry these ideas into action. Each had an impact upon the course of history that was powerful and undeniable; each illustrates the possible significance of the individual in history. At the same time, each applied the ideas of his time to the course of history, thereby demonstrating the reality of the role of ideas in human history. Finally, their three colonies, while vastly different from one another, were the chief germinal beginnings of a new society. Each man was conscious that he was building a new "nation," but never dreamed of the form and the spirit it would take; each one brought to this work distinct values and these were indelibly written into the character of the new nation that they founded: pragmatism, religion, and humanitarianism.

2

Gentlemen and Men of Property

WILLIAM BYRD
SAMUEL SEWALL
WILLIAM JOHNSON

by Louis B. Wright
National Geographic Society

Many reasons prompted emigration to the New World in the early periods of our history, but few motives were more powerful than the lure of easily procurable land. Land not only insured a livelihood but it held out the promise of status. In 17th-century England, however, land was hard to come by. Inherited property descended to the eldest son; little land came on the market, and when it did the price was beyond the means of most would-be purchasers.

But in the English colonies across the Atlantic, land in almost limitless quantities was available on terms not beyond the means of even a yeoman farmer. In Virginia and in some of the other colonies, any immigrant able to pay ocean passage for himself and his household was given 50 acres as a "headright" for each member of his family as well as for each servant. Anyone with a little capital could also purchase land at such modest prices that younger sons who had no hope of an inheritance at home could establish themselves overseas as landed proprietors.

From time immemorial, the possession of land in England had conferred a status. A yeoman with a farm in fee simple had a respected place in society. Larger holdings might insure that the owner would be classed among the gentry, hold county offices, and perhaps even sit in Parliament. Great acreages with many tenants usually meant that the possessor belonged to the upper aristocracy, frequently with a title of nobility. Thus land was a stepping stone in the individual's rise in the social scale.

Besides the acquisition of land, other opportunities in the colonies induced emigrants to try their luck overseas. Most came for the betterment of their economic lot, whatever it had been, and a few prospered in trade beyond their expectations. Traffic with the Indians for furs as well as fishing were the earliest sources of substantial revenue, but soon other avenues opened. In New England particularly, shipbuilding and shipping laid the foundations of many a family fortune. In South Carolina, trade for deerskins with the Indians of the highlands and the marketing of forest products (turpentine, rosin, and ship timbers) were combined with the production of rice and indigo to bring fortunes to Charleston gentlemen who feared no "taint of trade." In a new country, colonists experimented with any suggestion that seemed to promise a profit. At the same time they retained memories of the hierarchy and status that prevailed in the old country and frequently sought purposefully to reproduce the best of the social conditions they remembered.

The ideal of the English country gentleman had a persistent appeal, especially in the agrarian colonies. Much ink has been wasted by contemporary genealogists in trying to prove the aristocratic origins in England of American families; but this effort, frequently unconvincing, is far less important than a study of what they became once established on these shores and of how they achieved their status. For many colonial families, in a generation or two, were living in a state that gave them the right to be considered members of a rising aristocracy.

The word "gentleman" in the 17th and 18th centuries was a technical term connoting something more than a well-behaved individual, the usual definition at the present time. In England, at that time, a gentleman was normally a landed proprietor, with sufficient property to enable him to live without manual labor himself, though he might carefully supervise the workers on his estate. William Harrison, a writer in Shakespeare's day, made the point, however, that others besides landowners might expect to be designated gentlemen and have the right to be called "Master" (our word Mister). "Whosoever studieth the laws of the realm, whoso abideth in the University giving his mind to his book, or professeth physic [medicine] and the liberal sciences," or serves as a captain in the wars or benefits the commonwealth by his counsel, "can live without manual labor and thereto is able and will bear the port, charge, and countenance of a gentleman, he shall be called 'master,' which is the title that men give to esquires and gentlemen, and be reputed a gentleman ever after." A proverb of the day declared that "gentility is nothing but ancient riches," and some commentator observed that riches need not be very ancient. In colonial America riches could be very recent, indeed, to enable a man to write "Mr." in front of his name or "Esquire" after it.

During the 17th century a number of Virginia families emerged who were to play a prominent part in the country's later history. Such were the Lees, the Fitzhughs, the Carters, the Byrds, and a score of others. Few were more conspicuous than the Carters, who were both rich and prolific. The second of the name in Virginia, Robert Carter of Corotoman, known for his pride and wealth as "King" Carter, eventually acquired some 300,000 acres in that portion of the colony designated the Northern Neck. Serving as justice of the peace, colonel of the militia, member of the Council of State, rector of the College of William and Mary, and holder of other offices, Carter illustrates the devotion to duty that characterized the gentry of this period. Few emoluments went with these offices, which the holder occupied as a civic duty, and for the privileged this tradition carried with it a sense of responsibility. Carter managed to accumulate his land, not because he held public office, but because he served as agent for the Fairfaxes who held a royal patent for the proprietorship of all the Northern Neck.

*   *   *

Perhaps the best remembered member of Virginia's ruling class is William Byrd II of Westover, for he kept a well-publicized diary, wrote one of the most urbane narratives of the period (*The History of the Dividing Line*), occupied many high offices, and fathered a dynasty that has wielded political power to the present time.

Byrd's father, William Byrd I, who emigrated to Virginia sometime before 1670, was the son of a London goldsmith. His maternal grandfather, Thomas Stegg, was a ship captain in the Virginia trade who had already acquired land on the James River. After this grandfather was lost at sea, young Byrd went to live with his Virginia uncle, also named Thomas Stegg, and eventually inherited his property. Thus the first William Byrd came into possession of a substantial acreage and a trading business with the Indians, which he subsequently increased.

William Byrd I married Mary Horsmanden, the daughter of an emigré Cavalier. They sent their son, William Byrd II, to England to be educated at Felsted Grammar School in Essex; and, later, the father sent him to Holland. Here the son would learn about business from one of his commercial correspondents, and then serve for a term in the business house of Perry & Lane of London.

Eventually Byrd II entered the Middle Temple and was called to the English bar. Thus he received basic classical training in grammar school (essential, it was believed, for a gentleman), gained practical business experience, and came back to Virginia with the prestige of an English legal education. Furthermore, on the death of his father in 1704, he inherited a comfortable fortune, a thriving trade with the Indians of the interior, a family seat in Henrico County on the James, and the help of influential friends who saw that he soon received appointment to high offices in the colony. William Byrd II was already on his way to becoming one of Virginia's ornamental as well as important members of the ruling hierarchy.

In the course of his life Byrd made five journeys across the Atlantic to serve as the official emissary of the colony in dealing with governmental authorities in London. He employed the skills of a diplomat and a lobbyist in arguing for advantages favorable to Virginia. His stays were usually for long periods, in one instance for over five years, which gave him an opportunity to cultivate the friendship of important officials and friends among the British aristocracy. He was conscious of being a member of the gentry himself and was readily accepted by his English counterparts. When he returned to his plantation home at Westover he brought back portraits of these friends, ranging from scientific colleagues in the Royal Society (which he was invited to join) to the Duke of Argyle. A few of Byrd's Virginia neighbors smiled at his vanity in displaying his friendship with so many prominent Englishmen.

Byrd deserves an honored place as a man of letters, though he published little in his own lifetime. *The History of the Dividing Line,* on which his reputation earlier rested, was first published by Edmund Ruffin at Petersburg, Virginia, in 1841. A modern version of his *Prose Works* (edited by Louis B. Wright) was brought out in 1966.

Byrd is one of the best documented of colonial Americans. In addition to his literary pieces like *The History of the Dividing Line Betwixt Virginia and North Carolina Run in . . . 1728, A Progress to the Mines in the Year 1732,* and *A Journey to the Land of Eden, Anno 1733,* Byrd through much of his adult life kept a diary in shorthand in which he entered highly intimate details of these years. Three portions of this diary are now in print, and other portions, yet undiscovered, may appear someday. He also wrote numerous letters that throw light on himself and his times. His prose works are lightened with humor and have an urbanity and grace rarely found in other colonial writings.

But Byrd was more than a skillful author. He was the counterpart of the European virtuoso of the 18th century, the period of the Enlightenment. He was interested in science, in learning, in classical languages and literature, and in the world about him. He also cultivated the social graces that characterized the gentleman: hospitality, good manners, good conversation, music, and dancing. Much of the Renaissance tradition of the well-rounded man persisted in Byrd—and would find a culmination in Thomas Jefferson. With all his faults, which were numerous, William Byrd II personified the ideal of cultivation that distinguished Virginia's ruling class, an aristocracy that provided a leadership of extraordinary talent in a later generation when Americans were trying to hammer out the framework of a new nation.

Fortunately for our understanding of Byrd, the first of his known diaries begins as early as 1709. It was published in 1941 as *The Secret Diary of William Byrd of Westover 1709–1712* (edited by Louis B. Wright and Marion Tinling). A few excerpts illustrate his many-sided interests. Passages may be picked almost at random. This, for example, is the entry for October 31, 1709:

> I rose at 6 o'clock and read two chapters in Hebrew and some Greek in Lucian. I said my prayers and ate milk for breakfast. About 10 o'clock we went to court. The committee met to receive proposals for the building [of] the College [William and Mary] and Mr. Tullitt undertook it for £2,000 provided he might [take] wood off the College land and all assistants from England to come at the College's risk. We sat in court till about 4 o'clock and then I rode to Green Springs to meet my wife. I found her there and had the pleasure to learn that all was well at home, thanks be to God. There was likewise Mrs. Chiswell. I ate boiled beef for supper. Then we danced and were merry till about 10 o'clock. I neglected to say my prayers but had good health, good thoughts, and good humor, thanks be to God Almighty.

The opening sentence of the above is no surprise. A cultivated gentleman in the early 18th century was expected to know the classical tongues. Familiarity with Latin and Greek literature was taken for granted. But Byrd had more than a bowing acquaintance with these literatures. Owning a fine collection, he made constant use of his books. Since the press of work and the visits of neighbors made consistent reading problematical, he adopted the system of beginning his day with Greek and Hebrew. Occasionally he read some Latin author or something in Italian or French, but Hebrew and Greek were his normal pre-breakfast fare. This daily stint of Greek and Hebrew he maintained throughout his life.

Other items in this passage deserve comment. Already a member of the Council of State, which sat as the highest court in the colony, Byrd had gone to Williamsburg to attend a routine meeting of the Council. He belonged to a Council committee that let a contract for the erection of a building at the College of William and Mary. Further entries in the diary show his continuing interest in the College and in education. Like other members of his group, he was trying to provide for the perpetuation of higher learning, which our ancestors believed essential for an enlightened leadership.

Byrd's regret over forgetting to say his prayers is not mere rhetoric. An 18th-century gentleman of Byrd's class had a profound belief in the value of religion. A society without religion was, in his opinion, a contradiction in terms. Decency, decorum, and good order required men to show respect for religion, and a member of the ruling class had to set an example by going to church and observing at least the outward forms of worship.

Although Byrd's private life demonstrated many weaknesses of the flesh, he was sincerely religious. Classifying his beliefs is difficult. The rationalism that characterized many 18th-century intellectuals touched Byrd but did not envelop him, for his diaries not only record his daily prayers and those times when he neglected them, they also tell us of an insatiable appetite for sermon reading.

The randomly selected passage cited above indicates a few other things about Byrd. It shows his interest in people, his love of gaiety, his concern for his home, and certain peculiarities of diet. These things might be passed over as trivial if they were not indicative of wider interests that throw further light on the man.

An 18th-century aristocrat had to exhibit the social graces expected of a member of his class. But Byrd was no gilded butterfly. Colonial planters by and large were industrious and thrifty folk instead of the silken Cavaliers of popular fiction. Nevertheless, Byrd, like other members of his group, delighted in dancing and in the social gatherings that were part of life in Tidewater Virginia. To the end of his days he was never too tired to turn out for a ball at Williamsburg.

The excerpt above that records the presence of Mrs. Chiswell has more meaning than is at first apparent. Byrd clearly was interested in this pert and pretty woman. Three days later, on November 2, he again began his routine at 6:00 A.M., read some Hebrew and Greek, said his prayers, had milk for breakfast before settling some accounts. But in the evening, he continued,

> I went to Dr. [Barret's] where my wife came this afternoon. Here I found Mrs. Chiswell, my sister Custis, and other ladies. We sat and talked till about 11 o'clock and then retired to our chambers. I played at [r-m] with Mrs. Chiswell and kissed her on the bed till she was angry and my wife also was uneasy about it, and cried as soon as the company was gone. I neglected to say my prayers, which I should not have done, because I ought to beg pardon for the lust I had for another man's wife. However I had good health, good thoughts, and good humor, thanks be to God Almighty.

A wistful note later crept into Byrd's *A Progress to the Mines* when he reported a visit with Mr. and Mrs. Chiswell and found that Mrs. Chiswell, whom he had not seen in more than twenty years, had aged sadly.

Through a long life (he died in 1744) Byrd struggled to improve his plantation at Westover, to make a profit from the Indian trade that his father had developed, to increase his landed holdings, and patriotically to serve the colony of Virginia. Despite the multiplicity of his duties as a member of the Council, as a colonel of militia, and as a consultant in every important matter concerning the colony's welfare, he never neglected the improvement of his mind. He remained a student of the classics and a man of letters. In his library, one of the best in North America at the time, he found both delight and instruction. Other members of the ruling class shared many of Byrd's interests, his ideals—and some of his shortcomings. He was, then, typical of a small group who managed to dominate colonial society in Virginia.

*　　*　　*

In Massachusetts, the second region to be settled by the English, Samuel Sewall, another diarist, even more diligent in recording events than William Byrd, rose to prominence as a merchant and a jurist in the late 17th and early 18th centuries. Sewall's parents had emigrated from England in 1634 but returned to the homeland where Samuel was born at Bishopstoke in 1652. Nine years later, after Samuel had attended grammar school for a few years, the family returned to Boston. Samuel completed his secondary education and attended Harvard College, from which he graduated in 1671.

Massachusetts Bay in its early years had been dominated by the Puritan clergy. Its charter said that only "freemen" should vote. But to be admitted to the ranks of freemen, one had to be a church member in good standing; and in effect the clergy had succeeded in restricting the right to vote to church members. Joining a Puritan church was not easy. A candidate for admission had to stand up in open congregation and testify that he or she had experienced conversion. While young Sewall was a schoolboy in Boston, the churches found themselves hard pressed because members of the younger generation, who were unwilling to testify that they had experienced conversion, were clamoring to be admitted as freemen so they could vote. Consequently, in 1662, the churches adopted what was called the Half-Way Covenant. That is, unconverted children of church members were admitted to church membership and thus became freemen. Although these unregenerate members could vote, they were not permitted to take the sacrament of the Lord's Supper. This weakening of theocratic control of the colony influenced Sewall in the choice of a career.

After completing his education at Harvard, Sewall had to decide between becoming a minister or entering business. Had he graduated a generation earlier he undoubtedly would have chosen the ministry, a vocation then leading to power; but Sewall, though deeply pious, was also ambitious, and so he decided upon a career of business and politics. First, however, he served briefly as a Harvard tutor and "keeper of the college library."

Sewall's rise in the world was accelerated by a fortunate marriage in

1676 to an heiress, Hannah Hull, daughter of John Hull, the colony's master of the mint and a wealthy merchant. Hannah bore him 14 children, but her inheritance from her father, who died in 1683, helped to keep this numerous progeny from becoming a financial burden.

The term merchant in this time did not mean a tradesman who sold goods in a shop. A merchant was an importer and exporter of general merchandise which he then sold wholesale from his ships or warehouses. Although Sewall began keeping his famous diary in 1674, he tells very little about his business affairs. He displays far greater interest in social conditions in the community, the sermons he heard, and particularly the funerals he attended. Indeed, the diary often reads like a necrology as Sewall comments on the dead, lists the pall bearers, and reports on the funeral sermons.

In 1676 Sewall and his wife moved into his father-in-law's house on Washington Street, Boston, where he was to live for the rest of his life. Under the tutelage of John Hull, from this time onward, he "followed merchandise" (to use his own phrase) and prospered. He also quickly began to take on civic responsibilities and honors. During the outbreak of Indian hostilities known as King Philip's War, he served as a major commanding a detachment of Massachusetts troops. Three years later he became a member of the Ancient and Honorable Artillery Company, an organization known more for its social prestige than its military prowess. Many years later he was elected its captain. In the meantime, however, he served in 1683 as captain of John Hull's Company and in 1685 as captain of the South Company of Boston. He resigned his commission in the latter company in the following year because of an order to put the cross of St. George in the company's colors. To Sewall the cross was "popish" and idolatrous, such were his Puritan prejudices.

By 1684 Sewall was already a member of the Court of Assistants and presided as a magistrate, an office that started him on a long career as a jurist. In this period one did not have to be a trained lawyer to become a judge. Sewall, like many other colonial jurists, had never studied law but he had a fund of common sense and a deep concern for justice. In the same year that he became a magistrate, he was also appointed to the Board of Overseers of Harvard College. He was now firmly established in the political and social hierarchy of Boston where he would remain for the rest of his life with ever increasing honors and responsibilities.

Sewall went to England in November 1688 and therefore witnessed the "Glorious Revolution" of that year which deposed James II and crowned William of Orange and his wife Mary (daughter of King James). The purpose of Sewall's journey was to further his mercantile affairs, but he also attempted to assist the Reverend Increase Mather, who had gone to London to argue for a renewal of the colony's charter, which had been cancelled. Mather showed scant appreciation of Sewall's offers of help, which he thought officious. The King decided to grant a new charter but reserved the right to appoint the governor. Mather persuaded the King to choose Sir William Phips, who had married the widow of John Hull, Sewall's father-in-law.

Phips, a typical self-made man, was never accepted by the Boston social aristocracy; he had been knighted by James II for his exploit in discovering and raising in the Caribbean a Spanish wreck loaded with treasure. Although Phips had married a socially prominent wife, he never forgot his upbringing as a ship's carpenter and sea captain; he preferred the company of seamen, retained the manners and behavior of the quarter-deck, and showed a tenderness toward pirates who frequented colonial harbors. Perhaps Phips's most commendable act was his stopping the Salem witchcraft trials in which Sewall served as one of the judges.

Sewall's journal notes of his visit to London, which lasted from January 13 to October 10, 1689, reveal a side of the author not made explicit elsewhere in the diary. He recorded fewer funerals, since he knew fewer of the deceased in England and felt no duty to mention so many deaths. Although no less observant of the Sabbath, Sewall's travels from place to place left him less opportunity to listen to sermons. Nevertheless, he managed to find many non-Conformist preachers he knew by reputation, and he expressed his pleasure in hearing them.

What is otherwise recorded of his English visit throws light on Sewall's business activities. He visited an amazing number of relatives, some of whom owed him money, and carefully noted his collection of debts. Sometimes, in lieu of cash, he accepted gloves, silk stockings, and other light manufactured articles in payment. He had inherited land and rental property that he inspected, renewed leases, and attended to other business matters. All in all, he had a profitable and pleasant time.

Like any tourist, Sewall visited as many places of interest as time permitted and contrived to see a large part of England, from Plymouth to East Anglia, the Midlands, and of course London. On his way from Dover, his port of entry, he stopped at Canterbury; his Puritan prejudices, however, allowed him to say only of the Cathedral that it was "a very lofty and magnificent building but of little use."

Upon reaching London, Sewall at once sought out Increase Mather, official lobbyist for Massachusetts, and offered his unwanted help. When Sewall could spare time from business matters and from seeking out famous Puritan preachers, he saw the sights: the Guild Hall, Westminster Abbey, St. Paul's Cathedral and other churches, the Tower of London (and the zoo then kept at the Tower), and countless other spots that still attract visitors. Sewall displayed a particular curiosity about architectural specifications. He carried a folding yardstick and was forever measuring floor spaces. The Guild Hall, for example, he noted was 50 yards long and 16 yards broad. At Eton and Hampton Court, which he visited on May 8, 1689, he seems to have been chiefly interested in dimensions, for he noted in his journal: "Eton College Library, 69 foot long, the shelves four." At Hampton Court he took the trouble to measure some of the rooms open to visitors: "Queen's bedchamber, 24 foot square; King's public dining room, 32 foot and near square."

A gregarious man, Sewall contrived to find cousins or cousins of friends nearly everywhere, and he enjoyed the hospitality shown him. Puritan though he was, he was no ascetic and relished good food and drink, never refusing cider, ale, or wine. Near Southampton he dined at Cousin Jane Holt's and had "very good bacon, veal, parsnips, very good shoulder of mutton and a fowl roasted, good currant suet pudding, and the fairest dish of apples that I have ever eat in England." So it was on numerous occasions. Like William Byrd, he carefully enumerated the items of food and drink that were served.

In an age when the only means of travel was by coach or horseback, Sewall contrived to get around to many of the most interesting spots in England. At Winchester he looked up the librarian of Winchester College and gave him a copy of John Eliot's Indian Bible, which can still be seen there. Few sights escaped him as he rode across the land: Stonehenge, Salisbury—where he was more impressed by the original site of Old Sarum than by the cathedral—and numerous towns and villages on the road back to London. In late March he set out from London for a two week trip to Abingdon, Oxford, Warwick, Coventry, and other points of interest. If he thought of visiting Shakespeare's Stratford, he does not mention it. After all, Shakespeare was merely the author of profane plays. To relatives and friends along the way, Sewall gave gifts of sermons written by Increase Mather's learned son, Cotton, of Boston. Sewall must have brought over a bale of these pamphlet sermons, which he distributed widely. On April 3 he was shown the Bodleian Library in shape of an H, he reported, "a very magnificent thing. The galleries very magnificent, about 44 of my canes length and nearly 8 in breadth. . . . Mr. Gilbert gives us a pint of wine. Lodge at the Bear Inn."

Sewall was not one to go overboard in admiration of any sight. Visiting Cambridge in late June, he went first to Emmanuel College, from which many of New England's preachers had come. King's College Chapel, one of the architectural wonders of England, he dismissed as "very stately." He found St. John's College more interesting, especially its "library and many rarities, among which was a petrified cheese."

Finally on October 10, 1689, after much travel, many visits to relatives and friends, and important business transacted, Sewall sailed from Plymouth on a vessel aptly named *America*. He reached Boston on December 2, and immediately resumed his political, military, religious, and commercial activities. Soon after his return, Sewall was appointed a member of the provincial Council to which he was reelected every year until 1725 when he retired.

The Indians on the frontier, on instigation of the French, were giving trouble, and one of the first pieces of bad news Sewall heard after his arrival was an account of depredations in the interior. On February 8, 1690, he noted in his diary the massacre by Indians of 60 men, women, and children at Schenectady. Massachusetts mobilized its militia, and Sewall, formerly captain of the South Company, turned out for drill. On March 24 he recorded in his diary that "I go into the field, pray with the South Company, exercise them in a few distances, facings, doublings . . . told them the place I was in required more time and strength than I had, so took leave of them."

Two years later Sewall played a significant role in one of the most tragic episodes in colonial history, the Salem witchcraft delusion, in which scores of citizens were accused on the testimony of a group of hysterical or sensation-seeking teen-age girls. When Governor Phips reached Massachusetts in May 1692, more than a hundred persons were in jail or under indictment for the crime of witchcraft. He immediately appointed a panel of nine members of a commission of Oyer and Ter-miner, a special court, to bring those accused of witchcraft to justice. Sewall was one of the nine. His brother Stephen was clerk of the court. At the first sitting of the court on June 2, Bridget Bishop was convicted and sentenced to hang. Her execution followed on June 10. By the end of the summer, after many sensational trials characterized by flimsy "spectral" evidence that no modern judge would admit, 19 persons had suffered death. Even Increase and Cotton Mather, who had originally demanded that the court root out the heinous sin of witchcraft, realized that things had gone too far. With pressure from some of the more rational citizens of the region, Governor Phips in September stopped the trials.

Sewall says little about the witch trials in his diary. Clearly he was not proud of his role and felt uneasy in his conscience. Of the nine members of the court he was the only one to confess publicly his regret over participating in the miscarriage of justice. Five years later, on Jan-uary 14, 1697, he stood up in Old South Church and had the minister read a statement he had drafted in which he said he desired "to take the blame and shame of it [the witchcraft trials], asking pardon of men and especially desiring prayers that God . . . would pardon that sin." Many must have admired Sewall's courage in taking the blame upon himself, something none of the others involved showed a willingness to do.

On December 6, 1692, Sewall had been chosen one of the justices of the Superior Court of Judicature, a post to which he was constantly re-appointed until 1728 when he retired for age. On April 16, 1718, he was made chief justice. Sewall's judicial duties took much of his time, but he was never too busy to attend to other obligations expected of a civic leader of his station. He served as an overseer of Harvard College, judge of probate of Suffolk County, commissioner, secretary, and treasurer of the Company for the Propagation of the Gospel in New England and Parts Adjacent. Furthermore, he prized his commission as captain of the Ancient and Honorable Artillery Company. Again, he was conscientious about attending the funeral of nearly every prominent citizen of the region, male and female. His journal also records his attendance at church on nearly every Sunday and Lecture Day (Thursday), with a statement of the preacher's sermon text. A reader is left wondering how Sewall found time for his business affairs, but his journal gives few clues.

Sewall was oppressively pious, but this was characteristic of many of the old school of Puritans in Massachusetts. Times were changing, and Sewall frequently expressed regret at the increasing wickedness of the age. He was scandalized at "mixed dancing"; he was shocked at Cotton Mather's defense of wearing periwigs, especially his mention of so worldly a matter in the pulpit; he disapproved of boys playing tricks on April Fool's Day and on Shrove Tuesday; and he voiced approval when Boston's citizens failed to observe Christmas, a "Popish" festival.

The diary is full of moralizing. On January 13, 1677, for example, he observed: "Giving my chickens meat [food], it came to my mind that I gave them nothing save Indian corn and water, and yet they eat it and thrived very well . . . which much affected me and convinced [sic] what need I stood in of spiritual food. . . ." Almost every event provided an opportunity for Sewall to draw a moral. Another typical instance appears on October 1, 1697. At dinner someone knocked over and broke a bottle of spirits that "stood upon a joint stool." "I said 'twas a lively emblem of our fragility and mortality."

Sewall was one of the first New Englanders to protest against slavery and in 1700 published *The Selling of Joseph*, a tract expressing his views on the subject. In this he was a pioneer, for even ministers like Cotton Mather kept black slaves as household servants, and many merchants were engaged in the slave trade. To Sewall's credit, his mercantile activities did not embrace trade with Africa in which New England shippers bartered their rum with African chiefs for captives taken in tribal wars.

In addition to *The Selling of Joseph*, Sewall published other tracts on pious subjects. He also wrote verses that he circulated in manuscript among his friends. Books were among the imports brought over from England for sale, but Sewall rarely mentions them by title.

Sewall's own literary taste ran to the reading of sermons, which he distributed freely. A sermon in his opinion was an appropriate gift with which to court a lady when he was a widower seeking a wife. One of the most interesting episodes in the diary recounts his effort in 1720 to persuade Katherine Winthrop, widow of Wait Winthrop, to marry him. Sewall's second wife had died in May of that year. In the autumn he was vigorously pursuing his courtship, calling on "Madam" Winthrop as often as possible and taking her sermons as well as sweetmeats, almonds, gingerbread, and other small gifts. He provides a full account in his diary for September, October, and November. Madam Winthrop strung him along for several weeks, first encouraging him and then being distant. On October 12 he called and was discouraged to find that "Madam Winthrop's countenance was much changed from what 'twas on Monday, looked dark and lowering. . . . I got my chair in place, had some converse but very cold and indifferent to what 'twas before. Asked her to acquit me of rudeness if I drew off her glove. Enquiring the reason, I told her 'twas great odds between handling a dead goat and a living lady. Got it off." Ardent as was his pursuit, it came to naught. Madam Winthrop insisted upon Sewall's keeping a coach and he refused such an extravagance. The courtship cooled, and Sewall with some regret sought elsewhere for a wife. On March 29, 1722, he married another widow, Mrs. Mary Gibbs.

Sewall represented the best type of New England Puritan of the late 17th and early 18th centuries. He exemplified the bourgeois virtues embraced in what is now called the "work ethic." He believed that God would reward him with material blessings if he lived righteously according to the rigid Puritan concept of behavior. He insisted upon a life of diligence, thrift, sobriety, and abstinence from extravagant waste. To have a coach, which Madam Winthrop demanded, would have violated his principle of avoiding useless ostentation. The accumulation of wealth in Sewall's eyes was evidence of God's approval. So Sewall practiced piety, attended to his business but did not let it envelop him, and died on January 1, 1730, prosperous and in the odor of sanctity.

*   *   *

Few greater contrasts in character could be found than that between Judge Samuel Sewall of Massachusetts Bay and Sir William Johnson of New York. Sewall, a prosperous merchant and judge, gave little evidence of an interest in worldly affairs in his long diary. Recording vast numbers of sermons and funerals, moralizing about the hope of the hereafter, he gives the impression of being more concerned about the next world. Sir William Johnson, on the contrary, revealed little interest in the future life. In his utterances "God" was usually followed by the word "damn." It is true that he had some concern about religion, but his interest was in the practical aspects of missionary activities with the Indians. He had a profound interest in the fur trade, and his greed for land was exceeded by that of few other colonials. Before he died he had accumulated a princely estate of more than 1,000,000 acres in the Mohawk Valley and adjacent territory.

Sewall's interest in women was strictly within the bounds of matrimony. He occasionally mentions in his diary an observation that a young lass was "comely," but if his thoughts ever strayed beyond that, he never revealed it. It is true that after the death of his wife Sewall was soon pursuing a widow with offers of marriage—subject to her acceptance of his somewhat penny-pinching domestic arrangements. Johnson, on the other hand, was attracted by all sorts and kinds of women and felt no compulsion to resist female temptation. His interest in the opposite sex was apparently well known and unflagging. Even in his old age, on a peace-making mission to Detroit, his host, eager to please, assembled 30 of the most beautiful women in the area at a banquet in Sir William's honor. Included was Angelique Cuillerier (*dit* Beaubien), regarded as the most alluring temptress on the frontier. Johnson had been attracted by her before, and on this occasion he succumbed to a torrid love affair— but shrewdly sidestepped the lady's efforts to trap him into matrimony.

Johnson and William Byrd might well have understood one another, but there was a vast difference between them. Byrd, too, had an interest in the Indian trade inherited from his father; he had the same land hunger displayed by Johnson and other prosperous colonials; and he also had a weakness for women often revealed in his diaries—particularly when he was a widower in London. But Byrd had an acute sense of decorum and guilt lacking in Johnson. When lured by feminine wiles, as happened on frequent evenings in London, Byrd spent some of the next morning on his knees in the church of St. Clement Danes asking God's forgiveness for his transgressions. Johnson, as far as the record indicates, never showed remorse for any affair of the heart.

Johnson, born in 1715 in County Meath, Ireland, was a nephew of Vice Admiral Sir Peter Warren, already the owner of a considerable landed estate in New York's Mohawk River valley. His uncle sent William to America, probably late in 1737, to look after his property. The young man of 22 immediately saw the possibility of expanding the fur trade. He opened a trading post and began to make friends with the Indians. Soon he acquired land of his own and continued for the rest of his life to expand his holdings.

The secret of Johnson's success lay in his ability to get along with people, especially the Indians. He began by treating them fairly. They soon learned that Johnson would not cheat them—an unusual phenomenon in the traffic with aborigines north of Albany. Many rascally Dutch and English traders infested this and other frontiers. Johnson's honesty proved a highly profitable asset.

By the 1740s Johnson had already created quite an establishment of his own north of the Mohawk River on the site of Amsterdam, New

York, to which he gave the name Mount Johnson. A large stone house served as both residence and fortress. Because of this dual use it was frequently referred to as Fort Johnson. Not far away, in 1762–63, he built a vast manor house near the present city of Johnstown, New York. This commodious building and its outlying units provided space for the entertainment of all classes of visitors, from half-naked Indians to European dignitaries. Here, in Johnson Hall, the proprietor lived out his days in grandeur that might have excited the envy of many a titled Englishman.

Johnson's domestic affairs in the early years were informal and somewhat obscure. He took as housekeeper and companion an indentured German girl who bore him a son and two daughters. At some point he legalized the union to legitimize his children.

After his wife's death he brought into Johnson Hall a Mohawk squaw whose uncle, Hendrick, was a powerful chief. This informal union proved extremely useful to Johnson because it cemented his relations with the Mohawks. He had three more children by her. After her death, his next companion was her niece, Molly, the sister of an even more powerful chief named Joseph Brant. A woman of great strength of character, Molly Brant proved a highly useful helpmate and bore him eight children. The union, once again, helped to further Johnson's friendship with the Mohawks, and he was taken into the tribe as an adopted brother.

Johnson's greatest contribution to the development of colonial America was the enduring friendship he established with the powerful Iroquois confederation known as the Six Nations, of which the Mohawks were an especially influential unit. The original Five Nations were the Mohawks, Oneidas, Onondagas, Cayugas, and Senecas. Early in the 18th century an Iroquoian tribe known as the Tuscaroras was driven out of North Carolina after a disastrous war and joined the Iroquois confederation to make the sixth nation.

Johnson's relations with the Indians were sometimes tempestuous and not always satisfactory to him or to the tribesmen. But over a long period, until his death in 1774, he contrived to keep the Six Nations usually on the side of the English. To be sure, he suffered defeat. For instance, the Senecas, proving most difficult, came under French influence and defected. But Johnson at times was able to lure them back into the fold and prevent any enduring schism.

Johnson's skill in dealing with the Indians resulted from his knowledge of their language, which he learned to speak fluently, his intimate acquaintance with Indian psychology, and his own eloquence in addressing the Indians in the figurative and flowery rhetoric that characterized their own speeches. Johnson became one of the country's most skillful forest diplomats. When patience was required, he could sit around the council fires smoking and listening for hours at a time. When the situation dictated force instead of words, he could make an instant decision and act accordingly. The Indians respected him, and many showed him deep affection.

In the numerous conflicts of the 18th century between the English and the French, as they battled for dominance in disputed territories in the north and west, Johnson was always ready to take the initiative in any military action. Early in the Seven Years' War, which saw Braddock's defeat in the 1775 campaign for Fort Duquesne, Johnson led some 2,500 provincial troops with 300 or 400 Indian allies in an effort to block the French and their Indians from pushing down from Lake Champlain. His immediate objective was Crown Point, which he never reached. But he did succeed in defeating the enemy in a battle at Lake George, the only English victory in 1755. So pleased was the Colonial Office in London with this unusual good news that King George II created Johnson a baronet, a hereditary title that he was able to pass on to his son.

The Lake George battle, characteristic of many frontier conflicts in this period, throws a vivid light on Johnson and the qualities of his leadership. To whip up enthusiasm among his Mohawk allies, who came to the rendezvous near Albany, he painted his face like a warrior, danced the war dance, and then gave them a feast of roast ox from which he cut the first slice with his sword. He had need to stir his Indian allies, even his brother Mohawks, for they were at this time reluctant warriors. Despite the feast and a discreet ration of rum, the Mohawks sent along only some 300 warriors. Although in the subsequent battle a few fought bravely, most did little; one commented that they had come to see their English brothers fight. With levies of provincial troops numbering about 2,200, Johnson marched toward Lake George. The militia, farmers who had never been in action before, regarded their local officers with more respect than Johnson, the over-all commander. Discipline was difficult. Yet Johnson showed great tact in dealing with these raw recruits and their untrained leaders. He invited the officers to his headquarters, gave them strong lemon punch and good wine, and held joint councils of war.

The French commander, a German named Baron Dieskau, had almost as much trouble as Johnson with his own troops, more than 3,500 regulars, Canadians, and Indians. The Canadians were unruly and the French Indians gave Dieskau so much difficulty that he wrote his superior that "one needs the patience of an angel to get on with these devils." This problem, common to both sides during the wilderness wars, makes Johnson's role more significant, for he managed to exercise more control over the Indians than any other colonial leader.

Early in the battle Johnson received a bullet in his thigh and had to take to his tent. This wound would plague him the rest of his life. Dieskau, also severely wounded, was taken captive and brought to the British commander's tent. Dieskau later declared that Johnson ordered the surgeon to treat the Baron's wounds before having his own dressed. Johnson also saved Dieskau from the vengeance of the Mohawks, who tried to seize and murder him because of the death of Hendrick, their chief. Such was Johnson's gallantry toward a brave enemy. Francis Parkman, the historian, wrote rather disparagingly of Johnson's failure to pursue and destroy the fleeing French troops, but Johnson understood the limitations of his forces. Always a pragmatic warrior, he knew better than regular British army officers what could be accomplished in the forests with unreliable Indian allies and ill-trained militia.

In later campaigns Johnson was profoundly irritated by the superciliousness of British commanders-in-chief, particularly with Sir Jeffrey Amherst whom he blamed for the slaughter and disaster on the frontier during Pontiac's conspiracy in the 1760s.

The year following Johnson's creation as a baronet, King George II also named him "colonel of the Six Nations" and sole superintendent of Indian affairs north of the Ohio. In the south he had a counterpart in John Stuart. Johnson was allowed to name as assistant George Croghan, a loyal and ingenious fellow Irishman who helped to implement his Indian policies.

Johnson hoped to restrain white invaders of the Indian hunting grounds. In 1768, to be sure, he held a great council at Fort Stanwix where, outdoing himself in oratory, he persuaded the Indians to sign a treaty ceding large tracts on the frontiers from Virginia to New York for settlement by whites. But lands beyond a boundary established at Fort Stanwix would be reserved to the Indians for their hunting grounds for "as long as the rivers run." Johnson himself acquired desirable tracts, for which he was later criticized. But if he enriched himself, he showed no more land-greed than hundreds of other colonials, including George Washington. He merely had greater opportunities.

In his later years Johnson took increasing pleasure in the baronial life. His wealth had enabled him to provide Johnson Hall with all the amenities that an 18th-century gentleman could desire. Not one to stint himself of any luxury, he loaded his pantries and cellars with the best food, wine, and liquors that money could buy. Johnson Hall teemed with swarms of white retainers, black slaves, and Indians of uncertain status. Always present were numerous Indian girls, some handsome, some fat and squat. Johnson was not always terribly fastidious. It was reported by contemporaries that he had fathered in his time some three hundred children. Few of these, of course, inhabited Johnson Hall. When George Croghan's own wife was pregnant, he sent her off to what he referred to as "fruitful Johnson Hall." Croghan himself, though constantly in debt, sought to imitate his leader by a similar display of luxury. He named his own log quarters on Lake Otsego "Croghan Hall."

Sir William Johnson was one of the most colorful figures in colonial

America. In his youth handsome, jovial, and friendly, he remained into his later years a strong and stalwart figure capable of winning friends among New York's aristocratic grandees and the warriors of the Six Nations. Though hated by many unscrupulous traders, and disliked by the pacific Quakers of Pennsylvania, he was extravagantly admired by frontiersmen everywhere. They believed Johnson capable of performing miracles with the Indians. European visitors to the estate enjoyed their host's hospitality and also remarked on his skillful diplomacy.

Like William Byrd of Virginia, Johnson took pleasure in his library at Johnson Hall, where he accumulated more than 2,000 volumes, chiefly on scientific, historical, and political subjects. As early as 1749 he had ordered the works of Sir Isaac Newton and numerous scientific treatises. Later he left a standing order with his London bookseller for "all new books on history, philosophy [science], and the lives of men worth reading about." He was especially interested in works on agriculture, which he, as a large landowner, was eager to promote.

Although having had little formal education, Johnson was a literate man, read a great deal in his later years, and wrote with vigor and clarity. His reports on Indian affairs (preserved among the Johnson Papers in the New York Historical Society and elsewhere) show a keen intellect and remarkable powers of observation and discrimination. He contributed to the American Philosophical Society, and his communications concerning the customs and languages of the Indians of the Six Nations were printed in the Society's *Proceedings*. Until the end of his life Johnson continued his anthropological interests and investigated variations in Indian dialects. Late in life he also became a trustee of the New Jersey school that ultimately became Rutgers University.

Although Johnson showed little concern for religion in his own personal life, like other leaders of his generation, he recognized its civilizing influence. In the town that he established near Johnson Hall (now Johnstown, New York), he built an Anglican church at his own expense and provided a canopied pew for himself—in case he should need it. He also encouraged the clergyman of this church to adapt the prayer book for the use of the Mohawks. His religious support was not exclusively confined to the Anglicans, for he helped build chapels for the Dutch Reformed Church in the Mohawk valley.

Among his contemporaries, Johnson demonstrated a remarkable combination of traits. He combined the qualities of an 18th-century landed grandee and the typical frontiersman of a later day, now popularized in both history and legend. He displayed some of the characteristics of the cultivated gentleman and virtuoso of his period; he felt at home with the great gentry of New York like the Schuylers and De Lanceys; and he could entertain English noblemen and their ladies at Johnson Hall with grace and ease. He also could display on occasion the manners and behavior of the typical "squaw man" known on all the frontiers. This unusually versatile colonial leader died on July 11, 1774, shortly after a speech to the Mohawks characterized by his usual persuasive tact in which he urged the chiefs to control their men. Some said his death was caused by syphilis; others diagnosed his fatal collapse as apoplexy.

Although controversies between the colonies and the mother country had become acute at the time of his death, Johnson never swerved in his loyalty to Great Britain. Had he lived, he would have been a Tory loyalist, and his influence with the Six Nations might have made their adherence to the British cause even more dangerous to the outcome of the War of Independence on the frontier.

3

Changing 18th-Century Religious Attitudes

JONATHAN EDWARDS
BENJAMIN FRANKLIN
THOMAS PAINE

by Paul F. Boller, Jr.
Texas Christian University

During the 18th century the secularization of American life and thought proceeded rapidly and for more and more Americans the church was becoming less important with each passing day. "This *Worldly Spirit*," complained a Boston minister in 1733, "has in a great measure thrust out Religion, and given it a Wound which will prove *Deadly* unless infinite Mercy prevent. . . ." Religion was not dying; it was being transformed. The stern Jehovah of high Calvinism was gradually being replaced by the genial God of rationalistic Deism for many people and the doctrine of human depravity was giving way to a belief in the potentialities of human nature for good. The key words for increasing numbers of Americans were no longer grace, election, and redemption; they were freedom, independence, and natural rights. Jonathan Edwards, struck by the "extraordinary dullness in religion" around him, worked hard to stem the tide of secularism overwhelming the land, but while he was solemnly calling sinners to repentance Benjamin Franklin was busily spreading the gospel of reason and tolerance in his almanacs, newspapers, pamphlets, and journals. And toward the end of the century Edwards' worst fears were realized: in an outspoken freethinking (and enormously popular) book called *Age of Reason*, Thomas Paine abandoned Franklin's kindly tolerance for all kinds of religion and issued a bold declaration of war on organized religion in general and a militant call for universal Deism. Surely no three men could have been more unalike than Edwards, Franklin, and Paine when it came to religion. But their lives, too, were utterly at variance.

Compared with Benjamin Franklin and Thomas Paine, Jonathan Edwards lived a singularly uneventful life. Born in East Windsor, Connecticut, in 1708, the son of a Congregational clergyman, he entered Yale at 13, studied theology after graduation, had a church for a while in New York City, became assistant and then senior minister of the Congregational Church in Northampton, Massachusetts, led a great revival there in 1734–35, quarreled with his parishioners in 1748 over qualifications for church membership, left to take a post in the frontier town of Stockbridge, and then agreed a few years later to become President of the College of New Jersey only to succumb to smallpox shortly after reaching Princeton in December 1758. He never went abroad, saw military action, participated in politics, held public office, or became involved in burning social issues, and he never really learned much about America outside of his beloved New England. Franklin, by contrast, was printer, journalist, editor, civic leader, scientist, inventor, diplomat, and statesman; and Paine was also a journalist, politician, and humanitarian leader as well as something of an inventor and very much a revolutionary.

Edwards in a real sense never really left home. Franklin and Paine walked among the great both here and abroad and they both participated in momentous events on both continents. But Edwards traveled widely only in the City of God and the crises he encountered were largely spiritual. Though like Franklin and Paine he familiarized himself with the secular psychology of John Locke and the new physics of Sir Isaac Newton, he utilized his knowledge mainly to justify the ways of a Calvinistic God to man. In an Age of Enlightenment, he dwelt on mystery, miracle, and prophecy; in an Age of Reason he emphasized religious affections and saving faith. He remained quite other-worldly in an increasingly secular age and implacably opposed to the resolute this-worldliness of men like Franklin and Paine. He dedicated his life to restoring the faith of his Puritan fathers that Franklin and Paine were steadily undermining. But when he died, the drift of American thought was unmistakably away from Edwardseanism, especially among educated people in urban centers, toward the genial optimism of Franklin and even, in some cases, toward the militant freethinking of Paine.

Edwards, unlike Franklin and Paine, was a God-intoxicated man. His aim in life was "to lie low before God, as in the dust; that I might be nothing, and that God might be All. . . ." In sermons, essays, and treatises on Christian fundamentals, he depicted in loving detail the beauty, power, wisdom, and goodness of God and called on his parishioners (and people everywhere) to prostrate themselves before Him. God, he declared, had created the world and sustained it by his infinite power; He worked through secondary causes and natural law but intervened in His creation whenever He saw fit; He gave all men and women common grace with which to improve their natural abilities, but He also freely bestowed His supernatural grace on a chosen few so that they might possess the kind of faith in Christ that guaranteed them salvation. Edwards' God was both omniscient and omnipotent; He had foreknowledge of all that was to come because He had foreordained it through all eternity. He had created the world for His own glory and it was the duty of His creatures to reflect this glory back upon their Creator by continual acts of praise and worship. Edwards insisted that "the whole is *of* God, and *in* God, and *to* God, and God is the beginning, middle, and end in this affair."

In Edwards' predestined scheme, there was no room for human autonomy. Men and women could not choose their destinies for themselves; their fate lay in the hands of the Almighty. Edwards never doubted the absolute sovereignty of God after his conversion at college and he was convinced that the profoundest insights into the human condition were embodied in the Calvinist theology he learned as a boy in a Puritan parsonage. Above all, he insisted on the doctrine of original sin: the belief that because of Adam's sin in disobeying God all human beings were born weak and selfish, behaved wickedly, and fully deserved the eternal punishment He reserved for unrepentant sinners. Edwards thought that empirical evidence for human depravity appeared in all ages and countries and that the history of every community was a chronicle of almost unrelieved greed, cruelty, dishonesty, and oppression. But he was also convinced of the validity of four other Calvinistic doctrines that dealt with release from the consequences of sin: unconditional election (God arbitrarily selects a few people for salvation regardless of their merits); limited atonement (Christ died to save some, but not all, people); irresistible grace (people play no part in achieving salvation but passively receive God's saving grace); and the final perseverance of the saints (people who receive God's free grace never lapse from their regenerate state). There was no place for free will in any of this. The Calvinistic Five Points that Edwards expounded rested squarely on a belief in predestination.

Edwards thought that the doctrine of predestination, like that of total depravity, was intellectually compelling. Did not the great Newton declare that "every event has a cause"? And did not the causal necessity asserted by scientists rule out free will (that is, uncaused volitions) as emphatically as predestination did? In his celebrated treatise on *Freedom of the Will* (1754), Edwards argued that human choices always have motives, that people always act according to what seems best to them at the moment, and that what seems good in turn depends on a variety of hereditary and environmental causes. But though people's choices are motivated, not free, people themselves are nonetheless free so long as there are no obstacles to doing what they choose to do and if they are not forced to do things they don't choose to do. The volitions of both slave and freeman are causally necessitated, but the latter is nevertheless free to do things the former can never do. Freedom, in short, lies in overt action, not in internal volition, and with this kind of freedom comes responsibility for what one does. Given human depravity, the tendency of people will be to put themselves above God and their neighbors, choose and act selfishly, and commit the sins that merit God's punishment. And only God can interrupt the necessary sequence of causes and effects set in motion by the creation of the world and, by shedding His free grace on certain men and women, rescue them from the awful consequences of their evil-doing.

During the Great Awakening, the great colonial religious revival of which the Northampton revival was one phase, Edwards preached powerful sermons on the terrible fate awaiting sinners upon the day of judgment and called on his congregations to realize the enormity of their depravity and throw themselves utterly on the mercy of God. He even gave the impression at times that if people strove hard enough to resist their sinful temptations and dedicate themselves to God they might be rewarded by an act of grace. Strictly speaking, however, he did not make and could not have made any such promise. Human beings surely could not, according to his theocentric religion, coax the Almighty into altering His predestined plans. Salvation was in God's hands, not man's; to think otherwise was to depreciate His majestic sovereignty. It might be, indeed, that the profound sense of worthlessness, feeling of utter dependence on God, and loving faith in Christ that accompanied the conversion experience, as well as the greater ability to resist temptation following from conversion, were outward signs of invisible grace. It was important therefore to strive hard, by constant reflection on one's infinite sinfulness, for the experience of grace. But if it came, it was God's, not the sinner's, doing. Edwards' determinism was uncompromising, but he did not regard it as inconsistent with hortatory sermonizing. He preached predestination and called for repentance the way modern sociologists teach environmental determinism and call for social reconstruction. Above all, he preached a religion of the heart, insisted that doctrinal knowledge without emotional commitment was worthless, and made a psychological analysis of the conversion experience after the Northampton revival that, like his later treatise on free will, still commands respect. He was anxious for the church to be filled, not with formal or birthright members, but with people who had experienced the awesome crisis of conversion. One of the reasons his Northampton congregation decided to dissolve its connection with him was that he demanded too much religiously from them.

In his later years, Edwards devoted his energies to combatting what was loosely called Arminianism. The Arminians made a larger place for human enterprise in their scheme of salvation than the Calvinists did and their views became increasingly popular in Protestant religious circles during the 18th century. They rejected the Five Points because there was no place for human initiative in them, insisted that human nature was a mixture of good and evil tendencies and not predetermined to evil, and asserted that a conscientious person might, by his own efforts, as well as with the help of God, achieve salvation. By playing down God's arbitrary grace and stressing man's potentiality for good, Arminianism had the effect of raising man's status at the expense of God's. Edwards observed the spread of Arminianism (in the Church of England and among educated people in New England, particularly in eastern Massachusetts) with alarm. He was convinced that rejecting the doctrine of God's free grace was the first step toward deism, atheism, and the destruction of Christianity. In 1754 he published his massive treatise on free will with the hope of demolishing the Arminian heresy once for all.

*   *   *

Edwards' *Freedom of the Will* was a magnificent failure. Though difficult to refute, it did little to stem the tide of Arminianism in Edwards' day. The movement in America as well as in England was steadily away from Calvinism to Arminianism and then to deism and beyond. The evolution of Benjamin Franklin's thinking about religion was a perfect example of the kind of 18th-century religious trends that Edwards was combatting. Franklin, like Edwards, was born into an orthodox home in Boston, filled with books on "polemical divinity," baptized in the Presbyterian church, and instructed in the Calvinist "Quinquarticulars" as a child. But where Edwards spent his boyhood building prayer-booths, yearning for conversion, and striving mightily to accept divine sovereignty, young Franklin was learning to swim, make candles in his father's shop, perfect his writing style, and set type in his brother's printing shop. It would never have occurred to Edwards, as it did to Franklin, to urge his father to say grace over a barrel of fish once for all so he wouldn't have to do it each time the family ate fish at mealtimes. Or to suggest to a Presbyterian chaplain, as Franklin did later on, to dole out the soldiers' ration of rum right after divine service in order to improve church attendance. Unlike Edwards, Franklin discarded Calvinism with relief as a young man. He read some books attempting to refute deism and was promptly converted to the deist outlook. He was a "staunch doubter" at 16; at that age Edwards was immersed in theology. From Edwards' point of view, Franklin's thinking went steadily downhill after he became a deist.

When he was about 19, Franklin amused himself by writing a *Dissertation on Liberty and Necessity* (1725) which proved that predestinarian assumptions like Edwards' shut virtue as well as freedom out of the world. If God is all-wise, all-good, and all-powerful, and determines whatever happens, he argued, it follows that there can be no evil, no free will, and no morality in the world. No evil, because nothing happens without God's consent and what He consents to must be good because He is good. (Edwards had argued that God "permits" sin, though He hates it, for His own mysterious purposes.) No free will, because if man can do only what God predetermines him to do, he cannot choose on his own. No morality, because if men do not choose for themselves, "there can be neither Merit nor Demerit in Creatures" and "therefore every Creature must be equally esteem'd by the Creator." It would have been foolish, Franklin added, for God to have peopled the world with free agents, because if people had to make their own decisions they would never know what was best to do and they would have only one chance in 10,000 of actually hitting on the right action. A predestined world, though lacking in freedom and virtue, was a smoothly operating and harmonious one. Man should be grateful therefore that he is "Part of this great Machine, the Universe," that "his regular Acting is requisite to the regular moving of the whole," and that his choices and actions were governed by an all-wise Providence. Sowing a few wild oats in London, as Franklin was doing when he composed his "little metaphysical piece," as he called it, was presumably part of God's great plan.

Franklin eventually decided that his "Dissertation" had "an ill-tendency" because it was so cavalier about virtue, destroyed most copies of it, and wrote an essay on "the Providence of God in the Government of the World" (1732) in which he argued the case for freedom. In this essay Franklin took the line that predestination and prayer were incompatible. God would be malicious, he said, if He allowed people to pray in a world in which everything was foreordained. But God was good, not malicious, and people do pray, and the upshot must be that things are not utterly foreordained. (Edwards of course thought that both the rain and the prayers for rain were foreordained.) Franklin did not think that God left *everything* in the world to free agency, for that would make Him indifferent to His creation. So having rejected universal determinism and absolute freedom, he reached a compromise: God permits the laws of nature and the free agency of men to shape what happens in the world, but on occasion, not to leave the rewarding of virtue and the punishing of evil entirely to chance, He "interferes by his particular Providence, and sets aside the Events which would otherwise have been produced in the Course of Nature, or by the Free Agency of Men...." Franklin was convinced that God had imparted some of His freedom, along with some of His wisdom, power, and goodness, to men. But he did not so much argue the case for free agency as to show the incompatibility of predestination with human effort. Thereafter he took freedom for granted and abandoned metaphysical reasonings about it as exercises in frustration. Like most of his associates in colonial America he lost interest in Calvinistic issues and never again engaged in serious discussion of the predestination-free will question.

But if Franklin lost interest in theology, his interest in religion continued undiminished. He was unorthodox but not irreligious. In 1728, he drew up a little liturgy for his own private use entitled *Articles of Belief and Acts of Religion*. In it, he professed belief in "one Supreme most perfect Being" who was too infinite and incomprehensible for humans to be able to worship and who, as far as human praise was concerned, was "INFINITELY ABOVE IT." But the Infinite, according to Franklin, had created "many Beings or Gods, vastly superior to Man" who did comprehend and worship Him and who were wise, good, and powerful enough themselves to create suns and planets of their own to govern. Franklin wasn't sure whether these secondary gods were immortal; they might endure forever or they might die out and be replaced by other gods after many ages—but they deserved and welcomed acts of worship. Franklin reserved his devotion for the "wise and good God, who is the Author and Owner of our System" and he pictured Him as having some of the same passions as human beings and consequently pleased by praise and worship and hurt by neglect. Franklin was convinced that the God of our solar system was a "good Being" who created many things for the "Delight of Man" and who was pleased "when He sees His Children solace themselves in any manner of pleasant Exercises and innocent Delights." But without virtue, Franklin added, people could have no happiness in the world and so "I firmly believe he delights to see me Virtuous, because he is pleas'd when he sees me Happy." Having stated his "First Principles," Franklin went on to present an elaborate liturgy of adoration, petition, and thanks to the God of our planetary system. It is clear that the polytheism of Franklin's liturgy enabled him to accept the aloof and impersonal deist God (who created the great world-machine and then left it to operate on its own by the laws of nature) without entirely abandoning the personal God of traditional religion which, he thought, satisfied the "natural principle" all people possess "which inclines . . . to DEVOTION or the Worship of some unseen Power." But polytheism was no rigid belief for Franklin. Though he toyed all his life with the notion of a plurality of lesser gods under the direction of a Supreme Power (much as Newton did), he also frequently expressed monotheistic views. In his autobiography he declared that "there is one God, who made all things" and this was by no means unusual for him.

Franklin's *Articles* show that he was fond of ceremony and ritual. He was continually tinkering with traditional Christian forms, rites, and creeds and trying to make them more acceptable to freethinkers like himself. In 1773, he collaborated with Lord Le DeSpencer in revising the Anglican Book of Common Prayer, on which his *Articles of Religion* had been modelled, to make it more attractive to church-goers. Lord Le DeSpencer edited the liturgy and Franklin redid the catechism as well as the Psalms and together they succeeded in cutting the Anglican service in half. For his part, Franklin omitted the imprecatory Psalms which, he said, "appeared not to suit well the Christian doctrine of forgiveness of injuries," abbreviated the prayers for the visitation of the sick, and shortened the "Order for the Burial of the Dead" in order "to preserve the health and lives of the living." Franklin hoped the shortened service would bring more people into church but he later admitted that the "Abridgement of the Book of Common Prayer" attracted little interest. Nevertheless, he joined David Williams, an English political philosopher, in preparing another system of worship which was even more deistical than the "Abridgement." He also went to work on the Lord's Prayer, which he thought badly needed modernizing, and turned it in effect into a Deist's petition; proposed a new version of the Bible in modern English and rewrote some verses from Job as an example of what he had in mind; and composed new chapters for the Old Testament containing parables about brotherly love and religious toleration. His "Parable Against Persecution," presented as the 51st chapter of Genesis, recounts how Abraham turned a stranger away from his house because he worshipped a different God and then relented after being severely rebuked for his intolerance by Jehovah.

Franklin thought religious intolerance was the curse of humanity and he did everything he could as editor and civic leader in Philadelphia to combat it. In 1735, he vigorously championed Samuel Hemphill, a Presbyterian minister under fire for heresy in the Synod of Philadelphia; in 1740, helped secure a building in which evangelist George Whitefield (who had been barred from the city's pulpits) might hold forth; and in 1747, while organizing a voluntary military "Association" for the defense of Pennsylvania, warned his supporters against animosity toward the pacifist Quakers who "from their religious *Scruples,* cannot allow themselves to join us." In his autobiography, he expressed admiration for the Dunkers who, though much misunderstood, refrained from publishing their Confession of Faith lest it bind and restrict them and make them "unwilling to receive Farther Improvement." During the Hemphill controversy, Franklin evinced considerable anticlerical feeling, referring to the ministers who put Hemphill on trial as "Rev. Asses," but on the whole his relations with clergymen of all denominations were amicable. He was on excellent terms with Whitefield, though the Anglican revivalist's Calvinist views were much closer to Edwards' than to his own, and he told his brother: "He is a good Man and I love him." But when he invited Whitefield to stay at his home and the latter thanked him for making the offer "for Christ's sake," Franklin exclaimed: "Don't let me be mistaken; it was not for Christ's sake, but for your sake." Whitefield despaired of ever converting his journalist friend.

Franklin respected organized religion for its emotional as well as moral value and though not a regular church-goer himself (after all, he had his own private liturgy), he gave financial support, first to the Presbyterian and then to the Episcopal church in Philadelphia (where he had a pew from 1760 to 1790), observed Lent, probably took communion on occasion, urged members of his family to participate regularly in liturgical devotions, proposed fast days for colonial Pennsylvania, and suggested daily prayers in the Constitutional Convention of 1787. He also gave money for Whitefield's projects, helped establish the first Unitarian chapel in England, and contributed to a fund to keep the Jewish synagogue in Philadelphia from being auctioned for debt. After the Revolution, Franklin helped the American Protestant Episcopal Church establish its independence from the Church of England; he also advised the Holy See on the organization of the Catholic Church in the new nation and played some part in the decision of the Spanish Cortes to end the Inquisition. "The Catholics thought him almost a Catholic," observed John Adams. "The Church of England claimed him as one of them. The Presbyterians thought him half a Presbyterian, and the Friends believed him a wet Quaker." Franklin was of course none of these; he was a Deist who believed in God and immortality but did not accept either the divinity of Christ or the superiority of Christianity to other world religions. But he did believe in a superintending Providence and he thought churches performed a useful function in society and, as we have seen, felt a personal need for some kind of religious devotions himself.

Still, Franklin's religion was largely practical. He regarded the inculcation of practical morality as a religion's chief function. The "best service toward God," he told a friend, "is doing good toward men. . . ." He thought "works of kindness, charity, mercy, and public Spirit" were far more important than "holiday-keeping, sermon reading or hearing, performing church ceremonies, or making long prayers" and he was sure that Jesus also preferred the *"doers* of the Word, to the mere *hearers."* When his sister Jane expressed misgivings about his religion, Franklin referred her to a passage in Edwards' *Thoughts on Revivals* (1742) which placed such fruits of faith as "Self-denial, Righteousness, Meekness, and Christian Love, in our Behavior among Men" above such outward acts of worship as attending church, taking the sacrament, bowing, kneeling, and praying. From the beginning, Franklin enjoyed devising moral exercises as well as liturgies of devotion for himself. Two years before composing his *Acts of Religion,* he drew up a plan for regulating his "future Conduct of Life" in which he resolved to be extremely frugal, speak the truth in every instance, apply himself industriously to every task he undertook, and to speak ill of no man. A few years later he conceived an even more ambitious project for arriving at moral perfection consisting of 13 virtues—temperance, silence, order, resolution, frugality, industry, sincerity, justice, moderation, cleanliness, tranquillity, chastity, and humility—on which he was to rate himself day by day. He planned to concentrate on one virtue each week, thus making the rounds in 13 weeks and repeating the "course," as he called it, four times a year. He kept a record of his performance in a little notebook which he always carried with him, composed a little prayer to be used daily beseeching God's assistance in executing his resolutions, and followed out his plan of self-examination for a surprising number of years. He was dismayed to find himself "so much fuller of faults" than he had imagined and he admitted that the virtue, Order, gave him the greatest trouble, though he carefully drew up a schedule to follow for the 24 hours of each day. He also revealed in his autobiography that his list of virtues at first contained only 12, but a Quaker friend, informing him he was generally regarded as proud, advised him to add Humility to his list, which he agreed to do. Franklin thought there was "no one of our natural passions so hard to subdue as *pride*" and he confessed: "I cannot boast of much success in acquiring the *reality* of this virtue, but I had a good deal with regard to the *appearance* of it."

Franklin's emphasis on industry and frugality in his schemes of virtue led Max Weber in *The Protestant Ethic and the Spirit of Capitalism* (1905) to single him out as a perfect example of the bourgeois Economic Man of early modern times who identified godliness with hard work and by practicing the economic virtues—thrift, temperance, sobriety, frugality, and diligence—forged ahead rapidly in an expanding capitalistic economy. There was much in Franklin's writing illustrative of the Protestant or Puritan work ethic. For years, his *Poor Richard's Almanac* poured out preachy little admonitions like the following: "Early to bed, early to rise, makes a man healthy, wealthy, and wise"; "God helps them that help themselves"; "God gives all things to industry"; "Little strokes fell great oaks"; "Keep thy shop and thy shop will keep thee"; "No gains without pains"; "Idleness is the greatest Prodigality"; "Lost Time is never found again"; "Dost thou love life? then do not squander Time, for that's the Stuff Life is made of." Franklin also wrote essays on "Necessary Hints to Those That Would Be Rich" and "The Way to Make Money Plenty in Every Man's Pocket," and in his *Advice to a Young Tradesman* (1740) declared that the way to wealth "depends chiefly on two Words, INDUSTRY AND FRUGALITY." After the Revolution, he wanted the new nation to use coins inscribed with maxims from *Poor Richard's Almanac* as well as with Biblical injunctions. Franklin was no stuffy bourgeois devoid of *joie de vivre*. He included hedonistic as well as prudential maxims in his almanacs, wrote drinking songs ("For there can't be good Living where there is not good Drinking") as well as satirical, slightly cynical and sometimes ribald pieces, and enjoyed living lavishly in Paris where he developed gout. "Frugality is an enriching virtue," he once sighed; "a virtue I never could acquire in myself." In *The Way to Wealth* (1758), a compilation of *Poor Richard* maxims, Franklin has Father Abraham preach the gospel of thrift and industry to a crowd of people but he ends the book by reporting that the people "approved the Doctrine and immediately practiced the contrary, just as if it had been a common Sermon." Franklin regarded "the Pursuit of Wealth to no end" as foolish and while he thought that discipline and diligence were essential to the achievement of anything worthwhile, he also realized it was absurd to make them ends in themselves. He worked hard himself (though, as with all supremely talented people, there was something effortless about everything he did), but not all the time. He liked to swim, take air baths in the nude, participate in drinking sessions, and dally with the ladies. ("Somebody, it seems, gave it out that I loved ladies," he told his stepniece, tongue in cheek, in 1779.) If he was a "workaholic," his contemporaries were not aware of it. John Adams in fact thought him something of a rake and, when working with him on diplomatic missions in France after the Revolution, he was disgusted with the older man's late hours and generally frivolous behavior.

The Puritan ethic was unquestionably important to Franklin, but it represented only one side of his thinking. At 42 he was a rich man and he arranged to turn the management of his printing and bookselling house over to his partners so he could devote himself to science and public service. Yet he had always been concerned with non-pecuniary enterprises. While still building up his printing business, he found time to form the Junto club, a kind of adult-education society for young men; create the Philadelphia Library Company, the first subscription library in America; organize the Union Fire Company, the first in Philadelphia, and help establish the American Philosophical Society for scientific research and discussion. He also invented the Franklin open stove (which he refused to patent since he intended it for the benefit of mankind) and began his studies in electricity. After he retired, the pace of his scientific and civic activities increased. He founded the academy out of which the University of Pennsylvania developed, helped establish the Pennsylvania hospital, published *Experiments and Observations on Electricity* (1751), a path-breaking study which brought him fame in Europe rivaling that of Newton's, invented the lightning rod, studied the Gulf Stream, made numerous meteorological investigations, constructed a glass harmonica or organ which became popular in Europe (and for which Beethoven and Mozart composed music) and, after holding several local offices, began his long career as a public official outside of Pennsylvania: deputy postmaster general of North America, agent in London for several colonies, member of the Continental Congress that declared independence, commissioner in France negotiating the French alliance, member of the peace commission in Britain after Yorktown, and delegate to the Constitutional Convention. During an unusually long and busy life he also championed free speech, thought, press, and religion in his publications and in his last years lent his prestigious name to the burgeoning antislavery movement.

Franklin always remained something of a Puritan. He could not help thinking, particularly in his younger days, that poverty was an individual, not a social, responsibility, and that people were poor because of idleness and sloth, not because of fortuitous circumstances. He also occasionally expressed a gloomy view of human nature which Edwards would have heartily endorsed. In one of his rare speeches in the Constitutional Convention of 1787, he proposed a salaryless Chief Magistrate for the new republic. His reasoning: the two strongest human impulses are love of power and love of money and to unite both power and money in the presidency would attract people who were both greedy and power-mad and turn it into a monarchy. Yet Franklin was as much Deist as Puritan and he succeeded in shucking off much of the "sardonic optimism" (as George Santayana called it) of his Puritan heritage. He came to believe that people had innate benevolent impulses that could be nourished, as well as self-regarding instincts, and that with the help of a benevolent Providence they might learn to live together with generosity and goodwill in this world. He even came, perhaps because of his later association with French liberals, to take a social view of property. Private property, he declared, was "the Creature of public Convention"; natural right gave each men title to all the property necessary for the "Conservation of the Individual and the Propagation of the Species," but the remainder was "the Property of the Public, who, by their Laws, have created it, and who may therefore by other Laws dispose of it, whenever the Welfare of the Public shall demand such disposition." It was a point of view Thomas Paine, powerfully drawn, like Franklin, to laissez faire, was also to come around to in his later years.

When Franklin was an old man, Paine visited him in Philadelphia and was surprised to find him busily arranging books in his library. But Franklin told him it was his policy "to live on as if I was to live always." Franklin faced death, as he did life, with equanimity; he knew God was frugal and wouldn't waste anything He had created and he was confident that he would always exist in some form. Paine shared Franklin's belief in a benevolent God and a future state of existence, but he was far less patient with things as they were than Franklin and much more anxious to get on with the business of demolishing ancient superstitions and overturning reactionary social institutions. Once he showed Franklin a strongly worded attack on organized religion he had just composed and Franklin strongly advised him to tone it down or destroy it. But the older Paine got the harder he found it to tone things down. Freeing the mind from bondage to the reactionary past, he had concluded, took extraordinary efforts. Paine was closer to Edwards than to Franklin in his unwillingness to compromise with what he regarded as evil.

"Where liberty is, there is my country," Franklin once remarked. "Where liberty is not, there is my country," Paine, an enemy of oppression wherever he happened to be, is said to have responded. Paine was more militant as a Deist than Franklin was and he had far less tolerance for organized religion (and for the pecadilloes of human nature) than his friend Franklin did. He was a religious as well as a political revolutionary and he wanted to overturn ecclesiastical as well as political establishments. His aim was to replace conventional religion with a "religion of humanity" and hereditary monarchies and aristocracies with republican institutions based on the freely given consent of the governed. He thought Deism and republicanism went naturally together. Unlike Franklin, he didn't take even a passing interest in theological questions; he had the typical 18th-century rationalist's contempt for such matters. He did write a piece on "the absurd and impious doctrine of predestination" toward the end of his life but he could scarcely conceal his exasperation over having to bother with the subject at all. In Paine's opinion, human beings were—or should be—"free agents," that is, autonomous individuals who could express their opinions openly, carry out actions of their own choosing, and participate in social decisions involving their happiness and well-being. Paine did not try to argue the case philosophically; he thought it was obvious to reasonable people. His major concern was with social and political arrangements guaranteeing and expanding man's free agency. In 1792, he made a proud inventory of the causes that motivated his life: representative government, universal education, public support for the poor and aged, world peace, free trade, and the eradication of superstition. He summed it all up in *The Rights of Man*: "... my country is the world, and my religion is to do good."

*   *   *

It is customary to explain Paine's love of freedom and his hatred of war, slavery, and oppression by his Quaker background. His father was a poor Quaker corset-maker in Thetford, England, and though Paine never formally joined the Society of Friends, he always spoke with affection of his Quaker rearing. He praised the Friends for "their care of the poor of their Society" and for "the education of their children" and, while critical of them for not supporting the American Revolution, said he shared their detestation of war. In *Age of Reason,* that powerful blast against all organized religion, he praised the Society of Friends as the only sect that had not engaged in persecution and said he reverenced their philanthropy. And though he added that he couldn't help smiling at thinking what the world would be like if the Quakers, with their plain ways, had been consulted at creation, he singled them out as being closer to "true Deism in the moral and benign part thereof" than any other religion. Coming from Paine this was high praise indeed. In plain fact, though, Paine's militant rationalism was about as far from the Quaker's mystical Inner Light as it was from the Calvinism of Jonathan Edwards and George Whitefield he so detested.

The natural bent of his mind, Paine once said, was toward science. When he was a young man, he recalled, he purchased a pair of globes, began attending science lectures in London, and became friendly with an astronomer who belonged to the Royal Society. He also studied mathematics on his own, made scientific and mechanical experiments, and followed Franklin's electrical researches with interest. Shortly after coming to America in November 1774, he became part of the little scientific community centered around Franklin, Jefferson, and other members of the American Philosophical Society. Like Franklin, he was fascinated by inventions. While editing the *Pennsylvania Magazine,* he published reports on various new English inventions and he also invented things himself: a planing machine, a new crane, smokeless candles (with Franklin's help), and, above all, an iron bridge (in which Franklin was also interested). The universe for Paine was an immense machine and God a great mechanic. God was also an "Almighty Lecturer" who displayed the principles of science in the structure of the universe. Paine saw unerring order and universal harmony in every part of God's works and believed the laws governing the physical world were eternal. But moral truths for Paine were just as self-evident and immutable as scientific truths. He dismissed with scorn the notion that abstract ideas and general principles were human contrivances devised to facilitate human understanding; he thought of them as truths of divine origin which were accessible to reason (the highest authority) if it were given a free rein. His epistemology was both optimistic and authoritarian.

Paine thought the social, religious, and political institutions of the Western world were horrendously unscientific. Cumbersome, unwieldy, devious, and oppressive, they prevented people from apprehending things as they truly were and living naturally by them. He took upon himself the gigantic task of setting people right on basic principles and he had no Quaker humility about the validity of his opinions. "What I write is pure nature," he averred, "and my pen and my soul have ever gone together." Though his philosophy was based on ideas familiar to all educated and informed people in the West in the late 18th century (especially those of Locke and Newton), Paine thought it came from acts of pure reason on his own part and he sincerely believed he was a man of nature thinking about certain issues for the first time. Actually, only in the rigorous consistency and boldness with which he carried certain principles to their logical conclusion can he be considered original. But the lucidity, precision, and assurance with which he expounded his ideas gave them wide currency and his popular influence far outran his originality. "I am a *farmer of thoughts*," he once said, "and all the crops I raise I give away."

Paine had not intended to become a farmer of thoughts when he left his excise post in London and came to America in 1774 armed with letters of introduction from Franklin whom he had met a few months earlier. He came looking for a career in science or teaching. But he soon secured a position on the *Pennsylvania Packet* and quickly discovered that his natural talents lay in journalism. With the outbreak of the American Revolution, he thought he saw "a vast scene" opening in America with momentous consequences for the freedom of mankind and he joined the rebels. In addition to contributing *Common Sense* (which Franklin said had "prodigious effects" on the movement for independence from Britain) and *The Crisis* to the American cause, he served in the Continental Army and also worked for the Continental Congress. After the Revolution he looked back with pride on the part he had played in helping found "a New Empire raised on the principles of liberty and liberality." In 1787 he left his adopted country, mainly to promote his plan for a single-arch iron bridge in Europe, and he intended to return the following year. But he was soon caught up in the swirl of events in France and he ended by remaining in Europe, shuttling, for a time, between Paris and London, until 1802. The outbreak of the French Revolution, Paine thought, opened up an opportunity to extend "the principles of liberty and fraternity through the greater part of Europe" and he felt duty-bound to remain on hand to contribute his services to the revolutionary cause. In Paine's opinion, the French cause, like the earlier American cause, was the cause of all mankind and involved the freedom and rights of all men. During the French Revolution he did what he could to help: consulted with French leaders, served in the French National Assembly, and participated in constitution-making. Above all, he defended the principles of the Revolution in his forthright essays and pamphlets and tried to promote a republican revolution in England. When Edmund Burke published *Reflections on the Revolution in France* late in 1790, defending hereditary monarchies and established churches against the attacks of revolutionaries, Paine converted an essay he was working on into a massive assault on monarchical institutions and a defense of republican government which was published as *The Rights of Man* in 1791 and 1792. Paine's book touched off a storm of criticism among exponents of privilege and prescription and Paine was charged with everything ranging from ignorance, mendacity, and vulgarity on the one hand to recklessness, demagoguery, and downright anarchism on the other. The British government declared Paine's book seditious and proclaimed Paine an outlaw in December 1792.

But Paine remained imperturbable throughout. To him it all seemed as plain as day. To support the French Revolution—and the earlier American Revolution—was, he thought, the most natural thing in the world for a rational person to do. The fight for free institutions was grounded in the very nature of things. God, Paine insisted, had created the world and endowed every human being in it with a natural right to self-determination. He had given man, moreover, the precious gift of reason by which he was to apprehend the magnificent laws of nature He had set in motion for regulating creation and govern his life accordingly. Somehow, though, human beings in the course of long history had become almost utterly estranged from nature and nature's God. (Paine was no better than Edwards or Franklin at reconciling the existence of evil in the world with a benevolent Creator.) A small clique of self-interested men (priests and politicians) had succeeded by force and fraud in erecting formidable barriers, in the form of artificial and corrupt institutions, between man and nature. Not only did they concentrate power and wealth in their own hands and develop stupendous privileges for themselves that they transmitted to their heirs and favorites by means of hereditary institutions; they also deprived the majority of people of their natural God-given rights of free agency, equal opportunity, and political participation and kept them in a state of bondage and misery. Privileged elites and hereditary governments of all kinds violated the natural rights of man, according to Paine, and were absolutely contrary to nature; only republican governments, whose officials were chosen freely by the people and dedicated to protecting the rights of all citizens, had the sanction of nature and nature's God.

In America, Paine had not been much concerned with religion and his attitude toward the churches, even the Calvinistic ones, was generally benign, for most of them supported the Revolution. There was no "adulterous connection" between church and state in the United States, as there was in Europe, he observed, and religious diversity produced a great deal of tolerance (though Paine disliked the condescension implied in the word) and freedom in religious matters. In France, however, as elsewhere in Europe, things were different. Paine was appalled by the close bonds between Christianity and the old regime in France and he became convinced that organized religion had for centuries been one of the main enemies of the free mind. In 1794, he published the first part of *Age of Reason* (the second part came out the following year) to set people straight on religion as he had earlier set them straight on politics. He dedicated it to "my Fellow Citizens of the United States" and subtitled it "An Investigation of True and Fabulous Theology." By the latter he of course meant the kind of theology that people like Edwards cherished.

Paine's *Age of Reason* was a frankly anti-Christian book, greatly admired by freethinkers in Paine's day and ever since, but he wrote it to counteract atheism as well as orthodoxy. (This did not prevent Theodore Roosevelt from calling Paine a "filthy little atheist" many years later.) He was worried, he confessed in the preface to the book, lest, in the general overturn of established religious institutions and practices in France during the Revolution, people might "lose sight of morality, of humanity, and of the theology that is true." Paine made his own confession of faith at the outset. "I believe in one God, and no more," he announced; "and I hope for happiness beyond this life." He also believed in the equality of man, he added, and thought that religious duties consisted of "doing justice, loving mercy, and endeavoring to make our fellow creatures happy." He then announced that he most emphatically did not believe in the creeds professed by the Jewish, Roman, Greek, Turkish, Protestant or any other church and he exclaimed: "My own mind is my own church." All national institutions of churches, whether Jewish, Christian, or Turkish, he went on to say, were "no other than human inventions, set up to terrify and enslave mankind, and monopolize power and profit." The rest of *Age of Reason* was a sustained attack on the Bible and on Christian theology.

Paine had little but scorn and contempt for the Bible. He rejected it as the word of God, questioned the historical authenticity of the events recorded in it, and subjected its doctrines to scathing criticism. He went through the Old and New Testaments, book by book, reducing most of them to absurdity. Except for the Psalms and the book of Job, in which he admitted there was a great deal of sentiment reverentially expressed about the power and benignity of the Almighty, Paine had nothing good to say about the Old Testament. He dismissed it as a mélange of "obscene stories, voluptuous debaucheries, cruel and tortuous executions, and unrelenting vindictiveness" and declared that it had corrupted and brutalized mankind. He was no easier on the New Testament. He ridiculed the immaculate conception, the resurrection, the Trinity, and the admonition to love one's enemies (though he rejected the idea of revenge for injury) and dismissed the New Testament miracles as "degrading the Almighty into the character of a showman, playing tricks to amuse and make the people stare and wonder." Paine did, to be sure, speak respectfully of Jesus: "He was a virtuous and an amiable man" and "the morality that he preached and practised was of the most benevolent kind . . ." But he denied the divinity of Christ, saying he was no more the son of God than any other human being, and he pointed out that systems of morality similar to Jesus' had been preached by Confucius and some of the Greek philosophers many years before. He also declared that the Christian church had set up a system of religion utterly contradictory to the character of the person whose name it bore: "It has set up a religion of pomp and of revenue, in pretended imitation of a person whose life was humility and poverty."

Was there, then, to be no word of God? Was there to be no divine revelation for humanity? There was, indeed, Paine hastened to say. "The WORD OF GOD IS THE CREATION WE BEHOLD," he exclaimed, "and it is in this *word*, which no human invention can counterfeit or alter, that God speaketh universally to man." God's power, said Paine, was found in the immensity of the universe; his wisdom in the "unchangeable order by which the incomprehensible whole" was governed; his munificence in the abundance with which he filled the Earth; and his mercy in not withholding that abundance even from the unthankful. "In fine," said Paine, "do we want to know what God is? Search not the book called the Scripture, which any human mind might make, but the Scripture called creation." Paine did not accept the idea of "particular Providences" (interpositions by God from time to time in the affairs of men), as Franklin did, though he never doubted God's benevolent supervision ("general Providence") of the universe as a whole through the laws of nature. Nor did he trouble himself, as Franklin did, with composing prayers and liturgies of devotion; and he certainly did not think, as Edwards did, that religion was mainly a matter of the heart. Religion for Paine was purely a matter of reason, like science, with which it was so closely identified in his mind, and he thought human beings were worshipping God best when they were studying His creation and discovering how it was constructed. Science and religion were virtually interchangeable for Paine.

Paine's *Age of Reason* delighted freethinkers and appalled Christian believers everywhere. In some ways the book created a greater storm than *Rights of Man* had created and it alienated many of his former admirers in America. Devout people called it "The Devil's Prayer Book" and excoriated the author as an atheist, infidel, sot, adulterer, reptile, monster, and "lily-livered rogue." In 1801, when President Jefferson invited Paine to return to the United States from France on a government vessel, there was considerable indignation among the orthodox. "What!" exclaimed a Boston newspaper, "invite to the United States that lying, drunken, brutal infidel, who rejoiced in the opportunity of basking and wallowing in the confusion, devastation, bloodshed, rapine, and murder, in which his soul delights!" When Paine finally returned to America in 1802, to live out his remaining years, he was treated like a pariah. One coachman refused to accept so notorious an infidel as a passenger and the town of New Rochelle, where he went to live on some land the State of New York had given him as a reward for his Revolutionary services, denied him the right to vote even though Congress had made him a citizen during the Revolution. Even the Quakers held him at arm's length; when he died in Greenwich Village in poverty and obscurity in 1809, they refused to let his body be placed in their burial grounds. But Deism, it turned out, was not as seductive to Americans as Edwards had feared it would be. In the 1790s, it is true, there was a decline in church-going and a drift away from orthodoxy, and pious people feared that a wave of Deism was engulfing the nation, especially the colleges, and blamed Paine for it. But a Second Great Awakening was beginning to develop, even during Paine's last years, and it was soon to sweep hundreds of Americans back into orthodoxy and make good church-goers out of them.

*   *   *

Edwards would have rejoiced to see the Second Great Awakening overwhelm the tide of Deism in America. He might even have looked on the Second Awakening, as he did the first, as a sign that perhaps the millennium might begin in America after all. Franklin's hopes for America were quite different: his emphasis was on material progress, though he admitted that progress in morality, though less likely, was more important. Paine was the most hopeful of all. Despite the personal rebuffs he received at the end of his life and despite the setbacks to the cause of republicanism and to the "religion of humanity" he witnessed in both Europe and America, he never doubted that they would triumph some day in America and that the United States, by her example, would inspire other nations to develop free and rational institutions. Many Americans came to share Paine's hopes. In American religious circles, the 19th century marked a steady trend away from Edwardsean pessimism about humanity toward the kind of hopeful optimism concerning human nature that Paine espoused. In the 20th century, many of the things that Paine said about religion would seem commonplace in the increasingly liberal churches of the nation.

Still, after World War I, there was an unmistakable movement in American religious circles back to Edwardsean pessimism or at least back to Franklin's mixed views about humanity. Reinhold Niebuhr, America's best-known theologian after the 1930s, insisted, like Edwards, that the ancient doctrine of original sin contained important empirical insights into human nature. While not denying that there were rational and moral resources available to human beings (as Paine thought there were) that enabled them to develop self-governing institutions that safeguarded the freedom and happiness of citizens, Niebuhr also insisted there was an ineradicable impulse toward self-aggrandizement in all people (including the most idealistic) that had to be carefully hedged about with democratic checks and balances. "Man's capacity for justice makes democracy possible," declared Niebuhr; but "man's inclination to injustice makes democracy necessary." Edwards and Paine would have been puzzled by Niebuhr's statement. Franklin would have understood perfectly.

4

The Rights of Man and the American Revolution

SAMUEL ADAMS
THOMAS HUTCHINSON
JOHN DICKINSON

by James Kirby Martin
Rutgers University

Even with 200 years of historical perspective, the American Revolution stands as an elusive series of events; no consensus has emerged about what factors caused the Revolution. Likewise, the consequences of the momentous decision of 13 colonies to unite as one and break away from the sovereign British empire are still heatedly debated. To suggest that these issues could be settled here would be somewhat presumptuous. They cannot. But the personal histories of Samuel Adams, Thomas Hutchinson, and John Dickinson allow us to consider the role that conflicting personalities and perceptions of political reality played in hastening the disruption of the British empire. Personalities in conflict had a great deal to do with the pattern of revolutionary causation. In turn the furor those personalities generated gave birth to a basic alteration in political relationships which is still affecting the American experience.

The 13 Anglo-American provinces that chose to turn against their parent state in the mid-1770s were very much a part of the political culture shaping the 18th-century British empire. For its time it was an enlightened culture, even though the assumptions were clearly different from those that contemporary Americans hold as self-evident truths. Above all else two terms—*balance* and *hierarchy*—characterized the values

63

of that culture. Balance and hierarchy lent stability to political relationships and guaranteed all citizens, both in England and in America, their rights and liberties as freeborn Englishmen. However, the sense that established relationships were out of order led the pugnacious Samuel Adams of Boston to push with all his energies against the weight of imperial policy in the dawning years of revolution. A similar sense, but from a different interpretive point of view, trapped the urbane and scholarly Thomas Hutchinson into resisting the brute force of Samuel Adams and his "insurgent" cohorts. Adams pushed and shoved as the protagonist; Hutchinson resisted as the despised antagonist. Caught in the middle and nearly crushed for want of direction were citizens like John Dickinson, the moderate "Pennsylvania Farmer" who did so much to construct the intellectual grounds for American resistance but could not bring himself to sign the Declaration of Independence as a Pennsylvania delegate to the second Continental Congress.

The political culture of 18th-century Britons and Americans encased the perceptual differences that brought Adams, Hutchinson, Dickinson, and 2,500,000 other provincial citizens into open conflict with one another and with the home government of King and Parliament. Different personalities jostled against each other because of the multiplicity of interpretations that arose from a common body of political theory and explained what was going wrong with the system and what needed to be done. The placement of individuals in the imperial system affected their perception of political affairs. Adams concluded that revolution was necessary; Hutchinson chose the path of loyalism; Dickinson equivocated until it was almost too late. Behind this complex set of responses were varying perceptions of reality based on those assumptions about balance and hierarchy that gave form and meaning to the British political culture.

"Democracy" was a derisive term for the politically sophisticated in the pre-revolutionary British empire. The word did not refer so much to a system or a style of politics; rather it specifically denoted the masses of common citizens who inhabited society. More broadly, the 18th-century definition of "democracy," carrying over from the writings of Aristotle, reflected upon one of three socio-economic orders (or classes of citizens) in functioning societies. The *demos* or "general masses" needed to have their interests represented in at least one branch of government to give balance to overall policy formulation and decision-making; furthermore, the democracy needed representation to act as a counterweight against potential excesses by either or both of the two higher socio-economic orders—the monarchy and the aristocracy.

According to the most enlightened—though somewhat archaic and medieval—political science of those times, the English constitution embodied the quintessence of balanced government, mixing and blending the three socio-economic orders of monarchy, aristocracy, and democracy in the three working branches of government, as represented in the King, the House of Lords, and the House of Commons respectively. More than anything else, students of 18th-century political culture feared an imbalance in the distribution of authority and responsibility among the orders. They believed history demonstrated that too much monarchical domination in decision-making, without appropriate aristocratic and democratic checks through the other two branches of government, had the dangerous potential to destroy known *liberties* and to produce political *tyranny*. Capricious if not arbitrary royal rule would in time subvert the basic political rights and liberties of the aristocracy as well as the democracy. On the other hand, too much power in the hands of the democracy, the ordinary citizens, had the equally deleterious effect of forcing the body politic in *anarchical* directions. Imbalance in authority favoring the democracy would result in licentious behavior, threatening known liberties, as commoners vied with one another to grab scarce socioeconomic rewards, such as private or public property, higher social position, greater community prestige, or even raw power itself.

Too much democracy predictably would produce a reaction, a swing of the political pendulum back toward aristocratic and/or monarchical domination so as to end popular licentiousness and once again to restore peace and order in governance. In precise, rhythmic fashion, so characteristic of the thinking of the Age of Reason in Europe and America, the most stable polities carefully balanced the socio-economic orders of democracy, aristocracy, and monarchy in the branches of government so that no one order would gain ascendancy. It was the only way to avoid the extremes of tyranny or anarchy; the delicate balance guaranteed that the known rights and liberties of all citizens would then be secure from veiled threats and outright attacks.

These assumptions may be summarized in the phrase *hierarchical conception of balanced government*. It was not the familiar notion of checks and balances among executive, legislative, and judicial powers that we accept today as axiomatic for even-handed government. Rather there was the tacit awareness of an indivisible relationship among leadership in state and society. Every subject in the realm had his or her place; to violate that place was to threaten the very foundations upon which known liberties through the ages had been constructed.

Well read and politically sophisticated colonial Americans by the beginning of the 18th century were drawing analogies between the working parts of their provincial governments and the English model. Using somewhat faulty if not porous logic, prominent American leaders were claiming that governors represented and substituted for the monarchy; councilors forming the upper houses in Assemblies and serving as advisers to governors represented and substituted for the aristocracy; delegates to the lower house represented the general citizenry—the democracy.

The analogy was far from perfect. There was no resident titled nobility in the provinces; yet individual and family wealth did serve as the basis for distinction between the "lower sort" and the higher orders in the provincial social hierarchy. Prospering colonial families were forming themselves into community and colony-wide leadership elites. Committed to the proposition that success in the socio-economic sphere conveyed the right to legislate and to execute that legislation for the general citizenry, the provincial upper classes believed that only those of demonstrated capacity should rule, especially in those upper-hierarchy offices representing the monarchy and the aristocracy of wealth and social prominence in America.

Colonial leaders, though, did not restrict their claims to higher provincial offices. In common with the "better sort" in England, they believed in comprehensive political stewardship. *Deferential* attitudes assumed that common citizens would submit in matters of state to men who by wealth, occupation, birth, and/or social position had the breadth of vision to act in the best interests of the body politic, thereby preserving and enhancing liberties. Wealthy and prominent men were less likely to be corrupted by power and to turn the public trust to private advantage. Socio-economic betters had demonstrated that their intelligence was keener, their wisdom perhaps more fully developed. One colonial Virginian pungently summarized deferential assumptions when he wrote: "It is right that men of *birth* and *fortune*, in every government that is free, should be invested with power, and enjoy higher honors than the people. If it were otherwise, their privileges would be less, and they would not enjoy an equal degree of liberty with the people."

Deferential assumptions in an age when the educated placed such a high value upon balance and hierarchy for the sake of political stability guaranteed provincial men of wealth and standing a major voice in their governments. Consequently, the lower houses of America's 18th-century Assemblies were largely controlled by the "better sort" of provincials, from which positions they perceived themselves as legislating most ably and wisely for the commonalty of citizens. Even though legislative seats were elective and voting rights widespread, the candidates usually were acknowledged "betters" in the pre-revolutionary socio-economic milieu. From their seats in lower houses and from appointive positions in upper houses they formulated local laws and statutes. Normally these same leaders set the colony-wide tone in accepting or challenging broader imperial policies enunciated by King and Parliament and given visible presence through royal governors and other Crown officials in America.

Such in brief were the integrating assumptions and structural components of imperial political culture. Men on both sides of the Atlantic contended over the prerogatives of authority. They sensed that political stability depended upon balance among socio-economic orders in society and state. Most politically-active gentlemen envisioned themselves as guarding the entire community against those few insidious individuals who would corrupt the accepted hierarchical relationships in governments as well as destroy liberties for private and petty interests. The life of the system, or the known liberties of all citizens, depended upon avoiding tyranny from above or anarchy from below. Even before midcentury some Americans were becoming fearful that English policymakers were distorting the balance and threatening liberties. A major shift in the direction of imperial policy during the early 1760s confirmed the worst suspicions of such men; among them was Samuel Adams.

*   *   *

Nothing in the early life of Samuel Adams would have led his parents to suspect that their energetic young son would be remembered as the chief revolutionary agitator of the next and more rebellious generation. Born during 1722 in the bustling seaport of Boston, young Samuel could take pride in his father and mother, Deacon Samuel, Sr., and Mary Fifield Adams. The Deacon was a prospering maker of malt, enough so that he earned the honor of serving as a local justice of the peace. He had money enough to send his son to Harvard College, then representing a level of educational opportunity that very few 18th-century Americans enjoyed. Most friends assumed that young Samuel would become a minister, since he himself had a penchant for systematic theology with a strong Calvinist flavor. But it would be otherwise. Little is known about Adams the student, except that he had an undistinguished academic record and that the school authorities once disciplined him for "drinking prohibited Liquors." He graduated just before his 18th birthday, during a crisis that would destroy the family fortune and turn him into a bitter foe of many prominently-placed leaders and supporters of imperial policies in Massachusetts.

The family crisis centered on the Land Bank scheme that Deacon Samuel and other local leaders were sponsoring in an effort to keep the Massachusetts economy fluid. There was never enough hard money (gold and silver) in the provinces to sustain the expansive tendencies of local economic activity. As a result, ingenious colonists (when not bartering) supplemented the sparse money supply with varieties of fiat currency. The Land Bank represented one such plan. Subscribers like the Deacon pooled funds—and their capital provided a modest backing for a large issue of paper money bills, loaned out by Land Bank directors at six percent interest and secured with mortgages against the landholdings of borrowers. Such precautions were taken so that the money would maintain as much of its face value as possible when circulating through the marketplace before retirement from circulation.

These currencies, when issued in modest amounts, tended to hold their values well, but merchants generally eschewed fiat money for fear that currencies with inadequate backing might plummet in value at any time. They did not want to be caught short. Leading merchants in Boston, among them the wealthy Thomas Hutchinson, had little use for fiat currencies of any kind. They were demanding before 1740 that the Land Bank plan of Deacon Adams and his cohorts be completely eradicated.

If the younger Samuel Adams had a respectable family background, Thomas Hutchinson had an even more prominent heritage. The family traced itself back five generations in Massachusetts history to Mistress Anne Hutchinson, famous for her radical Antinomian views among the first generation of Puritan settlers. Hutchinson's father ranked among the wealthier merchants in the province; he even had the distinction of sitting with the Massachusetts Council for several years. Colonel Thomas and his wife Sarah Foster Hutchinson had 12 children, among them Thomas, Jr., who was born in September 1711. The boy grew up in the stately family mansion in Boston until the age of 12 when his parents enrolled him in Harvard where he was an eager student and especially interested in history. Emerging with a degree before his 17th birthday and designated class valedictorian, this young man of immense family distinction, intelligence, energy, and personal rectitude was about to face a most tumultuous and controversial career.

To complete his education the younger Thomas joined his father's mercantile house as an apprentice and soon distinguished himself by his own business acumen. Everything about this glamorous young man marked him for leadership. Before his 26th birthday, he was named a Boston selectman; a few months later he found himself elected to the lower house of the General Court, Massachusetts' Assembly. In this lower chamber Hutchinson made known his opposition to paper money schemes. Speaking out as he did and associating himself with wealthy gentlemen of the Boston mercantile community, Hutchinson lost his seat in the 1739 General Court elections. But it was only a temporary reversal in a burgeoning political career.

The Adams faction wanted paper currency, but the merchants frustrated their best laid plans through the intervention of Governor Jonathan Belcher, royal appointee and hard money man. The Governor issued a proclamation stating that any person holding an office under royal authority who acknowledged Land Bank notes in any transaction would be removed from office. Deacon Adams then resigned his commission as justice of the peace and attacked the royal powers; he charged the Belcher faction with insensitivity to local economic needs. The quarrel spread, and the battle lines hardened. Governor Belcher removed other commissioned militia officers and justices of the peace from office. But the Land Bankers responded with enough popular support to carry the 1741

General Court elections and recommended Deacon Adams and a few other loyal fiat money men to the Governor's Council. (In Massachusetts an unusual arrangement in the royal charter permitted those elected by the populace to the lower house in turn to elect the members of the upper house or Council.) Belcher peremptorily vetoed the General Court's choices. Thus the elder Adams was unable to gain entrance to the inner circle where he and his associates could more effectively defend the collapsing Land Bank.

The uncertainty of heated political turmoil completely undercut the value of Land Bank notes. Even original subscribers, including Deacon Adams, became fearful of accepting the notes in exchange for goods. Belcher, Hutchinson, and others had ruined the Land Bank in the name of secure and stable hard currency. In the process they undercut the personal estate of Adams, who not only lost his part of the original subscription but also remained liable for debts against the Land Bank. Deacon Adams died in 1748 knowing that his son would have to make his way in the world with creditors hounding at his heels. Despising men like Hutchinson who seemed to be in league with royal officials and opposed to legitimate local interests, young Samuel would in time find other ways to refurbish the tattered family reputation.

After graduating from Harvard Samuel Adams had demonstrated no aptitude for or interest in business matters. Apprenticed to a merchant, he failed to respond to direction or instruction. Sent home, his father gave him money to go into business for himself, but Samuel soon lost it by loaning the currency to a friend. In 1748 he was working for his father. Preferring to keep himself solvent by remunerations from local political offices and by earning just enough to keep food on the table, Samuel let the business drift after the Deacon's death. More than business pursuits, he enjoyed local politics—and he would become a craftsman in the politics of vilification.

Through his father's contacts Samuel Adams ingratiated himself with the Boston political leaders who opposed imperial officials and with their supporters in Massachusetts. In 1746 he won election to the local post of clerk of the market; in 1753 he became the town scavenger; shortly thereafter he took the job as collector of the local liquor excise tax, to be followed a few years later by the more important office of Boston tax collector. These local offices were important for many reasons. They gave him the opportunity to be in constant contact with the common people of Boston. For instance, he built friendships by being a most generous tax collector—in that he was reluctant to perform the duties of his office, especially when citizens were in dire financial straits. By 1765 when he left the tax collecting post, he was some £8,000 in arrears. No doubt some of the funds had gone to keep his family in clothes; but the deficit accumulated largely because Adams did not always collect. As a result, he had a host of friends who listened with gratitude when he talked politics.

Very few men in the 18th century could make their way as petty politicians, living each hour by currying favor with the people. It might have been different had the modest Adams family fortune not been decimated by the Land Bank fiasco. But that is conjecture. Both out of necessity and temperament Adams reached out and touched the "poorer sort." He lived meagerly and closely to the people. Described by one contemporary as a "plain, simple, decent citizen, of middling stature, dress and manners," Samuel Adams was cultivating a constituency despite the accepted canons about hierarchy, balance, and political stewardship.

* * *

While Samuel Adams thrived on petty offices, the "tall, slender, fair-complexioned, fair-spoken" Thomas Hutchinson moved in the larger imperial officeholding orbit. During the 1740s he won election after election to the lower house of the General Court, eventually becoming speaker. In 1749 the lower house elevated him to the Council for the first time. By 1760 Hutchinson had emerged as a major plural officeholder. He held a commission as a commander of the fort on Castle Island in Boston and had also served since 1752 as a probate judge as well as a justice of the Suffolk County court of common pleas. He relinquished the latter post in 1758, perhaps because he became the province's lieutenant governor by royal commission the same year. Seemingly Hutchinson had an insatiable appetite for prominent offices. This hunger soon was to coalesce his Boston enemies and fix Hutchinson as a prime agent in what some believed was a plot to destroy American liberties, regardless of the amount of enlightenment this leader from the "better sort" demonstrated.

Hutchinson's officeholding appetite bloated his judgment. In 1760 Massachusetts welcomed a new royal governor, Francis Bernard, who in one of his official acts had to appoint a chief justice of the Superior Court, the highest in the province. Several candidates presented themselves, but none more ostentatiously than James Otis, Sr., then speaker of the house. Otis had been promised the office by a former royal governor, long since passed from the scene. While Otis, Sr., presented his claim, his more famous son, James, Jr., emerging as a powerful attorney and provincial leader in his own right, broadcasted it about that if his father was not appointed to replace the deceased incumbent, he would personally "kindle such a fire in the province as shall singe the governor, though I myself perish in the flames." Governor Bernard mused over the matter carefully and then chose Thomas Hutchinson. As one contemporary chronicler stated it, the younger Otis retaliated by joining "himself to the party which was jealous that the views of [the Bernard] administration were unfavorable to the rights of the colony . . . and soon became its chief leader."

James Otis, Jr., and Samuel Adams became closer friends after this contest over the chief justiceship. That friendship had some roots in mutual dislike for, if not personal revulsion with, the favored Hutchinson. Their ties became more resolute once ministerial leaders in England made it clear that the era of "salutary neglect" was coming to an end. The Bernard and Hutchinson royal faction would be charged with implementing the reinvigorated imperial program of the 1760s. The Otis and Adams combination would lead Bostonians in their resistance to the impending tyranny of the new policies being articulated by Parliament. First it was Otis, Jr., who more visibly waved the banner of liberty and then, as the decade progressed, Samuel Adams emerged as the hallowed figure—as Otis began to develop serious psychological problems as well as to flail about on issues. Personal animosities, though, hardened factional lines long before Otis gave indication of losing his mental stability.

The abrupt change in imperial policy crystalized in 1765 with Parliament's promulgation of the Stamp Act, though a host of less well-known statutes signaled the new departure. Great Britain had for decades fought wars throughout the world to maintain and extend her empire. She emerged triumphant among the imperial nations of Europe in 1763 with the signing of the Peace of Paris, ending the Seven Years' War (known in its American phase as the French and Indian War). This conflict resulted in the elimination of France's claims from the New World. The French menace no longer lingered in Canada and to the west. Home officials thought that Anglo-Americans should be forever grateful, sufficiently so at least to share more directly in the costs of imperial administration. British leaders knew that the English national debt had risen from £75 million to nearly £130 million during the Seven Years' War. They realized that part of that enlarged debt went to the advantage of all Americans who would be more secure without French competitors in North America. Funds, too, were lacking to back up the decision to maintain a 10,000 man regular British army on the American frontier for the ostensible purpose of keeping peace between aggresive settlers and warlike Indians. The course of action seemed obvious: Parliament must tax the sometimes troublesome and less than appreciative colonists.

The decision to tax directly represented a bold departure from established policy. Heretofore Americans had paid a variety of duties on trade into imperial coffers. But direct taxes had been the prerogative of local American assemblies. Now Parliament was asserting full legislative sovereignty over all subjects of the realm. Fiscal stability at home and the presumed need for greater consolidation in imperial administration expressed itself perhaps too plainly in the 1765 Stamp Act.

The Stamp Act proposed to draw money out of provincial pockets by placing stamps on some fifty items, including newspapers, pamphlets, playing cards and dice, wills, deeds and other land sale documents, marriage licenses, college diplomas, bills of lading, and ship clearance papers. The price of stamps varied according to the nature of each item, but none of the listed commodities could be bought, sold, or used after November 1, 1765, without stamps. To make matters worse, Americans would have to purchase stamps with hard money, always scarce. Violators could be tried in vice-admiralty courts (where there was no trial by jury) as well as in regular civil courts. Comprehensive enough to affect all Americans, the Stamp Act seemed to violate a host of basic political liberties, including the right to trial by jury and to taxation only by representatives elected by the voting citizenry.

First reports of Parliament's approval of the Stamp Act arrived in the provinces during April 1765. There was ample time to organize resistance against both the taxation plan and those royal officials in the provinces, such as Francis Bernard and Thomas Hutchinson who would be charged with administering the tax in Massachusetts. Samuel Adams proved a most effective organizer. Attacking the Stamp Act was one way to get back directly at his old enemy, now ensconced as Lieutenant Governor and Chief Justice of the Superior Court. How much of the assault was in defense of liberties and how much represented an opportunity to crush old foes may never be determined. Both factors surely were operative for Adams.

During the summer of 1765 Samuel Adams called upon old friendships (some no doubt formed during his tax collecting days) and assisted in organizing Boston's Sons of Liberty. He brought together two warring groups of Boston ruffians, the North End and South End gangs, and molded them into a powerful tool of local resistance under the street leadership of a cobbler, Ebenezer Mackintosh. With an organized mob—one could be more polite and say "crowd"—of liberty-loving citizens ready to perform violent acts in defense of community interests, the scenario was set for the memorable August riots. The script was quickly completed when Bostonians learned that Andrew Oliver, the province's secretary as well as closely-tied brother-in-law and political ally of Thomas Hutchinson, was to be the Massachusetts stamp distributor.

Trouble began on the morning of August 14 when the local populace awoke to find hanging from the "Liberty Tree" effigies of Oliver and Lord Bute, previously ministerial head in England. A shocked Governor Bernard demanded that the effigies be torn down; but no one dared to touch them. In the early evening the Sons of Liberty took both the effigies to a warehouse recently constructed by Oliver. In short order they tore the building apart, perhaps because it was rumored that the warehouse would be the distribution center for the stamps. Next they carried wood from the building's site to a nearby hill and ignited the effigies amidst a thunder of cheers. With Oliver's gracious home nearby, the mob turned on it, ripping apart the first floor and drinking unsparingly from the wine supply in the cellar. The merriment lasted until midnight. Early the next morning, according to Hutchinson, Andrew Oliver, "despairing of protection, and finding his family in terror and great distress . . . came to the sudden resolution to resign his office before another night." Indeed, no one in Massachusetts dared to think about distributing stamps after Boston's August 14 riot.

If the local Sons of Liberty had only wished to check the administration of the Stamp Act, they would then have stopped rioting, having proven their point with force. But a false rumor began twisting its way through Boston's byways and alleys to the effect that Hutchinson through his royal offices had argued in favor of the tax. Worse yet, local gossips were stating categorically that Hutchinson had clandestinely helped write the legislation. Unconcerned with hard evidence, the Sons of Liberty appeared in moblike fashion twice again and on the evening of August 26 wrecked Hutchinson's lavish Boston residence, one of the finest in the province. Hutchinson described the scene as follows: "They continued their possession until daylight; destroyed, carried away, or cast into the street, everything that was in the house; demolished every part of it, except the walls, as far as lay in their power." No one knows who started the rumors, but Samuel Adams and his cohorts were not out in the streets suppressing the gossips.

During the fall, violence spread to other communities in the 13 provinces where mobs intimidated other stamp distributors into resigning their commissions. Adamant colonists began to plan a boycott of English goods if Parliament did not back down. Provincial assemblies and an intercolonial Stamp Act Congress sent petitions to England. These remonstrances reiterated the theme that taxation without representation threatened the very foundation of political liberties and was a violation of constitutional rights. As the Stamp Act Congress summarized it, since it was unfeasible for Anglo-Americans "from their local circumstances" to be adequately represented in Parliament, the one way to sustain "all the inherent rights and liberties" of Englishmen in America was for the sovereign Parliament to concede that only elective assemblies in the provinces could tax citizens. Given the rioting, the intimidation, the boycott, and the petitions, Parliament accepted the obvious. The Stamp Act could not be executed without forcing even more heated confrontations. In March 1766 Parliament repealed the tax, but not before declaring that it alone had "full power and authority to make laws and statutes of sufficient force and validity to bind the colonies and people of America, subjects of the Crown of Great Britain, *in all cases whatsoever.*"

These words provided little consolation to Thomas Hutchinson, back in Boston and looking for financial reimbursement for his home. For him the devastated residence served as a symbol of the common people's licentious behavior. When there were no appropriate aristocratic- and monarchical-like checks upon the branches of government, the uncontrolled populace would tear all institutions of society apart in a frenzy of anarchy. Hutchinson remained committed to balance among the social orders. Above all else, stability had to be maintained in the realm. In 1767 Hutchinson wrote despairingly that "the town of Boston is an absolute democracy," which seemingly could not be constrained by royal officials representing the higher socio-political orders. By 1769 his concern with maintaining the hierarchical conception of balanced government for the preservation of society led him to express the conviction that "there must be an abridgement of what are called English liberties. . . . I wish the good of the colony when I wish to see some further restraint of liberty, rather than the connection with the parent state should be broken; for I am sure such a breach must prove the ruin of the colony." These indiscreet words would later haunt him. After 1765 Hutchinson dedicated himself to keeping in check those whom he believed were seriously threatening the very stability and good order of Massachusetts. Separation from Great Britain, he was sure, would mean total anarchy.

Samuel Adams drew upon the same political heritage and assumptions, but he interpreted events very differently. In line with other insurgent activists, he was conjuring up a conspiracy aimed against American political liberties by unbridled ministerial tyranny. Ministers in England and their sycophantic agents in America were being corrupted by power. If anarchy resulted from too much power in the peoples' hands, tyranny resulted from too much power in the hands of the monarch and his ministers. In 1768 Adams wrote in the *Boston Gazette* that "when the People are oppressed, when their Rights are infringed, when their property is invaded, when taskmasters are set over them, . . . when placemen and their underlings swarm about them, and Pensioners begin to make an insolent appearance . . . In such Circumstances, while they have the spirit of freedom, they will boldly assert their freedom; and they are to be justified in so doing." Adams was not worried by popular licentiousness and anarchy; rather he feared tyranny. On more than one public occasion he alluded to Thomas Hutchinson as the man who would shackle Massachusetts in political slavery.

Thus the destruction of liberties from above convulsed Adams, while Hutchinson despaired of political ruin from below. To Adams the reinvigorated imperial program and the continued elevation of men like Hutchinson to high provincial offices, meant that there could be no accommodation with the Crown; in peril were such rights as taxation only by consent. Adams and Hutchinson were at the opposite poles of the same set of ideas. Their diverging interpretations of reality reflected their relative placement in the political and social milieu of pre-Revolutionary Massachusetts. In fact it was this very placement as well as their previous personal experiences that shaped the development of their perceptions and gave them meaning.

In 1765 Adams won election to the General Court for the first time; in 1769 Francis Bernard left the province to be replaced in the royal governorship by none other than Thomas Hutchinson. Unconsciously the first was becoming a revolutionary, the second a loyalist.

*   *   *

Like Adams and Hutchinson, John Dickinson grew up with many advantages. His father owned extensive property in eastern Maryland, Delaware, and Pennsylvania. On the family estate at Croisiadore, Maryland, Mary Cardwell Dickinson gave birth to John on November 13, 1732. Little is known about his childhood, except that the family moved to sparsely populated Kent County, Delaware, when he was eight. There this son of a prospering planter grew to manhood. He was "tall and spare" and "simple and unostentatious in his habits." The family placed a great value upon education and provided their son with a private tutor. By his 18th birthday John Dickinson had decided to begin legal training in Philadelphia. After a three-year apprenticeship in William Penn's provincial capital, he completed his legal education at the Inns of Court in London. Studying in England represented the sort of exposure that few Americans enjoyed; yet wealthier families like the Dickinsons knew that such educational advantages almost assured economic success for children who did not squander such opportunities. For four years John Dickinson went about his legal studies in London with unusual diligence and rigor. He was to become one of the finest legal minds in 18th-century America.

By his mid-twenties Dickinson's world had been made. He knew that the family estates would eventually belong to him. Moreover, he had passed the bar examination in Philadelphia, the most populous and thriving provincial city of the time. While Philadelphia would be the base for his legal practice, Dickinson often traveled to Delaware to watch over business activities on the family estate. His was the life of a wealthy gentleman planter and a talented legal adviser.

Like so many other well-educated 18th-century provincial gentlemen, John Dickinson considered it his duty to take an active part in politics and lead the citizenry in enlightened directions. Elected to the Pennsylvania Assembly in 1762, Dickinson appeared at first to blend in with the "Quaker Party" of Benjamin Franklin and others who pitted themselves against the "Proprietary Party" supporters of the Penn family. There was nothing of real distinction in Dickinson's early Assembly career, except that he split with Franklin in the latter's consuming desire to see Pennsylvania taken away from the Penns and turned into a royal province. Given the beginnings of the new imperial program in the early 1760s, he saw no particular advantage to having Pennsylvania fall directly under the aegis of the Crown. Persisting in his convictions, Dickinson refused to be intimidated by powerful Quaker interests.

Although John Dickinson's early years in the Pennsylvania political arena were lackluster, he was developing a reputation for independence of thought and action; and he deserved it. At no time in his life did John Dickinson depart from his values and ideals under the heat of transient issues and events. He believed that any person who wished to live well had to be reasonable and moderate, not only in dress and manners but also in the formulation and articulation of his opinions. Moderation in all things became the trademark of this wealthy lawyer-planter who at times could be independent to the point of indecisiveness.

John Dickinson earned an intercolonial reputation as a spokesman for the American cause during the fight over the so-called Townshend Duties, which were hatched in the mind of a ministerial leader, Charles Townshend. In June 1767 Parliament approved his scheme to draw tax monies out of colonists in the guise of trade duties. The British ministry believed that Americans in resisting the Stamp Act were objecting only to "internal" or direct taxes, not to "external" or indirect taxes which in this case were duties on trade goods for imperial revenue. Americans long had paid duties on varieties of imperial goods, but Townshend made it clear that the duties to be collected in provincial ports on British-manu-factured glass, red and white lead, paper, painters' colors, and tea would be used to defray the costs of imperial administration in the New World. With heavy-handed subtleness, Townshend and Parliament seemed determined to prove that colonists could and would be taxed.

Unified colonial resistance was slow in developing, largely because the Townshend Duties, unlike the Stamp tax, burdened only a few. Except for tea, the duties were on essentially luxury items, rarely needed by the vast majority of Americans. It would take untold energy and nearly two years to mount an effective intercolonial boycott of all British trade goods as one form of pressure on Parliament. In the meantime, John Dickinson forcefully and persuasively articulated the full ramifications of the American position on taxation. Literary conceit probably led Dickinson, the wealthy lawyer-planter from Delaware, to entitle the several newspaper editorials making up his closely-reasoned statements, *Letters from a Pennsylvania Farmer*. The editorials were read widely as other provincial newspapers reprinted what he first published in the *Pennsylvania Chronicle* during late 1767 and early 1768. Pamphlet copies were later circulated among the colonists. All along the Atlantic seaboard literate provincials toasted their "Farmer," who made Townshend's rationale for taxation by trade duties seem absurd to them.

Dickinson wrote to defend fundamental political liberties. He stressed that "the single question is, whether the Parliament can legally impose duties . . . for the sole purpose of raising a revenue, on commodities which she obliges us to take from her alone, or in other words, whether the Parliament can legally take money out of our pockets, without our consent." Duties to regulate the flow of imperial commerce with revenue being an incidental consideration were one matter and were perfectly acceptable by precedent. But duties that so obviously were for the purpose of taxation could not be accepted in any guise. "If they can," surmised Dickinson, "our boasted liberty is but 'a sound and nothing else.'" Payment of such duties signaled the end of liberty by ministerial tyrants and the beginning of political slavery.

All enlightened men, Dickinson continued, had to align and resist that desperate condition. He called for unity of colonial action while speaking out against those—like Samuel Adams—who instantly would resort to violence and destruction of property to carry their position. First and foremost, citizens had to petition through their governments for a redress of grievances. If constitutional methods did not work, then Americans should adopt measures that were slightly coercive but non-violent, such as trade boycotts and nonimportation agreements. The weapon of force through violence should be unsheathed only when all else failed. Dickinson, moreover, warned that violence would result in retaliation by King and Parliament. Ultimately the colonists would be the losers and "bleed at every vein," since the "Farmer" did not believe that the American provinces could stand alone among the nations of the world. The acceptable course of action was to petition for a revocation of duties first, that is after enunciating the basis of the grievance, and hope that the home ministers would yield to pleas for the preservation of liberties.

What Dickinson failed to perceive was that his tightly-drawn arguments about taxation would not be accepted by ministerial leaders. More than any other writer, he established that Anglo-Americans would not accede to taxation by Parliament, no matter how packaged. But he and indeed most other colonists in the late 1760s did accept the general principle that Parliament as the sovereign body of the realm could legislate in general terms for Americans. British ministers never appreciated the distinction because it implied divisible sovereignty. What they did understand in the heat of the moment was that the nonimportation agreements that colonists began to support in reaction to the Townshend Duties were seriously impeding the flow of goods from English to American ports. It was the threat of economic prostration in Great Britain that led Parliament in 1770 to rescind the Townshend program, that is except for the duty on tea. Indeed, the repeal turned out to be a pyrrhic victory for Dickinson; Parliament had recanted again, but not because ministers understood, appreciated, or accepted the reasoning behind his position. The violence and destruction that Dickinson worried about was not far off.

The remaining duty on tea precipitated the final crisis that both Dickinson and Thomas Hutchinson feared might ensue. Because of the tea duty, colonists found it convenient to purchase smuggled Dutch tea from local merchants. Injured by the serious decline in sales as a prime supplier of English tea, the powerful British East India Company sought from Parliament a drop in the price of its tea below that of Dutch brands, even with the tea duty added to the base price. The ministerial head, Lord Frederick North, saw many advantages to the plan. Not only would the Company lose some of its authority over political affairs in India in exchange for such trading concessions, but colonists would find it to their economic advantage to buy less expensive Company tea. Furthermore, when Americans bought the tea, they would have to pay the three pence a pound duty; they thereby would be accepting the proposition that Parliament had the right to tax them. In June 1773 Parliament approved Lord North's East India Company legislation.

Lord North's calculations proved incorrect. He reopened an old wound by violating a perception of reality which men like Samuel Adams held dear. The East India legislation seemed but one more element in the ministerial conspiracy to subvert and destroy American liberties. When two sons of Thomas Hutchinson were named among the tea agents for Massachusetts, it only confirmed the hardening belief that ministers and royal agents seemed bent upon a plot to put the colonists in chains. No economic advantage in pricing, however real, could outweigh what appeared to be a tyrannical act. East India Company tea had to be returned to England or its sale suppressed. The tea shipments en route would be seen as visible proof of a conspiracy by a corrupted ministry to aggrandize power at the expense of colonial liberties.

Even though tea agents had been named for many American ports and tea consignments went to several colonies, it was in Boston where once again a confrontation with far-reaching implications took place. Samuel Adams and his old enemy, Thomas Hutchinson, were in the vortex of the storm. This time local gossips were noising it about that Hutchinson was lining his sons' pockets with proposed profits from tea sales. Citizens were wondering whether anything could stop their governor in his quest for riches and power. Such thoughts must have been in the mind of the mob that formed in early November 1773 and tried to force the tea agents into resigning. But the Hutchinson sons and other agents refused; they had not as yet received commissions and were unwilling to renounce positions not formally authorized. Then the first tea ship, the *Dartmouth*, entered Boston harbor on November 28. The Boston committee of correspondence placed guards on the *Dartmouth* and the other two tea ships as they docked. Samuel Adams and other local leaders insisted that the vessels return to England without unloading; but a legal technicality and an obdurate Governor Hutchinson thwarted the demand.

Victimized for years by the vilification of Samuel Adams and his cronies, Hutchinson was determined to take a stand and face issues squarely. The Boston "democracy" had painted him as a foolish sycophant too many times. For the sake of stability and the preservation of imperial ties vital to the survival of America, Hutchinson would force the tea on his fellow Bostonians. A customs law stated that once a ship entered the Boston harbor, it had twenty days to unload its cargo and pay necessary trade duties. But if any vessel did not unload, then the customs commissioners were empowered to seize its goods and store them in warehouses on land until all duties were paid. As governor, Hutchinson could authorize vessels to leave port before the twenty-day period elapsed. But he refused to issue the necessary papers; and instead he called on the Royal Navy to block off the harbor. The tea ships could not escape. The period of grace was over on December 16; then by law the tea had to be landed. For once Hutchinson sensed a victory for imperial interests over the disorderly Adams crowd.

But Samuel Adams never took a political challenge lightly, especially when it came from Hutchinson. On the afternoon of December 16 a mass meeting turbulently tried to determine a course of action. No one seemed to know what tactics to pursue. Finally, Adams stood up and reportedly yelled: "This meeting can do no more to save the country." It was time for mob action. Several citizens disguised themselves as Indians, went to the wharves, and dumped into the harbor some 342 chests of tea worth nearly £ 10,000 sterling. This dramatic act of open defiance set the pattern of confrontation that accelerated rapidly.

Reports of the Boston Tea Party shocked the English ministry. As John Dickinson had warned, confrontation led to retaliation in the form of the "Coercive" Acts, passed by Parliament in the spring of 1774. One act closed the port of Boston to all commercial activity until the city's citizens paid for the tea; another vastly increased the authority of Massachusetts royal officials in constraining local legislative bodies; and a third afforded greater protection to royal officials by guaranteeing them trials outside Massachusetts if they harmed anyone in executing their duties. Even though tea ships had not been allowed to unload in other ports, British officials concentrated their wrath against Massachusetts, largely because of the destruction of tea and the recalcitrant record of insurgents like Samuel Adams.

This parliamentary reaction to the Boston Tea Party seemed like a massive assault on liberty, even to colonists outside Massachusetts. No longer was the conspiracy hidden. First Massachusetts would be put in chains; then the other colonies would become victims of political tyranny from England. American resistance in the fall of 1774 focused on Philadelphia and the first Continental Congress, where Samuel Adams was among the leaders pushing for a complete economic boycott in the form of the "Continental Association." Once the Congress met, chances for reconciling differences rapidly diminished as British ministers ignored its petitions and almost disappeared when, in April 1775, British regulars and "embattled farmers" clashed in open and bloody combat at Lexington and Concord.

The second Continental Congress met in Philadelphia under the shadow of conflict. Samuel Adams was there; so was John Dickinson. Relations with England had deteriorated to the point that the only real question facing the delegates was whether independence should be declared. Adams and many New England delegates were ready to face the issue, but John Dickinson with a larger following still insisted that every avenue to a possible reconciliation of differences be explored. Dickinson and his adherents were able to control the Congress for nearly a year. They believed, as had Thomas Hutchinson, that the provinces could not survive as a viable nation. And they feared that the licentiousness of unlettered common citizens would result in internal economic, social, and political chaos in all the colonies. Consequently, the reconciliationists demanded that petition after petition be sent to King and Parliament. When Congress organized the Continental army in the summer of 1775, Dickinson insisted that a document be directed to the King explaining such apparent belligerence. The "Declaration of the Causes and Necessity for Taking up Arms," written by Dickinson and Thomas Jefferson, stated that the purpose of the army was not "to dissolve that union which has so long and so happily subsisted between us." Rather the Continentals would defend American lives, property, and liberty until "hostilities shall cease on the part of the aggressors, and all danger of their being renewed shall be removed, and not before."

And so it went during the next several months. The Dickinson group, clearly committed to upholding American liberties, would not allow open insurgency to become overt revolution. The Adams men, though, barely tolerated what they perceived as faint-heartedness. John Adams, another Massachusetts delegate in league with his cousin Samuel, no doubt stated his kinsman's misgivings when he wrote of Dickinson that "a certain great fortune and piddling genius, whose fame has been trumpeted so loudly, has given a silly cast to our whole doings. We are between hawk and buzzard."

The weight of events, especially spreading military confrontations, finally undermined the Dickinson group. In the debates over the Declaration of Independence Dickinson again reiterated his concern for political stability. He feared what other nations would do with "this stranger in the states of the world." He projected images of civil convulsions in the colonies unless "first we . . . establish our governments and take the regular form of a state. These preventive measures will show deliberation, wisdom, caution, and unanimity." Dickinson pleaded, but the other delegates found his arguments wanting. For them reconciliation had become a delusive impossibility. The moment had come for the birth of a new nation. Convinced to the end that formal revolution must be avoided at all costs, Dickinson abstained in the vote of July 2, 1776, approving the Declaration of Independence. His name does not appear among the signers.

*   *   *

Dickinson's failure to back the American cause in 1776 was less serious than Thomas Hutchinson's miscalculation of late 1773 in challenging the Boston insurgents to a showdown. Hutchinson believed that the integrity of the empire was at stake; at some juncture the Adams group had to be defeated if the vital, indeed life-sustaining cord, was to be maintained with Britain. But Hutchinson chose the wrong moment to assert his will against the Boston "democracy." The Tea Party was a challenge that English ministers could not ignore—and save face. Like Hutchinson, John Dickinson could not imagine that the colonies could long survive as an independent nation. If not torn apart by enemies from without, then civil turmoil and political insurgency by the licentious democracy would undermine any attempt at nation-building from within. The imperial connection meant stability, security, balance, and order; neither man wanted to face the next day without those elements. Perhaps for both it was a failure of vision.

Cast as tyrant when he saw himself as a defender of the British constitution against the turbulent masses, Hutchinson received in late 1773 a special leave from the governorship to go to England. He was tired of the political battles. Sailing in June, he hoped to return soon to his beloved native land. But the opportunity never came. As the imperial crisis intensified and insurgency turned to revolution, Hutchinson became *persona non grata* in Massachusetts as the primary symbol of the ministerial plot. First Boston's revolutionaries seized his property; then they declared him an enemy to the state and marked him as one who could never return to his home upon penalty of death. Thus Hutchinson lived on in London, first a knowledgeable celebrity among the ministry and then as a friend of other loyalist refugees who had not fared so well as he in escaping. In his last days Hutchinson's consuming passion was once again to be with his friends and neighbors in New England. He died at his London home on June 3, 1780, at the age of 68, despised to the end as a purveyor of offices, a power-hungry fiend, and a destroyer of liberties. The soothing effect of time has been a more reasonable judge.

Despite his seeming apostasy, John Dickinson did better. He finally cast his lot with the American cause, devoting himself to finding the constitutional means of building a stable, orderly American republic.

There were those who taunted him because of his refusal to sign the Declaration of Independence, but none could attack him as an enemy of American liberties. Yet they had to admit that Dickinson remained consistent during the revolutionary crisis in his position that liberties could only be preserved when there was a restraining hand on the potentially turbulent and anarchical citizenry. Thus Dickinson worked first to create a strong national government through the Articles of Confederation. Failing in that but remaining active in Delaware and Pennsylvania politics, he joined the distinguished group of nationalists who drafted the Constitution of 1787 and carried it to the citizenry as a document that truly would draw the 13 struggling states more closely together into one nation.

Since national unity was one key to stability, Dickinson seemed satisfied that the more-powerful national government resulting from the Constitution of 1787 could control popular anarchy. By remaining with the American cause despite his qualms and anxieties, Dickinson ultimately was able to assist in formulating the kind of constitutional settlement that he so wanted before a formal declaration of independence. For the rest of his life the "Farmer" generally eschewed politics, preferring to live on his estates. He was satisfied that the Constitution gave the republic every hope for survival, regardless of internal or external political pressures. John Dickinson died in 1808 at the age of 76 knowing that the experiment in nation-building was working.

If Dickinson in 1776 seemed for a moment to lose his way by recoiling at the thought of a complete severance of ties with Great Britain, Samuel Adams appeared to lose his political compass permanently after 1776 once the prelude to revolution was over. Adams was in many ways a driven man in his hatred of Thomas Hutchinson. For years he had resorted to every imaginable tactic in attacking his visible and well-placed adversary. One energizing source of that rage was the Land Bank controversy, which seriously undercut the Adams' family financial base. The Hutchinson clique even then seemed to be destroyers of liberty and political tyrants operating with the backing of imperial officials. Having personalized the area of disagreement, every significant issue after that time, so Adams thought, seemed to cast Hutchinson more and more in the role of ministerial sycophant and tyrant. Hutchinson's presence in so many high Massachusetts offices during the 1760s and early 1770s heightened tensions and abetted political disequilibrium. He was always there, representing the conspiracy from above. Adams again and again sought his humiliation and political destruction, characterizing him as a power-hungry enemy of the "democracy" of common citizens. When Hutchinson's downfall came in 1774, it was too late to regain political equilibrium. Too many leaders on both sides of the Atlantic had become involved in the larger ramifications of that struggle.

Rejoicing in Hutchinson's departure, Samuel Adams seemed thereafter to grope for political focus. He worked diligently for independence; but once it had been declared, Adams drifted in opinionated fashion from one personality and issue to the next, making few significant contributions either as a representative in the Continental Congress during the later 1770s, as a state senator in Massachusetts during the 1780s, or as the governor of his state for a brief period during the 1790s. There was no longer any person or group to rail against with sustained credibility. An old friend stated in the 1780s that Adams had "become the most arbitrary and despotic Man" in Massachusetts, a rather ironic comment given the latter's many venomous attacks on Hutchinson. When Adams died in October 1803 at the age of 81, Bostonians came out for a grand funeral procession. Obituaries spoke of a man who had fought diligently for liberty but who later in life had become an anachronism in the political arena. Adams the agitator, then, earned no real distinctions in postrevolutionary Massachusetts.

But the efforts of Samuel Adams as the protagonist in the revolutionary crisis should not be clouded by his failure to distinguish himself after 1776. Because Adams and others pushed, shoved, and challenged the British empire and its rulers, colonists gained the opportunity to rethink traditional assumptions about hierarchy and balance in state and society. The socio-political orders of monarchy and aristocracy rapidly lost their importance without the imperial connection. Some men started to speculate about an open political arena where the people themselves rather than stewards from higher orders would control decision-making in all branches of government, would enunciate and defend liberties, and by extension would shape the nation's destiny. Popular sovereignty was in the air. The question in 1776 seemed to be how far constitution-makers could go in allowing the people to govern themselves. Among other factors the fear of popular rule, reflected in the thoughts of men like John Dickinson, moderated the majority of the first state constitution-makers. They preferred constitutional checks on the common citizens. But a seed was being planted, a seed that transcended the rather petty and vituperative defense of liberties as conducted before 1776 by Adams and his associates. It was the seed of self-government by the citizenry itself through popular sovereignty. That was an emerging concept of political possibilities that became a very real part of the American Revolution. It would take time for the seed to sprout and grow. It would mean a fundamental change in the definition of democracy. But that too in time would flower.

5

Philosophers of the New Republic

THOMAS JEFFERSON
JOHN ADAMS
ALEXANDER HAMILTON

by Henry Steele Commager
Amherst College

No other people are as fortunate in their founding fathers as are the American. What a galaxy of statesmen presided over the birth of the American nation, and presided, too, over its formative years! Benjamin Franklin and George Washington, Thomas Jefferson and James Madison, Alexander Hamilton and John Adams, James Wilson and Thomas Paine —why, we have not been able to match them in 200 years! And, what is no less astonishing, the generation that won independence and created the nation, lived on for another half century. Continuity thus was woven into the very fabric of that nation that had been born out of revolution.

It was Washington who contributed most to the creation of the nation, for he was not only the Father of his country, but its symbol as well. Jefferson and Hamilton were "the movers and shakers," the men who put their stamp on ideals and on institutions, who set the pattern for the America of the future. John Adams, overshadowed a bit by both of them, was both a collaborator and a foil.

It is Adams, Jefferson, and Hamilton who command our attention. They fought together in the Revolution, they served together in the Washington administration, they helped to lay the foundations of our national institutions—not least of which are the political parties. Yet they

84

were not a triumvirate; each was distinctive and independent, each made his own contribution—or perhaps, at times—counter-contribution. It is the differences that interest us, differences that, in the limited American theater, seem dramatic and even fundamental. But it is easy to exaggerate these differences, to assume that because they seem fundamental in an American context they were indeed fundamental and irreconcilable. What is historically most important is that these statesmen were on the same side in the great events of the 70s and the 80s: on the side of revolution, independence, commonwealth-making, and nation-making. To put it somewhat simply, they were on Washington's side. No one of them was tempted to be a Loyalist, none opposed independence or the philosophy that justified it, none challenged the new federal constitution, none withheld his support from the new government that guided the nation through the treacherous waters of the 90s. We attach the term "Republican" to Jefferson and "Federalist" to Hamilton and Adams, but it was Jefferson who said, in his Inaugural Address, that "we are all Republicans, we are all Federalists"; it was Hamilton who assured the peaceable election of Jefferson over Burr in the crisis of 1800; it was Adams who eventually associated himself with the Republican Party. We take much of this for granted, as we take consensus for granted in our history, but you do not find anything like this in the Europe of the Age of Revolution. Edmund Burke was not a champion of revolution, nor William Pitt, and the British revolutionaries for their part were either silenced or—as with Paine and Joseph Priestley—driven out. Nor was the situation different on the Continent. Adams, Jefferson, and Hamilton wore out their hearts and their lives in the same cause: and both of Adams' associates could have subscribed to what he said in that moving letter to his beloved wife Abigail, written on the day after he had voted for independence:

> I am well aware of the toil, the blood and treasure, that it will cost us to maintain this declaration and support and defend these States. Yet through all the gloom I can see the rays of ravishing light and glory. I can see that the end is more than worth all the means, and that posterity will triumph in that day's transaction.

We must then be constantly on guard—especially in an enterprise of this nature—against the professional vice of the historian; that of being more impressed with what men say than with what men do, and of looking for motives rather than looking at conduct. Both Adams and Hamilton sounded a good deal more High Tory than they actually were in their political character. Both tended to look on the people as a mob, and to identify American commoners with the mobs of the Old World; both feared democracy and were inclined to approve a class society. Hamilton thought the British system the most nearly perfect in the world; he thirsted for monarchy and was ready to argue that corruption was an essential part of the beauty of that government. If Adams did not go quite that far, he nonetheless confessed that "chance was better than choice" and a hereditary prince better than an elective. Hamilton rejoiced in the military, yearned to don a uniform and to lead an assault on the ramparts of the enemy; Adams did not. But both detested the French Revolution, rejected the possibility of genuine equality, and thought talk of progress mostly cant. Jefferson, too, was given to hyperbole. Did he really mean that the tree of liberty must be watered with the blood of martyrs? Was he really ready to scrap all constitutions every 20½ years because each generation should make its own constitution? Was he really persuaded that there was a plot to establish a monarchy in the United States? We must remember, rather, that whatever Hamilton said in that famous speech at the Constitutional Convention on June 18, 1787, it was he who led the fight for ratification in New York State and who bore the major burden of writing the *Federalist Papers;* that however much he endorsed the British Monarchy and admired the British Empire, he fought to destroy them both and to set up a system without King or Colonies. So with Adams: he detested the French Revolution and Napoleon but risked his presidency to prevent a war with France; he did not oppose the liberalization of the Massachusetts Constitution he had originally written; and he ended up— thanks in part to the Hamiltonians—in the Jeffersonian party. As for Jefferson, he proclaimed the doctrine of state sovereignty in the 1798 Kentucky Resolutions and hinted at secession, but proved in the end the most ardent nationalist of all; he adored France and Italy but was ready to pray for an ocean of fire between the Old World and the New; he was a communicant of the Anglican Church, but helped topple it from its established position in Virginia.

It is their creativity that impresses us most, perhaps because we are so shamefully unable to emulate it. Together with their associates in Revolution, they created every important political and constitutional institution in our history: six generations have added nothing of importance in this realm, and we are still living on the capital they piled up in that remarkable quarter century between the Declaration of Independence and the inauguration of Thomas Jefferson. Adams, Jefferson, Hamilton, and their associates did far more than win independence; they *"realized* the theories of the wisest writers." They confronted the problem of how men make government—of how government "derives its powers from the consent of the governed." And they responded to it with the constitutional convention, the basic institution of democracy. They also confronted the problem of how men can limit government, and responded with written constitutions, separation of powers, Bills of Rights, and judicial review. Organizing 13 independent States into a single nation, they invented the first successful federal system in history. They faced the challenge of the organization and administration of what was in effect a colonial empire west of the Alleghenies, and solved the intractable problem of imperial-colonial relations by the simple device of doing away with colonies altogether and recognizing western territories as equal commonwealths in the federal system. They banished the spectre of religious wars by providing not only for complete toleration but also for separation of church and state. They made impossible, so they thought, the danger of a Cromwell or a Napoleon by subordinating the military to the civilian authority. They did not do away with slavery, but that was not the fault of the American *philosophes,* and certainly not of Jefferson and Adams who regarded the institution with loathing.

Another common denominator—far more prominent in the New World than in the Old—was a commitment to freedom of the mind; freedom from the tyranny of the church or of the state, freedom to follow the teachings of science wherever they led, freedom from ignorance, from authority, from the past. No one put this better than Jefferson, or more eloquently: "I have sworn upon the altar of God eternal hostility against every form of tyranny over the mind of man." Adams shared this passion for freedom, though rather for himself than for others; Hamilton took it for granted, but contributed little to it.

Their objective was, of course, to liberate the minds and the energies of men; to enable them to achieve what God or Nature had so clearly intended that they should achieve; to persuade them to conform so perfectly to the laws of Nature that the errors and corruptions which had for so long afflicted mankind would fall away, and man would enter a golden age. In Europe that was impossible, and there only the most infatuated *philosophes* talked in this fashion. Adams thought it was impossible in America, too, for he had little faith in Progress and none in Utopia. Hamilton would have put the matter in more secular terms: an enlightened government—defined as one that is managed by men like himself—could indeed solve most of the problems that afflicted most societies, could create an orderly system of political economy. Beyond that he was reluctant to go. With Jefferson this objective was of paramount importance and its realization a consuming passion for 50 years.

Already the differences are beginning to emerge, differences that in the Old World would have assigned each of them to warring camps, for there Hamilton would inevitably have been like his fellow American, Count Rumford, advisor to one of the Enlightened Despots; Adams, for all his misgivings about England, would have gravitated to Dr. Samuel Johnson and his circle; Jefferson—alone of the three—would have been, and indeed was, at home with the *philosophes.*

*　　*　　*

Thomas Jefferson was born in 1743 in the county of Goochland (now Albemarle) on what was then the Virginia frontier. His father, Peter Jefferson, was a surveyor who had helped run the boundary line between

Virginia and North Carolina. A man of substance and position in his own right, he had married into the powerful and distinguished Randolph family. From childhood, then, Thomas belonged both to the frontier and to the tidewater. Through his father he was familiar with that great West for which he later became the pre-eminent spokesman; through his mother he had entrée to the best society of colonial Virginia, which had some claim to be the best society in America. As a young man Jefferson studied Latin and Greek with the Rev. James Maury, who first initiated him into the pleasures of learning, an initiation he never thereafter betrayed. At the age of 17 he enrolled in the little provincial college of William and Mary; there he had the good fortune to study under the distinguished mathematician and philosopher, Dr. William Small, who introduced him to the pleasures of natural science and to the attention and favors of Gov. Fauquier and George Wythe—most distinguished of Virginia lawyers who later became the first professor of law in America and Chief Justice of the Commonwealth of Virginia. It was heady company for a lad from the frontier, but Jefferson proved himself ready for it. At the age of 24 Jefferson was called to the bar; in seven years of practice he rose to be one of the leaders of the bar and, more importantly, found time to collect the ancient laws and the judicial cases of the Virginia courts, thus early displaying that talent for the practical and the scholarly that characterized him for the next half century. In 1772 he married Martha Skelton who brought substantial estates and gave him four children. Already he had begun to build what was to be the most beautiful house in America, Monticello, for his talent for architecture and gardening emerged as early as did his talent for law, politics, agriculture, science, and learning. In 1769 his neighbors had sent him to the House of Burgesses; that began a public life that stretched over a span of 56 years. Like John Adams, he was early caught up in the controversy with the mother country and like him, too, contributed to that controversy a pamphlet of lasting value in our literature: the *Summary View of the Rights of British America*. In 1774 the Burgesses chose him as a delegate to the Continental Congress; he returned there in 1776 to achieve immortality.

Clearly there is no more cosmopolitan figure in the whole of our history than Jefferson, this man who could sit "gazing for hours at the Maison Quarrée, like a lover at his mistress" and then reproduce it in the State Capitol at Richmond; who was not only America's most ardent disciple of Palladio, but reproduced two of that great Italian architect's masterpieces, the Villa Rotunda and the Villa Malcontenta—in his own exquisite Monticello and then adapted the master's style to that great architectural achievement, the University of Virginia; who delighted in gardens as in temples, villas and stately homes, and studied these in France, Italy, and England; who laid out the gardens at his own University, and kept a fascinating garden book throughout his life; who imported exotic plants from every quarter of the globe; and who confessed that "no occupation on earth is so delightful to me as the culture of the Earth, and no culture comparable to that of the garden." At another time it was music that was "the dearest passion of my heart," and Jefferson delighted in the opera and the chamber music of Paris, compiled a large collection of music—alas, lost—and himself played the fiddle. He had other passions, too—how did he find time for them all?—a passion for "natural philosophy," which we call science, and he added to it both on the practical and the theoretical side; for book collecting, and he amassed the largest and best selected library in America and refounded the Library of Congress after its destruction by the British in 1814; for classical literature. He translated what he needed of Sophocles and Euripides, and to the close of his life sprinkled his correspondence with quotations from the Greek and the Latin. No other American of his generation contributed so richly to the arts as did Jefferson. Hamilton could design a state, but imagine him designing its capitol building as well: there is no evidence, indeed, that for all his passion for high society Hamilton had any interest in the arts. John Adams was a farmer, but imagine him visiting the vineyards of the Loire or the Moselle, or laying out the gardens of a university. Though he did write into the Constitution of Massachusetts an admonition to the Legislature "to cherish the interests of literature and the sciences," he resolutely put aside all temptations to indulge in the arts: as he wrote his Abigail in 1780

> I must study politics and war that my sons may have the liberty to study mathematics and philosophy. My sons ought to study mathematics and philosophy . . . commerce and agriculture, to give their children the right to study painting, poetry, music, architecture, statuary, tapestry, and porcelain.

But 30 years later he was prepared to dismiss even such study as flummery. "Statues, paintings, panygerics, in short all the fine arts, even music and dancing," he wrote, "promote virtue while virtue is in fashion. After that they promote luxury, effeminacy, corruption, prostitution, and every species of abandoned profligacy."

Jefferson mixed romanticism with classicism and provinciality with cosmopolitanism. His romantic view of America had decisive political connotations. It was Jefferson, after all, not Hamilton or Adams, who rejected Europe—the European past, and the European present. His admiration for the Old World rested on nothing so corrosive as envy of, or longing for, those institutions that perpetuated the rule of his class; his antipathy on nothing so vulgar as a sense of discomfort, resentment of snubs, the difficulty with the language, exasperation at being considered a provincial. It was precisely the glitter, the charm, the social seductions that put Jefferson off. His isolation rested, after all, on moral grounds. Writing from Paris in 1785 he warned against sending an American boy abroad to study:

He acquires a fondness for European luxury and dissipation, and a contempt for the simplicity of his own country; he is fascinated with the privileges of European aristocrats and sees, with abhorrence, the lovely equality which the poor enjoy with the rich in his own country . . . he is led, by the strongest of all the human passions, into a spirit for female intrigue, destructive of his own and others' happiness . . . and learns to consider fidelity to the marriage bed an ungentlemanly practice. . . .

Nor did he ever depart from these views. It was Jefferson who, for all his affection for France, supported the Neutrality Proclamation; Jefferson who warned against "entangling alliances" with the countries of Europe; Jefferson who first used the Embargo as an instrument for peace; Jefferson who called for a "wall of fire" between the Old World and the New; Jefferson who urged on President James Monroe that doctrine that came to bear his name. Listen to him after 50 years in public life:

Our first and fundamental maxim should be never to entangle ourselves in the broils of Europe. Our second never to suffer Europe to intermeddle with cis-Atlantic affairs. America has a set of interests distinct from those of Europe, and peculiarly her own. She should therefore have a system of her own, separate and apart from that of Europe. While the last is laboring to become the domicile of despotism, our endeavors should surely be, to make our hemisphere that of freedom.

Certainly no other American was so thoroughly suffused with Enlightenment philosophy or contributed so much to it as Jefferson, and no other so symbolized the American Enlightenment. His commitment and his conduct was all of a piece. What he said at the beginning of his career in Philadelphia where he wrote the Declaration of Independence, in Virginia where he drew up the Revisal of the Laws, he also said at high noon as Secretary of State and Vice President and President, and in retirement at Monticello as the evening shadows fell. The very last letter he wrote breathes the same commitment to freedom, the same faith in progress that he had professed in his youth. It was on the occasion of the 50th anniversary of the Declaration and, as it turned out, the beginning of his own immortality:

May it be to the world what I believe it will be, the signal of arousing men to burst the chains under which monkish ignorance and superstition had persuaded them to bind themselves, and to assume the blessings and security of self government. That form which we have substituted restores the free right to the unbounded exercise of reason and freedom of opinion. All eyes are opened, or opening, to the rights of man. The general spread of the light of science has already laid open to every view the palpable truth that the mass of mankind has not been born with saddles on their backs, nor a favored few, booted and spurred, ready to ride them legitimately. These are grounds of hope for others. For ourselves let the annual return of this day forever refresh our recollections of these rights and an undiminished devotion to them.

From time to time Adams would allow himself this kind of sentiment, but mostly he looked with deep misgivings on the rhetoric of revolution, and as for Hamilton, he was far less interested in the rights of man than in the power of government. The differences were more than rhetorical; they were, or became, philosophical. Let us explore these differences.

*   *   *

And let us begin with one of those great controversies that erupted again and again in the 18th century and did so much to illuminate the mind of the age: the Ancients versus the Moderns, Nature versus Civilization, Mercantilism versus Physiocracy, the causes of the Rise and Decline of Empires and—of primary interest to us—Was America a Mistake?

It was an old question, this, one that had its origins in the discovery of the New World and that had raged, in various forms, over the following three centuries. By the time of the Enlightenment, Europe had in a sense come to terms with America, and no one now debated whether man had violated the will of God in lifting the veil on the new continent, or whether the Indians were indeed human beings, or whether there had been a single or multiple creations. But even the most enlightened of the *philosophes* had not wholly rid themselves of the notion that America was somehow inferior to Europe, its climate miserable, its flora and fauna degenerated, its people enervated, stunted, and doomed to permanent inferiority. Why was America so backward? Why had it never produced a civilization? Why was its effect so malign even on those Europeans who migrated there? These questions came not only from crackpots but from distinguished historians like Abbé Raynal, whose *Philosophical History of . . . the Europeans in the East and West Indies* was one of the most influential books of its day.

It was in 1780 that a young Secretary to the French Minister in Philadelphia, Francois Barbé de Marbois, forwarded to all the American governors a list of inquiries designed to provide his government with useful information about the new United States. The questions covered pretty much everything except politics—geography, natural resources, native races, the economy, commerce, and even history. Only one Governor bothered to answer this formidable set of queries, and that was the busiest of them all, Thomas Jefferson. Even he might not have troubled to do so, had it not been for a lucky accident. Riding around one of his farms, Poplar Forest, Jefferson fell off his horse and was for some weeks incapacitated. It is to that horse—and Jefferson's inveterate habit of making use of every moment—that we owe his reply to Marbois, the *Notes on Virginia.*

"This country," he wrote, "affords to philosophic view an extensive, rich and unexplored view." It is the philosophic view that make *Notes on Virginia* one of the great books of our literature, one of the important books of the whole Enlightenment. For Jefferson answered not only the formal queries, but thought up others of a more philosophical character—and answered them. The *Notes*—how desultory that sounds!—covered not only obvious things like geography and geology and commerce and finance, but also population (one of the crucial indices to civilization and population in the Enlightenment age), religion, education, slavery, and law; they included dissertations on the native races, the Negro, the past and the future of the State and, by implication, of America. In the end the *Notes* added up to a repudiation of the European animadversions against the New World, a celebration of religious liberty, an attack on slavery, a ringing declaration of scientific and intellectual independence, and a theory of History that subtly shifted the center of gravity from the past to the future. It probed the American character, and presented, more fully than any other treatise of the time the agenda of the American Enlightenment.

What then of the native races? What of Europeans in the American climate? Here the story was the same. After all, Americans knew the Indians as European scientists did not, and of all Americans none knew them better than Jefferson, who has some claim to be the father of American ethnology. No one of his generation, unless it was his friend and disciple Albert Gallatin, contributed more to our knowledge of the Indian than did Jefferson—certainly not Adams, certainly not Hamilton, who had no interest in them, either scientific or practical. The Indian, Jefferson made clear, was a product of climate as men were everywhere—climate as environment and climate as social and economic organization. An almost perfect product of that climate, he was perfectly adapted to it. The Indian was ardent and brave, strong and agile, resourceful and sagacious. Physically he was a splendid specimen: he had ardor and virility, the ability to withstand a hostile environment, and to provide for all his necessities; he had even— and here Jefferson yielded to that romanticism never far from the surface of his mind—eloquence and nobility of character.

But the nub of the matter was, of course, what happened to Europeans when transplanted to the New World. Were they indeed enfeebled by the new climate, distracted by the importunate necessities of the struggle for existence, hopelessly isolated from the centers of civilization? So said Corneille De Pauw, who claimed that "through the whole length of America, from Cape Horn to the Hudson Bay, there never appeared a philosopher, an artist, a man of learning whose name has found a place in the history of science." Even the friendly Abbé Raynal repeated the canard: "How astonishing that America has not yet produced a single good poet, an able mathematician, or a man of genius in any one of the arts or the sciences." Nonsense, said Jefferson. We have produced in one generation a Washington, a Franklin, a Rittenhouse—he might have added a Jefferson but let others do that: can France, with six times the American population, show six comparable men? But what is more to the point, we have produced a wholesome society, one where there are few extremes of wealth and of poverty, where there are few who are without schooling, where none live in fear of tyranny, where happiness is generally suffused. Look aside from the achievements of empires and armies and navies; Americans "have given hopeful proofs of genius of the nobler kinds which arouse the best feelings of man, which call him into action, which substantiate his freedom, and conduct him to happiness." Here is the Jeffersonian test of civilization—something that eluded not only the monarchs and the *philosophes* of the Old World, but Adams and Hamilton, too—the test not of power but of freedom and happiness.

There was not only happiness, there was progress too, progress such as no Old World people could display. For the new United States was set off from all other nations, something that vindicated—you can take your choice of these explanations—either the special favor of Providence, or the special good fortune of climate, or the special virtue of the American people. Jefferson, Adams, Hamilton all might give lip service to the first explanation without putting much stock in it; all, too, might endorse the second, though Hamilton had little faith in climate and much in government; only Jefferson would accept the third.

*   *   *

John Adams was born in Braintree, Massachusetts, in 1735, of a family respectable but not yet distinguished. His Yankee forebears had been farmers, and their days were spent in the routine of planting and harvesting, schoolroom, town meeting and church. Adams himself, notwithstanding more than half a century of public life, never departed very far from this routine, for he kept the ancestral homestead in Braintree and did not think it beneath his dignity to pitch hay in his meadows. John's father had been clever enough to marry a Boylston of Boston, just as John himself was clever enough to marry a Quincy of Boston; the marriages were happy but the relationship between Braintree and Boston was always an uneasy one: as John's great-grandson, the famous historian Henry Adams, was to write, there was a "hereditary warfare between State Street and Braintree." For all their worldliness, the Adamses were unregenerate provincials with their roots deep in their own soil. At 16—not uncommonly young for those days —Adams went off to Harvard College, graduating, without any special distinction, in 1755. A brief experience with school teaching persuaded him that he preferred the public to the private life, and within a year he managed to get himself admitted to the colonial bar under the auspices of the powerful Jeremiah Gridley of Boston. Though Adams was eventually to be appointed Chief Justice of Massachusetts, his interest in the law was never professional; the law opened to him, as to so many others, a path to public life that was always his meat and drink. As early as 1765 Adams plunged into the controversy with the Mother Country with a *Dissertation on the Feudal and Canon Law,* which attracted widespread attention, and in no time at all he was hobnobbing with men like Gridley, James Otis, Sam Adams, and others who were leaders in the anti-Hutchinson faction of colony politics. He was elected to the General Assembly, he rejoiced in the Boston Tea Party, he was chosen a delegate to the First Continental Congress; by 1775 he was so prominent in revolutionary activities he was one of the few radicals specifically exempted from the blanket pardon George III was ready to extend to the American rebels if only they would promise to behave themselves. Already it was clear that John Adams was the kind of man who would never be counted on to behave himself.

Unlike Thomas Jefferson, however, Adams had no faith in the virtue of man, not even of man in America, and he did not believe that even the most favorable climate could overcome man's innate perverseness and corruption. "There is no special Providence for Americans," he wrote, "and their nature is the same as that of others." As he surveyed the history of mankind, he found men and governments everywhere the same—men the same in their passions, greed, ambition, venality; governments the same in their propensity to tyranny. No other colonial political philosopher was so completely the prisoner, almost the victim, of History. It is all set forth in those three tumultuous volumes of the *Defense of the Constitution of the United States* and a fourth volume called *Discourses on Davila.* Almost every page plagiarized from older histories. No matter, it came out as Adams anyway. Adams saw in History "eternal, unchangeable proof" of the corruption and depravity of man. What a contrast to Jefferson, who was quite as much at home in history as was Adams, who had read the same books, but who rejected almost contemptuously the "Gothic idea that we are to look backwards rather than forwards, for the improvement of the human mind, and to recur to the annals of our ancestors for what is most perfect in government." The Earth belongs to the living, not the dead, Jefferson insisted and so, too, mechanisms controlling government and prosperity. This was something Adams could never understand, for his instincts were not only conservative but almost antiquarian.

History, Adams knew, was philosophy teaching by examples. What lessons did it teach, what that Americans should take to heart?

That men are irremediably corrupt, the creatures of passions and of interests;

That neither education nor religion could control the appetites of men; nothing but "force and power and strength" in the State;

That though all men are the same in their moral depravity, they are not equal, but incurably unequal in their physical, intellectual, social, and economic character, and that this inequality is the point of departure for any sound political philosophy;

That these basic inequalities divide every society between the few and the many: that the few were the rich and the well-born, the many were the masses of society whose lot would never be greatly improved;

That these divisions in society were distinguished chiefly by ownership of property, which in turn compels those who control it to exercise the tyranny of property—Adams preferred the term "dominion";

That the tyranny of property was matched, however, by the tyranny of the majority who were without property;

That the only way to protect both society and liberty from these twin tyrannies was by contriving a system of checks and balances so elaborate that they would inevitably frustrate corruption;

That "nothing but three different orders of men, bound by their interests to watch over each other, and stand the guardians of the law" could achieve the balance essential to the preservation of liberty, and that this threefold balance was that of an independent executive and two legislative bodies, each with a veto upon the other two;

That such a balance was far more than a mere political contrivance; it was rooted in natural law, for these three branches "have an unalterable foundation in Nature";

And finally, annotating it all—an annotation Adams shared with Hamilton—that the British Constitution was "the most perfect combination of human powers in society which infinite wisdom has yet contrived and reduced to practice for the preservation of liberty and the production of happiness."

Now it is hard to know whether to be more impressed by the narrowness of this entire argument or by its palpable irrelevance to the American experience. It was directed almost entirely to a single problem and with a single solution and that one of utmost simplicity. The problem was, basically, the innate depravity of man; the solution that of counteracting depravity by mechanical contrivances. Never, apparently, did Adams ask himself the most elementary of questions: how could merely mechanical obstacles really frustrate the ambitions and aggressions of men who were irremediably selfish and corrupt? But perhaps even more astonishing was the almost total inapplicability of the Adams argument to the American scene. Had Washington, had Franklin, or Jefferson, or Madison, or John Jay, or George Wythe, or Charles Carroll, or Benjamin Rush—had John Adams himself—most of them rich (by the simple standards of America) and all of them, surely, "well-born," succumbed to the temptations of power? Had they sought to enrich themselves at the public expense, to prolong their tenure of office, to subvert the Constitution or the laws? Could fatuity go any farther? Indeed it could, for here is Adams writing to Dr. Rush at the very time Washington was ascending to the Presidency: "Have not our Parties behaved like all Republican Parties? Is not the history of Hancock and Bowdoin, the history of the Medici and Albizi?"

What is startling is not only Adams' failure to understand the irrelevance of his major argument to the American scene, but his concentration on that one argument and that one solution as the beginning and the end of political wisdom. That the purpose of government was to preserve liberty was nowhere challenged, but was it the only purpose and, for that matter, was it the only method? Adams, to be sure, did make one contribution not so much to political theory (for the theory welled up from the New England town meetings) as to political practice; he was perhaps the first to "realize" the principle of popular sovereignty in the processes of constitution-making through the device of a popularly elected constitutional convention and subsequent popular ratification. Other than this, what is most impressive is perhaps the paucity of Adams' contributions to the solution of those great questions that confronted the American people in the early years of the Republic. To the solution of the problem of federalism—in many ways the toughest of them all—he made no contribution; indeed it is not clear that he even understood it. Nor did he have anything to contribute to the vexatious problem of the organization of the West and the necessity of transforming potential colonies into coordinate states: indeed, throughout his long life he remained curiously indifferent to the trans-Appalachian West and even to the native inhabitants, in contrast to Jefferson's almost obsessive preoccupation with the Indians. He was a lawyer and, technically, Chief Justice of Massachusetts, but gave so little thought to the judicial power that he did not even include the judiciary in his philosophy of the separation and balance of powers. And though Adams had himself drafted the Massachusetts Declaration of Rights, he showed no interest in a federal Bill of Rights and, as President, signed and enforced those Alien and Sedition Acts that palpably violated the guarantees of the First and the Fifth Amendments.

"Author of the Declaration of Independence, the Virginia Statute of Religious Liberty, and Founder of the University of Virginia." This was the epitaph Jefferson wrote for himself. His passion for freedom in all its manifestations suffuses the *Notes on Virginia*, especially those chapters devoted to slavery, to education, and to religious freedom. Listen to his answer to the innocuous Query XVII: "The Different Religions received into that State?"

> The rights of conscience we never submitted, nor could we submit [to the coercion of laws]. We are answerable for them to our God. The legitimate powers of government extend to such acts only as are injurious to others. But it does me no injury for my neighbour to say there are twenty Gods, or no God. . . . Reason and free enquiry are the only effectual agents against error. . . . they will support the true religion, by bringing every false one to their tribunal. . . . It is error alone which needs the support of government. Truth can stand by itself. Subject opinion to coercion, whom will you make your inquisitors?

The great Statute of Religious Liberty bore out the promise of these observations, but with an additional touch of eloquence and of passion:

> Truth is great, and will prevail if left to herself, she is the proper and sufficient antagonist to error, and has nothing to fear from the conflict unless by human interposition disarmed of her natural weapons, free argument and debate, errors ceasing to be dangerous when it is permitted freely to contradict them.

Nothing that Adams wrote or said can match this; nothing, needless to say, that we have from the pen of Hamilton is its equal. They were, each in his way, devoted to freedom, but it was freedom from Britain, from awkward political regulations, from the tyranny of the majority. It was not freedom as Jefferson cherished it. Adams feared the tyranny of George III and of the military, but he feared even more the tyranny of majorities, and he has some claim to have introduced that pernicious concept into American political thought. He was not responsible for the illiberal attitude of the Massachusetts government toward dissenting sects, nor for its retention of many of the prerogatives of the Congregational establishment, but he was wholly unable to understand why the Quakers or the Baptists should object to those arrangements. Indeed, he tried to fob off on the distinguished Quaker, Israel Pemberton, the argument that "the laws of Massachusetts were the most mild and equitable establishment of religion that was known to the world"; and he dismissed the powerful Isaac Backus and his Baptist followers as troublemakers. With the passing of years John Adams' illiberalism grew upon him, and the climax was his endorsement of the narrow and vindictive Alien and Sedition laws of 1798. In their disregard for the guarantees of the Bill of Rights and their acceptance of arbitrary executive authority, these laws went well beyond anything that the British had tried to impose on the American colonials. Hamilton was critical of the measures, but on grounds of political expedience only; Adams did not even doubt their expedience.

On that one great issue of the paradox of freedom and slavery that glared ceaselessly upon the American people, Adams and Jefferson were in substantial agreement on philosophy but not on policy. Both detested slavery on moral grounds and deplored it on practical grounds. But Adams, so far as the present record reveals, was content to refrain from public (though not from private) judgment, to avoid overt attack on the institution, and to let history take its course. That was doubtless natural enough in one who had so little faith in the improvability of human nature and who was persuaded that all men were the creatures of passions and interests. Adams was a member of the committee to draft the Declaration of Independence, but made no effort to retain Jefferson's fiery denunciation of George III for perpetuating slavery and the slave trade. As Vice President, in 1796, he reprobated a petition from the Quakers denouncing slavery, because he felt that it could have "no other effect than to stir up sectional animosities." The Missouri crisis of 1819–20, which Jefferson called "a firebell in the night" that "filled him with terror," persuaded Adams that humanity dictated the adoption of "every measure of prudence for the extirpation of slavery from the United States," but that "the same humanity requires that we should not by any rash act or violent measures expose the lives and property of those who are so unfortunate as to be surrounded with these fellow creatures . . . without their own fault." While Adams' abhorrence of slavery was genuine and deep, it did not lead to action.

Jefferson saw the fatal consequences of slavery at firsthand, and it is not perhaps astonishing that his response should be bolder and more effective. In his *Notes on Virginia,* "The whole commerce between master and slave," he wrote, is

> . . . the most unremitting despotism on the one part, and degrading submissions on the other. Our children see this and learn to imitate it. . . . The man must be a prodigy who can retain his manners and morals undepraved by such circumstances. And with what execration should the statesman be loaded who, permitting one half the citizens to trample on the rights of the other, transforms those into despots, and these into enemies, destroys the morals of the one part and the *amor partriae,* of the other. . . . I tremble for my country when I reflect that God is just; that his justice cannot sleep forever, that considering numbers, nature, and natural means only, a revolution of the wheel of fortune . . . is among possible events; that it may become probable by supernatural interference. The Almighty has no attribute which can take side with us in such a contest.

At the time he published his *Notes on Virginia,* no one had contributed more to the struggle against slavery in his own State, and perhaps in the nation, than Jefferson who was himself a slaveholder, and whose private relationship to slavery was marked by ambiguities almost inescapable in a southerner. As early as 1770, in an obscure local case that involved the freedom of a third-generation mulatto, Jefferson had pled that "we are all born free" and that slavery was contrary to nature; the court dismissed the argument out of hand. Time did not reconcile Jefferson to the paradox of a society proclaiming freedom and perpetuating slavery. Six years later he vainly tried to identify the political rights of Americans with the personal rights of Negro slaves, but the Continental Congress was not ready for such sentiments, and the passage, which meant so much to Jefferson, was omitted from the Declaration. That fall Jefferson returned to the Virginia Assembly. His proposed Revisal of the Laws of Virginia contained the bold proposal of the emancipation of all slaves born after 1800 with the added provision that those born slaves should be "brought up at public expense to tillage, arts or sciences." Two years later he introduced a bill putting an end to the importation of slaves, "which passed without opposition, and stopped the increase of the evil by importation, leaving to future efforts its final eradication." In 1784, he had proposed the total abolition of slavery in all the vast territory west of the Alleghenies—a proposal that lost by only one vote, but that was subsequently incorporated, for the territory north of the Ohio, into the Northwest Ordinance of 1787. Nor should we forget that it was President Jefferson who signed the bill which, at the earliest moment permitted under the Constitution, permanently outlawed the importation of slaves to the United States.

Yet Jefferson and Adams for all their differences of politics, philosophy, and temperament had much in common. Both were in a sense provincials, with their roots deep in the soil. Both were schooled in classical literature and history and drew their intellectual juices from that schooling. They had agitated and labored for independence and won it; together they had served their newly found country at home and abroad; each of them helped create a commonwealth; and each had served the new republic and General Washington. By the 1790s they had drifted apart—the Alien and Sedition Acts and the Kentucky and Virginia Resolutions dramatized how far apart—and there was a long hiatus in their association, a long suspension of their friendship. But "I have always loved Thomas Jefferson," Adams wrote in old age, and Jefferson responded with one of his most felicitous letters:

> A letter from you calls up recollections very dear to my heart. It carries me back to the times when, beset by difficulties and dangers, we were fellow laborers in the same cause. . . . Laboring always at the same oar, with some wave ever ahead threatening to overwhelm us, and yet passing harmless under our bark, we knew not how we rode through the storm with heart and hand, and made a happy port. . . .

And the ancient friendship was renewed, and with it the most fascinating correspondence in the history of American politics.

*   *   *

We know almost everything we need to know about the family, childhood, and education of John Adams and Thomas Jefferson, but our knowledge of the youthful Hamilton is meager. He was born on the island of Nevis, in the British Leeward Islands, in 1755, perhaps in 1753. His mother, Rachel Faucette, the daughter of a French Huguenot physician on the island, had left her husband after five years of unhappy marriage, and attached herself to an indigent Scots merchant, James Hamilton: there is no record of marriage, but the family lived together until Rachel's death in 1768 when it appears that Hamilton abandoned his son who was thereafter dependent on the uncertain aid of relatives and on his own resources. We know little about his boyhood, except that he worked for a merchant on the island of St. Croix, picked up a desultory education with a local Presbyterian dominie, and was early fired with an ambition that never deserted him or left him in peace. In 1772 he found his way to America and the next year wound up in New York as a student in King's College where he quickly distinguished himself by his energy and address. A handsome, brilliant, and ebullient young man with a lively sense of his own worth, Hamilton quickly attracted the attention of men of power and influence. For all his admiration for the British constitution—an admiration that persisted to the end—Hamilton quickly joined his fortunes with the patriot cause, and as early as 1774 emerged as one of the leaders of that cause in the colony of New York. A series of pamphlets early displayed his talent for literature and for logic; his zeal for military action commended him to those who were preparing for possible war, and early in 1776 he received a commission as commander of an artillery company authorized by the Provincial Convention.

"Mine is an odd destiny," he wrote to one of his few intimates, Gouverneur Morris, in 1802:

> Perhaps no man in the United States has sacrificed more or done more for the present Constitution than myself; and contrary to all my anticipations of its fate, as you know from the very beginning, I am still laboring to prop the frail and worthless fabric. Yet I have the murmurs of its friends as well as the curses of its foes for my reward. What can I do better than withdraw from the scene? Every day proves to me more and more that this American world was not made for me.

He was, alas, right: his contribution to creating the American world was prodigious—who except Washington and Jefferson contributed more?—but the American world was not for him. He owed much to King's College and he was the most trusted of Washington's lieutenants; he fought before the redoubts at Yorktown; he married into the aristocratic Schuyler clan of New York and glittered with the glamor of that family socially, as he glittered with his own well-earned glamor professionally. He was the most effective of all those who labored to create a strong union out of what was a rope of sand, and he was successful. With Madison he provided, in the *Federalist Papers,* the best commentary on the art and science of politics in 18th-century literature. He was the guiding intelligence of Washington's administration, carrying through, almost single-handed, a program of economic nationalism unmatched elsewhere in that century for boldness and effectiveness. He was the organizing genius—and the avenging genius, too —of the Federalist Party. He helped shape the American nation and government in his own image, but he lacked faith in that nation or in its government ("a frail and worthless fabric").

No Hamilton did not really belong in America. He belonged in Britain, which he admired above all other nations: there he might have been another Camden, another Fox, another Pitt. He belonged in Europe, which had expelled his mother's people, and which would never have given an opportunity to a young man whom John Adams called "the bastard son of a Scots pedlar." What he really admired was not just the British Constitution but Enlightened Absolutism. He did not like Washington, but confessed that "he was an aegis very necessary to me"; might he not have been happier with a Frederick the Great, a Louis XV, a Gustavus III, a Joseph of Austria? His purpose was not to sweep away ancient injustices or archaic institutions, nor to promote the happiness of men; it was to strengthen the power and augment the wealth of the state.

Nationalism meant to Hamilton the dignity, the authority, the power, the wealth, of the state. To this end he was ready to sacrifice all other considerations. He was ready to wipe out state lines and consolidate the union; he was ready to enlarge the authority of the executive, for "energy" was the prime requisite of good government; he was ready to sacrifice the supposed interests of the people to the very real interests of the state. He had a genius for bringing order out of administrative chaos; he admired the military and believed in war as an instrument of national policy; he was prepared, like Karl Fredrick of tiny Baden, "to make his subjects into free, opulent, and law-abiding citizens whether they liked it or not." Born in the West Indies, Hamilton never understood that deep attachment Americans had first for their colony and then for their state. Trained in a counting-house and in the law, he had little feeling for the land or for farming and no sympathy for that peculiarly Jeffersonian form of physiocracy, agrarian democracy. A parvenu who had pulled himself up by his bootstraps and then married into the Hudson River aristocracy, Hamilton had no interest in the people and no patience with the romantic pretentions of democracy. He was prepared to reprobate the "spirit of persecution" against Loyalists, but at the same time to call for laws restraining "seditious and incendiary publications . . . if levelled against any officer of the United States," since it was more important to preserve "confidence in the officers of the general government" than in the principles of the Bill of Rights. He helped draft the American Constitution but had no faith in its permanence; he helped create the Federalist Party, but never understood the unique character of American politics, and instead of following the Jeffersonian policy of merging all ingredients into a single political organization, he embraced the British practice of fomenting factionalism within his own party.

He was, in short, a man who had faith only in his own star and his own genius, and in the end it was his lack of faith in the American people that destroyed him. He did not believe in duelling and had no desire to fight Aaron Burr but accepted the challenge of Weehawken for the highest of motives—just such motives as might exalt a sovereign. He was sure that the American union was falling apart; he believed that he and he alone could save the American people from ruin; he was persuaded that if he were to command their support and allegiance, he must prove himself a man of courage and of honor. For this gross misjudgment of the American situation and the American character he paid with his life.

It is in the light of these traits of character that Hamilton's relations with Adams and Jefferson take on firmer contours. In his deep distrust of human nature, his detestation of democracy, and his readiness to embrace a class society, his admiration for the British Constitution and his horror of the French Revolution, his advocacy of a strong executive, his keen sense of the economic basis of politics, he was closer to Adams than to the master of Monticello. Yet he neither liked nor trusted John Adams: nothing in his own experience disposed him to appreciate the homespun, the provincialism, the garrulousness, the pugnacious honesty, or the intractable Puritanism of the man who threatened to take *his* party away from him, and it was not merely differences on foreign policy—deep as they were—that persuaded Hamilton to risk destroying the Federalist Party to deny Adams the presidency in 1800.

To the end of his life, Hamilton's attitude toward Jefferson was ambivalent: he thought his great rival weak, devious, cunning—and dangerous; at the same time he displayed a grudging admiration for him. Certainly Hamilton found it easier to understand, even to work with, Jefferson than Adams. When he read the Kentucky and Virginia Resolutions, he burst out that this was the spirit which, unless crushed, would destroy the union; but when the crunch came, just two years later, it was to Jefferson that Hamilton threw his support, not to Aaron Burr. As he wrote James Bayard, "I admit that his [Jefferson's] politics are tinged with fanaticism; that he is too much in earnest with his democracy; that he has been a mischievous enemy to the principal measures of our past administration; that he is crafty and persevering in his objects; that he is not scrupulous about the means of success, nor very mindful of truth; that he is a contemptible hypocrite, but"—and this counterbalanced the whole damning indictment—"he is as likely as any man I know to temporize, and the probable result of such a temper is the preservation of systems which, being once established, could not be overturned without danger to the person who did it. To my mind a true estimate of Mr. Jefferson's character warrants the expectation of a temporizing, rather than a violent system." And then a postscript that spoke volumes: "Add to this that there is no reason to suppose him capable of being corrupted."

Yet this acceptance of Jefferson—an acceptance colored, we cannot help thinking, by the fact that socially Jefferson represented what Hamilton wanted to be—was nevertheless misleading. For Hamilton's philosophical differences with Jefferson were both more extensive and deeper than his differences with Adams. It is not fortuitous that there is no Jefferson-Hamilton correspondence to compare with that of Jefferson and Adams, or that Jefferson should name Bacon, Newton, and Locke, while Hamilton would nominate Julius Caesar, as "the greatest men the world had ever produced."

It is perhaps sufficient to list the philosophical and pragmatic differences that divided these two great founders of the American republic.

There was, first, an ineradicable difference of temperament that permeated both the characters and the philosophies of the two men. Jefferson was by nature sanguine, buoyant, hopeful, and indefatigable. "I am among those who think well of human nature," he wrote. "I believe, with Condorcet, that man's mind is perfectible to a degree of which we cannot as yet form any conception." Hamilton's view of human nature was, by contrast, dour, sceptical, and misanthropic. He thought the idea of perfectibility one of the vagaries of a romantic imagination. He assumed the worst of men, and appealed—in this he was not unlike Adams—not to their better natures, but to their passions and interests; to him practical statesmanship was the successful manipulation of these interests.

But with Jefferson the concept of perfectibility was not a romantic fancy but rested on logical and scientific foundations. Here we have a second difference between the two men, and one that permeated their thinking and their conduct. Jefferson's conclusions were dictated by the teachings of science and Hamilton's by practical calculations; here Jefferson was one with the *philosophes* who provided the ideas of the Enlightenment, while Hamilton may be identified with the administrators who sometimes, but not often, put those ideas into effect. It was Professor William Small who made the greatest impression upon the youthful Jefferson; it was with the members of the American Philosophical Society—of which he was a long-time President—such as David Rittenhouse and Drs. Franklin and Rush that Jefferson was most at home; it was Old World scientists such as Dr. Priestley, Helvetius, and Lavoisier he cultivated abroad. Nor did he himself fail to make important contributions to science, especially to the science of agriculture. When he tried to lure Priestley over to America "to drink the cup of knowledge with us" at the new university he was already planning, he listed as "first among the objects to be taught botany, chemistry, zoology, anatomy, surgery, medicine, natural philosophy, agriculture, mathematics, astronomy, geography." And at the close of his life he could still write with enthusiasm about "the most extraordinary of all books"—one that explained Dr. Flourand's experiments on the function of the nervous system.

But there was more to science than sheer intellectual delight. For if you accepted the almost universally endorsed Newtonian principle of natural philosophy—that those cosmic laws that governed the movement of the stars in the heavens and the tides in the oceans, the circulation of blood in the body, and the functioning of the eye—also governed the operations of politics, law, administration, the economy, and morality, then you could look forward with confidence to the achievement of ultimate perfection. Man had but to use reason to conform to these laws and thus solve all the problems that confronted him. In a more immediate way, science was of particular importance to Americans, since it taught them how to adapt to a new world—how to drain the swamps, clear the forests, accommodate the plow to its soil, the axe to its trees, the canoe to its streams; how to transfer old plants to new soil, and how to domesticate plants that grew wild; how to cope with the diseases of a strange environment; how to guard against the excessive cold of the North and the excessive heat of the South —all the things that helped create a society that was healthier, more long-lived, and more progressive than any heretofore known to history. These were the things that made for civilization, and that provided a scientific basis for Jeffersonian idealism and optimism. Thus science was an essential ingredient in that Jeffersonian philosophy that affirmed that the New World was an improvement on the Old, that America was opening a new page in history, and that in the abundance and the richness of land, the potentialities of science, and the rewards of general education there was a far more solid basis for faith in progress than a Turgot or a Condorcet had imagined.

All this was part, too, of an even deeper difference, one that went to the very heart of social philosophy. Hamilton was not interested in science, or the philosophy of progress or in such notions as happiness or popular education, because with him the center of gravity was the state. What did interest him was the power and wealth of the nation, the energy of government, the efficiency of administration.

These different philosophies of government were dramatized by the very different attitudes toward two governmental instrumentalities, one very old, one new: the military and judicial review. Though Jefferson had helped precipitate one war, he was a man of peace. He was all but ready to liquidate both the Army and Navy upon becoming President; later he persuaded Congress to impose an embargo on both imports and exports as a substitute for war—a plan that turned out calamitously, in part, at least, because he thought too highly of human nature. Notwithstanding all the high offices he held during his long life, it is relevant to observe he was always *Mr.* Jefferson, but that Hamilton preferred to be *Colonel* Hamilton. Hamilton confessed early that he loved to hear the whistle of bullets; one sometimes thinks that he all but concocted the "Whiskey Rebellion" just so he could display the power of the new government and lead the militia against the rebels. When, at a later time, he imagined open resistance to the Alien and Sedition Acts from Virginia, he warned the Secretary of War that "whenever the government appears in arms, it ought to appear like a *Hercules*, and inspire respect by the display of strength."

As for that uniquely American instrument of strong government, judicial review, it was Hamilton who first perceived its potentialities and who first and most powerfully formulated its logic. Not even Chief Justice John Marshall would improve on the argument of No. 78 of the *Federalist Papers*, one of the great contributions to jurisprudence of our literature. Jefferson approved of an independent judiciary, but the notion that independence somehow implied superiority was alien to his political philosophy. Yet his opposition to judicial review, especially when exercised by the federal judiciary, was tardy, and flawed by personal considerations, for it was not really until Marshall made *Marbury* v. *Madison* a vehicle for a personal attack on President Jefferson and his Secretary of State, James Madison, that Jefferson awoke to its dangers. To this day it is not quite clear whether Jefferson rejected judicial review more because of its undemocratic or its partisan nature: more, that is, because it substituted the judgment of the one non-democratic branch of the government for those of the two democratic branches, or because Justices Marshall and Joseph Story used it so palpably as a weapon to preserve Federalist policies after they had been repudiated at the polls.

The most ostentatious contrast between Jefferson and Hamilton was in their attitude towards the economy. Neither was primarily an economist; both were statesmen who proposed to use the economy to achieve larger ends—with Jefferson social, with Hamilton political. Both sublimated the economic activities with which they were most familiar into moral principles. Jefferson was not converted to physiocracy by French thinkers: it was because he was himself a farmer who had lived all his life in the agreeable society of farmers and planters, that he found so much to commend in physiocracy. Hamilton was not attracted to mercantilism by studying the classics of these economic doctrines; rather he gravitated to mercantilism because it best fitted his political preconceptions.

The difference went deep and its consequences were far-reaching. Jefferson wanted to make sure that the new United States would remain an agrarian democracy into the most distant future. "Those who labor in the earth," he wrote in the *Notes on Virginia*

> are the chosen people of God, if ever He had a chosen people, whose breasts he has made His peculiar deposit for substantial and genuine virtue. . . . Generally speaking the proportion which the aggregate of the other classes of citizens bears in any State to that of its husbandmen, is the proportion of its unsound to its healthy parts. . . . While we have land to labor, then, let us never wish to see our citizens occupied at a work-bench, or twirling a distaff. . . . For our general operations of manufacture, let our workshops remain in Europe.

This commitment to agriculture led Jefferson to look ever westward for the future of the Republic, persuaded him to forego his constitutional scruples and acquire Louisiana, strengthened his determination to acquire New Orleans and West Florida as essential for the control of the Mississippi and the prosperity of the West, and justified a policy of geographical isolation. For Jefferson shared with most physiocrats the conviction that the growth of commerce and trade would inevitably lead to the acquisition of colonies and of an empire, to a great military organism which would devour the substance of the people or subvert their government. In short what Jefferson feared was the Europeanization of America through mercantilism.

Unlike the French physiocrats, however, Jefferson was able to do something about it. Almost alone of the great agrarians of that age, he stood not in the shadow of power but at its center. As a member of the Virginia Assembly, he took the lead in abolishing those remnants of feudalism—primogeniture and entail, and his program of disestablishment of the church carried with it the ultimate forfeiture of its glebe lands. His proposal to grant 50 acres to every adult male who was landless was rejected, but while it failed in Virginia it succeeded on a larger theater, for the acquisition of Louisiana doubled the agricultural domain of the nation and—together with those enlightened ordinances for the Northwest that Jefferson helped write—guaranteed a flourishing agrarian republic in the West.

Hamilton envisioned an economy not unlike that of most Old World nations, one in which agriculture, manufactures, commerce, banking worked together to assure self-sufficiency, encourage immigration, stimulate the growth of cities, assure financial solvency, enhance the national wealth, and strengthen the national government by making it increasingly the arbiter of the economy and the guardian of major economic interests. Thus the United States would be able to hold her own with other nations, strong enough to bargain on terms of equality with the great powers of the Old World. Thus she could protect her interests against those threats history taught were inevitable. To achieve all this, Hamilton recommended creation of a national bank; assumption of state debts in order to attract the support of security holders to the central government; and encouragement of manufactures by tariffs, bounties and monopolies. To the Jeffersonians this program conjured up the spectre of re-creating at home conditions long familiar abroad: the growth of great cities with all their poverty and misery and vice; the emergence of a capitalist class that would eventuate into a class society; the struggle for markets that would encourage the growth of the military; the penetration of the central authority into every nook and cranny of the economy. There were social implications, too, in Hamilton's argument that in his system "the farmer might experience a new source of profit and support from the increased industry of his wife and daughters," and that it would make certain that "in general women and children are rendered more useful, and the latter more early useful, by manufacturing establishments, than they would otherwise be." It is of course misleading to read back into the 18th century modern attitudes toward child labor, but it is not misleading to recognize that the successful implementation of the Hamiltonian program entailed a shift in the center of gravity from countryside to city, and from local to central political controls.

Jeffersonian agrarianism and Hamiltonian mercantilism involved different concepts of life and of society. Jefferson's was romantic—by implication anyway—individualistic, simple, egalitarian, and close to nature and to all that nature intended for a virtuous and enlightened people. Hamilton conjured up a shift from farming to industry, from rural to urban, from isolation to involvement, from a classless to a class society, from a mild and passive government to one that would inevitably aggrandize power over society and economy alike. Clearly Jefferson was most in touch with reality in the early years of the Republic. But it turned out that it was Hamilton who anticipated the future, and by anticipating it hastened its approach. Clearly Jefferson presided over the birth of the Republic; Hamilton presides over its maturity. But do not feel sorry for John Adams. He presides over the most famous family in American history, and to a member of a generation that thought its obligation to posterity the most solemn of all obligations, that is sufficient glory.

6

Self-Portraits:
Three 18th-Century Women*

JANE FRANKLIN MECOM
ELIZABETH SANDWITH DRINKER
ELIZA LUCAS PINCKNEY

by Anne Firor Scott
Duke University

> [Collections of letters] heap up in mounds of insignificant and often
> dismal dust the innumerable trivialities of daily life, as it grinds itself out,
> year after year, and then suddenly they blaze up; the day shines out, com-
> plete, alive, before our eyes. . . .
> —Virginia Woolf, "The Pastons and Chaucer"

Colonial history has so long been written in terms of high achievement,
of economic development, of David-and-Goliath conflict, that it is easy to
forget how small a part such things played in most individual lives. From
the standpoint of ordinary people, the essential theme of the 18th-century
experience was the fragility and chanciness of life. Death was omnipresent.
Three children in one family die on a single day from epidemic disease;
fathers are lost at sea; adolescents mysteriously waste away; mothers die
in childbirth; yet life goes on to a constant murmur of "God's sacred will
be done." In these circumstances, how is the meaning of life perceived?
What social structures do people build to sustain the spirit? What are the
central values? What is the texture of daily life?

---

* Condensed from a considerably longer essay in R. Bushman, B. Solomon, and
N. Harris, eds., *Uprooted Americans: Essays in Honor of Oscar Handlin* (Boston: Little, Brown, 1979).

The life histories of three colonial women give some clues.

The three are Jane Franklin Mecom of Boston, Elizabeth Sandwith Drinker of Philadelphia, and Eliza Lucas Pinckney of Charleston. Taken together their lives cover nearly a century, from 1712 when the first was born to 1807 when the youngest died. Their experience encompassed three cultures—Puritan, Quaker, and plantation—and covered a broad spectrum of colonial social classes. Each created a self-portrait, two in letters, one in a journal she kept from the time she was 22 until a few days before her death. Many things went unrecorded. Yet the documents that have survived bring us into the midst of daily experience, and reveal, from time to time, these women's most deeply held cultural values.

*   *   *

Jane Franklin Mecom, youngest of Josiah Franklin's seventeen children, was born in 1712, six years after Benjamin. Because she became her brother's favorite correspondent, we know more about her than about any other woman of her social class in eighteenth-century Boston.

She was eleven when Benjamin made his famous getaway, and embarked upon the career that would make him the archetypal self-made American. In old age both looked back with favor upon their early childhood: "It was indeed a Lowly Dweling we were brought up in but we were fed Plentifully, made comfortable with fire and cloathing, had sildom any contention among us, but all was Harmony: Especially betwen the Heads —and they were Universally Respected, & the most of the Famely in good Reputation, this is still happier liveing than multituds Injoy."[1]

Their parents were remarkable people, and such education as offspring get at home, both had gotten. The childhood things Jane Mecom singled out were central values all her life: a good reputation and the respect of the community.

At the age when her brother had run away to begin his climb to fame, Jane Franklin married a neighbor who was a saddler. Her brother sent a spinning wheel, an appropriate gift for a seventeenth child who could expect no dowry. The best efforts of both spouses would be required to keep up with a growing family, since for a quarter of a century every second year brought a new baby. Three died in infancy, but nine survived to be fed, clothed, and trained for self-support.

By the time we catch another glimpse of Jane Mecom she was already thirty, living in a house owned by her father, taking in lodgers and caring for her aging parents. Her twelve-year-old son was learning the saddler's trade and she was searching for apprenticeships for the younger ones. Between caring for parents, children, lodgers, and her husband's shop it is no wonder that her only written word from this period is a postscript to a letter her mother wrote to Benjamin. His letters to her began a pattern that would last a lifetime, as he spoke of sending "a few Things that may be of some Use perhaps in your Family."[2]

Busy making his own way in Philadelphia, he took time to find an apprenticeship for his namesake, Benny Mecom. Benny, Franklin wrote, "has many good qualities,"[3] but diligence was not one of them. Indeed, Jane Mecom was deeply concerned lest Benny never learn to work. He never did, at least not steadily, and would cause his mother anxiety as long as he lived.

We get our next clear glimpse of Jane Mecom when she was 51 and entertaining her brother in her own house. While he was there she enjoyed what would ever after be her measure of "suitable Conversation," and shone, however briefly, in the reflected glory of Dr. Franklin. The fact that he chose to domicile himself with the Mecoms, rather than with the affluent and welcoming "cousen Williams," says something about the quality of her conversation, or, perhaps, about his sensitivity to her feelings.

That interval of pleasure was brief. Four of the 12 Mecom children were already dead; now Sarah, at 27 a "Dear and Worthy child," died, leaving a husband and four children who promptly moved into Jane Mecom's house. Within six months two of the four grandchildren were dead. She was still grieving for them when Edward Mecom, her husband of 38 years, also died. Two years later she lost her youngest and favorite, Polly, at 18: "Sorrows roll upon me like the waves of the sea. . . . I have now, in the first flow of my grief, been almost ready to say 'What have I more?' But God forbid, that I should indulge that thought. . . . God is sovereign and I submit."[4]

In 1766 she was 55. Of five surviving children the oldest was 34 and the youngest 21, but none was in a position to support a widowed mother. Two sons had been bred to the saddler's trade; one had died and the other gone to sea. Peter, a soap-boiler like his grandfather, showed signs of the mental illness that would eventually incapacitate him, and the feckless Benjamin was not earning enough to support his own wife and children. Her son-in-law was an unskilled workman, hard put to take care of his two children. The daughter who still lived with her was a melancholy and sickly young woman.

Jane Mecom's thoughts turned to self-support. She continued to take in lodgers and her brother sent from England a small stock of trading goods which arrived just as Bostonians decided to boycott English goods in protest of the Stamp Act. Poverty, she concluded, "is Intailed on my famely."[5]

She was acutely aware of her dependence on her brother and tried to repay him with reports on life in Boston. "The whol conversation of this Place turns upon Politics and Riligous contryverces," she wrote. With his reply he sent her a set of his philosophical papers, which she proudly read.[6]

Her letters began to grow longer and more revealing; she began to speak more freely, range more widely, and fill out—for us—the scanty self-portrait belatedly begun.

An admirer of Thomas Hutchinson, Jane Mecom was no early patriot.

By 1774, however, "Proflegate soulders" harassing citizens on the streets of Boston pushed her closer to the rebel position. The battle of Lexington finished what the soldiers had begun, as she packed such goods as she could carry, and took refuge in Rhode Island with her brother's friend Catherine Ray Greene.

In the fall of 1774 Franklin came home and took his sister for a prolonged stay in Philadelphia. His wife had died, and Jane was able to be helpful to him until he went to France. General Howe's decision to occupy Philadelphia sent her back to her granddaughter's house, where she was "much Exposed & . . . under constant Apprehensions" that the British would invade.[7]

Yet the British were not as troublesome to her as a personal crisis brought on by wartime inflation. The country woman who cared for her son Peter suddenly demanded more money for that service than Jane Mecom had or could get. Dependence on her brother was galling enough when he anticipated her needs; now she had to ask for help. Her spirits felt "so deprest" that she could scarcely write, but what else could she do?

Relief came in a painful guise: Peter died. Accustomed as she was to accepting God's will, Jane Mecom reflected that Peter had been "no comfort to any won nor capable of injoying any Himself for many years."[8]

At the same time she had heard nothing for five months from her daughter Jane Collas in Boston, and began to worry lest this last remaining child might be going the way of her brothers into insanity. Apologizing for burdening a busy and important man, she wrote her fears to Franklin: "It gives some Relief to unbousom wons self to a dear friend as you have been & are to me. . . ."[9]

Her daughter was, it turned out, physically rather than mentally ill, but sick or well she was never able to live up to her mother's standards of energy and enterprise. "You say you will endeavour to correct all your faults," Jane Mecom wrote in 1778 when Jane Collas was already in her thirties, and proceeded to outline what those faults were: a tendency to look on the dark side of "God's Providence," an inclination to despair and to extravagance, laziness and a lack of ingenuity in working to meet her material needs, an unseemly fondness for company. She also tended to lie abed late, which her mother found "a trouble to me on many accounts." To top it off, she aspired to gentility without the means to support her aspiration.[10]

Nine children had survived infancy and none had fulfilled their mother's hopes. Most had died in early adulthood. Benjamin simply disappeared during the Battle of Trenton and no trace of him was ever found. The fate of her children pushed Jane Mecom to a rare moment of questioning God's will: "I think there was hardly Ever so unfourtunate a Famely. I am not willing to think it is all owing to misconduct. I have had some children that seemed to be doing well till they were taken off by Death. . . ."[11] But one must accept these things or go mad.

In the late seventies the long train of bereavement, displacement, and struggle abated for a while. Her granddaughter Jenny Greene was a most satisfactory young person whose conversation and attention comforted her and whose husband she respected. Though there was no neighbor for two miles, many visitors dropped in. She herself never left home unless someone sent a carriage since "I hant courage to ride a hors."[12] She made and sent to Franklin several batches of crown soap according to a secret family recipe for his friends in France, took care of Jenny Greene in successive lyings-in, helped with the babies, supervised the household, and, from time to time, sold "some little matter" from the small store of goods she had brought from Boston in 1775. "My time seems to be filld up as the Famely I am in Increases fast," she wrote. She was sixty-eight and energetic, though "as I grow older I wish for more Quiet and our Famely is more Incumbered as we have three children Born since I came & tho they give grat Pleasure . . . yet the Noise of them is sometimes troublesom. . . ."[13] She knew "but little how the world goes Except seeing a Newspaper some times which contains Enough to give Pain but little satisfaction while we are in Armes against each other. . . ."[14] In spite of the inflation and the losses the Greenes were suffering, her life was pleasanter than it had been since childhood. "I contineu very Easey and happy hear," she wrote in 1781, "have no more to troble me than what is Incident to human Nature & cant be avoided in any Place, I write now in my own litle chamber the window opening on won of the Pleasantest prospects in the country the Birds singing about me and nobod up in the house near me to Desturb me. . . ."[15]

Life had taught Jane Mecom to be wary when things were going well. Ten months after that happy note her granddaughter died, and at 70 Jane Mecom was suddenly again the female head of a household of young children who needed "some person more lively and Patient to watch over them continualy"; but since there was no one else, she did it anyway.[16] Fortunately she found them a comfort as she grieved for her beloved grandchild, sacrifice to the age's custom of unbroken childbearing.

Her brother's first postwar letter included a "grat, very grat, Present," for which she thanked him extravagantly, adding that his generosity would enable her to live "at Ease in my old Age (after a life of Care Labour & Anxiety). . . ."[17]

By 1784 she was back in Boston, in a house owned by her brother, where she was able to "live all ways Cleen and Look Decent."[18] She had leisure to read and write, a minister she respected with whom to discuss theology and other things, and the care and companionship of her granddaughter Jenny Mecom. Her grandchildren and great-grandchildren were often a source of pride and pleasure.

With her brother in Philadelphia, correspondence quickened. He was still concerned that someone in the family be trained to carry on the tradition of the crown soap. She had thought earlier of teaching her son-in-law Peter Collas, whose difficulties in earning a living had become almost ludicrous. Whenever he took berth on a ship it was promptly captured. But she had decided that the soap required a man of "Peculiar Genius," and that Collas was not.[19]

She wished Franklin well in the federal convention, and when the Constitution arrived in Boston she reported that while some quarrelsome spirits opposed it those of "Superior Judgement" were going to support it.

A ship captain friend took a favorable report of her to Philadelphia, for which she was grateful: "The Gratest Part of my time when I am sitting at home I am apt to Imagine as Samson did when He lost his Hare, that I can Arise & Shake my Self & Go forth as at other times but on Tryal Like him I am wofully disappointed & find my Feet cripling & my Breath short, but I am still chearful for that is my Natural Temper."[20]

In January 1788, replying to his request for a "very peticular" account of how she lived, she provided a detailed description:

> I have a good clean House to Live in my Grandaughter constantly to atend me to do whatever I desier in my own way & in my own time, I go to bed Early lye warm & comfortable Rise Early to a good Fire have my Brakfast directly and Eate it with a good Apetite and then Read or Work or what Els I Pleas, we live frugaly, Bake all our own Bread, brew small bear, lay in a little cyder, Pork, Buter, &c. & suply our selves with Plenty of other nesesary Provision Dayly at the Dore we make no Entertainments, but some Times an Intimate Acquaintance will come in and Pertake with us the Diner we have Provided for our selves & a Dish of Tea in the After Noon, & if a Friend sitts and chats a litle in the Evening we Eate our Hasty Puding (our comon super) after they are gone; It is trew I have some Trobles but my Dear Brother Does all in His Power to Aleviat them by Praventing Even a wish, that when I Look Round me on all my Acquaintance I do not see won I have reason to think Happier than I am and would not change my neighbour with my Self where will you Find one in a more comfortable State as I see Every won has ther Trobles and I sopose them to be such as fitts them best & shakeing off them might be only changing for the wors.[21]

Six more years of life remained to her. The new Constitution was inaugurated, George Washington took office, merchants and politicians concerned themselves with their own and the nation's prosperity, foreign conflicts flamed and threatened. Jane Mecom, for her part, worried about Benjamin Franklin's illness with "the stone," and prayed for his tranquillity. Their correspondence ranged around topics mostly personal and family, and reflections on life as they had lived it. "I do not Pretend to writ about Politics," she said, "tho I Love to hear them. . . ."[22]

Franklin's death in 1790 was a blow, but she was now 78 and prepared to be philosophical about this, as she saw it, temporary separation from her best friend. In his will he provided for her, and when she died four years later this woman who had lived so frugally was able to leave an estate of a thousand pounds to Jane Collas (in trust—she still worried about her daughter's extravagance!) and to her 15 grandchildren and great-grandchildren.

When the historians came to treat the years covered by her life they dwelt on wars and politics, on the opening of land and trade and manu-facture, on the economic development of a fertile wilderness, the rapid growth in population, the experiment in representative government. But life as she perceived it was mostly made up of the small events of which great events are composed: of 21 years of pregnancy and childbirth which, multiplied by millions of women, created the country's rapid population growth; of the hard struggle to "git a living" and to make sure her children were prepared to earn theirs; of the constant procession of deaths which was the hallmark of her time; of the belated prosperity and happiness that came to her in old age. What added up to a wilderness conquered, a new nation created, was often experienced by individuals as a very hard life somehow survived. It is only in retrospect that all the separate experiences together create something we call "economic development," or "manifest destiny," or simply, "history."

The events of Jane Mecom's life might have destroyed a weaker person, but some combination of natural resilience, good health, belief in the vir-tues of diligence, industry, and ingeniousness, and firm faith that God had good reasons for all the pain and sorrow that befell her, carried her through. Perhaps her final judgment on the whole experience was summed up in that sentence: "Every won has ther Trobles and I sopose them to be such as fitts them best & shakeing off them might be only changing for the wors."

*   *   *

Jane Mecom's life emerges full of interest from the most fragmentary records. Elizabeth Drinker, by contrast, left the most detailed record of any eighteenth-century American woman, one that provides an intimate view of daily life among the tight little community of Philadelphia Quakers.

Born Elizabeth Sandwith, of Irish inheritance, she was orphaned in her teens. In 1759, when she was 24, she began a laconic record of how she spent her time ("Went thrice to meeting; drank tea at Neighbor Callen-der's") which gradually grew into a journal wherein she recorded the de-tails of her life and speculated upon them. The last entry was made a few days before her death in 1807.

As a child she had had the good fortune to go to Anthony Benezet's school, and she knew English, Latin, and French. To a solid basic educa-tion she brought an inquiring mind—science and medicine were particu-larly fascinating to her—and a touch of intellectual (though not religious) skepticism.

At 26, after a long courtship, she married Henry Drinker, a widower her own age, who after an apprenticeship to a merchant firm and the requisite trading voyage, had been taken into the company.

For 13 months the journal lay untouched but for one minor entry, and by the time she began to keep it regularly again "my dear little Sal" had joined the family. For the ensuing 19 years pregnancies, miscarriages, births, deaths of four infants and the weaning and raising of the other five formed the principal focus of her life. Henry, for his part, was on the way to becoming one of the busiest men in Philadelphia, constantly "from home" on business or on Quaker affairs, for his progress in business was paralleled by his gradual accumulation of responsibility in the world of the Friends.

As child after child was born and lived or died, the journal became in part a medical record. Capable of serving as midwife for her friends, Elizabeth Drinker could do little to ease her own very difficult childbirths, "lingering and tedious," as she called them. She liked to nurse her babies, but was often forced for reasons of health to put them out to nurse. Though the family could afford the best doctors in Philadelphia, she was an independent-minded practitioner herself who often went contrary to their advice. When one of her sons fell out of a tree and broke a collarbone, she was pleased to find herself able to help the doctor set it. When newly acquired indentured servants (often under the age of ten) arrived with the itch and with lice and without smallpox inoculation, she undertook to deal with all these problems. Her husband and children fell ill with astonishing frequency. Along the way she read weighty medical books and speculated, sometimes in conversation with her good friend Benjamin Rush, about the cause and cure of various diseases.

The conflict with Great Britain marked a turning point in her development. Quakers tried to remain aloof, both for religious reasons and because those who were merchants had much to lose. One consequence was that in 1777 Henry Drinker and a number of others were arrested and taken off to prison in Winchester, Virginia. At 42 Elizabeth Drinker was suddenly the head of a household composed of her sister Mary, five children, and five indentured servants, and the British army was about to occupy Philadelphia. While she dutifully trusted that "it will please the Almighty to order all for the best," it was clear that she would have to lend Him a hand, and she prayed for resolution and fortitude.[23]

There were daily challenges. Barrels of flour disappeared and rumors of widespread looting sped through the town. "Tis hardly safe to leave the door open," she noted. "I often feel afraid to go to bed." Henry's business affairs had to be attended to. One of her servants was first "very impertinent and saucy," and then ran away altogether with an audacious British soldier. Meeting the soldier on the street, Elizabeth Drinker confronted him, demanding that he pay for the servant's time. The British began commandeering blankets, and other things. Horses were stolen; wood was scarce; other servants disappeared, to the point that "we have but 9 persons in our Family this winter; we have not had less than 13 or 14 for many years past."[24]

As if they had overheard her, the British authorities arranged to enlarge the family again by quartering a certain Major Crammond, his two horses, two cows, and a Hessian stableboy in the Drinker household. The major kept the family awake with late dinner parties.

Her husband's return was quickly followed by the British evacuation. People who had been too friendly with the enemy were now turned out of their houses, their goods confiscated, and a few, including some Quakers, hanged. The Americans were worse than the British in expropriating what they wanted (calling it taxation), and good furniture, pewter, blankets, and provisions were hauled off under their eyes. Servants continued to disappear. When news of Cornwallis's defeat arrived, Quakers who refused to illuminate their houses in celebration were subjected to a mob. Seventy panes of glass were broken in the Drinkers' house.

By the time the treaty of peace was signed, she, like the new nation of which she was somewhat reluctantly a part, had reached a new stage of life. "I have often thought," she wrote in later years, ". . . that women who live to get over the time of Childbareing if other things are favourable to them, experience more comfort and satisfaction than at any other period of their lives."[25] When that was written in 1797, she was certainly commenting upon her own life, which by our standards would not seem to have been precisely one of comfort, whatever it might have enjoyed of satisfaction. Though her last child had been born when she was 46, illness continued to be a major theme of the Drinker experience through the rest of her life.

Eleven pregnancies had left her own health uncertain at best; her son William had tuberculosis; Henry Drinker was a constant victim of intestinal disorders and even more of the heroic treatment he received for them; one child had yellow fever and the whole family lived through three yellow fever epidemics; everyone sooner or later had malaria; in the household someone, husband, children, grandchildren, or servants, was always ill. Yet this seemed to interfere very little with the daily routine. Sick people entertained visitors along with the rest of the family, and those down with chills and fever one day were riding their horses off to the country the next. To the 20th-century mind the whole situation is quite baffling.

Though she regularly worried about the ill health of her daughters, all three married and began at once to have children of their own. One daughter, the youngest, caused a family crisis by running away and marrying "out of meeting" a perfectly respectable young Friend whose only disability, apparently, was that he did not wear the plain dress. Henry Drinker took a hard line: no one was to visit the miscreant daughter. After a few months Elizabeth Drinker defied him, noting without contrition: "I feel best pleased I went."[26] Henry finally relented, and Molly and her husband became part of the growing clan of sons and daughters and in-laws.

Elizabeth Drinker attended each of her daughters in childbirth, assisting the midwife and the doctor. After a hard time with Sally's fourth, she recorded that she had slept only two of the preceding 50 hours and noted that she was "much fatigued, bones ache, flesh sore, Head giddy, etc. but have at the same time much to be thankful for."[27] Mother and child had both survived.

Two years later Molly and Sally were in labor at the same time. Sally's delivery was a very hard one; Molly's baby was stillborn. "The loss gives me great concern, not only being deprived of a sweet little grandson, but ye suffering of my poor Child, who lost, what may be called the reward of her labour . . . [and who] may pass through, if she lives, the same excruciating trouble a year the sooner for this loss."[28] In 1799 Sally was in labor with her sixth child and very depressed. Elizabeth Drinker tried to cheer her, reminding her that she was now 39 and that this "might possibly be the last trial of this sort, if she could suckle her baby for 2 years to come, as she had several times done heretofore. . . ."[29] It is odd that Elizabeth Drinker should have offered this particular argument, since she herself had twice become pregnant while nursing a baby, but it was standard advice from mothers to daughters in the 18th century. Neither she nor her daughters made any bones about their dislike of pregnancy and childbirth, though it seems in no way to have diminished their affection for the children themselves. Indeed, rather the contrary, since the burgeoning family was the center of Elizabeth Drinker's life. Children, in-laws, and grandchildren moved in and out of the house daily and formed the subject for much of what she wrote. All her children lived nearby and visited each other as well as their parents constantly, sharing carriages, lending servants, sharing summer houses, exchanging children.

The Drinkers included servants in their conception of family—bound boys and girls or indentured adults. Often they came as children of seven or eight. Once there were three black boys under ten at the same time. Elizabeth Drinker gave them careful attention, mending their clothes and trying to teach them. "I have much to do for the little black boys; these small folk ought to be of service when they grow bigger, for they are very troublesome when young. . . ."[30] Pretty bound girls were likely to flirt, or, worse, to get pregnant. One, who had lived with them since she was ten, gave birth to a mulatto baby, at the Drinkers' expense. There followed much soul-searching as to what the child's future should be, but it died before they could decide.

There was no doubt in her mind that the "poorer sort" were different from herself, yet some of her former servants were close friends who came back often to visit. When one favorite servant came down with yellow fever, the family reluctantly decided to send her to the yellow fever hospital where, of course, she died. The matter weighed on Elizabeth Drinker's conscience.

She recognized that much of the comfort and satisfaction of her later life was because of Mary Sandwith, who never married, and who chose to care for household things, leaving her sister free to "amuse myself in reading and doing such work as I like best."[31]

The natural world interested her greatly; insects, butterflies, and turtles were brought for her inspection by children and grandchildren who knew of her curiosity about such things. Eclipses fascinated her. She speculated as to the causes of all sorts of natural events and loved to read about science.

Her reading, indeed, was prodigious. She felt constrained to note in her journal that it was not her sole occupation, but it was certainly an increasingly important part of her life as she grew older. She kept lists of books read, and they encompass most of what 18th-century Philadelphia had to offer. She read Mary Wollstonecraft's *Vindication of the Rights of Women* and noted that "in very many of her sentiments, she, as some of our friends say, *speaks my mind.* . . ."[32] Then she read William Godwin's memoir of Mary Wollstonecraft, and modified her opinion: "I think her a prodigious fine writer, and should be charmed by some of her pieces if I had never heard of her character."[33]

She read Tom Paine and abhorred what she took to be his dangerous principles. She took *Gargantua and Pantagruel* from the library and, after one quick look, hastily sent it back. She was equally shocked by Rousseau's *Confessions*. She read Swift, and seven volumes of Sterne, tracts by Madame Roland, dozens of religious books, Plutarch's *Lives*, and on and on.

While she read and wrote, children and grandchildren (by 1804 there were 17) moved steadily in and out; often 20 people came to dinner. Friends from other towns arrived for the Yearly Meeting and lodged with the Drinkers. Henry continued to be the busiest man in Philadelphia, and she remarked that if good works would take a person to heaven he would certainly get there. She was not in the best of health herself, but was "seldom Idle." Every year she took stock on the first of January, and was surprised to find herself still alive. More and more she enjoyed solitude, a thing which had been disagreeable to her when she was young.

As she grew older her interest in politics quickened. When John Adams came to town as President her feelings were at war with her Quaker principles. "He went by our door attended by the Light-horse and a few others. Tho' I am not for parade of any sort, in ye general way, yet on this occasion, everything considered, I should have been pleased to see a little more of it."[34] In 1800 she took note of the disputed election and of Jefferson's popularity in Philadelphia.

Friend after friend died. The last pages of the journal recorded an endless succession of deaths and funerals, accompanied by the small sense of triumph that oneself was still alive. Sally's death at 46 bore heavily on her spirit. I have had nine children, she mused, and now my first, third, fifth, seventh, and ninth are all dead.

She fell and bruised herself and the doctors wanted to bleed her, "which I would not comply with."[35] Old age had brought the courage to resist their violent treatments, of which she had long been rightly skeptical. On the eighteenth of November in 1807 she noted in her journal that the weather was clear and cold, and the moon out. One grandson dropped in; she sent William to make the rounds of all the family dwellings. He came back to report that, but for one toothache, all were in good health. With her world thus in as good order as it could be, Elizabeth Drinker died.

She had lived 72 years, born in a prosperous colony when no more than three quarters of a million people lived in all British North America; she died a citizen of a nation of nearly seven million. Her own town had grown remarkably and had been the scene of the Declaration of Independence, the Constitutional Convention, and the early years of the new government. James and Drinker, her husband's firm, had exemplified in microcosm much of the mercantile history of the colony and the new nation. Her son, who sailed off to India, and her son-in-law, with a yen for the backwoods, were both part of much larger movements.

Yet for Elizabeth Drinker, observant, thoughtful, well-read person that she was, life almost began and ended with family, work, and religion. From the day Sally was born until the day she herself died, she was deeply concerned with the welfare, first of children, then of grandchildren. She was never without a child in her house and never ceased trying to teach them the ways of righteousness. She abhorred idleness and made sure that her journal noted this fact lest some future reader think she spent all her time reading books! And, like Jane Mecom, she believed the Almighty knew what He was about.

Her descendants continued to flourish in Philadelphia, and it is pleasant fantasy to imagine the shock (but secret pleasure too) with which Elizabeth Drinker might read part of their story in Catherine Drinker Bowen's *Family Affair.*

*   *   *

Born in the West Indies, almost midway between Jane Mecom and Elizabeth Drinker, daughter of an army officer whose family had owned land in South Carolina and Antigua for three generations, Eliza Lucas came from more favored circumstances than either of the others. The contrast between Jane Mecom's rough-hewn prose and phonetic spelling and her equally rough-hewn handwriting and the elegant language, copperplate penmanship, and ritual formality of Eliza Lucas's early letters is re-markable. While Jane Mecom's friends and relatives included people in almost the whole range of the social scale and Elizabeth Drinker belonged to the solid middle class, with Eliza Lucas we move to the top of the scale.

There had been money to send her "home" to England for a careful edu-cation, and when she was 17, her father had settled her, along with her mother and her younger sister, on one of his plantations in Carolina while he carried on his duties as governor of Antigua.

We can see Eliza Lucas clearly in her youth, and an astonishing young person she was. As vigorous and enterprising as the young Franklin or the young Jefferson, for five years she taught the three Rs to her sister and the slave children, experimented with new plants, dealt daily with overseers and factors, wrote long letters on business matters to her father and to his business associates, taught herself law and used her knowledge to help her neighbors who could not afford a proper lawyer, and read so much in Locke, Boyle, Plutarch, Virgil, and Malebranche that an old lady in the neighborhood prophesied that she would damage her brain.

A touch of humor and of self-deprecation was all that saved her from being unbearably didactic when she wrote to her younger brothers or younger friends. With older people, especially her much admired father, she was witty and straightforward.

So she continued happily as his agent, writing dozens of letters, dealing with the factor and with the agent in England, supervising planting, in-structing overseers, paying debts, and contracting new ones. "By rising early," said this female Poor Richard, "I get through a great deal of business."[36]

The social life of Charleston appealed to her less than the work of the plantation. "I own," she wrote, "that I love the vigitable world extremely."[37] The most visible consequence of her love affair with vegetables was the development of indigo as a major export crop for South Carolina. At her father's suggestion she began to plant indigo seeds, and when, after several failures, a crop was achieved, she worked with servants he had sent from Antigua to refine the process by which it was prepared as a dye.

A true exemplar of the Enlightenment, she believed religion and right reason could coexist, and said that "the soports of the Xtian religion" en-abled her to view life's hazards with equanimity. She endeavored to resign herself to events as they came, since "there is an all Wise Being that orders Events, who knows what is best for us," and she believed in subduing the passions to reason.[38]

Migraine headaches hardly slowed her down. It occurred to her to plant oak trees against the day when South Carolina might run out of hardwood. In a careful letter she compared the agriculture of England and South Carolina, somewhat to the advantage of the latter, and observed that "the poorer sort [here] are the most indolent people in the world or they could never be so wretched in so plentiful a country as this." Indolence was, in her view, close to a deadly sin.[39]

This precocious young woman who found men her own age dull—"I don't trouble my head about them"—was intrigued by the intelligent conversation of a man in his forties. Carolina's first native-born lawyer, Charles Pinckney. She had met Pinckney and his wife soon after her arrival. He lent her books, encouraged her to report to him on her reading, and enjoyed the discipleship of so eager a pupil. Once, in 1741, she absentmindedly signed a letter to him "Eliza Pinckney."[40]

Three years later in December 1744, Mrs. Pinckney died. On May 2, 1745, Eliza wrote her father thanking him for permission to marry Charles Pinckney and "for the fortune you are pleased to promise me." She also thanked him for the pains and money laid out for her education, which "I esteem a more valuable fortune than any you have now given me." She assured him that Mr. Pinckney was fully satisfied with her dowry.[41]

To a cousin who had warned that she was so particular she was bound to "dye an old maid," she wrote: "But you are mistaken. I am married and the gentleman I have made choice of comes up to my plan in every tittle . . . I do him barely justice when I say his good Sence and Judgment, his extraordinary good nature and eveness of temper joynd to a most agreeable conversation and many valuable qualifications gives me the most agreeable prospect in the world. . . ."[42]

She bore with equanimity the talk of the town about their somewhat precipitate marriage, but was righteously indignant when gossip told it that the late Mrs. Pinckney had been neglected in her last illness. Writing to that lady's sister she said firmly that she would never have married a man who had been guilty of such a thing.[43] As she had earlier striven to please her father, so now she made every effort to please her husband. "When I write you," she told him, "I . . . desire . . . to equal even a Cicero or Demosthenes that I might gain your applause."[44]

Her father seems to have worried lest the strong-minded independence in which he had reared her might not sit well with a husband, and she reassured him that "acting out of my proper province and invading his, would be inexcusable."[45] She and Pinckney apparently agreed that her proper province was a spacious one.

Her self-improving urge was as strong as ever. She wrote a long list of resolutions and planned to reread them daily. With God's help she hoped not to be "anxious or doubtful, not to be fearful of any accident or misfortune that may happen to me or mine, not to regard the frowns of the world." She planned to govern her passions, improve her virtues, avoid all the deadly sins, be a frugal manager while extending hospitality and charity generously, and make a good wife, daughter, and mother and a good mistress of servants. At the end of this long list of injunctions to herself for ideal behavior she made a typical note: "Before I leave my Chamber recolect in General the business to be done that day." Good advice for any administrator.[46] Once she noted that "nobody eats the bread of idleness while I am here."[47]

Her married life was as busy as her single life had been. In ten months Charles Cotesworth Pinckney was born. Eliza could see "all his papa's virtues already dawning" in the infant. A friend in England was asked to find a set of educational toys described by John Locke, while his father set about designing toys to teach the infant his letters. "You perceive we begin bytimes," Eliza added, "for he is not yet four months old."[48]

A second son was born and died. Then came Thomas and Harriott. Though Eliza Pinckney had slave nurses to suckle her infants, she was intensely preoccupied with the training, education, and shaping of her children.

In 1752 political maneuvering deprived Charles Pinckney of his seat as chief justice of the colony and he left for England to serve as South Carolina's agent there. The family took a house in Surrey; the boys were sent to school and Harriott was taught at home. It was a good life, and she was in no hurry to return to South Carolina.

Increasingly concerned by developments in the Seven Years' War and fearful that France might take over a large part of North America, the Pinckneys decided to depart for America, and to liquidate their Carolina estate. To this end they sailed the war-infested sea in 1758, taking Harriott and leaving their sons in school. But three weeks after they landed Charles Pinckney was dead. Eliza Pinckney at 35 was once again in charge of a large and complex plantation enterprise. It was just as well, she thought, to have so great a responsibility; otherwise the loss of this most perfect of husbands would have undone her.

In letter after letter she recited Pinckney's virtues; his religious dedication, "free from sourness and superstition," his integrity, charm, and good temper, "his fine address"—she thought she would never find his like again.[49]

It was for the children she told herself (and them) that she worked so hard, overseeing the planting, buying, and selling, writing ceaselessly to England (in several copies since no ship was secure), nursing slaves through smallpox, supervising the education of Harriott. She expected reciprocal effort from her sons. She wrote Charles Cotesworth: ". . . though you are very young, you must know the welfare of a whole family depends in a great measure on the progress you make in moral Virtue, Religion, and learning. . . . To be patient, humble, and resigned is to be happy. It is also to have a noble soul, a mind out of the reach of Envy, malice and every Calamity. And the earlier, my dear boy, you learn this lesson, the longer will you be wise and happy."[50]

She thought highly of female talent. Harriott was "fond of learning and I indulge her in it. It shall not be my fault if she roams abroad for amusement, as I believe 'tis want of knowing how to imploy themselves agreeably that makes many women too fond of going abroad."[51] Indeed, Harriott's education continued to be one of her chief joys: "For pleasure it certainly is to cultivate the tender mind, to teach the young Idea how to shoot, &c. especially to a mind so tractable and a temper so sweet as hers. . . ."[52]

In 1768 Harriott at 19 married a 35-year-old planter, Daniel Horry, and set about replicating her mother's career. In her own well-organized household five slaves had each their appointed tasks; none was idle and none, she said, overworked. She herself was constantly industrious.

Her mother, meanwhile, fell ill and lay four months in her chamber, but was too busy to die. A friend in England wanted seeds of all the trees in Carolina, and she was happy to oblige. She decided to modernize her plantations, working harder, she said, than any slave. She revived silk-making experiments, and endeavored to teach the skill to other women.

In such good order, then, were the family affairs in 1769 when Charles Cotesworth Pinckney came home from his 16-year sojourn in England, already an American patriot. He was at once admitted to the bar and in a month had been elected to the South Carolina Assembly. A year or so later Thomas arrived to join him. The children for whom she had seen herself as working so hard were all launched. But public affairs were in turmoil, and in 1775 both her sons were commissioned in the first regiment of South Carolina troops. Their business affairs remained in the hands of their mother and sister, who were quite prepared to carry on while the men went to war.

It was 1778 before the full force of hostilities reached the Pinckneys. They had chosen Ashepoo, the family plantation belonging to Thomas Pinckney, as the safest place for all their valuables. It was a bad guess. Augustine Prevost's forces burned it to the ground on their way to Charleston. British troops, moreover, impressed horses, took provisions, and commandeered houses. Eliza Pinckney had to take refuge in the country. In the midst of all this stress Thomas was wounded, Charles Cotesworth, already suffering from malaria, was imprisoned, and two grandchildren were born. In 1780 the British captured Charleston, and by that time plenty had given way to pinched poverty. She owed 60 pounds to a creditor in England and could find no way at all to pay it. For a while it seemed that the fruit of 30 years' hard work was all lost.

Even before the war ended, however, it was clear that Eliza Pinckney's labors had accomplished much more than the building of a prosperous planting interest. She had created an enormously effective family. Planting and business, important as they were, had always taken second place to the upbringing and education of her children. Now, as adults, the three saw themselves with her as almost a single entity. The men, at war, often wrote their mother twice a day. Harriott, who had been Tom's close friend and confidante before he was married and whom he had always treated as an intellectual equal, continued after his marriage as his business agent and political adviser. For both brothers she managed plantations (as well as her own, after Daniel Horry died), handled money, and looked after their wives and children. They in turn took time from their pressing military duties to oversee the education of her son.

After the war the pattern continued. Both Pinckney men moved into public service. Charles Cotesworth was a member of the Constitutional Convention; Thomas was elected governor of South Carolina by an overwhelming majority and was in office when the state ratified the Constitution. Both were part of the developing Federalist party. Each was to be a foreign envoy and to give his name to important treaties. These careers were made possible by the labors of their mother and sister.

In 1792 Eliza Pinckney developed cancer, and almost the entire family proposed to accompany her to Philadelphia, where a physician with considerable reputation in that field was to be found. She refused to go if they all came along: she could not risk the whole family on one ship. So, while Charles Cotesworth and his children reluctantly remained in Charleston, Harriott took her to Philadelphia. It was too late. She died and was buried there, George Washington at his own request serving as one of her pallbearers.

Building notable families was one of the things American colonials had to do for themselves when they came away from England. Franklin and Drinker were to become well-known family names because of the work and the public service of their men. Pinckney, too, became famous as a consequence of the public service of Thomas, Charles Cotesworth, and their cousin, also Charles. But the family was created and sustained, and developed a strong sense of itself as a consequence of the work, the vision, the exhortation, and the constant attention of Eliza Pinckney.

*   *   *

The records left by these three women take us to the heart of daily life: to scenes of childbearing and nerve-racking struggles to keep babies alive, to scenes of mysterious illness and sudden death, of wartime stringencies and dislocations, to the struggle to "git a living" or—at another level—to get rich. Through their eyes we see the chanciness of life and begin to understand the central role of kinship in providing such security as was possible in a world so filled with uncertainty.

Different as these women were, each put family at the center of life. Eliza Pinckney and her three children viewed the world, not as individuals, but *as a family*. By the time she died the family had a full-fledged "tradition" for many of its activities, and doubtless no one remembered that it had all been created in two generations.

The Drinkers were equally knit together by kinship. The sons-in-law were brought into the family business and encouraged to help each other.

When one had business reverses the whole family helped out. The cousins were grouped around the grandparents and encouraged to see the family as their most basic commitment.

Jane Mecom's life was shaped by her relationship to Benjamin Franklin, but beyond the two of them lay a wide network of Franklin kin, in-laws and cousins in various degrees. In-laws were addressed as "sister" and "brother" and were entitled to at least formal statements of affection. They clearly recognized some members of the clan as more "valuable" than others, but blood created a responsibility even for ne'er-do-wells. While historical demographers argue about nuclear and extended families, we must pay close attention to the actual experience of families, and beware of false dichotomies.

No one who reads these pages will doubt that women's lives were different from those of men. In a day when contraception was all but unknown there is no mystery about a sexual division of labor that allotted men tasks in the public sphere and women those that could be carried out at home. Each of these women was pregnant within a month after marriage, and two continued to bear children into their late 40s. Eliza Pinckney's family was unusually small for the time, but she was widowed at 35.

All three of these women were as much involved in raising the second generation as they had been with the first, and Jane Mecom, for a time, was responsible for four great-grandchildren. Grandmothering was an important part of their lifework.

All three believed in work as a moral value. They reserved their strongest criticisms for indolence in any form, and none of them saw old age as justification for idleness. For Jane Mecom and Elizabeth Drinker, "work" was largely domestic, though both dealt also in some mercantile ventures. Jane Mecom ran her own little shop for a while, and Elizabeth Drinker kept accounts for her husband's firm. Eliza Pinckney's work encompassed the larger world of plantation trade. Through most of her life she was busy with shipments, payments, factors, and the like, while she also planned and supervised the actual production of rice, indigo, silk, and the hundred other products of the relatively self-sufficient plantation. Though nominally working for others, first for her father, then for her husband, and finally for her children, she seems not to have felt any inhibition about acting in her own name and making her own decisions. The fact that legal ownership belonged to her father or husband was of no great operational significance.

Woman's life in the 18th century was fundamentally influenced by marriage. In a day when conventional wisdom had it that for both men and women it was wise to marry close to home, all three did so. But the luck of the draw varied widely. There is little record of Edward Mecom's life, but circumstantial evidence suggests that Jane Mecom might have done better on her own. Elizabeth Drinker admired Henry, and his success in business provided her with a life of material comfort. As she grew older he was gradually replaced at the center of her emotional focus by her son William, and her other children and grandchildren preoccupied her mind.

Eliza Pinckney never remarried after her husband's death. During her marriage she had played the role of the properly subservient wife; widowed, she assumed the role of head of the family and continued to make vital decisions even when her sons were grown and had families of their own. With their help she created the "Pinckney Family."

These were only three of millions of women who lived and worked and died in colonial America. In this age of statistical sophistication, it is a bold historian who builds any case upon three examples, yet these women exemplify cultural values that were shared by many of their contemporaries. In their experience we see much of the common life of 18th-century woman, no matter what her social class. In another sense, of course, all three were uncommon women, whose achievements tell us something about the possibilities as well as the probabilities for women in their day and generation.

Notes

1. Jane Mecom to Benjamin Franklin, Aug. 16, 1787, in Carl Van Doren, ed., *The Letters of Benjamin Franklin and Jane Mecom* (Princeton: Princeton University Press, 1950), p. 296. Note her use of the plural *Heads*.
2. *Ibid.*, p. 52.
3. *Ibid.*, p. 43.
4. The original of this letter is lost. It is here reprinted from Jared Sparks, ed., *The Papers of Benjamin Franklin*, VII (New Haven: Yale University Press, 1965), 515n. Sparks corrected spelling and punctuation.
5. Van Doren, *Letters*, p. 114.
6. *Ibid.*, pp. 106–107.
7. *Ibid.*, p. 183.
8. *Ibid.*, p. 189.
9. *Ibid.*
10. *Ibid.*, p. 174.
11. *Ibid.*, p. 171.
12. *Ibid.*, p. 197.
13. *Ibid.*, p. 208.
14. *Ibid.*, p. 210.
15. *Ibid.*
16. *Ibid.*, p. 214.
17. *Ibid.*, p. 221.
18. *Ibid.*, p. 245.
19. *Ibid.*, p. 206.
20. *Ibid.*, p. 263.
21. *Ibid.*, p. 306.
22. *Ibid.*, p. 322.

23. H. D. Biddle, *Extracts from the Journal of Elizabeth Drinker* (Philadelphia: Lippincott, 1889), p. 49.
24. Typescript of manuscript journal, Historical Society of Pennsylvania, Dec. 7, 11, 14, 1777. Cited herafter as Ms. Journal.
25. *Ibid.*, Feb. 26, 1797.
26. Biddle, *Extracts*, pp. 292–293.
27. Ms. Journal, Apr. 5–8, 1795.
28. *Ibid.*, June 14, 1796.
29. *Ibid.*, Oct. 23, 1799.
30. *Ibid.*, Dec. 26, 1794.
31. *Ibid.*, Jan. 1, 1802.
32. *Ibid.*, Apr. 22, 1796.
33. *Ibid.*, 1799 (n.d.).
34. Biddle, *Extracts*, p. 313.
35. Ms. Journal, Jan. 1, 1807.
36. Elise Pinckney, ed., *The Letterbook of Eliza Lucas Pinckney* (Chapel Hill: University of North Carolina Press, 1972), p. 7.
37. *Ibid.*, pp. 34–35.
38. *Ibid.*, p. 49.
39. *Ibid.*, pp. 29, 19.
40. *Ibid.*, pp. 39–40.
41. Harriott Horry Ravenal, *Eliza Lucas Pinckney* (New York: Scribner's, 1896), pp. 69–70.
42. *Ibid.*, p. 94.
43. Eliza Lucas Pinckney to Miss Bartlett, Manuscript Division, William R. Perkins Library, Duke University, Durham, N.C.
44. Ravenal, *Pinckney*, p. 90.
45. *Ibid.*, p. 100.
46. *Ibid.*, pp. 115–118.
47. *Ibid.*, p. 245.
48. Eliza Lucas Pinckney to Miss Bartlett.
49. Pinckney, *Letterbook*, pp. 100–102.
50. *Ibid.*, p. 168.
51. *Ibid.*, p. 142.
52. *Ibid.*, p. 181.

7

New Currents
in American Protestantism

TIMOTHY DWIGHT
CHARLES G. FINNEY
WILLIAM E. CHANNING

by Milton Cantor
University of Massachusetts, Amherst

Between the Revolutionary years and the industrial takeoff of the mid-19th century, great and fundamental changes occurred in American society. Outwardly, the old colonial institutions of family, church, political faction, social class seemed stable enough, but in reality all of them were gradually coming apart at the seams. Their unravelling, moreover, paralleled that of the rural community itself; and, in combination, had the effect of freeing men from the constraints of traditional social values. Small wonder that many of the religious orthodox found the Revolution fatal to the old morality.

Meanwhile, to turn to politics, the Federalists dominated the nation's political life in the 1790s. They distrusted the ordinary man and affirmed the wisdom of a ruling elite—unlike Jefferson's rising Republicans, with their confidence in public opinion and popular rule. These Federalists had recoiled from the execution of the French King, the subsequent Terror, and the seeming destruction of religion, even if it were a Catholic faith. Jacobinism came to seem not merely anti-Catholic, but anti-clerical and even anti-Christian as well. Voltaire and the *philosophes*, so it seemed, had let loose doctrines that any breeze might sweep across the seas and infect America's increasingly fragile religious and political communities. To a mounting number of both Federalists and Congregationalists it seemed that the respectable people, those of property and standing, might ultimately suffer the fate of France's aristocracy. Anti-Jacobinism, then, became a highly attractive ideology for many Americans. More than ever before, in the generally prosperous 1790s, the possibility of mob uprising and social revolution lurked as the spectre at the feast.

Believing in the rule of moral man, as they of course defined him, the Federalists evoked a basic and deeply embedded Protestant piety and inevitably lured New England's Congregational clergy into their camp. Many of this clergy had been prominent in resisting English tyranny from mid-century onward, and the American revolution had simply enhanced their good name. They had been, for instance, the immediate beneficiaries when New England Anglicans, owing to their Toryism, were cast in the villain role during the War of Independence. But Congregationalism, the first religion of New England, began to show signs of slippage. Its growth was the slowest of any denomination in Massachusetts during the 1780s and 1790s. Nor did ethnic and population changes help it—as Irish Catholic migrants began to settle in the growing seaport towns. A swarming and largely foreign working class, mostly Irish and "papist," new working class organizations, and riotous urban conditions called for immediate restraints—by the "strong arm of the law," declared Lyman Beecher, the prominent Congregational minister.

A host of votaries shared such ministerial apprehensions about the growth of new denominations; the more permissive ways of the world; the seeming erosion of the old community and the concomitant rise of commercial centers that encouraged seemingly un-Christian life styles; the decline of morals—the drunkenness, vice, Sabbath-breaking; the influx of new Irish immigrants who quickly identified with the "licentious" Republican Party.

The old "Congregational way" was also plagued by mounting doctrinal problems, with New England's urban ministry beginning to rework the traditional Calvinism. Influenced by Enlightenment currents, this ministry was increasingly drawn toward belief in a benevolent Providence. By 1825, to jump ahead momentarily, schism would come to what had been *the* established church of the northeast—in the form of Unitarianism. Itself a product of growing urbanity, enlightenment and self-confidence, Unitarianism gained adherents among the wealthy and educated of New England's seaport cities—and won over most of the faculty and students at Harvard College. Defectors from orthodoxy were drawn to the newest of denominations by its Arminianism, which emphasized human agency and human will rather than divine will and guidance; by its Arianism, the ancient heresy that questioned the doctrine of the Trinity; or by its overtone of 18th-century Christian rationalism. Calvinist Congregationalism, then, would fragment after 1800, with followers of Reverend Samuel Hopkins, who were strongest in central and southern Massachusetts, joining orthodox Calvinists in the Berkshires against the rising menace of religious liberalism in the coastal counties.

*   *   *

Among the most alarmed of New England's Congregationalists was the Reverend Timothy Dwight, President of Yale College (1795–1815). Dwight was convinced that the United States was being subverted by an international conspiracy, the Bavarian Illuminati—"those enemies of Christ"—and by the infidelity and immorality of Revolutionary France. The latter was "a kind of suburb of perdition . . . ," he warned. "Her embrace is death." He asked a Fourth of July audience in 1798: "Shall we, my brethren, become partakers in these sins? Shall we introduce them into our government, our schools, our families? Shall our sons become disciples of Voltaire and the dragoons of Marat, or our daughters the concubines of the Illuminati?"

Timothy Dwight, then 40 years old and possibly Connecticut's most respected citizen, was born in 1752. For over a century before, the family fortunes had been interwoven with the history of Massachusetts. On his father's side, he came from five generations of farmers, yeomen, and public servants—men who tilled the soil, served the community, sturdily believed in the God of John Calvin. His maternal line also had impressive Congregational credentials. Dwight's brown-eyed, dark-haired mother was the third daughter of no less than Jonathan Edwards. It was in Edwards' Northampton, a town nestled in the Connecticut Valley, that Timothy grew up, the first of a brood of 13 children.

Young Timothy had a bookish cast of mind. He was early taught to love God, to walk strictly in the narrow way of the Ten Commandments, to be acutely aware of the differences between right and wrong, to know his own depravity. At the age of six, this proper grandson of the great Edwards had already learned that good conduct was unavailing, that he was predestined, that his fate was in the hands of a righteous, inscrutable, justly angry God. And yet, as his deeply reverent mother taught, he must model his conduct on that of Jesus.

Timothy's formal education also began at six—down the road at a local grammar school. Gradually he developed a thirst for knowledge that would never be satisfied. His world slowly expanded. He studied everything that came his way, especially Latin, and made astonishing progress. He ransacked his father's library, devoured histories of Greece and England, and wrestled with accounts of early New England settlements and the first Indian wars. Outgrowing Northampton's limited educational facilities, which had been augmented by his mother's tutoring, the 12-year-old was shipped off to Middleton, Connecticut, where he would be prepared for college under the supervision of the town's minister. Yale accepted him in 1765, at age 13. While enjoying card playing and under-graduate pranks, Timothy continued to read voraciously. He graduated in 1769, remained at Yale for graduate studies, and supported himself by teaching grammar school, a common practice for young men fresh from college.

In 1771, Timothy Dwight became a tutor at his Alma Mater, remaining at this post for six years. With two other tutors, he championed the cause of belles lettres and provoked an intellectual ferment unprecedented in the life of the little provincial college. In addition to teaching Yale's rough country boys, he labored over a gigantic epic, "The Conquest of Canaan," which was typical of the mock-heroic poems of that day. Working long hours by candlelight, he subjected his eyes to strains from which they never fully recovered. Indeed, he was forced to rest them by taking a moratorium from books.

The roar of cannon would further lengthen his exile from the library. Called to fight in the Revolutionary conflict, Dwight's period of army service was a short one. It included a leave to deliver the 1776 "Valedictory Address" to Yale's graduates. A model of that stirring and optimistic nationalism then drenching American letters, the address prophesied that the empire of America would be the most glorious of all, the last and the brightest of time, the final kingdom, God's glorious plan fulfilled. By 1777, with the death of John Dwight, his soldiering came to an end. He received a license to preach, becoming army chaplain to General Samuel Parson's Connecticut brigade. He found time for another nationalist paean, "Columbia, Columbia, to glory arise," which cheered the soldier audience who heard it. Finally putting the army forever behind him, he moved into the old Northampton homestead with his wife and small child.

Timothy Dwight had become the main support for a large family of younger brothers and sisters. He managed two large farms, but still had energy enough to teach school and continue his studies in literature and philosophy. Moreover, the young minister-schoolmaster-farmer was elected Northampton's representative in the State legislature in 1781. But it was a short tour of duty, for he received a call to the Congregational ministry at Greenfield Hill in Connecticut and put the dust of North-ampton behind him.

By the mid-1790s, Dwight had acquired a national reputation. Though minister of a small rural church, he was celebrated for his preaching, poetry, political satires, and liberal educational policies. His sermons, often composed while hoeing in the garden, usually were delivered extemporaneously, owing in part to his congenitally feeble eyesight. They were renowned for their broad and searching rhythms, their eloquence and power, and the rich, mellow voice of the preacher.

Loyalty to Yale as well as unquestioned ability made Dwight an obvious candidate for the school's presidency when Ezra Stiles died in May 1795. Heeding "an important call of Divine Providence," Dwight was inaugurated in September 1795, a date that marked a new era in Yale's history.

At Greenfield, and later at Yale, Timothy Dwight was convinced that his country was in danger. He had long recognized that "benevolence toward man" was a Christian virtue having the highest priority. And such charitable impulses, that sense of noblesse oblige axiomatic of Puritanism, were in the hands of the wise and good—to be directed toward the community itself, especially toward one's social inferiors. Dwight continually practiced moral and social stewardship, and believed that he was thereby doing God's great work. It follows that he would support foreign missions for Africans, tract societies—so popular in Jacksonian society—and all the products of the Christian tradition. He encouraged a number of charitable and missionary agencies—and they in turn absorbed some of the religious energies catalyzed by revivalism and by an ethic of benevolence. Dwight himself helped establish the Missionary Society of Connecticut; he was a founder of the American Home Missionary Society; and he was a committed member of the American Board of Commissioners of Foreign Missions. He assisted the campaigns for prison reform and poor relief; indeed, he helped any agency working toward the alleviation of human distress. So he also endorsed a school for young Negro girls, commending three socially prominent New Haven ladies who would teach them how to read; he even helped raise a "considerable fund" for the school.

Education and religion were Timothy Dwight's lifelong concerns. Both were essential, he believed, to the dissemination of knowledge and piety, qualities absolutely necessary to the community that wished to enjoy divine favor. "Without churches," he declared, "men will be vicious of course; without churches they will be ignorant." Such sentiments suggest the same fear of social change, the same dread of spiritual contamination, the same belief in orthodoxy so important to his Puritan ancestors. And it was important, too, to Connecticut's orthodox, the Standing Order as it was appropriately called, that mix of the Congregational elect and solid Federalists. They would stand athwart the terror of the French Revolution, now horridly stalking New England's shores. And they would combat the "unAmerican" party of Jefferson that was then threatening national security, and frustrate the democratic masses—tradesmen, mechanics, small farmers, mostly "infidels"—already clamoring for greater political power in Connecticut and the nation.

Dwight's views recalled those early Puritans who had steeled their hearts by the fires of faith, those who had sought order, social stability, the discipline of the senses, and the maintenance of the cohesive community. Much like the Puritan fathers, he assumed that government was ordained by God and must dispense the divine law. Everything he had been taught argued that religion alone could guarantee that high level of public morals essential to good government. Everything that he saw about him, in the four frenetic post-Revolutionary decades, suggested the breakdown of the old religious life. He would, it followed, lead the host of the righteous against Arminianism, Arianism, Catholicism, and French philosophy. He would champion the moral renovation of society through sumptuary legislation and a quiet revivalism. Recalling Yale's undergraduates to the original mission of Connecticut's settlers, he proclaimed: "This land was settled by Christians. God brought his little flock hither; and placed it in this wilderness, for the great purpose of establishing permanently the church of Christ in these vast regions of idolatry and sin, and commencing here the glorious work of salvation. This great continent is soon to be filled with the praise, the piety, of the Millennium."

Dwight would use revivalism as a practical weapon in the crusade to restore religious orthodoxy. Moreover, he subscribed to most of the tenets of the New Divinity men who had revised and liberalized Calvinism. He even rejected the Half-Way Covenant by which persons who could make no claim to a conscious regenerate experience were admitted into the church and their children were allowed to take the baptismal rite. But more adroit than the followers of Edwards, he was willing to compromise, and his moderation helped overcome objections to his appointment at Greenfield Hill and to the Yale presidency. Nevertheless, he worked successfully toward the gradual elimination of the Half-Way Covenant in Connecticut's Congregational churches.

In addition, Dwight held to nearly the entire battery of Biblical truths. He accepted the story of the Flood and believed in the existence of Adam and Eve. But he refused to endorse the orthodox claim that Adam's children carried his sin. They had Adam's propensity to sin, to be sure, but did not bear his depravity or his guilt.

Dwight was closer to his grandfather and to Calvinist orthodoxy on the question of future rewards and punishments. He drew a vivid picture of the horrors of Hell and the bliss of heaven. He knew, furthermore, that straight was the way and narrow the gate, and repentence and regeneration in earthly life was necessary before entry into the celestial city; the unregenerate on earth would not be rewarded with heaven. But unlike the implicitly man-centered theology of revivalism, Dwight was convinced, at least in his early ministerial years, that only God could transform the sinful nature of man by His benevolence.

At the outset, then, Dwight was much like his fellow Yale man, the Reverend Samuel Hopkins of Newport, Rhode Island. But Hopkins was more a theologian than Dwight, now the recognized leader of the New Divinity clergy. Dwight was relatively unconcerned with speculative thought per se. His mind was more receptive than creative. He was practical and commonsensical, a man with a job to get done. Hopkins, much more unbending, and much like Jonathan Edwards, insisted upon God's absolute sovereignty and man's utter moral powerlessness when it came to faith and repentence. So at the outset did Dwight, but he increasingly moved away from this antinomian cult of helplessness. Quite understandably, he emphasized Bible reading, church attendance, and meditation, and connected them with man's ultimate hope for conversion. Man, Dwight insisted, must become aware and be convinced of his sinful state. He must pray to God and ask forgiveness, since only He could deliver man from sin and eternal punishment.

Dwight, therefore, preached the sovereignty of God but would enlarge man's moral and intellectual agency. Beyond what his grandfather might affirm, predestination was a diminished thing: man had the ability and the absolute obligation to "make great effort." Dwight's emphasis on the practical carried him toward a "system of duties"—the duties of a Christian life on Earth—which was enmeshed in a utilitarian notion of happiness far removed from Edwards' insistence upon depravity and exclusive dependence upon God.

It is ironic, then, that Dwight also fought a lifelong battle to revive his grandfather's faith, to halt the lamentable decline of morals, to save the Standing Order, to revitalize Congregationalism in New England. And the irony is embedded in the implications of revivalism, which assumed that human nature was not inherently depraved. Jonathan Edwards' theological system had not only claimed man was sinful by nature, but that any attempt by an unconverted heart to seek God's grace was a defiance of His will. It is, in fact, almost impossible to combine Edwardsean theology—which imputed inability to believers, which literally claimed that the unconverted could not even pray properly, which inspired a cult of passive obedience, which called for the sheer surrender of man to his Creator—with the contrary assumptions of revivalists that every person can help himself. Dwight nearly pulled off the impossible. In an age that had clearly lost much of its moral earnestness and inner convictions, he tried to finesse the issue in the interest of bringing people into a conversion experience—of reawakening the sense of sin, of turning men's hearts again toward God.

Again like his grandfather, Dwight was goaded by contemporary indifference to religious faith in New England, by the prevalence of irreligion and immorality. He had, after all, a fiercely proprietary interest in the region and it compelled him to use revivals as a means of restoring religious convictions and worship. So in 1806, he became president of the Connecticut Religious Tract Society, which had as its sole objective "the promotion of evangelical religion." And he would be the single most important early leader of Connecticut's Second Awakening. He knew, of course, that the First Awakening, which Jonathan Edwards had led in New England, was marked by egregious emotional excesses, an "enthusiasm," and hoped to avoid it. In any case, he initiated a quiet revival in 1801. It was, he believed, a mighty weapon in the ceaseless struggle against infidelity.

Previously, in 1795, infidelity at Yale had been Dwight's overriding concern. When he took over the reins, Yale was in his estimation a "ruined college." One contemporary found it in "a most ungodly state"; another observed a dreadful "state of disorder, impiety, & wickedness." Probably little had changed since Dwight studied there, beyond the deepening fears of Connecticut's Standing Order. Yale certainly seemed the same physically: four motley buildings set on the commons, along with a few shade trees, a nearby barbershop, some taverns, a jail, and a few boarding houses. But Dwight believed things had changed. For one thing, undergraduates seemed to be indulging excessively in pranks, profanity, petty thefts, intemperance and gambling, and one and all had to be combatted. However, "Pope" Dwight, as Connecticut's Republicans had begun to call him, gave higher priority to other transgressions; namely, denial of the Scripture, desecration of the Sabbath, propagation of heresy.

Dwight was determined to recapture this Congregational bastion. Yale did indeed begin to hum under his leadership and it would be transformed over the next two decades. Dwight served as both President and professor of divinity. He introduced new texts, new subjects, new methods, new professorships—most significantly in chemistry, a field then in its infancy. Owing to his skilled maneuvering, new lands were purchased for new buildings; the library holdings were doubled; the College's endowment increased; medical and divinity schools had their start; and good relations were established with the State legislature.

Equally important in Dwight's scheme of things was his successful campaign against dwindling chapel attendance, the appeal of the Enlightenment, the popularity of Tom Paine and Ethan Allen whose writings the farm boys devoured, especially when religion, priestcraft, and the Genesis version of creation were being arraigned. The new President struck hard and uncompromising blows at such heretical thoughts in lectures on "evidences of Divine Revelation." Furthermore, his campaign for moral purification eventually would have its rewards. The handsome and magisterial Dwight, with his broad-brimmed beaver hat and imposing presence, commanded respect. Some students, like Lyman Beecher, even loved him. And the President helped his own cause by building bridges to them. He eliminated fines for infractions of College rules, substituting private admonitions and personal suasion. Eventually, discipline was such that fines were unnecessary. Some students, possibly only a handful, admired his capacity to broaden their education and intellectual horizons even while restoring orthodoxy. And restore orthodoxy he did—by encouraging free and open discussion of religious doubts, inviting students into his house, especially those concerned with their salvation, and debating undergraduates on the truth of the Bible versus the agnosticism of Tom Paine and English rationalists.

Rare was the occasion when Dwight failed to proclaim the meaning and beauty of the Bible. In a four-year cycle of discourses on Christianity, he explored its nature and defended it against assaults from those who despise God and know "a priori that there is nothing beyond the grave." Dwight's sonorous and extemporaneous sermons avoided jargon as well as complex theological issues. Gradually, he brought Yale's rowdies and sceptics back to the "service of God." By 1797, in a period of rising revivalism in Connecticut, Dwight sponsored the Moral Society, which students willingly joined and which stimulated religious debate on campus. In 1801 Yale experienced another mild Awakening and in 1812, during still one more revival, Dwight converted nearly a hundred boys.

For Dwight, as we have seen, religious revivalism and political orthodoxy were inextricably enmeshed, with religious faith yoked to social stability, and Federalism, the politics of the Godly. He had long felt this way. The collapse of stable government during and directly after the American Revolution had greatly troubled him. So had the subsequent currency depreciation which contributed, he felt, to social instability. Understandably, he had turned to the cause of strong central government. His sermons frequently combined Federalist panic toward France and its Jeffersonian followers with an apocalyptic vision presented in millennarian rhetoric. Dwight's July 4, 1798, address, "The Duty of Americans at the Present Crisis," was delivered during the cold war with France. It called the roll of fallen republics and proclaimed the New World a unique refuge of pure religion. Three years later Dwight would become a prominent political satirist in the service of God and Federalism.

By now Dwight's belligerent message was familiar throughout New England and beyond it. Any preacher who predicted that Republican victory would mean the deflowering of Connecticut females by Jeffersonian democrats was bound to win the attention of pious Federalists. The latter had long been convinced that the Republicans were morally depraved and Jefferson's 1800 victory was a galvanic shock to those who had made Jacobinism, the Illuminati, and conspiracy theories household words. Now they looked to Dwight for further guidance and he was not timid about giving it. Indeed, he was happy to declaim against French and Jeffersonian infidelity and subversion from the rooftops of New Haven. For over two decades he would battle in the cause of true religion, good morals, and sound government—seeking to save Yale College, the State of Connecticut, and the New England he loved.

*　　*　　*

Perhaps the most prominent evangelist of the Second Awakening was Charles Grandison Finney. Born a Connecticut Yankee in 1792, Finney was the son of a Revolutionary army veteran and an heir of 17th-century Puritanism. Following the westward trail of many earlier New Englanders, his parents took their two-year-old son to Kirkland in the central part of New York State—into what was then part of the Burned-Over District, so called because of the innumerable religious fires that had already scorched it. Young Charles Finney attended the common schools of the frontier that was Oneida County and then, in 1812, he returned to his birthplace in Warren, Connecticut, for a high school education. For the first time he encountered formal religious teaching, which he largely ignored. Rather than seeking to enroll at Yale, he chose to go instead to New Jersey where he taught school for two years. He contemplated establishing a private school in the South, but nothing came of it. With no other prospects in view, Finney, now a 25-year-old man, decided to study law. Returning to Adams, New York, he easily read through some dusty law books in a local attorney's office, joined the bar, and settled down to practice.

Six feet two, physically impressive, and in robust health, Charles Finney seemed content with life. He was rightly popular with his peers; he played the cello, loved Shakespeare, sang solos in the church choir, enjoyed horseback riding, and excelled as a marksman. George Gale, the energetic young Presbyterian minister of Adams did not believe the sinful Finney would ever be converted but worked on him nonetheless. And then, in October 1812, Charles Finney had a conversion experience; he was then nearly 29 years old. Sitting in his law office, he had a vision of confronting Christ and received, as he described it, "a mighty baptism of the Holy Ghost." So overwhelming were successive waves of feeling that he cried out: "Lord, I cannot bear any more; I shall die if these [feelings] continue." His violent conversion also included a vision of Christ on the main street of Adams as well as an encounter with the Lord in the nearby woods where, as he recounted it, "I could feel the impression, like a wave of electricity going through and through me."

Out of this sudden and spectacular mystical experience came Charles Finney's single-minded determination to enlist in Christ's army and to preach his gospel; his lucrative law practice was forgotten. During the course of his conversion, Finney realized that salvation was complete only when he consented to give up his sins and accept Christ. There was no need to wait for God's regenerative power to enter him; no need for probationary good works. It was his "decision" to make—and he did so. In lawyer's language, he stated, "I have a retainer from the Lord Jesus Christ to plead his cause, and," he told a client, "I cannot plead yours."

Finney next brought Adams' townsfolk together in a meeting house and gave them no rest until all but one were converted. After a week without food and sleep, his feelings were as inflamed as ever. In this giddy state of mind he met Reverend Gale at the church door, and an "ineffable" light flooded his soul and he found himself sobbing hysterically. But this personal state of elevation was a passing phase, and his real mission began to take shape: he would forge an evangelical Christianity, first locally, in Adams, Evans Mills, Antwerp, and Gouverneur, and then in the State's larger cities. And this handsome, sandy-haired preacher with burning convictions would have phenomenal success by appealing to the practical and common sense tastes of the area's shopkeepers and farmers.

Finney did not graduate from a major seminary or pass through a university theology course and thereafter few revivalists would go this route. He had been urged to enroll at Princeton, where Gale had been trained and the local Presbytery even offered to pay his expenses. But Finney refused: "I plainly told them that I would not put myself under such an influence as they had been under; that I was confident that they had been wrongly educated, and they were not ministers that met my ideal of what a minister of Christ should be." A superbly contemptuous statement, it was a straw in the wind. In 1823, with understandable reluctance, the Saint Lawrence Presbyterian licensing board examined and ordained him. The following year, the Female Missionary Society of the Western District of New York commissioned this imposing man with the hypnotic blue eyes to thunder the Word.

From the beginning, Finney relied upon the Bible and worked toward a religious faith based on scriptural literalism. For him, the most important religious agency was the revival and it had been perfectly designed, as he understood it, to convince the unconverted of their sinfulness, thereby beginning the process of repentence and conversion. A revival, he insisted, must dwell "on that class of truths, which hold up man's ability, and obligation, and responsibility. This was the only class of truths that would bring sinners to submission." And by "submission," he meant conversion, which had three stages: conviction, repentence, reformation. Finney rejected Reverend Gale's contention that salvation was for the elect. Not so, the novitiate declared, it was for all men. His gospel, then, was close to that of Dwight, who would liberalize the old Calvinist view of God's arbitrary will and emphasize His transcendant goodness.

Revivalism was to split Presbyterian ranks, with the absolutist Old Light ministry eventually bringing charges against many New School revivalist preachers. Finney seemingly didn't care. He went ahead as if there were no stopping him. For his part, the theological critics could literally go to Hell; his successes in conversion, his results, were what counted and they validated his methods. This rebuttal was more than sublimely defiant; it said something about Finney's pragmatic criterion, indeed, his opportunism. He firmly believed that conditions demanded a new religious emphasis, even if at a cost of abandoning strict Calvinism and doctrinal distinctions.

As a rampaging frontier revivalist, Charles Finney broke all the rules. In a score of sermons, he emphasized human agency in the work of an individual's redemption; he maintained that God was benevolent and reasonable; he affirmed man's ability to know God. Open your souls to the Lord, he exhorted audiences: the Holy Ghost did not miraculously enter a man and alter his debased condition. Agreeing with the now deceased Yale President, Finney believed that man could not save himself, that God alone knew who He had willed to salvation. But salvation, Finney thundered in 1834, "is the work of man. It is something for man to do. . . . It is a man's duty. It is not a miracle, or dependent on a miracle in any sense." Man could save himself by an effort of will, Finney was fond of asserting: "The agency is the sinner himself. . . . The conversion of a sinner consists in his obeying the truth. It is therefore impossible it should take place without his agency. . . ." Man, by virtue of his conscience and of "all things that conduce to enlightening the mind, chooses God's way and at that very moment [conversion] God accepts him and he is born into the Kingdom [regeneration]."

Finney ranged across New York State at a time when the Erie Canal was bringing urbanization and a new wealth into the region. And in the process the upstate farmers and townsfolk saw their isolation end, their communities fragmenting, their verities being corrupted by new and alien ideas. Nostalgia for their lost world and fear of the new made the old inhabitants grist for every revivalist who came down the sawdust trail. Finney comforted them, fueling a religious enthusiasm that swept across the Burned-Over District like wildfire. He expressed perfectly ante-bellum moralizing theology and he made clear to his listeners the relation between man as a moral agent and God as his moral governor.

Finney's message, delivered in plain and powerful rhetoric, was uncomplicated. Vice was sin, not merely bad intention, he explained to penitent and unrepentant alike. And sinners would suffer the fires of hell. He portrayed its horrors with enormous energy and imaginative invective: the fiery lake filled with burning wretches moaning and screaming through eternity. Unquestionably he believed in this vivid picture and so did his hearers. There was indeed a personal devil as well as a personal God. Such a message was presented without erudite discourse or ornamentation or equivocation. Finney could not abide the timid and moderate preacher. He rejected the orthodox view that the sinner could not repent. Repudiating "cannot-ism," he deplored the jingle: "You can and you can't; you will and you won't; you're damned if you do and damned if you don't."

From the outset, the manipulative preaching of this back-country amateur created a sensation, the more so because of his innovations. He

was willing to scrap traditional worship in order to get across his Arminianized Calvinism; he spoke at outdoor meetings, barns, and schoolhouses;
he departed from the regularly scheduled times for religious services; he
made extensive use of the "protracted meeting," which went day and
night for a week or more; he introduced the "anxious bench," to which
came the most promising potential converts, who were culled from the
mass of parishioners, to subject themselves to special exhortation and
prayer, he encouraged women to pray and to testify in meeting, though
St. Paul had admonished their silence in the churches; and he openly
encouraged the "fallings" and "weepings"—those well-known physical
manifestations of revivalism—though avoiding incitement to bodily convulsions such as "jerking," "rolling," "jumping." Nonetheless, some of these
"exercises" were present at his gatherings, especially in the early phases
of his work. Small wonder, when he believed that "mankind will not wake
until they are excited." And Finney would excite men. He was perhaps the
most American of all contemporary preachers, and his practical, nonsec-
tarian, implicitly anti-Calvinist message inevitably stirred things up. It
struck an immediate responsive chord.

Wherever Finney went, men and women crowded around the pulpit,
begged for mercy, pleaded with him to stop, reacted with hysteria. "If I
had a sword in my hand," he contentedly exclaimed, "I could not have
cut them down as fast as they fell." After successful revivals in Rome,
Utica, and Auburn, New York, Finney seemed like the wave of the future.
He was emerging from the back country as a power to be reckoned with.
This tall, long-armed preacher could gesticulate; he could bully—and
triumphantly announce that "he beheld the angels of God sealing their
eternal doom"; he could thunder; he could literally frighten people into
submission. But Finney could also persuade with a lawyer-like brief.
Nonetheless, it was his whirling arms, his flailing of unbelievers, his
passion that worried both conservatives and urban revivalist preachers.
The Unitarian Henry Ware, for example, watched disgustedly Finney's
"abject groanings, his writhing of his body." Actually, Finney's emotionalism became more muted as he neared New England, and he began to
caution himself against loud praying and bench pounding. But conservatives were not persuaded. The man was a menace. They objected to his
emphasis upon "free and full salvation," worried over the connection
between revivalism and social reform, were affronted by handbills that
proclaimed his coming "by command of the King of Kings," and of course
they opposed his methods.

The Reverend Lyman Beecher, himself an acknowledged revivalist
leader, was aghast. Finney, emerging from western obscurity, was now
standing on the border of New England. "I know your plan," Beecher
declared, "and you know I do. You mean to come into Connecticut, and
carry a streak of fire to Boston. But if you attempt it, as the Lord liveth,

I'll meet you at the State line, and call out all the artillery-men, and fight every inch of the way to Boston, and I'll fight you there." So frightened were Beecher and other conservative clergy that they held a meeting at New Lebanan, New York, on July 18–27, but Finney decisively bested them in debate. He was not to be curbed. Indeed he was remorseless, "made for action" as Beecher reported, and his only pausing was for marriage to Lydia Andrews in October 1824. Crossing over from New York State, he assaulted—and there is no other word for it—Wilmington; Lancaster, Philadelphia, where he spoke nightly for a year; Rochester, for three months of meetings attended, among others, by lawyers, bankers, judges; New York City; and, finally, Boston. Beecher couldn't fend him off—not when earlier meetings in the East failed to produce the legendary "outbursts." As a consequence, a number of deacons and ministers sought to have him speak. Beecher himself surrendered—even to the point of expressly inviting Finney into his own Hanover Church; and Finney drew large crowds and aroused great excitement. And then he advanced into Connecticut where, *mirabile dictu,* some of the settled clergy endorsed his presence.

In 1832, this phase of itinerant revivals came to an end when Finney accepted a pulpit at the Broadway Tabernacle Church in New York City. The church itself had been especially built for him by Lewis Tappan, the New York merchant prince and reformer. Three years later, he became Professor of Didactic, Polemic, and Pastoral Theology at Oberlin College in Ohio. Founded by a band of pious New Englanders and open to Negro students as well as to women, Oberlin primarily prepared ministers for frontier duties. Finney, however, continued to make occasional evangelical forays from there, including two trips to England. There was also a six-week campaign at Boston's Park Street Church in 1857, which more than any previous appearance signalled the approval of revivalism by New England's Congregationalists. And he continued to make religious news. He scored unparalleled triumphs whenever welcomed to New York City. After Reverends Albert Barnes and Lyman and Edward Beecher were tried on heresy charges, Finney became a Congregationalist, leaving Presbyterianism in disgust. Finally, in 1850, he was appointed President of Oberlin.

These Oberlin years were important ones. For some time, Finney's confidence in the conversion experience had been shaken by the large number of backsliders. To be sure, he unwaveringly believed that a divinely ordained assignment had been given him, but the ambiguous results of these revival conversions were confusing. These results indicated that conversion itself was not enough; it did not lead to that exalted Christian life demanded by evangelical Christianity. He was forced to the dismaying conclusion that sainthood might not be for everyone who experienced a "decision." Disillusioned, he began, first at the Broadway Tabernacle and then at Oberlin, to work out a theology of his own. It emphasized God's perfection as its ideal and selfless love as its central proposition. All the converted, he declared, "should aim at being holy and not rest satisfied till they are as perfect as God." Man could grow in Grace, Finney told his students, until they reached a state of virtual sinlessness. He called it "entire sanctification" and in effect it amounted to a second conversion or "higher blessing." Christian perfection fed that hunger for holiness that existed among Protestants. But it meant a willful abandonment of revivalism and Finney's fellow evangelists charged that this doctrine of divine government smacked of heresy. Finney, once again, therefore, proved an extremely divisive figure and contributed to the tensions within the ministry that led to recurring schisms.

Charles G. Finney and the revivalists helped undermine Calvinism in one way; Unitarianism did it in another. Coming from a different direction—eastern Massachusetts to be precise—and with its own distinct emphasis, Unitarianism would also call into question the Congregationalist positions on sin, depravity, free will, and the granting of grace. From modest beginnings in the 1790s, it would become a separate sect and eventually take over a considerable number of the oldest Calvinist churches in New England.

Harvard men and Boston merchants bulked large among the Unitarians. They were part of a distinctive social and intellectual class, an "elite of wealth and fashion," so Harriet Beecher Stowe reported. The church of this cohesive and patrician elite was destined to be only a small backwater in the tidal wave of religious awakening then sweeping across the country. Nor were Unitarians competitive with the evangelical sects. They did not wish to be. They distrusted religious emotionalism, since they believed its hysteria robbed men of their reason. They held that man needed only to follow his conscience, cultivate the higher faculties, educate himself, and model his life on Jesus. They believed, as the old jest had it, in the fatherhood of God, the brotherhood of man, and the community of Boston; and he who was born in Boston did not need to be reborn.

*   *   *

Unitarianism's greatest leader, William Ellery Channing, was born in April 1780—and not in Boston, but in Newport, Rhode Island, a community whose wealth had derived in large part from the notorious rum and slave trade. His father, the State's Attorney General, had a flourishing law practice as well as a family of ten children. Generally too busy to spare time for his sons and daughters, he nonetheless was a strict disciplinarian who believed children should be infrequently seen and never heard. Not surprisingly, the boy looked elsewhere for guidance and affection, and received both from his maternal grandfather, William Ellery. Young

Channing was sent to school early because his mother was in poor health and, when old enough, was enrolled in the local boarding school of Master Robert Rogers, a disciplinarian who bequeathed a hatred of flogging to Channing and apparently little else.

The slight but muscular schoolboy was fond of solitary ways, usually content to play alone with his kite or to take a lonely walk on the beach. But he was also exposed to some of the leading personalities and best minds of the day. Ezra Stiles, the family minister before Yale called him to its presidency, was a greater influence upon young Channing than any other man, except possibly Grandfather Ellery. There was also the Reverend Samuel Hopkins, though his gloomy Calvinism repelled the sensitive boy. The Channing house, moreover, was a center for both social gatherings and Federalist political activity, and to it came, among others, John Jay and George Washington.

Young William Ellery Channing also had a close-up look at both slavery and the rum trade along Newport's wharves. Indeed, there were domestic bondsmen in his own house, some of them possibly brought home by his highly respected merchant grandfather who imported slaves. Lawyer Channing never openly opposed slavery and would manumit his own black domestics after the Revolution. Very conceivably, it was at this point in his life that young Channing began to develop that sensitivity for human beings which later made him an abolitionist.

As childhood passed into adolescence, William Ellery Channing prepared for college—in the household of his uncle, Reverend Henry Channing in nearby New London, Connecticut. The latter was a clerical maverick who ardently supported revivalism and adamantly denied the divinity of Christ. Under his tutelage, young Channing was further liberated from Calvinism. In 1794, at age 14, he enrolled at Harvard, where his classmates and friends included Joseph Story, a future Justice of the Supreme Court; William Emerson, father of Ralph Waldo Emerson; and Joseph Tuckerman, who would become his beloved colleague in the Unitarian ministry. Harvard was then not quite ready to go over to Unitarianism but the bracing winds of religious liberalism were clearly affecting faculty and students alike. Few if any of them were unacquainted with the readings of Bishop Berkeley, David Hume, the idealism of Richard Price, or the appealing men of the Edinburgh Enlightenment like Francis Hutcheson.

The same unsettling social and political conditions Timothy Dwight encountered when he took over the presidency at Yale were also present during Channing's years in Cambridge. "The old foundations of social order, loyalty, tradition, habit, reverence for antiquity," values that Channing held sacred, "were everywhere shaken, if not subverted." As at Yale, Harvard's Federalist teachers and overseers saw infidelity in every troubling development, including student pranks and Jacobinism. Channing's Federalist background placed him squarely in the camp of the opponents of the French Revolution. His grandfather also fed his Gallophobia. Jacobinism, for this gentle, slender schoolboy, was "synonymous with a dishonest, immoral, factious, and disorganized man."

Graduated in 1798, William Ellery Channing was restless and unsettled. While having learned much under Harvard's willows, he was still uncertain in religion. Sentiments had not yet hardened into convictions, nor had knowledge matured into philosophy. He was nothing formed or clear, merely a learned young man who had still to ask critical questions and to feel his way toward "spiritual things." He was even uncertain about a career to pursue when he met David Randolph of Virginia, then visiting Newport. At the latter's invitation, he went south to Richmond, to tutor the Randolph children. Richmond, far away from the confines of New England, was a window on a larger world. Channing commended Virginians for their manners and for loving "money less than we do." Without "their sensuality and their slaves," they'd be the "greatest people in the world." For once again he had encountered Negro wretchedness, even on the relatively humane Virginia plantations, and it hardened his sentiments that slavery was an affront to God. His rigid Federalist persuasion, on the other hand, began to soften—to the extent of opposing President John Adams' military preparedness against France as well as the Alien and Sedition Acts. Whatever hours were his own after completing the day's chore of educating 12 children he spent in reading—mostly Rousseau and Godwin—despite failing eyesight, by candlelight. Cultivating loneliness and privation, he adopted a spartan existence. He wore improper dress, slept on the bare floor, neglected to eat, and punished the flesh as a way of exorcising his "shameful" passions. The stress and strain of these "sore trials" produced hallucinatory moments and a deep and moving conversion experience; he would be "a servant of God."

But first Channing had to recover from his weakened physical state. In 1800 he decided to leave Virginia and return to Newport, a pale and emaciated young man badly in need of rest. Both at home and later at Cambridge, he devoted most of his hours to preparation for the ministry. His orthodoxy satisfied the Cambridge Association, and he was licensed in the autumn of 1802.

Short, slender, with stooped frame and worn appearance, Channing gave an impressive initial performance at Medford's First Church in October 1802. Listeners unanimously observed "that wonderful voice—so distinct and strong and sincere"; and the sermons themselves—so plain and undogmatic. Soon Channing was preaching in Boston, at the large and fashionable Brattle Street Church and before the Federal Street Church congregation. Both churches needed a minister and extended invitations to him. Channing accepted that offered by members of the old wooden Federal Street Church and was ordained on June 1, 1803. He would remain there almost 40 years and during that time would travel very far from the Calvinism and Federalism of his youth. In fact he would become the acknowledged leader of American Unitarianism.

Channing loved Boston and knew its patricians, those who had made this "hub of the universe" a center of charity, culture, wisdom, and stability. He invariably associated with the city's moderate, cultivated, cool-tempered ministers who had Arminianized Calvinism and were slowly making Boston their stronghold. Such ministers emphasized the ethical elements of love and good conduct in a Christian's life. And so did Channing. He had not yet broken with orthodoxy, however, and as late as 1807, he thought man's depravity "should be most deeply and painfully felt." But he was moving toward the camp of religious liberalism and had concluded by 1812 that Calvinism "chills the best affections," that it could have a "dreadful influence" on "susceptible minds." He would come to virtually deny the existence of Hell, and to believe in the perfectibility of man, and hold to a concept of God in man's image. Confident of man's destiny, he exclaimed, "I do and I must reverence human nature."

Most of these views were incorporated in Channing's famous and widely circulated 1819 Baltimore sermon, a 45,000 word statement that was perhaps the most comprehensive and most subtle expression of the Unitarian position. A stirring call to the colors of liberal Christianity, this manifesto opened with a clear assertion of God's beneficence, the significance of Jesus as a divinely appointed model for mankind, the love of God for man, and the dignity of man himself. An expression of the secular humanitarianism that had been developing in New England, the sermon rejected the doctrine of election, the Trinity, dogmatic scriptural authority, and all religious agencies that curbed man's freedom. Channing wished men would engage in a "deliberate, devout, fearless study of God's word."

Countless sermons followed. They all dwelt on aspects of the doctrinal synthesis of 1819. Human reason had centrality in most of them, but it was not unequivocally affirmed. There were, to be sure, beautiful tributes to reason, as would be expected of an advocate of rational religion and Christian humanism. "Christianity," he declared, "is reason in its most perfect form." That "ultimate reliance of a human being," Channing further stated, "is and must be on his own mind." Even revelation was based on reason, he stated in 1828. But such claims were hardly an absolute for a minister who declared that the spiritual message was not to be found in book or creed but in "the human heart"; nor for one who asserted elsewhere that man's "rational nature is from God" and that Christianity was miraculous in origin. Unlike the English Unitarians and the American Transcendentalists, Channing never considered Jesus as merely human; he always insisted on the special divinity of Christ as the first of the sons of God. But, like the Transcendentalists, he exclaimed: "In ourselves are the elements of divinity."

Reason, then, was obviously a very inclusive term for Channing, at once intellectual and spiritual. This maddening ambiguity was aggravated by his proximity to Transcendentalism. He came close to their treatment of reason as a faculty to be exercised in feeling; he shared their belief in a self-directed life; he agreed that his Unitarian colleagues had "a want of vitality and force." However, he was unwilling to go the entire route with these young men and women who, recalling Jonathan Edwards' "sense of the heart," would turn religion into an ecstasy, a saturnalia of faith. Channing was troubled by their tendency to substitute private inspiration for Christianity; he balked at their conviction of an actual union of Self and the Divine. Channing's own note is nonetheless clear in his claim of man's "likeness to God," of "impenetrable mystery in every action . . . in the universe," presumably impenetrable to the thrust of reason.

Unitarian rejection of Calvinism, and its cautious belief in man's capacity for perfectibility, strikes a chord familiar to Charles Finney and to evangelical Christianity. It was consonant as well with the spirit which animated many of the communities that mushroomed in these decades, the golden age of utopian experimentation. Channing would not accept social predeterminism any more than he had endorsed religious predestination. Men could manipulate their society and alter the character of their institutions. Indeed, man himself "was also equally improvable, for he was endowed with reason, will, and conscience, inwardly impelled by God's decree to seek betterment."

Social-economic change, it followed, could ultimately be effected only through perfection of the individual and only through voluntary action. Channing himself was not much of a joiner. "Let not the individual enslave his conscience to others," he exhorted. He affirmed the principle of Fourier's "association," and cautiously endorsed Brook Farm as well as Adin Ballou's Hopedale Community but, always the supreme individualist, he warned that any and all organizations, public or private, ecclesiastical or secular, had "a tendency to fetter men, to repress energy." He emphasized instead self reform and "self-determination" above all.

By 1830 Channing was the chief ornament of the Unitarian pulpit, but he was also the paradigm of the high-minded Protestant who had been reared in the spirit of charity and liberality. He had increasingly emphasized the social value of the Bible, the importance of inculcating morality, and the need to evangelize the entire nation. To this end, he published the *Christian Disciple,* a journal of liberal Christianity. In addition, he was a member of the Boston School Commission, a founder of the Harvard Divinity School, a member of the Harvard Corporation, a pioneer in adult education, and an advocate of publicly-supported schools. He always displayed great concern for the education of the children of the poor. He was a friend and confidant of Horace Mann and influenced Mann's elementary school reform proposals for Massachusetts. In large measure, Elizabeth Peabody owed her interest in kindergarten reform to the "personal exertions of Dr. Channing."

There was more. Channing did not limit his reform energies in any direction. Rather, despite recurrent ill health, he engaged in a strenuous array of activities. He grew bolder with the years. Encouraging Dorothea Dix, he allowed her to prepare the moving "Memorial on the Condition of the Insane" in his study. He championed penal reform and the abolition of capital punishment; and he informed his proper middle-class parishioners that the criminal caught the infection of vice from the respectable element in society. He drew up the petition in defense of Abner Kneeland who was jailed for atheism, for he "would call that mind free which calls no man master." And none was more vehement than Channing in condemning the sins of property.

Like so many practitioners of religious benevolence, Channing struck hard at war, urban poverty, intemperance, and slavery. He was, for instance, the heart and soul of the Massachusetts Peace Society whose 22 founders first met in his study. Although believing wars of self defense were justified, he held that war itself was "a tremendous evil" and that the "profession of a soldier . . . is immoral."

Channing's reaction to urban poverty was even more ambivalent. Most ministers, as of old, attributed it to idleness and immorality, and to deficiencies of character. His own analysis, which was a model religious response, blamed poverty on the poor themselves and showed little sympathy for the urban poor or for factory operatives. But he did on occasion concede that "a man half fed, half clothed . . . will be too crushed in spirit to do the proper work of a man," and he did believe workers "must share more largely in the fruits of their toil." Like his co-religionaries, Channing mostly urged "self-culture" upon workers; however, he also campaigned for more practical reforms—such as new approaches to juvenile delinquency; "manual labor schools," like the one Tuckerman proposed; abolition for imprisonment for debt. Channing also helped organize, in 1824, the Association of the Members of the Federal Street Society for Benevolent Virtues, an agency typical of that extraordinary array of voluntary societies from Boston to Baltimore which channelled the anti-pauperism energies of merchant elite and Christian liberals alike.

Always seeking to avoid controversy and notoriety, to live above the clamor of political and theological strife, Channing approached the slave controversy with the same desire to appear "mild and amiable" and "not mingle with the contentions of the world" that had guided him in all reform efforts. Hardly a militant, therefore, he shunned a meeting with William Lloyd Garrison, whose verbal fury scandalized proper Bostonians after 1830, and his early anti-slavery critiques were wooden and labored. The Abolitionists were admittedly "a noble set of men," but intemperate and excessive as well. Still slavery was "essentially evil"; and he would abolish it—in the North by statute and in the South by moral suasion and voluntary action, by appeals to reason and conscience. By 1835, however, Reverend Samuel May chided him on neglect of the great issue: "Why, Sir, have you not spoken before?" and evoked this admission: "I acknowledge the justice of your reproof: I have been silent too long." And he was not silent again. By 1836, he was attending a session of the New England Anti-Slavery Convention and attacking Cincinnati's anti-abolitionists who had destroyed James Birney's anti-slavery press. He spoke at Faneuil Hall in the following year, at a mass meeting protesting the murder of Elijah Lovejoy, the Illinois printer. He signed petitions for the elimination of slavery in the District of Columbia; in 1839 he defended the Abolitionists who called "the slaveholder hard names"; and two months before he died, in an 1842 Lenox, Massachusetts speech, he violently arraigned the "evil" and "outrage" of slavery.

Such sentiments distressed his Federal Street Church members who regarded them as an endorsement of Abolitionism. Channing struck hard at these gentlemen of standing and property who made "gain ... their God" and would sacrifice human rights to it. But the congregation prevailed and had virtually cast him out by the late 1830s. It was a bitter blow. He was forced to give up cherished personal associations and endure hostility from friends of a lifetime. Nonetheless, he had no regrets. It had been a privilege "to have lived in an age so stirring, so pregnant, so eventful." And he had moved with the age. His decade-long journey from moderation to militancy on the issue of slavery was matched by a similar emancipation from conservatism on other reform issues—much as he had evolved from a tentative and cautious young man who held to religious orthodoxy to a bold spokesman against it in his middle years. And in the course of this devolution to reform, to radicalism even, Channing, more than most, questioned the goals and values—such as materialism—held by his countrymen. He loved quiet and preferred to "work alone," but in the end none spoke braver or wiser words to his generation, none were superior in ability to galvanize belief in the certainty of human improvement.

*   *   *

Channing's commitment to reform was hardly unique. In varying degree, Dwight and Finney both shared it, as did most evangelical ministers; witness the near-universal clerical concern for temperance and educational reform. Moreover, all three ministers eventually concluded that emotion was superior to reason—though its victory was not clear-cut with Dwight or Channing; all would nonetheless assent to Dwight's judgment about the evanescent nature of metaphysical speculation; all would appeal to the "heart" and to plain common sense. Nor were their inconsistencies, we have seen, limited to the contrasting virtues of reason and faith. Each vacillated between the useful and the intuitive, science and miracles, self-reliance and divine guidance, social reform and rugged individualism, social obligations and otherworldly concerns, secular humanism and religious benevolence. None held unswervingly or consistently to a single lifelong position—not Channing, the moderate religious and social reformer; not Finney, the pietistic radical and the social conservative; not even Dwight, whose abiding conservatism drenched every aspect of his life and thought. Each in differing degree reflected that cultural and social mix characteristic of all those who lived in the first 50 years after the Revolution—between the afterglow of the Enlightenment and the dawn of American romanticism. From the former, they drew something of their faith in progress and in education; from the latter, their trust in humanitarian evangelism and in the possibilities of man.

8

Gentlemen Democrats
at Home and Abroad

ALEXIS DE TOCQUEVILLE
SAMUEL F. B. MORSE
JAMES FENIMORE COOPER

by R. Jackson Wilson
Smith College

Down the stretch of United States history running from George Washington's inauguration to Abraham Lincoln's assassination, no development was more obvious and exciting to Americans than the survival and triumph of their republican democracy. Lincoln was astonishingly skilled at finding words to sanctify facts, and he never exercised his skills more effectively than when he put together phrases like "dedicated to the proposition that all men are created equal," or "government of the people, by the people, and for the people." By the 1860s, Lincoln's phrases—for all their peculiar grace—captured only the commonplace understanding of most politically conscious men and women in America: theirs was a society whose essential meaning was to be sought in their experiment in the practice of human equality.

Lincoln's words have droned through the minds and mouths of so many school children for so long a time that they have an almost ritual character. It is not easy to be curious about what they really meant, and even more difficult to remember that an important misunderstanding was just below their surface. For the nation's "fathers" had not "conceived" the nation as a democratic enterprise. "Democracy" to them was a word to be seldom used and usually as a fright-word, another name for mob rule. The notion that all men are created equal was an abstraction for

Thomas Jefferson and for most of his contemporaries, an appeal to an almost metaphysical principle. Functioning democracy was a phenomenon of the 19th century, not of the period of the Revolutionary years, a fact of life younger than Lincoln himself.

By the time of the Civil War, of course, democracy had become an article of faith in the United States. And one requirement of the faith was that the idea of "government of the people" be rudely pushed back in time, enfolded into the 18th-century Revolution. This reverent picture of our national history had the odd effect of ignoring one of the great mental efforts of Americans born *after* the Revolution: their own awkward, halting, but monumental attempt to comprehend the seeming triumph of Democracy in their political and social lives.

This effort was especially trying for those who—by birth, talents, education and fortunes—were marked as gentlemen. There was, of course, no American "aristocracy"; the Constitution itself forbade titles of nobility. But there were thousands of Americans who were persons of "refinement" and "quality." There was, in other words, a self-conscious elite whose members thought of themselves as set apart from the enveloping democratic mass. The gentleman might be a planter in the South, or a merchant in New York or Philadelphia; he might be a landowner along the Hudson or the Connecticut, or he could be a lawyer or a minister in New England. But however they were situated, gentlemen in America in the decades after 1820 understood one thing very clearly: an 18th-century social order that had entitled men like them to the automatic deference of their social inferiors was dying. A new world was being born in which they had lost access to power and position, a world that jostled them rudely and embarrassed them by its roughness, its crudity, and its lack of controlled expectations.

One logical response to such deep and threatening changes would have been to repudiate democracy in both theory and practice, to ask simply for the return of a time when ministers could be confident of their congregations' regard, gentlemen on the street would not be insulted, manners would have their supposedly ancient social value, and styles of dress would still mark men and women in recognizable ranks. But, after about 1820, this response had become unworkable. To reject democracy in favor of "aristocratic" values would brand any gentleman (even in the South) as a mere crank. None of the political parties of the period—Democratic, Whig, or Republican—had room for anti-democratic ideas; and no tradition of religion, no scholarly career, no learned profession served as a barrier to the tide of equality. For any educated and articulate member of the elite—any person of "breeding"—accommodation to Democracy was an urgent necessity. A generation of American gentlemen (and European gentlemen, too) had to come to terms, to adjust to the ominous, powerful and encircling fact of equality.

One outcome of this encounter between an anxious elite and a triumphant social "principle" was the emergent gentleman democrat, a temporary but interesting social type. Before 1820, the type could not flourish; there was simply too little democracy to form it. After 1870 there simply were not enough self-conscious gentlemen. But from about 1825 until the Civil War, gentlemen democrats turned out a sizeable body of political essays, novels, speeches, histories—even poetry and paintings—dealing with an absorbing dilemma: how could they consent to the mounting democratic tide and still preserve the manners, graces, and social stability they thought had belonged to an older "aristocratic" world?

*   *   *

To those Americans grappling with this dilemma, the distinction between the stereotypes of "democracy" and "aristocracy" parallelled another contrast: between the United States and Europe. And so it seemed, too, to Europeans who believed they could read some of their own future in the American experience. Europeans, especially in England and France, were almost as preoccupied with democracy as Americans. Simple antidemocratic opposition was a more frequent option for Europeans; but an option that had its costs, and endorsed less often than Americans have supposed. Like their American counterparts, French and English aristocrats had to learn ways of accepting, rationalizing and even seeming to promote the new democratic ethic. And they were inevitably drawn to two momentous events: the great Revolution in France, with its Napoleonic sequel, and the Revolution of 1776 in the United States, with its own democratic sequel. The French Revolution made the democratic force seem as destructive as it was powerful. The American experiment appeared to offer more hope.

More than any other European of his day—and perhaps more than any European since 1776—Alexis de Tocqueville strained to read the European future in America. The outcome was *Democracy in America,* a massive and intricate analysis of American life that Tocqueville published in two parts in 1834 and 1840, and which Americans ever since have read more seriously than any other large analysis of their society.

Tocqueville was only 25 when he came to the United States, and only 30 when he published *Democracy in America;* but he wrote with a loftiness and majesty that earned him an enormous and quick reputation. His American readers, especially, found him far more balanced, detached and therefore "objective" than most foreigners who wrote about the United States—the easily offended English travelers, or the other Frenchmen who often romanticised America out of existence. But, in fact, *Democracy in America* was written not in loftiness and detachment, but with intense involvement. In many important ways, *Democracy in America* was a kind of projective autobiography. The book contained an implicit but important statement of what Tocqueville thought he was and might become socially and politically. His observations of particular facts, and his grand generalizations about the nature and meaning of American life all hinged on a perception of his own "delicate" (as he called it) position in French society: a gentleman, decidedly, but a gentleman trying to find ways to be a democrat.

In his introduction to the first volume, Tocqueville made a gloomy estimate of the state of affairs in France. He identified two important types of Frenchmen advocating two different social strategies. There were, first, men of "high and generous characters . . . virtuous and peaceful individuals whose pure morality, quiet habits, affluence and talents fit them to be the leaders of the surrounding population." But these gentry had fallen into a simple-minded, futile opposition to the democratic "novelty." On the other hand, there were democrats in France, anti-aristocratic men who assumed the role of "champions of modern civilization." But these *arrivistes* were nasty, pragmatic and utterly without principle. They were attempting (as any aristocrat would complain) to place "themselves in a station which they usurp with insolence."

These linkings of aristocracy with conservatism, democracy with social "unworthiness," were a "misery" to Tocqueville, they made a world

> where nothing is linked together, where virtue is without genius, and genius without honor; where the love of order is confounded with a taste for oppression, and the holy rites of freedom with a contempt of law . . . and where nothing seems to be any longer forbidden or allowed, honorable or shameful, false or true.

By birth, education and attitude, Tocqueville was an aristocrat. He was Alexis Charles Henri Clerel de Tocqueville, a member of the Norman nobility. His grandfather and his aunt had gone to the guillotine during the Revolution, and his own parents had been put in prison. His family had reentered public life only when Napoleon was overthrown and the Bourbon monarchy restored. After he became a lawyer, Tocqueville himself had accepted an appointment as a minor magistrate from the Bourbon monarchy. And when the Bourbons were again overthrown in 1830, Tocqueville felt compelled to leave either the government or the country —which prompted him to ask for a slightly fabricated assignment: visiting the United States to study its prison system. Tocqueville's identity, in other words, was clearly with the old regime—with order, stability, hierarchy, manners and taste and breeding. Indeed, he personalized these qualities—to the extent that even Gustave de Beaumont, his friend and colleague on the American tour, could twit Tocqueville on his excess of genteel reserve: "a manner a little cold, and too reserved in society;

too much indifference toward persons who don't please him, and an attitude silent and calm, too close to dignity."

It was no incidental thing, then, that the July Revolution of 1830, which replaced the Bourbons with a constitutional monarchy, made Tocqueville feel his position in France to be "delicate." Almost any democrat would have welcomed the revolution, especially since it was fostered and supported by one of the saintly figures of both French and American republicanism, the Marquis de Lafayette. But Toqueville's inheritance and his sensibilities were too deeply conservative. At the same time, however, he was too interested in politics and too concerned with finding a role for himself merely to withdraw. He needed most of all a strategy of reconciliation between his ancestry and what he had already come to see as the irresistible force of democracy. And if French society offered no ready clues toward such a strategy, then perhaps the United States might.

Tocqueville thought the problem out carefully before he and Beaumont left France. He brooded over the history of France, and he read carefully and widely about America. Even before arrival in the United States, he had already reached some fundamental intellectual conclusions. Tocqueville later began *Democracy in America* by referring to American equality as a "novel object" that "struck me forcibly during my stay in America." But this opening was disingenuous. He had decided, before embarking, that democracy was the most important force in world history, and that equality had made the most important and rapid inroads on the old "feudal" culture in the United States. And he had already decided, too, that if democracy had had beneficial social consequences anywhere, it was probably in America. So he went looking not for "novel objects" but for confirmations of a position that he had read about and reasoned toward in France—in response to French stimuli, not American.

Tocqueville's philosophical position was really quite simple, and not very original. From aristocratic beginnings, society in Europe was moving steadily and inevitably toward democratic ends. The old ways, perfected around the 12th century, had emphasized order, hierarchy, and subjection of plain people to a powerful and brilliant aristocracy. Men then had to pay a high price for social order: cruelty was a frequent feature of aristocracy, and suffering and ignorance the portion of the poor. But there had also been rewards: "the pursuit of luxury, the refinements of taste, the pleasures of wit, and the cultivation of the arts." Above all, men had felt bound together. The nobility could be benevolent and the people felt a deep attachment to their betters. Men understood who they were and what their obligations and rights were. "The social state thus organized might boast of its stability, its power, and, above all, its glory." Tocqueville almost never described the aristocratic state of society without obvious wistfulness and nostalgia; if he were now going to embrace democracy, the embrace would be gingerly and fastidious, the embrace an aristocrat might give a yeoman ally with whom his lot was cast by crisis.

Against the old order, which represented for Tocqueville a fixed point of beginning, the democratic tide had been breaking steadily for seven centuries. And, he reasoned, there was no way to turn it back. One of Tocqueville's subtle ways of accepting democracy without surrendering his refined bearing was to describe it as an impersonal force over which he and men like him had no real control. So Tocqueville objectified democracy, made it into an abstract power, a force to which he could succumb—a virgin submitting innocently to an irresistible seduction:

> The gradual development of the principle of equality is . . . a providential fact. It has all the chief characteristics of such a fact: it is universal, it is lasting, it constantly eludes all human interference, and all events as well as all men contribute to its progress . . . The whole book that is here offered to the public has been written under the influence of a kind of religious terror produced in the author's mind by the view of that irrestible revolution which has advanced for centuries in spite of every obstacle and which is still advancing in the midst of the ruins it has caused.

Here was the key to Tocqueville's objectivity, the reluctant objectivity of a man accepting what he could not avoid, counting its costs, stoically seeking some redeeming features in it. But the detachment was a function of passion, not indifference: the "ruins it has caused" were not merely historical facts to Tocqueville; they were personal. His ancestors' tragic sufferings at the hands of the Revolution were acted out again, almost as farce, in his own life. When he was forced to take the oath of allegiance in 1830 to the constitutional monarchy, he was self-consciously wracked:

> I have just taken the oath! [he wrote his wife] and I will count this day as one of the unhappiest of my life. For the first time since my birth, I have to avoid the presence of persons whom I esteem. Oh! Marie, the idea of it racks me! How my voice changed as I uttered those three words! I felt my heart beat as though it would burst from my breast.

This was the dramatic stance of a 25-year-old who had given in, sacrificing his "honor." From this point of shame, an almost logical chain led Tocqueville to and beyond *Democracy in America*. If he could believe that he had sacrificed family honor to an irresistible "force," then his heart need not "burst"; giving in to a vast tendency of history would provoke less guilt than surrendering to ordinary human beings. But the logic led forward. If the democratic force could be shown to have even one grand and good outcome—in the United States, if anywhere—then it just might be a force that a young man of aristocratic hauteur could accept and move with. And if he could perform such an intellectual somersault, then he could return to France and pursue a career in democratic politics without shame—not only without shame but with a positive mission, explaining the new world to the old, the future to the present, democracy to his fellow aristocrats.

The quasi-logical character of Tocqueville's dilemma helps explain one of the most striking peculiarities of *Democracy in America*. It had the form and manner of a geometry textbook: a schedule of theorems about democratic society. And, as in a geometry, the demonstrations were more important than the particular political planes and angles serving as examples. In both senses, American democracy was exemplary: it was the most favorable case of a general type; but it was also *only* an example, a case in point. This did not mean that Tocqueville's observations were not astute; in fact, he was a cunning observer precisely because he knew what he was looking for. He also knew where to look. He talked mostly to literate members of the American elite—who would also provide him with his American audience. *Democracy in America* was a book on the logic of democracy, written by an anxious young aristocrat, helped along by refined Americans. It was a class book, both in its origins and its reception, a genteel endeavor (which may help explain Tocqueville's great vogue after World War II among America's refined and anxious intellectuals).

Tocqueville found much to celebrate in American democracy. Though lacking elegance, the manners and morals of the people were sound. Property was respected and secure. The middle class, which he believed dominated society, was really conservative, since it (like Tocqueville) thought of democracy in America as a finished product, an inheritance from the 18th century, to be protected and secured. Because of their widespread political participation, Americans were much more sophisticated than most Europeans. Literacy was almost universal. Women and children were better off than in Europe—single women, in particular, though married women had some special problems. In general, Americans had developed an acute sense of political and social responsibility that could replace the vanished hierarchical stability of the aristocratic old regime. American constitutions, both state and federal, were cleverly designed to balance opposing forces and tendencies in democracy. The United States, in other words, satisfied Tocqueville's expectations.

But the logic of his situation required that democracy have faults; if it were both irrestistible and excellent, then what role could he and gentlemen like him play except that of spectator? And so Tocqueville set out to discover failings in democracy as well as successes. And his discoveries—even more than his positive observations—read like deductions from abstract principles. Democracy, he argued, made every man into a facsimile of every other, and this created the danger of gross mediocrity. Similarities between men also had the paradoxical effect of establishing distance between them; similar people suffered from feelings of alienation: they did not *need* society, and so they easily fell into isolated "individualism." But their isolation, in turn, made them constantly anxious about their social identity. And to try to control their anxiety they tried to control each other's lives. Americans, however, had given up all the old means that aristocratic society once used to enforce control, so they resorted to control by "public opinion." This, in turn, laid democratic societies open to the awful "tyranny" of public opinion.

Such masterly balancing of admiration and acceptance of democracy on one side and suspicion and resistance on the other was not merely a personality trait of Tocqueville's, or a simple triumph of reason over passion. For Tocqueville, as for any other member of what Mark Twain hilariously called "the quality," such balance between class instinct and political necessity was both difficult and precarious. Under pressure, Tocqueville (like gentlemen democrats in America) could revert quickly to aristocratic instinct. In an unpublished "confession" that he entitled "My instincts, my opinions," Tocqueville faced this truth about himself:

> Experience has proved to me that almost all men, but most certainly I, return more or less always to their fundamental instincts, and only do well those things that conform to these instincts. Let's try, sincerely then, to discover where my *fundamental instincts* and my *genuine principles* lie.
>
> My mind has a certain taste for democratic institutions, but I am aristocratic by instinct, that is to say I despise and fear the mob.
>
> I passionately love liberty, legality, respect for rights, but not democracy. There are the depths of my soul.

Hundreds of Americans, democrats by opinion and gentlemen by instinct, would have read his confession with quick transatlantic sympathy.

*　　*　　*

During the summer of 1830, when Alexis de Tocqueville was undergoing his humiliation in Paris, and making the decision to visit the United States, an American gentleman in Rome was beginning his own period of reflection about the meaning of being an American in a democratic age. Samuel Finley Breese Morse was, like Tocqueville, a man of refinement. Morse would later have a huge reputation as the inventor of the telegraph and of the code that still bears his name. But for the moment he was an artist, in Europe to study and copy, to try to revive an artistic career that had begun 15 years earlier with great promise. During 1830–31, Morse reversed Tocqueville's geographical movements: he went from Rome to Paris during Tocqueville's first summer in the United States, returning to America in 1832, the same year Tocqueville went back to Paris. The paths of the two men crossed intellectually, too. Morse was straining in a European setting to discover the significance of being an American democrat, just as Tocqueville was using the United States as a way of defining his European identity. For both men, the years were momentous and anxious; and for both American democracy was an opportunity as well as a peril.

Morse was, by American standards, as much an aristocrat as Tocqueville. He was the son of a well-placed minister and scholar, Jedediah Morse of Charlestown, Massachusetts. Jedediah Morse was the author of famous and influential books on American geography, a passionate and well-known defender of Congregationalist orthodoxy, and pastor to an important congregation. A graduate of Yale, friend of scholars and university presidents, he was learned and impeccably distinguished. Nor was he unique among the Morses in such honors. A great-grandfather had been president of Princeton, and one of his grandfathers was a judge. The Morse name had been in New England since the 1630s. The family was Federalist in politics long after Federalism had become hopelessly identified with New England reaction. Morse had, in other words, a "nest of associations"—in Henry Adams' nice phrase—that marked him from birth as a member of the elite.

A mild tension always existed between Morse's background and his own ambitions. Even at school, he found it difficult to submit to the dark discipline of the family's Calvinism. He liked to skate, to shoot, to pick blackberries and, above all, to draw. But there were always parental admonitions: keep death and the fate of the soul uppermost. When he was 14 and away at school, Morse received a letter from his mother about the death of a Boston girl:

> She ate her dinner perfectly well and was dead in five minutes after. Her name was Ann Hinkley. You see, the importance of always being prepared for *death*. We cannot be too soon or too well prepared for that all-important moment, as this is what we are sent into this world *for*. The main business of life is to prepare for death.

Within the Morse family, such ideas were not isolated religious sentiments. They expressed a world view. For Jedediah Morse, and for men like him, society was in crisis. Jeffersonianism in politics, Unitarianism in religion, the French Revolution, unruliness in Boston streets, the capture of Harvard College by men of "liberal" ideas—all these and half a dozen related tendencies spelled impending disaster. Change was everywhere, almost all of it bad. Foreign ideas, democratic nonsense, frivolity and irreligion were rife. And, it was clear to men like Jedediah Morse, members of the elite must use every opportunity to root out evil, rationalism, and loose morals. Charlestown, Massachusetts, was in fact a rather calm community during the first two decades of the 19th century, but the disturbed Morse household passed through days of gloom and fear quite like the anxious moments of Tocqueville's family of Bourbon loyalists. Jedediah Morse was a gentleman, but he was certainly no democrat. His son had to learn to try to be both; however, such learning was never free of the lurid, fearful social reflexes of the family.

How could it be otherwise, when one experience after another confirmed these reflexes? When Morse, while at Yale, was reprimanded for his frivolity and wastefulness after he went shooting a little too often? Or when his desire to become an artist was turned aside by his parents, and he was forced for a time to accept a dull apprenticeship to a bookseller? Or, when his parents finally consented to let him go to England to study art, his mother warned him that the theater, Madeira, and cigars were "ruinous to both soul and body," and that Americans studying in Europe were a lot of "dissipated infidels"? Morse was indelibly marked by all this experience; he could not even court his first wife without warning her to beware of her soul's state:

> I might flatter you, dear, I might tell you that your amiable disposition and your correct conduct would certainly recommend you to God, that you need only to go on, live correctly, be charitable, and you have nothing to fear. But think, my dear, what a part I should act: I could see one whom I loved so tenderly resting in false security, and I could live with her through life, and when death separated us, know for an awful truth, that if I was saved, we were separated *forever*. Could I love you, dear girl, if I could do this?

Such attitudes were an American equivalent of the Tocqueville family's Bourbonism. Within Morse's lifetime, religious ideas like his father's were transformed, and became primarily the property of revivalism— which appealed more and more to the lower middle-class and to the poor. But when Morse was growing up, Protestant "fundamentalism" still belonged primarily to respectable families, especially in New England. It was still the religion of a sector of the American elite.

Morse first definably parted with his father's world while studying art in London, during 1811–15. The United States and England were at war for most of these years, and Morse underwent the odd experience of being an enemy alien. He responded naturally enough by becoming staunchly patriotic, defending his country's war policies, and praying for American victories. But this natural response set him at odds politically with his own family. Like most New England Federalists, his father opposed the conflict and thought of it as a trick of the Jeffersonians, the party of infidelity. And his mother wrote him in 1812 to bewail the Republicans' war policy: "We rejoice that you are at so great a distance from our wretched, miserably distracted country, whose mad rulers are plunging us into an unnecessary war." And so when Morse, writing home, confessed that he favored the war, the implication was plain: "Some of you at home, I suppose, will call me a democrat."

Morse's political break had nothing to do with American domestic realities. Being a "democrat" meant nothing more to him in 1812 than being a patriot. He retained the values of the gentleman: Calvinism, fear of social change, distrust of "the people." He continued to identify with the Democratic Party, even in the years when the Party was being redefined by Andrew Jackson. But the identification was always casual, and did not involve him directly in politics. During the 1820s, for example, he busied himself with painting instead.

But even painting had ideological implications. Morse's career as an artist contained a double danger to his identity as a gentleman. In the first place, there was the growing notion that artists were "dissipated." And he was far from that. And, secondly, there was still a lingering identification of the artist as a craftsman, the practitioner of a trade that was beneath a gentleman's standards. Morse struggled against both dangers. And fortunately the solutions to each were identical. He painted only noble and "refined" subjects, designed to improve the morals of his audience—surely a fit occupation for any gentleman. And he painted portraits of the elite. First in New England, then in Charleston, South Carolina for several years, and finally in New York, Morse painted Americans who, in class terms, were indistinguishable from those with whom Tocqueville passed most of his time in America. Morse had a great deal of trouble making money as an artist. But he never dropped the dress, the style, the manners and the relentless dignity of the gentleman. After 1823, he settled in New York, where his friends were the cream of society. And painting subjects like President James Monroe and the fabled Marquis de Lafayette would hardly induce social unease.

In 1829, when Morse returned to Europe for more study—leaving behind, this time, his father, mother, and dead wife—he was a man with a low level of explicit political concern, a nominal democrat, a practised gentleman and a successful (if poor) painter. He settled in Rome, and began an unanticipated process of political awakening. Almost everything roused Morse. Rome, to him, was an old, "aristocratic" world of Catholic superstition and ritual, of ignorance and poverty and, above all, arbitrary subjection. Much as it had been in England during the War of 1812, his consciousness of American identity was heightened. Morse was especially intrigued by the Church's architecture and art, its ritual, and its hold on the imagination of its people. But he was also repelled. Gradually, he became preoccupied with the ideology of his own citizenship. He become a heated republican and democrat, not out of any awareness of American conditions, but in response to his encounter with European and with Catholic "autocracy."

Morse's political conversion was completed during the revolutions of 1830 and 1831. Lafayette, the subject for two of Morse's portraits and the type of aristocratic republican to be revered, lent his name and influence to the July Revolution. But he also supported an attempt by Poland's republicans to free themselves from Russian control. At the same time, a revolutionary army in Italy tried to bring down the Church government of the Papal States. An excited Morse set out for Paris, the center of the revolutions. Lafayette received him warmly, and initiated him into an exclusive "Polish committee."

Morse's experiences in Italy and Paris prompted the straightforward and obvious conclusion: a great struggle was in progress between republican freedom and autocratic tyranny. The United States, he thought, was the purest example of republicanism; and, conversely, Roman Catholicism represented the purest form of autocracy. Europe was already torn between these contending forces, and American democracy might also soon fall prey to the sinister, always advancing, power of the Church. "American liberty," Lafayette warned, "can only be destroyed by the Popish clergy." And Morse took the warning to heart. Returning home much more politically conscious than when he had left, he became a partisan of freedom and equality—of everything that smacked of republicanism. Now he was also required to combat the autocratic menace, to become a gentleman democrat in politics.

To Morse, back in New York, the enemy was not just an abstract and distant Popish danger. More alarming, he believed, was the growth of ignorance, poverty and plain boorishness at home. That New Yorkers would not buy paintings prompted genteel bitterness as well. "There is nothing new in New York," he wrote his friend James Fenimore Cooper, "except that they are not the same people that are driving after money, nor the same pigs at large in the street. Come prepared to find many, very many things in taste and manners different from your own good taste and manners."

Morse was caught between two worlds, geographically, ideologically, and socially. His own ideals of "refinement" and order clashed with what he considered to be American realities. But Europe was too full of popery and "aristocracy." Like Tocqueville, Morse often thought of Europe and the United States as abstractions. When the abstractions became too concrete, both men had an instinctive weakness for the old and the European. In Europe, Morse could be captivated by the picturesqueness of peasants; in the United States, pigs in the street were an offense. His nearest approach to ideological wholeness was in Paris, in the elegant company of Lafayette and other gentlemen, both European and American, giving wholehearted support to distant revolutions. The contradictions inherent in his position as a gentleman democrat were so deep that Morse could rail against the "tyranny" of the Church over Italian peasants, but at the same time see no evil in the practice of slavery in the United States.

During the disturbed political decade of the 1830s, these difficulties and contradictions focused on a single problem. European immigrants were flooding the United States, many of them Irish and Catholic. This immigration offended both Morse's gentility and his "democracy." The immigrants had none of the virtues he still believed were the core of "good taste and manners." But, Morse believed, the immigrants were also a threat to republican democracy, since they were easy prey for the Roman conspiracy. And so he entered politics as a distressed amateur. He ran for Mayor of New York City twice, in 1836 and 1841, under the colors of the new Native American Party. His platform was simple: a Jesuit conspiracy was at work, organizing immigrants into a political tool. Once this goal was accomplished, he claimed, "Anarchy ensues; and then the mass of people, who are always lovers of order and quiet, unite at once in support of the strong arm of force for protection; and despotism resumes its iron reign." Morse lost both elections badly—as he did again in 1854 when he ran for Congress.

Morse's alarmed nativism was not a repudiation of his theoretical democracy. He believed that democracy had to be protected *from* the people, whose abstract "sovereignty" was always being undercut by their weakness and poor "taste." And if defense of such an abstract democracy in effect required repudiation of "the people," then Morse would do it— confident that, in the long run, he was only fighting to preserve the good order and good manners necessary to the survival of republican democracy. Underneath—as with Tocqueville—there was always class instinct, ready to assert itself in any difficult moment. In an unpublished note very much like Tocqueville's private "confession," Morse laid out his rejection of Jean-Jacques Rousseau's principle that "Man is born free":

> I repudiate his fundamental postulate. There is not a living thing born into this world which is at its birth so utterly dependent, more perfectly enslaved, as man. [This] is the source of error of the Dec. of Indep., the equality paragraph.

*   *   *

James Fenimore Cooper, gentleman and writer, reached Paris for the first time in the summer of 1826, his 37th year. By October, with the generous help of Lafayette, Cooper had penetrated well into the upper reaches of French society. "I go to soirées," he wrote a friend, "where Princesses and Duchesses are as plenty as hogs in the streets of New

York." In truth, fastidious gentlemen like Cooper and Morse were probably much more numerous in New York streets than the pigs they fussed about. And Cooper probably exaggerated the estimated number of princesses of Paris, too. But his observation was more than a pair of miscounts, and more too than a joke to amuse a refined correspondent. He was beginning a seven-year stay in Europe, and it was a time of ideological tension for him as it had been for Morse and Tocqueville.

Like most other genteel Americans, Cooper was both fascinated and shocked by Europe. He gloried in his contacts with aristocracy, but made the almost routine American observation that Europe was a very mixed blessing. France, he said shortly after arrival, was a "strange country made up of dirt and gilding, good cheer and soupe maigre, bed bugs and laces." Europe set Cooper to thinking about America in a more systematic way than he had at home. He wrote his first work of non-fiction, *Notions of the Americans*, in Europe. And his attitudes toward American democracy became both more conscious and more troubled under the pressure of these seven years of European experiences. Like Morse and Tocqueville, then, Cooper became preoccupied with democracy in an international context; as with them, his perceptions of America were shaped at least as much by European as by American realities. Upon returning home in 1833, he was filled with doubt about republican democracy, and even more troubled over his status as a gentleman and his career as a novelist in democratic society.

The decor of James Fenimore Cooper's own life was gilding, good cheer and laces—not dirt, thin soup, and bed bugs. His ancestry was not so distinguished as Morse's; he was the son of the founder of Cooperstown, New York, a self-made man who accumulated a large fortune through land speculation. But William Cooper was a solid sort, who eventually became county judge, Congressman for two terms (as a Federalist, like Morse's father), and owner of an estate worth about $750,000, a huge fortune by the standards of the day. The family tried to educate young James suitably at Yale, but he studied little and pranked his way into dismissal in 1805. He was 16 and needed a career, so his father sent him to sea as a common sailor for a year in preparation for a naval officer's life. Cooper was commissioned a midshipman in 1808 and served until 1811.

Then, when James Fenimore Cooper was 22, his life reverted into a more gentlemanly channel. His father had died, leaving him $50,000 immediately and an interest in the entire estate. And he married Susan DeLancey, whose family was even richer and more aristocratic than Cooper's. He built a large home in Westchester on DeLancey land, and settled into the life of gentleman farmer with a few entreprenurial interests on the side.

This quiet pattern was broken in 1820, when Cooper began to write novels. The first was done on a dare, but once started he was obsessively efficient. Cooper published almost a book a year for the next six years, including *The Spy, The Pioneers,* and his greatest popular success, *The Last of the Mohicans.* He also moved into New York City, at about the same time Morse did, and for the same reason: the city was the most obvious place to pursue a literary or artistic career. Cooper was even more closely identified with the upper reaches of New York society than Morse. He began a dining club, called simply The Lunch, which served as a resort for New York's most talented and elegant men of letters, money, or power.

Like Morse (who also belonged to The Lunch), Cooper had broken with family tradition to become a Democrat. But being a Democrat in New York still meant associating with men from refined Hudson River families who ran the Party. The shift was not ideological, and Cooper was not greatly concerned with the social implications of politics. For him, Andrew Jackson was a southern gentleman and military hero, not a leader of democratic masses. And Cooper was much more interested in the reputation his books were gaining at home and abroad than in the development of democracy.

It was only when James Fenimore Cooper carried overseas his social credentials, his reputation and his concern for refinement that the problem of being both a gentleman and an American democrat began to agitate him. Just two years after he arrived in France, he published *Notions of the Americans,* two longish volumes devoted to explaining America to Europe—and to any of his countrymen who needed instruction, too. The book was begun for an odd reason. Lafayette, whom Cooper had met in New York when Lafayette made a triumphal tour of the United States in 1824, asked him to write an account of the tour. It would be difficult to make such a book interesting, but Cooper began anyway, out of courtesy and gratitude for Lafayette's social efforts on his behalf. *Notions of the Americans* took a peculiar shape, however, and one to which its original purpose was almost irrelevant. Cooper invented a travelling European nobleman, "The Count de - - - - -," who carried on an unrelenting correspondence with aristocratic friends in England and France about his travels in America. The "Count" was, in other words, a kind of fictive Tocqueville, three years before the fact.

The "Count's" perceptions were indeed very similar to some of Tocqueville's. He learned that "equality" had liberated Americans from foolish aristocratic notions and cruelties, that the democratic mass was serious, hardworking, inventive, generous, and decent. Equality had not erased the privileges of wealth and talent: gentlemen were still held in careful and gentle esteem by Americans. And gentlemen themselves had learned to live comfortably with democracy: their manners and dress were characterized by a republican simplicity reminiscent of their great national hero, Washington, the very model of the aristocratic republican. Cooper's explicit conclusions were commonplace, as were his contrasts between American democracy and European society. And his patriotic conclusion prefigured Tocqueville's awe at the inevitable triumph of democracy and of America which, in the last word of *Notions of the Americans,* was "irresistible."

On its surface, *Notions of the Americans* was not a problematic book. Its position on democracy was clear; its patriotism unambiguous; its picture of American government, manners and morals uniformly favorable—except for occasional dark spots, like slavery, which Cooper regarded as a "scourge." But as an event in its author's life, it was very perplexing. While at work on *Notions,* Cooper was very much involved in Parisian high society and worked hard to develop a courtly life style. His letters home were full of detailed descriptions of his social successes —like the grand ball at the house of Count Pozzo de Borgo, to which he escorted a real princess:

> As for the party, it was magnificence itself. Sixteen or seventeen rooms open, and many of them princely. The rooms were crowded, perhaps 1,500 people, including everybody most distinguished at Paris. The Princess and myself [!] came away at 1 o'clock, like sober people. My servant told me that 600 carriages had entered the court at 12 o'clock.

Cooper had made something of a habit of having his servant count the carriages. And he kept remarkably careful track of the aristocratic personages whom he met at Lafayette's weekly soirées. In such a setting, *Notions of the Americans* was quite eccentric: a defense of Cooper's own "democratic" society, yes, but prompted by the request of a Marquis, published anonymously in Europe, told in the form of letters of a fictive nobleman, directed obviously to an elite audience, and written by a man for whom European princesses appeared more frequent and congenial than New York hogs.

This striking disparity between the ideas of *Notions of the Americans* and the circumstances in which it was written should have made its readers cautious. The book aimed at one essential point: there was no real conflict between democracy and aristocracy in America, because both plain people and the elite have managed to preserve the best features of aristocratic society while shedding its abuses and oppressions. But the point was mildly dishonest. The novels Cooper had already written about America were dense with conflict between the values of gentlemen and of democrats. Even when Cooper wrote about "noble" men of poor birth and circumstances—like Natty Bumppo, the scout, hero of the Leatherstocking novels—the nobility was almost a miracle, a striking exception to class realities, not a typical trait of plain men. And the scout's very nobility constantly brought him into conflict with the demands for social order inherent in Cooper's idea of civilization. Cooper always had Leatherstocking come out the loser in these encounters, and Cooper's own values were normally represented by a gentleman, judge or squire who was "forced" to impose social discipline on the scout. Novels like *The Spy*, Cooper's second, published in 1821, had also been peopled by unruly, dangerous, disrespectful crowds of the poor and ignorant, obvious threats to the decent classes—the very kinds of people that *Notions of the Americans* chose carefully to ignore. The book was the gesture of a man deeply caught up in a Parisian world and anxious to picture his homeland as a place where "true" aristocracy could flourish within a wholly decent and restrained democracy.

Cooper traveled for two years after the publication of the *Notions*, but, with the July Revolution of 1830, hurried back to Paris. For the next two years, he was more politically active than he had ever been at home. He headed the Polish Committee, wrote essays defending American government and republican institutions in general, and watched with fascination as Lafayette and the republican liberals first seemed to have won, then gradually lost power to the new monarchy they had helped create. But James Fenimore Cooper the republican did this watching from an elegant two-story apartment in what his wife called "a very *distingué* part of the Town." Support for this life style came from his books, which he still churned out almost once a year. His royalties were very considerable: income from his British publisher was almost $20,000 for 1831 and 1832.

Finally, Cooper was ready to leave Europe. In 1833, with four Swiss servants, he set sail in "three state-rooms *en suite* built expressly for us, and near the centre of the ship, so that I hope the *maladie de mer* will not be killing." Cooper came home already troubled about the United States. His republican sentiments had earned him some very harsh reviews in the European press, and a number of America's Whig papers had reprinted the attacks. And so, before disembarking in New York, Cooper was prepared to notice great "changes" in his homeland, to "retire" as a novelist, to buy back his father's great house, "Otsego Hall" at Cooperstown, to take his family, servants, and expensive Persian rugs there—away from the instabilities and crudities of New York. The "change," of course, was at least as much in Cooper himself as in America. And what he chose to regard as a sudden "decline" in American manners was a decline not from the America he had actually known in the 1820s, but from the abstraction he had invented in *Notions of the Americans*.

Men looking for trouble seldom have any trouble finding it. Within months, Cooper was involved in newspaper feuds about himself, his work, the actions of Andrew Jackson's administration, and United States relations with France. In these feuds, Cooper, the Democrat, found himself cast by Whig papers as a Europeanized snob who, being spoiled by seven years abroad, was unable to tolerate the realities of American life. These charges had some truth to them. He was impatient with democracy, and he shared Morse's refined horror of New York's pigs and "nouveaux" entrepreneurs. It was a great consolation to buy his father's country seat and raise the ceilings three feet so he could put in Gothic windows to make the big house seem even more venerable.

Cooper's belief that American democracy had undergone a great corruption and decline got its strongest confirmation from a quarrel that he had deliberately provoked. The townsfolk had for years picnicked freely on a point of land owned by the Coopers and jutting into Lake Otsego. Cooper fretted about this incursion onto his family's "immemorial" rights. Finally, in 1837, he announced in the local Democratic newspaper that he intended to enforce the family's title to the Point. The first public reaction was an angry town meeting at which the local library was even asked to remove his novels from its shelves. The second was another newspaper war in which Whig papers in Cooperstown, Albany, and New York flayed his aristocratic pretensions. The third result was *The American Democrat* (1838), a book cataloguing the failures of American democracy.

In *Notions of the Americans,* Cooper had foreshadowed many of Tocqueville's optimistic assessments of the United States. In *The American Democrat,* he echoed many of Tocqueville's negative judgments. Cooper was still a theoretical democrat, to be sure. But now he was even more the gentleman, afraid of the tyranny of public opinion and of what he now saw as the dangerous conflict between rich and poor, gentry and people, order and anarchy. Most of all, he had decided, the public was to be feared: "The publick, then, is to be watched, in this country, as in other countries kings and aristocrats are to be watched." *The American Democrat* was an extremely abstract book, in which mere concepts like "classes," "men of cultivation," "the people," and the "the spirit of our institutions" collided on a blank geometrical plane. But its intentions were clear: to announce the collapse of the old, fictitious truce, stated in *Notions,* between democracy and aristocracy that had kept social peace.

The American Democrat was also a kind of schematic outline for two sets of novels: *Homeward Bound* and *Home as Found* in the 1830s, and a trilogy on a family of New York gentry, the Littlepages, in the 1840s. In these novels, aristocratic families recognizably like Cooper's found themselves in nasty encounters with democrats of all descriptions: ruthless entrepreneurs, demagogic politicians and journalists, Yankee farmers as crude and grasping as William Faulkner's family of Snopeses, and pretentious *nouveaux riches* whose manners merely betrayed an uncouth (and therefore democratic) obsession with the external badges of class. In all these encounters, Cooper's gentlemen could only be what they were: patient, moderate, and humane. They also turned out, as often as not, to be ineffectual, and to end in graceful retirement from scenes of action they could no longer control or even soften. In Cooper's world, there was no real alternative to democracy; he apparently shared an American consensus on that point. But the consensus was not always a willing one. Like many other gentlemen, Cooper felt himself born out of time, trapped in a world that had to be approved because it was the only one going, trapped too in the necessity to use the language and forms of democracy even when the purpose was to criticize or repudiate it.

Cooper never confessed, even privately, that he was no democrat. Nor did he ever formally reject the "equality paragraph" of the Declaration of Independence. But he did live a somewhat withdrawn life, interested himself more and more in religion as a check on the democratic "principle," and became visibly more bitter with the course that his country seemed to be taking. It was appropriate that he completed the Leatherstocking cycle of tales (which had begun with Natty Bumppo as a 70-year old man) with a pair of novels that retreated into the hero's youth. *The Pathfinder* and *The Deerslayer* pushed back into time and deeper into wilderness, to a period when there was less painful conflict between the hunter's "natural aristocracy" and the distressing "realities" that Cooper chose to see in American democracy. In the young Deerslayer, moving with efficient grace through his forests, Cooper could find imaginary relief from those selective "realities"; the novel ended with Cooper reflecting sadly that:

> We live in a world of transgressions and selfishness, and no pictures that represent us otherwise can be true; though, happily for human nature, gleamings of that pure spirit in whose likeness man has been fashioned, are to be seen, relieving its deformities, and mitigating, if not excusing its crimes.

For at least 50 years before Cooper wrote this ending to Leatherstocking's inverted career, it had been an axiom of American politics that the survival of republicanism depended on the "virtue" of the people. As the republicanism of the revolutionary generation was transformed into the democracy of the 1830s and 1840s, the people's "virtue" became an even more urgent need. But Cooper had concluded, finally, that there was very little virtue to be found in men in general. Leatherstocking, who was a magnificent accident of nature, represented, finally, no more than a consolation, a "gleaming" of light in a dark and distrusted world.

*   *   *

There was nothing in the actual history of the United States that *drove* Cooper (and Morse like him) to such a conclusion. The "people" were probably as virtuous on the whole in 1840 as they had been in 1800. It would have been just as easy, as a matter of experience, for Cooper to have decided that his Cooperstown neighbors were sturdy, decent yeomen, and to have thrown Three Mile Point open to their picnics, thereby fulfilling his own generous prophesies in *Notions of the Americans.* Morse, in a similar way, could have welcomed the Irish to New York as potential recruits to a new democratic culture. And Tocqueville could have seen any Paris crowd as the vanguard of a new awakening for France, instead of a fearsome mob. Men exercise a real choice in their perceptions, and their neighbors can become (within wide limits) symbols of almost any ideological fact or proof for almost any political theorem. Gentlemen's democracy, as it developed during the decades before the Civil War, was a paradoxical and unstable ideology. Men like Morse, Tocqueville and Cooper attributed a vague and elusive decency to "the people." But instead of building confidence, this hope could just as easily lead to fear—fear that the virtues so essential to the success of democracy might fade with alarming speed. In the end, it was fear, not hope, that governed the minds of most gentlemen democrats.

Soon, events would make the social perceptions of this trio of gentlemen democrats almost irrelevant. Immigration, geographical expansion, industrialization and urbanization—all punctuated by Civil War—transformed the face of the old republic much more radically than the short-term "declines" of the 1830s. The reflections and activities of gentlemen democrats were rudely treated by the processes of history, and the preoccupation of Tocqueville, Morse and Cooper with the international logic of democracy became half-relevant, almost antique.

9

Moral Man and Moral Society

LYMAN BEECHER
BRIGHAM YOUNG
HENRY D. THOREAU

by Charles A. Barker
The Johns Hopkins University

Lyman Beecher, Brigham Young, and Henry David Thoreau were three Americans who staked their lives on convictions they imagined would make society good. Two of them, Beecher and Young, won considerable support in their lifetime. Today Beecher is largely forgotten, Young continues to have followers, and Thoreau has emerged as a sort of patron saint for those who question the coercive power of the State.

The hope all three entertained, that their ideas would improve the behavior of human society, often fails to raise sympathy in 20th-century minds. A generation ago Reinhold Niebuhr, already beginning to be honored as the greatest American theologian in two centuries, expressed modern doubt about social regeneration, in *Moral Man and Immoral Society*. To be sure, Niebuhr restated Christianity's hope concerning individuals: by God's grace, His children on Earth can be, and often do actually become, just, altruistic, loving, and good. But society is different. The national state is especially incapable of altruism, for by its nature it cannot transcend self-interest. And self-interest and the sovereign power the state exercises with violence are inseparable parts of a lump of immorality. There is no regeneration in it.

This judgment has hung on. Not at all the unique position of one theologian, but an attitude widely heard during the 1930s, it re-echoes today.

But it has never prevailed; and it seems less near doing so now than before World War II. Indeed recent social movements have sung a different tune. "We shall overcome." Today is too early to say whether our present crop of social injustice and violence will reinforce Niebuhrian pessimism or will relight the hope never extinguished that, once moral bottom has been hit, an upturn may be expected.

All this bears on the men who appear in the next three sections of this chapter. Were the immoral-society view to govern us, we should have to prejudge two of them—Lyman Beecher, churchman, reformer, and educator, and a man of the modes of his time, and Brigham Young, leader, organizer and policy-giver to the Mormons—to have been fools. For both of them literally expected that the law of God would imminently prevail. Still taking the Niebuhrian line, we should have to think well of our third principal, Henry David Thoreau, the member of the Transcendentalist circle who had the most to say about law and society. For, though he spoke in a time of superpatriotism, the decades of the 1840s and 1850s, he totally defied the state and denied any virtue in politics.

Still and again, if the immoral-society view perhaps expects too much virtue of a few individuals, and too little of most, and none of organized society as a whole, we may approach our three "movers and shakers" with expectations more nearly equal. Supposing that all persons are affected by circumstance, we may well notice at the outset that every one of our three began life in New England, the region most productive of moral ideas. The religious genius of New England—from Anne Hutchinson to Ralph Waldo Emerson, Jonathan Edwards to Mary Baker Eddy—has been proliferation and variety. We may reasonably look to each of our three, not alone to Thoreau, for something of what our time has learned to call "alienation." Lyman Beecher, Puritan held over from colonial Puritanism; Brigham Young, migrant and outpost builder; Henry Thoreau, devotee of solitude —the three raise just that question.

*   *   *

Among the situations in history Lyman Beecher shares with Brigham Young and Henry Thoreau is that of having been the number-two man in the work with which he is identified. This condition is self-evident in the other cases as well: first Emerson, second Thoreau; first Joseph Smith, second Brigham Young. With Beecher the situation is less familiar, but the fact is that in Connecticut's moral-reformist history he was doubly a number two. He was second to President Timothy Dwight of Yale College, the man after whom he consciously modelled. In the 1790s Dwight had started the Connecticut work among students; 20 years later Beecher tried much the same reforms on the body of citizens. He also came second, in the sequence of thought rather than the sequence of time, after his friend and fellow Yale man, Nathaniel W. Taylor. From the pulpit of Center Church on New Haven's Green just in front of the college, and later from his chair of theology in the new Yale Divinity School, Taylor spoke brilliantly the lines of the "New Haven Theology." A variant of Edwardsean belief, it stressed man's free and sufficient "ability," under God, to live on Earth according to His law. Thus Taylor qualifies as the main theorist, and Beecher, accepting the theory, became its leading proponent.

Son and grandson of blacksmiths in lower Connecticut, Beecher began life on a social footing considerably lower than the famous Unitarians, who were born to such Harvard names as Channing and Emerson and whose careers would run parallel to his own. But there was no lack of Puritan content in Beecher's background. A Beecher had crossed the Atlantic with John Davenport, the founder of New Haven; Lyman himself was born and brought up in nearby Guilford, fronting on Long Island Sound. He entered Yale College just before President Ezra Stiles finished. This means that he breathed the twin currents of air that swept over post-Revolutionary Yale: first, the warmth of new currents from the Enlightenment to which Stiles had opened the windows, and second, the sharp wind of evangelism and of vigorous experimental science that entered with President Dwight. The combination made Yale popular; for some years it outstripped Harvard in student numbers and institutional growth. Long a home of nationalist feeling—for instance, of the Connecticut Wits—the college now made special contributions to social solidarity. Its science served the people of Connecticut, and its theology, the still-established Congregational Church.

Beecher's ministries took him away from New Haven. For the first decade of the new century, he served in a farming hamlet on upper Long Island, where he became restless, with too little money and too few chores. So when at age 35 he was called to Litchfield, a commercial town on the inland road from New York to Boston, he was delighted. It presented him with pleasant prospects: there were fine houses and gardens; Judge Tapping Reeve, who had more or less engineered Beecher's coming, had already established there his famous law school, the first in America. The new church was magnificent. Steeple and doors and windows, pulpit, and balcony supported by columns, all made the building inspiring. This was what Lyman Beecher wanted his church as an institution to be.

At the time of Lyman Beecher's new beginning, the United States from southwest to northeast was experiencing the Second Great Awakening. If measured by the influence of revivalism on society, the second Awakening was more important than the first, the very well-known one in the 1730s and '40s, of which Jonathan Edwards had been the great theologian. Generally speaking, where the 18th-century Great Awakening had strained near to breaking the century-old alliances between colonial churches and colonial governments, the 19th-century awakening sought almost the opposite: to impel the churches and the state and local governments into sympathetic efforts of reform. "Home missions" became everywhere important: training ministers; setting up churches, schools, and colleges in the West; supplying every encouragement to new settlements to nurture Christian youth who would be ready to meet their obligations, whether as churchmen and citizens or as creditors and debtors. From region to region the many churches acted differently, according to their organization. The four or five largest churches—the Congregationalists, Presbyterians, and Episcopalians, who had been numerous for more than a century; and the Methodists and Baptists, who had come to outnumber those three—accounted for a multitude of boards and commissions assigned to various undertakings of social action. Above all else the urgencies of population increase prevailed; if statistics are convincing, during the first half of the 19th century the United States was on the way, at last, to becoming surely and massively Christian.

Lyman Beecher's Connecticut had its small intense share of the excitements and hardships of growth. Farmers were moving west; debtors were numerous and noisy about their grievances; clergymen were losing, and politicians were gaining in public esteem. The State's Congregational church, as in Massachusetts but nowhere else in the Union, still received tax money to support it; but embarrassingly that church was proportionately losing strength to the Methodists and the Baptists. Likewise the Federalist Party, the members of which were characteristically Congregationalists, was falling behind. Such adverse and challenging, but not yet critical, conditions were the reverse side of the coin that drew Lyman Beecher to Litchfield.

What he could do for his parish, and for Connecticut, occurred to him in terms of his training and recent experiences. On Long Island Beecher had tackled intemperance within his congregation. In and around Litchfield, it was a bit astonishing for him to hear that the same abuse existed in all classes, but conspicuously among the clergy! The farmers, mechanics, and manufacturers of the community all needed, in Beecher's words, "to diminish the quantity of ardent spirits consumed in their several employments." He thought that they should substitute "other palatable and nutritious drinks" and that "compensation" should be given, "if necessary, to laborers who will dispense entirely of the use of ardent spirits." But first of all, it was up to the ministers and magistrates to improve. "Let ministers, and churches, and parents, and magistrates, and all the friends of civil and religious order . . . unite their counsels and their efforts, and make a faithful experiment."

These words by Beecher come from a committee report. Organized action followed. Whatever the substance of the abuse—whether the degradation that alcoholism now often accounts for, or something less—the writer does not know. We do know that, locally, other ministers joined Beecher, and public complaints diminished; that, nationally, excessive drinking challenged revivalist preachers in all regions; and that, historically, the churches tackling the problem preceded the first state legislative action in Maine by decades. We know also of Beecher that, while over and above parish routines he made temperance his first reform, he moved quickly on other causes. Before he arrived in the community, ministers had gone about raising money for the education of young women and for training men for the ministry. These efforts he promptly picked up. And in 1813 he took the principal lead in launching the Connecticut Society for Good Morals. Literally borrowing the name, the new society otherwise imitated one that Timothy Dwight had sponsored at Yale to Christianize student behavior. It spread a network across the state. Beecher served on the directing committee; the president was an ex-governor; the vice-president was Judge Reeve, Beecher's friend as well as parish associate. The program concerned manners as much as morals. It condemned blasphemy; it urged moderation of speech; it proposed strictness in keeping the Sabbath. In his 1827 farewell sermon to the people of Litchfield, Beecher uttered a kind of benediction on all that he and they had tried to do in their 15 years together: "Philosophers and patriots, statesmen and men of wealth, are beginning to feel that it is righteousness only which exalteth a nation." He quoted Revelations: "And He that sat upon the throne said Behold, I make all things good."

Finally, before summing up Lyman Beecher's efforts in Connecticut, an event of 1818, not something he did to the state but something the state did to him, requires a brief explanation. Much against his will, but according to the wishes of non-Congregationalists and more modern Congregationalists than himself, the convention that drew up a new constitution separated church from state. In his own retrospection: "I foresaw what was coming," he later reminisced. "I saw the enemy digging at the foundations of the standing order. . . . I went with deliberate calculation to defend it." The decision by the convention hurt. "For several days I suffered what no tongues can tell." Yet somehow he recovered. On learning that Congregationalist colleagues felt relief not to be tied to the government, he decided that he did too. Soon and surprisingly he pronounced disestablishment to be *"the best thing that ever happened to the State of Connecticut."*

By present-day standards, Connecticut's agricultural, commercial and early industrial society seems almost incredibly simple; and so do its social problems and its leading social reformer. What could have been more shallow for a learned clergyman, who believed that through God's church His will could be done on Earth, than the program of the Connecticut Society for Good Morals? What change of mind (quite apart from the merit of the matter) could have been more facile than Beecher's, about the relations of church and state?

Still and again, such questions suggest more about the distance of a century and half between him and us than they do about the work of Lyman Beecher, or about Connecticut, or about the subject of this chapter—19th-century approaches to reform. Beecher did start statewide social reform in Connecticut. Soon after his departure, under such leaders as Henry Barnard and Horace Bushnell, systematic programs of education, some of them tax-supported and some of them church-sustained, succeeded well. They owed something to him; he had preached reform with enormous impact, and men had followed where he led. It was a tribute to Beecher when, in 1827 at age 52, he was called to Boston. The Hanover Street congregation, inviting him, asked of him just what he was prepared for—revivalist preaching of the New Haven doctrine. Rendered the more attractive by a good salary at a good address, the new situation compares at first glance with the Litchfield one in 1811, but in larger dimensions.

Yet there were also deep differences. Connecticut was known as America's "land of steady habits." Not Massachusetts and especially not Boston. In eastern Massachusetts religious ferment, strong enough to dissolve Christian orthodoxy with regard to the doctrine of the Trinity, was two generations old. Meanwhile social dislocations, owing in part to the rise of textile factories and exacerbated by Irish immigration, produced class conflicts worse than those in Connecticut. Both phenomena bore on Beecher's career. Naturally the religious one, now developed to the stage of open harassment between the Unitarians—who called themselves "liberal Christians"—and the conservative Congregationalists, was the first to draw his fire.

He arrived expecting and ready to battle the Unitarians. During the previous decade, in common with Taylor in New Haven, he had sensed that the liberals would extend their effort to capture control of Congregationalist parishes all the way into Connecticut. The two had taken protective measures; Taylor's anti-Unitarianism goes far to explain the founding early in the 1820s of the Yale Divinity School, a counteroffensive with Taylor himself in command. From his citadel on Hanover Street, Beecher likewise counter-attacked. His congregation was only one of several in Boston that supported the Andover Theological Seminary, the two-decades-old opposition school to the Harvard School of Divinity. But, because his own New Haven theology favored more social reformism than did Andover doctrine, Beecher thought himself better prepared than his allies to understand the liberals and to demolish their ideas forthwith.

He led off with the old vigor. His preaching brought recruits to his congregation, promoted the missionary movement, and launched in the city and surrounding region a revivalistic campaign to compare in intensity with that of the 1740s. But any success he may have had against the Unitarians is dubious. Because Unitarian minds were closed to his ideas of regeneration, Unitarian ears did not hear his revivalist pleas. He failed to return many, if any, Unitarians to the fold of mother Congregationalism; he probably curtailed their growth. Rather than answering, they ignored him, a reaction that was hard to take.

The sector of Boston's social problems that most concerned Beecher was the startling increase of Roman Catholicism, largely but not altogether a product of immigration. No different from his ancestors, to whom the nearest Catholics in numbers were the French in Quebec, he conceived the Boston Papists to be enemies to be destroyed. As he envisaged them, Catholic ritual was archaic, the secrecy of confessional and convent was conspiratorial, and church authority was erosive of American freedom. In this mix of history and prejudice, Beecher abandoned the restraints that had moderated his assaults on evil in Connecticut; he became a rabble-rouser. One of his sermons, which alleged sexual misbehavior between priests and nuns, seems to have helped to incite, or at the very least to have shared the spirit of, the mob that broke into the Ursuline convent in Charlestown and burned it. This was the single most violent act in the anti-Catholic turbulence of the period, that guerilla warfare of the seaboard cities that historian Ray A. Billington has ironically called "the Protestant Crusade."

Partly because of this climax, rather anticlimax, of his pulpit career, Beecher's Boston period appears the most counterproductive part of a lifelong effort to make his people good. At this turning point of his life, while approaching 60, his mind once again seems not to have worked philosophically. In Boston the trouble was that, along with his total attachment to Congregationalism, he displayed no tolerance at all. Working for his denomination he gave no thought to the merits of Unitarians or Unitarianism, or to the merit of having them around. Still less did he comprehend or even begin to consider the value of welcoming Roman Catholics as neighbors.

Beecher moved to his last post of responsibility in 1832. While in Connecticut he had feared the movement to the frontier as a process upsetting institutional and moral stabilities, but his decision now to go to Cincinnati awakened in him the feeling (common among those who went there) that the Old Northwest had become the last best hope for the Christian republic. In Cincinnati he was given charge of a leading Presbyterian congregation and the presidency of Lane Theological Seminary. The latter was a combined Congregational and Presbyterian training center for ministers, a recent institutional product of the Second Great Awakening and of the temporary union between the two churches. Possibly contemplating the origins and ideals of the New Haven colony two centuries earlier, he managed to convince himself that Cincinnati would become America's London.

Soon after arrival Beecher ran into a second round of urban conflict. Some of his sermons disturbed the old-school Calvinists of his congregation. They brought him to trial for heresy, slander, and hypocrisy. Though the charges and the defense were very specific, procedures were relatively loose—as they were for all church trials at the time because ecclesiastical law was unsophisticated and trial officers rarely if ever were experienced. Heresy, consequently, had to be whatever the officers declared. Thus Beecher's ordeal stretched out; he was tried first before the local presbytery, second before the synod, and finally before the nationwide General

Assembly. In the end he was found innocent and returned with honor to his appointments. But the trial was a hard beginning for Beecher in the West. After his own intolerance in Boston he may have had coming to him some anguish on behalf of his own belief. Certainly, he bore a great deal for his faith in the work of his 60s and 70s.

His more famous ordeal in Cincinnati, the best-known episode of his life, occurred at the Lane seminary. During the early 1830s, when the antislavery movement was rising among the churches and the religious journals of the North and Northwest, his students insisted on meeting and discussing the subject. They were just across the river from Kentucky, and the South's peculiar institution had high and distressing visibility. But Lane's trustees, who were a mixed body of clergymen and businessmen, wanted quiet: "Education must be completed before the young are fitted to engage in the collisions of active life." Consequently it was wrong for the prospective ministers even to talk, and they forbade the meetings. During this discourse President Beecher temporized. For most of his life he had been indifferent to slavery; but, before leaving New England, he had come to favor the Negro colonization movement, which aimed to settle American blacks in Liberia. (In point of fact, white Southerners saw colonization as a means of removing free Negros from their midst.) Thus he was identified with a very slow method of emancipation and with a movement that acted out the common racist assumption that blacks were not to be assimilated as equal to whites in American society. Even so, Beecher did favor the students' demand, and when he finally insisted that the meetings be permitted, his trustees acquiesced.

Unfortunately Beecher's courage came late. The students at Lane walked out—the earliest and most memorable social protest of that kind in pre-Civil War history. They crossed the State northward to Oberlin College. There they were welcomed into an institution that not only had a few black students but also stood as the nation's principal academic citadel of antislavery. Oberlin was under the presidency of Charles G. Finney, who had been Beecher's rival in evangelism in the East. Moreover, the College immediately started its own theological seminary and its own "perfectionist" school of theology. In encouraging social reform, its ideas would carry considerably further than the New Haven theology. Thus in Ohio as in Connecticut, Beecher's cautious starts in reform and education were overtaken by men of larger commitment.

Unhappily for any sense of climax or culmination about Beecher's career, the long years before and after his retirement contained no memorable innovations and no successes that came near to matching his goals. After the tensions within church and seminary that upset his life during the early years in Ohio, the adversities of depression hit him in the late 1830s. In addition the strains of antislavery involvement mounted on him, as on all churchmen in the Old Northwest during the 1830s and 1840s. Instead of culmination, Lyman Beecher's later career brought him an increment of dignity, the reward—without either conspicuous success or conspicuous failure—of sustained effort made in a faith that was always sincere.

One special aspect of his life requires a kind of appendix because in a way it projects him ultimately into public affairs. President Abraham Lincoln, it may be recalled, once greeted Beecher's fourth daughter, Harriet (who was also the wife of his old close colleague at Lane, Calvin Stowe), as the woman who by her book had brought on the Civil War. She was one of his 13 children to whose upbringing he had contributed greatly, both during years of happy marriage and years of widowhood. His oldest daughter, Catharine, as founder of a school and a missionary of women's education, is a larger figure now than her father in the history of education; probably she is larger than Harriet in the history of women's freedom and participation in society's work.

Beecher also fathered seven sons, every one of whom grew up to be a Christian minister, just as he wanted. Though today not one of them seems as important as their two famous sisters, one is well remembered, Henry Ward Beecher. For years the country's best known preacher, honored with the charge of the rich Plymouth congregation in the rich suburb of Brooklyn of the nation's richest city, he built on a talent that he would seem to have inherited from his father. As adapter of current thought, Darwinian evolution, to Christian doctrine and as preacher of moderate social reform, he echoed Lyman Beecher's effort to shape the New Haven theology to social improvement.

*　　*　　*

Brigham Young's number-two, but hardly secondary, position in Mormon history owes nothing to the date of his birth. He entered the world in 1801, four years ahead of "The Prophet," Joseph Smith. Both were Vermont farm-village boys and while young were part of the large migration from upper New England to western New York. They had no family connections. But where Smith began well before 20 to have uncommon religious experiences and by 25 had transmitted to the world the Book of Mormon and founded the Church of Jesus Christ of Latter-Day Saints, Young was 31 when converted to that church and 43 when he took charge. The two lives first came together in the fall of 1832 when Young visited the Prophet at the Mormon settlement in Kirtland, Ohio.

Thus the top two Mormon leaders were born in one state, taken to another state, and then worked together in a third state, where the folkways of New England religion persevered. Just how tenaciously they did so, Lyman Beecher's career illustrates well. But, the other side of the coin, religious innovation, occurred as well. The so-called "Burned-Over District" of upstate western New York, where Joseph Smith grew up and Brigham

Young came into manhood, somehow became the special breeding place of radical faith. For instance, besides the Mormons there were the Oneida Perfectionists, who outdid all others in restructuring family organization and sex arrangements, and the Seventh-day Adventists, whose ideas about the calling of the saints were vivid and often upsetting. And in the same region the older churches competed with one another in revivalism, using Charles G. Finney's "anxious bench" and other new methods of conversion. "I am the way," became the repeated, essential message, not simply of radical leaders such as Joseph Smith, William Miller (another Vermonter), and John Humphrey Noyes, but of many another. It was a departure, but not a far departure, from the evangelical norm. Although Lyman Beecher was never caught saying so, that was just about what he meant.

Among the special revelations of the period, Smith's Book of Mormon is by far the most imposing. It declares that tribes of Israel, whose fate is unknown to to Jewish history, were the forebears of the American aborigines. This was nothing new: many Americans, Lewis and Clark among them, had long since entertained such an idea of red Indian origins. But the Book of Morman filled in the story in ways that gave it religious potency. In rough similarity to the historical books of the Old Testament, it chronicled complex wanderings and wars among the tribes. Jesus Christ was recorded as not only having come to Palestine with His message of salvation but also to America centuries ago. But His rule was accepted no more this time than on His first coming. Wars continued, with bad Indians exterminating good until only one tribe of the good, the Nephites, survived. Finally that tribe too was annihilated, excepting a short remission for Mormon, its chief. God then punished the evil victors by darkening their skins. (Here was established Mormonisms's special belief in the primacy of the white race; Joseph Smith and his successors would never recruit Negroes and Indians only to a limited extent for their new church. But, in truth, it was hardly more than a variation on the common 19th-century belief that God had made His creatures different, some high, some lower.) Thus the Book of Mormon concludes with a new picture of human destiny: American aborigines, like the ancient Jews from whom they were descended, had specially received the Savior; and like the Jews they had rejected Him. Among all the people of Earth, the readers of Mormon's book were now given a new New Testament. Like the early Christians receiving the Gospels and the church, they were called of God to lead all whites and Indians who would follow into righteousness during this life and beyond.

This remarkable book, and then over the years a flood of revelations, came to the Mormons in complex ways. (Smith had 133 revelations as compared with only one by Young.) According to Smith, he had early received directions for unearthing near his home the original Book of Mormon—the text Mormon himself had inscribed on plates of gold just before death. Next Smith was enabled by miracle to read the text and authorized to render it into English. Almost of equal importance to himself, to Brigham Young, and to all their successors in Mormon leadership, Smith received continuing instructions from God, instructions which were to shape Mormon policies. One group of these instructions placed the government of the church on a totally authoritarian basis. Joseph Smith identified himself as the "first president" in a council of three presidents. Another set of revelations set Mormon rules about marriage. During the 1830s God approved the plural marriages Joseph Smith had already made; in 1843 He sanctified plural marriage for any male approved by the church. (Strictly defined, Mormon "polygamy" should be called "polygyny," for extra partners were not allowed to females.) Thus Smith received and Young inherited two unique provisions of privilege: namely, one-man supremacy in the Mormon hierarchy and movement and as many women as they cared to marry. Over the years Young took 27 wives, 24 of them as a polygamist. He sired 54 children.

When his time came, Brigham Young proved no man to hold back. Within a year after becoming first president, he began his great act of moving his people far to the west, where they would be quite independent and he would be practically sovereign.

About six years were required to make the enormous transition. Before Joseph Smith was assassinated in 1844, the Mormons had been settled for several years in Nauvoo, Illinois, where they built a prospering community. Even so, as the violence of that year demonstrated, they had not achieved security; they had not outlived their previous condition as a rejected tribe. But Smith and Young had made one special provision of strength: a system for bringing converts from Europe. It quite reversed the usual way of American missionaries. Where the old churches, generally speaking, were based in the east and looked to the west for converts (in Oregon, in China) the Mormon movement looked east to the working classes in Europe—at first to the United kingdom, then to the northern, later to the central and southern parts of the continent. In today's language, the Mormons as an American counter-culture sought recruits in Europe's subculture. With polygamy they appealed to women. To be sure, a missionary's plea must often have seemed startling to women; namely, that they join a new church with some likelihood of sharing a new husband in the bargain. The message bore comforts nevertheless. The church provided immediate aid for making the transatlantic and transcontinental journey; marriage, whether single or plural, was guaranteed and was sure to be sanctified. Above all, in the mind of the convert, the church signified life among saints on this Earth.

With female reinforcement coming in large numbers and male immigration not short, Brigham Young's situation invites comparison in the American history of immigration with that of Governor John Winthrop, two centuries earlier. Like Winthrop in the role of principal manager of settlement in New England, Young could not escape separatism; schismatic groups of Mormons broke away. Neither did he avoid Indian fighting and killing. But like the great migration of the Puritans during the 1630s, that of the Mormons in the 1840s belongs to the history of heroism. Its size and success separated the Mormons forever from the insecurities of Joseph Smith's years. The Mormons did not worry unduly about their isolation in what was Mexican territory until 1848.

At this point the designation "theocracy"—which means government by God and implies a ruling high priest or other deputy for Him, is no longer to be avoided. Notwithstanding that the treaty of peace with Mexico in 1848 so redrew boundaries that Utah became a part of the United States, Brigham Young retained an ample supply of power. As if to confirm this fact, President Taylor appointed First-president Young to be the first governor of the territory that was created by act of Congress in 1850. If in theory such authority was incompatible with theocracy—there being no claim of divinity in the presidency of the United States—it neatly filled out on the secular side Brigham Young's consolidation of strengths. Certainly, in the most honored theocracy in American history, the Massachusetts Bay Colony, Governor Winthrop had had many advantages besides theory; but never had that church-and-state combination been as total and solid as this Mormon one.

On the church side, the church-state of Deseret (as the Mormons called it for years) developed as population growth demanded and as Brigham Young directed. As naturally as the now world-famous Temple and Tabernacle rose in stone and wood in the center of Salt Lake City and as small houses of worship were built in every farming settlement, so was the church hierarchy constructed, downward and outward from the first apostle to the people. From the presidency of 3 and the apostolate of 12 at center, church lines of command and invigoration reached the "wards," as the congregations under their "bishops" were known. Two religious brotherhoods, called Aaronic and Melchizedek, introduced some of the secrecy and comradeship that Masonry gave to eastern Protestants and reinforced the whole Mormon system.

On the governmental side of the theocracy, economic problems made early and urgent demands. The first need, posed by the unaccustomed climate, was water for very dry land. As to irrigation, Young and his colleagues can hardly have had any previous knowledge except from their Bibles. So his starting operation, which was laying out eight thousand acres of flatland in rectangular five- to ten-acre plots and directing the whole manpower of the community to dig intersecting canals, seems wonderfully imaginative and right. So also does his scheme of administration. He had plots distributed by lottery. Residential lots, with irrigation, were distributed in the city; and later on, as population growth required, the system was extended. Lotholders were sometimes required to plant fruit trees or shade trees or both. Today the regularity and beauty of Salt Lake City, a man-made oasis in a mountain-and-desert location, owes much to these beginnings.

The Mormons carried their ways of planning into their underlying institutions. All lands were assigned in usufruct, not in fee: that is, farmers and householders were given the role of steward rather than owner. Likewise the yield of grain was placed under a system of tithing. This meant that the product of a farmer's toil went 90 percent to him and ten percent to the community. By way of the church's tithing office, which was very close to President Young's own residence, the Mormons thus built up a durable food supply, insurance against lean years. Memory of the system would come to a second life during the 1930s in the New Deal's plan for an ever-normal granary.

Perhaps Brigham Young's three practices of theocratic management of the economy—landholding in usufruct, farming by irrigation, and tithing —did not strike him and his colleagues as being particularly connected in moral logic to polygamy. But the connection is evident in Utah's early history: for as a matter of course within the church "celestial marriage" was arranged early rather than late, often between teen-agers. And, as the female converts arrived, probably about 20 percent of the males took more than one wife. Few other Mormons matched President Young's total of 27, but others well up the hierarchical ladder counted wives in two digits. Concerning all this, it would be hard to certify that the harem-situation stories, which often appeared in American journals against the Mormons, contained no pebbles of truth. But the closer accounts indicate Mormon marriage to have been characterized by discipline, labor, child-bearing, and harshness rather than ease. Quite as plots of land were distributed in a way to encourage high productivity, so also were women converts placed on arrival. Conceivably, other arrangements could have been tried, say, religious sisterhoods living in convents. But for durable marriages and the birth and raising of legitimate children in that time and place, the moral common sense of Mormon polygamy is hard to doubt.

Far distant as Brigham Young's Utah was removed from its New England origins, the Mormon theocracy proceeded, almost Puritan style, with education. Again as in the 1630s, a "university," secondary schools, and primary schools were provided early.

In Utah, as in states of colonial origin, compromises were made in time between the interest of the church and the interest of the state. Radical economic policies and polygamy were abandoned. Thus, when normal American statehood finally arrived, half a century after the Mormon migration, tax supported, secular government followed as in the east. Church and state, separated by law but not fully divorced in practice, managed to mix, even to blend, their efforts.

In final hindsight, Brigham Young continues to look somewhat like the tribal leader, a kind of Moses of the 19th century. He and his people crossed the country, part of a huge and enveloping migration of peoples. But uniquely in America they stayed loyal to their inspiration and kept their community identity. To be sure, their women lost out in personal and economic freedom; but, just possibly they were more often fulfilled. Certainly the Mormons built a city of beauty, an unusual thing in that age. As to the common culture, they pulled themselves high by their bootstraps with their schools—and with music, dance, and theater, which departed from old Puritan ways.

Measured beside the other principals of this chapter, Lyman Beecher and Henry Thoreau, Brigham Young succeeded far beyond their success as immediate changer of the moral order in which he and his people lived.

*   *   *

Where Lyman Beecher and Brigham Young spoke from pulpits, Henry David Thoreau (1817–1862) won an audience much more slowly through writings supremely well done. In his lifetime, outside his home circle at Concord he reached very few people. But today, over a century later, his ideas and his identity have carried around the world.

We know the proximity of Thoreau to Emerson as Transcendentalism's number-two man in the 1840s. In the Concord circle, he was, in fact, the only native of that village. His studying at Harvard, his longest period ever away from home, gave him the very best preparation, under William Tyrrel Channing, for a literary life. Immediately after graduation in 1837 he taught school for a time, and he soon made the trip from which, ten years later, he drew his first book, *A Week on the Concord and Merrimack Rivers*. Having become close friends with Emerson, he lived in his home starting in 1841. Two years later, when he began his second longest residence away from Concord, he went as tutor to the household of Emerson's brother William on Staten Island in New York.

Though in college Thoreau ventured some teen-age defiance of discipline, he became no radical, nor did he mark up a high record as student. But he did become known as the most widely read member of his class; likewise, a decade later, he was probably the best-read member of the Concord group if one does not count Theodore Parker. After Harvard, German and Greek (taught to him by the mystical poet Jones Very) were always available. And when one examines the Oriental interests of the Transcendentalists in the Neoplatonism of the Middle East or in the Bhagavad-Gita and other wisdom literature of India, there is Henry Thoreau with his quotations in order. About his mind opening wide to his great neighbor Emerson, the only questions are those of detail. It would be pleasant to know, for instance, whether Thoreau sat in the audience when Emerson, in his first Harvard address, "The American Scholar," admonished the students against bookishness and in favor of intellectual "action." Altogether certain is Thoreau's lifelong, admiring, and loving attitude toward the number-one Transcendentalist. During the years that surrounded Thoreau's graduation from college, Emerson brought out Transcendentalism's philosophical charter, *Nature*, and, besides "The American Scholar," he gave the equally famous Harvard address wherein he advised divinity-school students and professors against the ministry as a career. That independence-declaring, nature-loving, now fully self-reliant Emerson gave Thoreau his model, philosopher, and friend.

Literary work began for Thoreau with contributions to the *Dial*, the journal edited first by Margaret Fuller and then by Emerson. In company with such older, distinguished people as Bronson Alcott and Theodore Parker, and with Emerson and Miss Fuller themselves, he contributed both poetry and prose.

His essay on "Friendship" was one piece. When Emerson assumed the editorship, Thoreau assisted at that work. Yet for all his elevated connections and opportunities during the first eight years out of Harvard, this postgraduate period has for Thoreau the look of a young man at loose ends. Those months of tutoring in New York did uncommonly widen his vistas. There he became acquainted with reformers: with Horace Greeley, when the New York *Tribune* was two years old; with Lucretia Mott, five years before the women's rights convention at Seneca Falls; and with Henry James, Sr., then studying Swedenborg. But only after returning to Concord would Thoreau take the step that would carry him directly to self-realization.

On July 4, 1845, just a few days short of his 28th birthday, Thoreau withdrew from society. Physically he moved only a very short distance, from the center of Concord village to the edge of Walden Pond. But spiritually he reached solitude. He was ready to take whatever time might seem right under wilderness conditions—26 months later he decided to return.

Of course his principal work, *Walden*, published nine years from this time, was the appropriate product of the period of observing and thinking. But the direction of his ruminations appears also in earlier, lesser writings. One of those writings, which to millions has seemed not a lesser writing at all, *Civil Disobedience*, flowed directly from his reaction to the outbreak of war with Mexico. As Thoreau tells the story, on a beautiful summer-day walk through Concord on a berry-picking expedition, he ran into a friend, the town constable, Sam Staples. The officer interrupted him with a reminder that his poll tax was long overdue: "Henry, if you don't pay I'll have to lock you up pretty soon." To which Thoreau replied, "As well now as any time, Sam." Perhaps he was angry, as another report says; but, according to *Civil Disobedience*, he was philosophical while in jail, as surely he ought to have been. For by intention he had been withholding payment since 1843. In that year Bronson Alcott, his friend and the schoolmaster and philosopher of child-nature, had refused the tax and had been jailed. The Massachusetts measure had posed the issue of principle. But in 1846 the Mexican War had changed the frame of reference. It aroused Thoreau, as it did many others who had doubts about slavery or about war as an institution.

Already leaders of the antislavery movement were advocating tax refusal. Abolitionists feared that the coming acquisition of Mexico's northerly and westerly domains would lead to transplanting slavery there. Tax refusal seemed to them, as it has to 20th-century radicals, to offer a way of resistance. But how could refusing to pay a tax locally, one enacted by State lawmakers and executed by Concord authorities, restrain conquests by forces that were authorized, paid, and directed from Washington? Thoreau's own words give us his reasoning. "I quarrel not with far-off foes, but with those who, near at home, cooperate with, and do the bidding of, those far away, and without whom the latter would be harmless. . . . I do not hesitate to say, that those who call themselves Abolitionists should at once effectually withdraw their support, both in person and in property, from the government of Massachusetts. . . . Any man more right than his neighbors constitutes a majority of one already. . . . Under a government which imprisons any man unjustly, the true place for a just man is also a prison. The proper place today, the only place which Massachusetts has provided for her freer and less desponding spirits, is in her prisons. . . . I was not born to be forced. . . . I quietly declare war with the State."

These passages go far to justify the claim that has been made by modern anarchists, that Henry Thoreau qualifies philosophically as an anarchist. Yet *Civil Disobedience* contains a countervailing conviction as well, the almost universal confidence in the nation that men of Harvard and men of Concord especially loved to assert. Again Thoreau's own words are not to be improved upon. As for the state and local government that surrounded him: "I have never declined paying the highway tax, because I am as desirous of being a good neighbor as of being a bad subject; and as for supporting schools, I am doing my best to educate my countrymen now." Directly to the point of the federal system, he acknowledged that the "Constitution, with all its faults, is very good; the law and the courts are very respectable; and even this State and this American government are, in many respects, very admirable, and rare things, to be thankful for." Thoreau's final word gives off an almost millennialist gleam: "I please myself with imagining a State at last which can afford to be just to all men, and to treat the individual with respect as a neighbor. . . . A State which bore this kind of fruit, and suffered it to drop off as fast as it ripened, would prepare the way for a still more perfect and glorious State, which also I have imagined, but not yet anywhere seen." In this mode appears the Thoreau who wanted to be a reformer, or a "re-former" as Emerson himself proposed.

Thoreau had courted imprisonment. He won publicity from it; but it falls short of an heroic event. His aunt paid the tax at once. He was released after just one night. Thus he resumed the life he had chosen, to be, in Emerson's phrase, "a bachellor of Thought and Nature." Certainly it is easy to think of his two years at Walden as experimental work leading to a degree. It is yet easier to think of *Walden* as a thesis, to record his findings; the famous first chapter, "Economy," particularly qualifies as a summary of backgrounds and procedures. Thoreau had said when he was 20 that Mosaic law is wrong about the work-week. "The seventh should be man's day of toil, wherein to earn his living; the other six the Sabbath of the affections and the soul—in which to range this garden and think." Not only did the traditional work ethic offend him, but also, much more, the new industrial spirit. In a book review, before *Walden*, he levelled his charge. The book before us, he said, "aims to secure the greatest degree of comfort and pleasure merely. . . . There is far too much hurry and bustle, and too little patience and privacy, in all our methods." Not different in logic from white contemporaries in the South, who reasoned that slavery provided a better system of labor than hirelings working with machines, Thoreau offered an anti-industrial way of living.

He was very exact about it. In that opening chapter on "Economy," he published his personal records. On the debit side, for examples: $28.12½ for building materials for his cabin; $8.74 for store provisions to last eight months. On the credit side: $36.78, from the sale of vegetables he had raised but not consumed and from payment for doing neighbors' odd jobs. And so on. In the end he found himself $25.21¾ out of pocket, which he balanced against 26 months of leisure, comfort, and health. By contrast he had observed surrounding him his "townsmen, whose misfortune it is to have inherited farms, houses, barns, and plowing tools. . . . Who made them serfs of the soil? . . . The mass of men lead lives of quiet desperation. . . . There is no play in them, for that comes after work." Many later chapters tell us what "play" meant to Thoreau: they speak, for instance, of life in "The Bean Field," of our "Brute Neighbors," and of "Winter Animals." In *Walden* work and play, observation and meditation, and all else move rhythmically, according to nature's four seasons.

Not for everyone but for men who will venture, the literal meaning of *Walden* seems to be that life can be rich and good. Recently critics have told us how much more and other than an economic solution the book contains. One of them, Charles R. Anderson, insists persuasively that *Walden* is truly a poem and that the ultimate concern of it is human regeneration. Here we see that passages are linked together in feeling, though logically they are as far apart as the opening ones about costs and earnings and the closing ones about sunrise and the life of insects. Thoreau managed beautifully the emotional distance between the everyday comity that man can establish with nature and nature's evidences of "resurrection and immortality." *Walden* marks him as America's best spokesman, so far, for living in love of nature.

*   *   *

Thoreau's phrase, "circumventing the state," voices a prime intention of his, a necessity, he was sure, for a moral man and for a moral society. The phrase applies, though differently, to Brigham Young. In the Utah utopia, he and his people escaped the authority of the United States for years. Beecher, a man of the religious establishment, of course was no circumventer. And yet, in today's retrospect his commitment to the church as the instrument of improving both humanity and society makes clear how different he was from most Americans now. It shows some cousinship of the spirit, a quarreling cousinship, with the other two. For all three, morality for mankind and morality for society were not disjoined but were joined —New Haven style, Salt Lake City style, or Concord style—in Christian faith.

In the 1960s and 1970s, as American fondness for strong government waned, and as among the young moral idealism waxed and moved toward the left, Henry Thoreau seemed more than ever special and the most prophetic of the three. Since the later 19th century he has been a household name to outdoorsmen, to conservationists in general, and especially so to wilderness lovers. With the passage of time he has become a hero to pacifists. To Martin Luther King and his followers, *Civil Disobedience* stated the best method of social protest. During the 1940s his moral outreach—by way of Mohandas K. Gandhi, into India's independence movement—carried the farthest ever, to a land very non-American and halfway around the world.

If one chooses to believe that moral ideals do in fact have long life in society, not apart from but in enhancement of their life in the hearts and minds of individuals, the ideas of Henry Thoreau offer supreme encouragement.

10

Patterns and Mentors: American Women before the Civil War

LUCRETIA MOTT
MARGARET FULLER
HARRIET BEECHER STOWE

by Barbara Welter
Hunter College, C.U.N.Y.

"True Womanhood" was firmly defined and enshrined between the American Revolution and the Civil War. During the same period women insisted on reforms in the family, the church and the state which affected their role and status. These early reformers did not challenge the definition of True Womanhood; still less did they contradict it. They offered instead a series of amendments that would demonstrate the strength, the power for good, and the resourcefulness of the American woman. Only a small handfull of women during the ante-bellum period emerged, either in person or through their writing, as mentors and models in their own right. They provide examples of the way in which True Womanhood co-existed with reform.

The lives of three American women furnish examples of the True Woman as reformer, innovator, and conservator. One of the intellectual pastimes of the 19th century was the codification of vast masses of phenomena into manageable categories. The French educator, François Delsarte, in this way classified all human expression into three spheres: the gestures of Soul, Mind, and Life. Accordingly, Lucretia Mott serves here as the Soul, Margaret Fuller as the Mind, and Harriet Beecher Stowe as the Life. All three played a role as mentor to the women of the period, and yet each adhered scrupulously to many of the firmly established patterns of womanhood.

*   *   *

Lucretia Coffin was born in Nantucket in 1793, one year after publication of Mary Wollstonecraft's *Vindication of the Rights of Woman*, which she would later call her "pet book." The Quaker community on the island, with which Lucretia's family had been associated since its founding, was hospitable to the ideas of equality and justice among classes, races, and sexes. The absence of Nantucket's men on long whaling voyages meant that women had to assume many traditional male functions. The Quakers granted women the right to be recorded as ministers and to receive the Spirit of light and inspiration. Although it is thus possible to find in Nantucket the geographical and spiritual origin of many reformers, it is hard to know why Lucretia went even beyond this liberal tradition in her later life. She herself thought the question irrelevant. "I grew up so thoroughly imbued with women's rights," she said, "that it was the most important question of my life from a very early age."

When she was 13 the family moved to Boston and two years later Lucretia enrolled in the Quaker-administered Nine Partner's School, near Poughkeepsie, New York. She became an assistant teacher at 17 and had occasion to note personally one blatant form of discrimination: women teachers were paid substantially less than men who performed the same tasks. Later she would see this incident as one which encouraged her to claim for her sex "all that an impartial Creator had bestowed upon it," but which benighted man had capriciously removed.

In 1809 the Coffins moved once more to Philadelphia, and James Mott, who had assisted at the Friends' School in Poughkeepsie, was hired to work in Thomas Coffin's hardware store. Two years later James and Lucretia were married. Between 1812 and 1817 they had six children, one of whom, her first-born son, died in infancy. The child's last words, "I love thee, Mother," were always remembered by her with tears, and throughout the rest of her otherwise happy life she mourned him. Many years later she wrote, "Dear little soul! How sorry I am that I did not oftener lay aside my sewing, and take him and love him." Although many women had similar losses, the tragedy was never a commonplace of 19th-century life, and, in the case of Lucretia Mott, it served both as a reminder of the brevity of life and the need for compassion for those with similar sorrows.

After three years of preparation, Lucretia Coffin Mott was officially recorded as a minister in the Society of Friends. Almost from the beginning, she attracted notice by her intensity and directness. She rarely used notes, and her listeners were convinced that her words were direct responses to the prompting of the Spirit. Quaker practice is significant. It meant that Lucretia Mott came from a tradition which allowed women to speak out in public. She was thus spared the problem of other female reformers who were accused of "unsexing" themselves when they ascended a lecture platform. Perhaps of all the hurdles which faced the emerging woman's movement, the proscription against speaking in a public place was the most important psychologically; Lucretia's growing fame as a speaker served to break the barrier and inspire confidence in more conventional women. Typically, she wasted little time on justifications for what *she* did. Instead, she spoke of the duty of those who had convictions to express them without fear of the consequences.

The early years of marriage were filled with business reverses and continual childbirth and childrearing, along with all the domestic chores which they entailed. Painfully conscious of the precarious nature of their finances, Lucretia intermittently taught school in order to earn money. Later she reflected that these lean years and "trials in early life were not without their good effect in disciplining the mind, and leading it to a just estimate of worldly pleasures." Her chosen motto, to which she adhered in each of her concerns and reforms was, "Truth for authority, not authority for truth." Her own poverty, coupled with the tragedy of her child's death, had liberated her from that preoccupation with money-making so typical of 19th-century Philadelphia. From 1825 on she refused to have anything to do with goods manufactured with slave-grown material and, after some years of patient prayer brought her husband to share this conviction, although it meant giving up whatever small profit James Mott had finally been able to make from his textile business. The implacability of Lucretia's will prevailed over his fears. Once she perceived a "manifest duty" there was no stopping her. From 1830 until his retirement in 1852 he would deal only in wool. A granddaughter and biographer wrote of Lucretia's energy and resolution "which in a less disciplined character might have been willfulness." But her grandfather, a much gentler person who was subject to bouts of discouragement and depression, was the perfect foil for all his wife's decisiveness, as good a listener as she was a speaker: "*His* life made *hers* possible."

From 1830 Lucretia Mott considered herself a social, not a doctrinal, member of the Society of Friends. James and Lucretia found themselves on the "Hicksite" side of the 1827 "Great Separation" among American Quakers, although Lucretia felt that "practical righteousness" rather than theological doctrine was the spiritual standard of Quakerism.

As the children grew older Lucretia could travel more frequently "in truth's service." Increasingly her words turned toward slavery. Some Friends, unwilling to cause unnecessary trouble, complained that she "lugged in" the unsavory topic when she could well have avoided it. In reply, Mrs. Mott declared, "If our principles are right, why should we be cowards? Why should we wait for those who never have had the courage to maintain the inalienable rights of the slave?" An anti-abolition mob burned Pennsylvania Hall and then sought her house for its especial vengeance. The Motts displayed great courage by remaining at home to confront the rioters. Fortunately for them, the rioters were distracted before getting there. It was, she wrote, "a searching time. I had often thought how I would sustain myself if called to pass such an ordeal. I hope I speak it not in the spirit of boasting when I tell you, my sisters, I believe that I was strengthened by God. I felt at the moment that I was willing to suffer whatever the cause required."

Lucretia Mott was one of the founders of the Philadelphia Female Anti-Slavery Society in 1833, when the American Anti-Slavery Society (AASS), organized the same year, refused to allow women members. The formation of such a separate group was not unprecedented, since most Protestant churches had women's auxiliaries for fund-raising and missionary activities. However, it was a statement of female solidarity, which not all the women abolitionists shared. Lydia Maria Child, for example, opposed all "female" societies, which resembled nothing so much as "half a scissors." The AASS, however, reconsidered and amended its charter in 1840, in time to send Lucretia Mott as a national delegate to the World's Anti-Slavery Conference in London.

Elizabeth Cady Stanton also went to this Conference, having been appointed a local delegate. The American women were denied seats and were relegated "behind the bar." In the ensuing debate and frenetic caucusing which went on between the American and the more conservative Foreign Anti-Slavery Society, Mrs. Stanton had the opportunity to observe Lucretia Mott in action. Removed from official participation though she was, Mrs. Mott emerged as the most powerful figure of the group. Indeed Mrs. Stanton, then an awed and excited young woman, saw in her mentor what she had hoped for but never believed she would find. The very contrast between the slight figure in the sober grey dress—the hands patiently clasped or busy knitting—and the sincerity, strength, and unconventionality of her speeches, captured the imagination of many delegates. Mrs. Stanton wrote, "Mrs. Mott was to me an entirely new revelation of womanhood. I sought every opportunity to be at her side, and continually plied her with questions, and I shall never cease to be grateful for the patience and seeming pleasure, with which she fed my hungering soul."

Throughout the woman's movement one reads of this moment of recognition, when some young woman becomes aware that the ideas and aspirations which had been regarded by her family and even herself as delusions or sinful temptations, were in fact shared by other women. Recurrently, in the memoirs of the second and third generation of those women who would devote themselves to removing the disabilities and restrictions placed on their sex, we read of the critical importance of this first meeting. It confirmed that they were not alone and they were not mad. From this meeting between Elizabeth Cady Stanton and Lucretia Mott came the Seneca Falls Convention of 1848, when woman's "Social, civil, and religious condition and rights" would for the first time be debated in public in the United States.

And yet Lucretia Mott fulfilled every popular conception of the truly domestic woman. Even those who were most suspicious of her ideas gave her full credit for being an admirable housewife and a devoted wife and mother. The secret of her ability to combine a private and public life, she herself felt, came from a rationalization of tasks into the essential and the nonessential. "Being fond of reading, I omitted much unneccessary stitching and ornamental work in the sewing for my family, so that I might have more time for this indulgence, and for the improvement of my mind." Every minute was used, and time was as frugally dispensed as any other commodity in her economical housewifery. Before each meeting she attended, she did the day's cooking, cleaning, and organization; and she often worked on the mending while waiting her turn to speak. She believed that only by scrupulously fulfilling her allotted tasks could woman be regarded seriously when she chose to go beyond them. To the present-day feminist, this concept may seem unfortunate; but Lucretia probably judged her contemporaries, both men and women, shrewdly. Because she could not be faulted as a wife and mother, she had a better chance of being heard as a reformer. Historical truth is often highly irritating and all too frequently illogical.

But the logic that propelled Mrs. Mott and the other women who organized the Seneca Falls Convention is completely understandable. Having done what they could in their allotted sphere and being sensible and intelligent, they felt that their tasks of imposing order and justice had to extend beyond the home. For Lucretia Mott, removal of restrictions on woman's role was not for the purpose of creating a "new woman," but rather to liberate the "True Woman" from artificial restraints that hampered her ability to perform the duties of her sex most fully and effectively. At the Convention, which took place in the Wesleyan Chapel in July 1848, Mrs. Stanton's wishes prevailed, and suffrage for women was announced as a specific goal. Mrs. Mott had demurred at its inclusion in the list of avowed goals. Most historians attribute this refusal to timidity and to the generation gap between the older and the younger women. While those reasons might have existed, her major objection to the suffrage issue lay in her Quaker heritage and her deep-seated distrust of government itself. One year later she wrote, "Far be it from me to encourage women to vote, or to take an active part in politics in the present state of our government. Her right to the elective franchise, however, is the same, and should be yielded to her, whether she exercises that right or not. Would that man, too, would have no participation in a government recognizing the life-taking principle—retaliation and the sword."

To Lucretia Mott, the vote seemed a mere accident of woman's condition, to be approached only after reforms in the more substantial areas of education, equal pay, and justice in the courts. Her own goal was to train women "to take a dignified place in the world, to be rational companions, to share the responsibility of life." Having a realistic view of human nature, she was often distressed at the triviality and lack of concentration of American women. The woman's movement could not and did not immediately create a race of perfect women. "Thou wilt have hard work to prove the equality of women with men," she wrote to Mrs. Stanton, "Facts are so against such an assumption, in the present stage of woman's development. We need not however admit inferiority even tho we may not be able to prove equality." As one who drew inspiration from Divine guidance, she was remarkably unvisionary in her approach to reform. Always clear-eyed, even about her own deficiencies, she often saw it as a painful but necessary duty to check the rhetoric and enthusiasms of her friends within the movement.

Although Mrs. Mott resisted writing down her ideas, she could occasionally be stung into written protest. In 1849 the critic and author Richard Henry Dana gave a series of inspirational talks on "Shakespeare's Women," in which he spoke hyperbolically of the importance of maintaining woman's role and status in order that she might fulfill her high destiny. Lucretia Mott responded to his glorified picture of women with a "Discourse on Woman," in which she rejected "the kind of homage that has been paid to women, the flattering appeals which have too long satisfied her." Drawing on Biblical evidence that required from women the same behavior as from men, she called for reforms that would make woman what God intended her to be. The removal of the "disabilities and disadvantages, religious, civil and social, which impede her progress," she affirmed, would not "unsex" women, but would rather at last allow her to proceed on the path marked out for her on Sinai. She dealt with critics of her own actions and those of her colleagues by insisting on the right of women to be reformers. "If she is to be satisfied with the narrow sphere assigned her by man, nor aspire to a higher, lest she should transcend the bounds of female delicacy, truly it is a mournful prospect for woman. We would admit all the differences that our great and beneficent Creator has made, in the relation of man and woman, nor would we seek to disturb this relation; but we deny that the present position of woman is her true sphere of usefulness." Though disparaging the vote in the present state of government, she was willing to admit that it might be worth more if women also exercised it: "Who knows, but that if woman acted her part in governmental affairs, there might be an entire change in the turmoil of political life?" Above all, she reserved her scorn for those women who hung back from the call to action, although she mingled it with pity for beings "enervated, their minds to some extent paralyzed; and like those still more degraded by personal bondage, she hugs her chains." For Lucretia Mott, the bondage of the slave and the bondage of women were equally wrong, perversions of the teachings of Jesus. It had been given to her to see these errors and it was her duty to make others see them too.

From the time of her husband's retirement until his death in 1868 Lucretia maintained her interest in reform. James wrote ruefully to a friend, "Lucretia has numerous calls almost daily from all sorts of folks, high and low, rich and poor, for respect, advice, assistance, etc. etc. I am sometimes amused to hear the object of some of the calls; it seems as though some people thought she could do any and every thing." She particularly protested those laws that prevented a woman from inheriting property after her husband's death, in favor of her children, who then assumed the "pious duty of 'keeping' Mother." To such a son, who had complained of his obligation, she wrote, "Did not her industry and frugality in her department entitle her to an equal ownership with her husband in homestead and farm? Should it not be said that she allows thee to live here with her?" She maintained a sharp eye for those innocuous-seeming conventions which she saw as symptoms of concealed injustice. Her voice could be heard in an audible whisper at the end of every wedding service she attended, "I pronounce you to be husband and wife," instead of "man and wife," a phrase suggesting that marriage entailed special responsibilities for women that men need not assume.

Until her death in 1880 Lucretia Mott was a prominent member of the reform hierarchy and provided vigorous counsel when her opinion was asked. She gloried in being called "the most Belligerent Non-Resistant." "I have no idea," she responded, "because I am a Non-Resistant, of submitting tamely to injustice inflicted either on me or on the slave . . . I am no advocate of passivity." Shortly before her death, when an editorial praising her role in reform movements was read to her, she commented tartly about the danger of "premature obituaries," and then added, "I'm a very much over-rated woman—it is humiliating." This praise continued after her death, when she became a prototype of the first generation of women to devote their lives to sisterhood. Although an early biography hailed her as "the Greatest American Woman," her role now is overshadowed by the more active and secular careers of Elizabeth Cady Stanton and Susan B. Anthony. Yet Lucretia was unquestionably important because she came so early to reform and because she served as a model for others to follow. Her standards were high; her thinking clear on all the major issues; and her convictions—about the right of women to preach and to be educated and the right of the slave to have freedom—were strong and tenacious. These were wedded to a mild contempt for those women who didn't lay their own carpets.

*   *   *

Many of those contemporaries who remembered Margaret Fuller after her short and dramatic career had ended, recalled the "Queen of Cambridge" with awe and admiration. For though she lived to be only 40, she was an extraordinarily vital and enduring presence in ante-bellum America. She managed, at one time or another, to alienate almost everyone—her family, her friend Emerson, the proper ladies, and the organized reformers. Her book on *Woman in the Nineteenth Century* was a catalyst for the early feminists, and she was often quoted even by those who disapproved of her. Although part of no formal movement, she shared the convictions of many reformers. Her primary interest was in her own intellectual and emotional development and in that of womanhood as a whole. The most individualistic and iconoclastic of women, she felt an almost mystical bond of sisterhood with all the members of her sex and a deep respect for the conventions of True Womanhood.

Sarah Margaret Fuller, the oldest child of Timothy and Margaret Fuller, was born in Cambridge in 1810. Timothy Fuller was a man for whom great things had been predicted, but his life became a series of disappointments, of which Margaret's birth was one; he wanted a boy. Ignoring any objections and brooking no opposition to his plans, as was his settled manner whether in politics or in his family, Timothy gave his daughter a classical 18th-century education. Although she came to appreciate the value of learning habits of study and a curriculum light-years in advance of any of the "dame schools" or fashionable seminaries for young ladies, she never failed to blame her father for sacrificing her health and "natural childhood," to his own iron-clad will.

After having passed through an intense "crush" on a young Englishwoman who gave her a window on a world beyond the confines of strict parental upbringing and a Puritan heritage, Margaret received her only formal education outside of her father's library; she was enrolled for two years at the Misses Prescott School in Groton. At boarding school her world narrowed again and the 14-year-old Margaret was scorned as a fat, nearsighted, incomprehensibly arrogant adolescent. In an autobiographical story of her experiences at the Misses Prescott, there is a lurid tale of malicious mischief designed to win affection and approval, followed by a confrontation and by brain fever, and equilibrium regained with the help of a wise female teacher. Although most biographers accept this work as completely factual, there is a strong possibility that Margaret incorporated a typical ruse of autobiographical fiction by inventing a denouement appealing to her and to her readers.

Released from school, she returned to Cambridge to enjoy the company of young Harvard undergraduates, who found her an engaging and precocious conversationalist, a voracious reader with a passion for learning and experience, and an interesting companion on long walks or rides in the countryside. Unfortunately they apparently did not see her as the bluestocking belle who would make a good New England wife. Mrs. Eliza Farrar could understand why. A guest at one of Timothy Fuller's parties in 1826, she watched Margaret appear in a singularly unbecoming pink satin dress. Mrs. Farrar had already established herself as a teacher to young American girls; her etiquette manual was one of the most practical of the pre-Civil War period. She took Margaret in hand, tight pink dress and all, and encouraged her to acquire a social and cultural polish that would enhance her intellectual achievements. But her pupil confided to her diary that she was resigned to being "bright but ugly." Nonetheless, as a young woman, Margaret showed that pragmatic spirit and ingenuity for which Yankees were becoming famous, and made the most of what she had.

The company of James Freeman Clarke, Frederick Henry Hedge, and other Harvard undergraduates resulted in knowledge and in a series of enduring friendships for Margaret. After her father, permanently frustrated in his attempts to secure high elected or appointed political office, moved the family to Groton in 1833, her correspondence with these friends provided one of her only links with Boston intellectual life. During a two-year period the Fuller family suffered from most of the misfortunes the 19th century could produce. Mrs. Fuller retreated further into invalidism, the two older boys left home and wandered from one unsatisfactory venture to another, the youngest child died and another brother seemed destined to be "intractable." Margaret, meanwhile, weary with coaching the other children, who were not always willing pupils, and with helping her father on his political history, fell seriously ill. She was still convalescent when Timothy Fuller died of cholera, and the family faced that most persistent problem of widows and orphans, financial disaster. Thus, Margaret's period of self-education was terminated; she now needed to earn a living.

In fall 1836 Margaret accepted Bronson Alcott's invitation to teach Latin and French in his school and supplemented her income with private language classes for young ladies. The following year she joined the Greene Street School in Providence, won over to exile from Boston by the offer of $1,000 a year, then regarded as an extraordinarily lucrative salary. For two years she devoted herself to the increasingly uncongenial job of teaching. Although interested in the girls she taught, she resented the time given over to paper work and "gabbling" in public, time better spent in some effort more worthy of her ability. Returning to Boston in 1839, she determined to make a living by her pen and to make her mark upon the century.

Margaret by now had accepted the probability of remaining single, although the life of a New England spinster was a dreary one. She longed for a man who could accept her mind, spirit, and body, but she had long since given up on finding one. As she confided in her diary, "With the intellect I always have, always will overcome, but that is not half the work. The life, the life! O my God, shall the life never be sweet?" At the same time, having had the role of vestal virgin thrust upon her, Margaret was quick to exploit its possibilities. Because she need be no one's "half" she could continue her development in search of a "perfect whole and harmony."

Margaret, after 1839 and until leaving for New York in 1844, had a series of public "conversations" on "Woman" with Boston women. Their purpose was "to systematize thought, and give a precision and clearness in which our sex are so deficient"; and in them she stressed the role of woman as guide, critic, and inspiration. Their major importance was in the impact they made upon those who otherwise might not have been aware of the possibilities for change in this era. Margaret found her real voice in these lectures. She moved from personal anecdote and homely detail to vaulting fantasy and, as she moved, drew her listeners with her. The class discussion, which she encouraged, displayed her talent, rare but wonderful in a teacher, for making students confident of their own ability, rather than of hers. This woman, so often condemned as arrogant, drew forth in halting, unaccustomed words the thoughts of the women in her audience. The thrust of her talks, whatever the subject, was the power of the individual to change the self and the world.

The Transcendentalist periodical, the *Dial*, began publication in 1840, and Margaret was its first editor. For five years her friendship with Ralph Waldo Emerson had been an important source of inspiration to her, although she lamented the coldness with which he responded to some of her enthusiasms. She was now an equal of Emerson and of those in his circle. Transcendentalism, after all, theoretically allowed no distinction between the sexes. Each individual was divine; and if Margaret brought ridicule on herself when claiming that no one was more divine than herself, it was nothing more than sound doctrine for this Emersonian circle. Her first publication in the magazine, "A Short Essay on Critics," established her in the role of literary as well as intellectual teacher and commentator. She also contributed to the nationalism of the age by insisting upon an American literature, one worthy of the land and the genius of its people. And if she was sharp-tongued in reviewing some of the nation's novelists, poets, and essayists, it was only because she insisted on nothing but the best for a country so promising. Some of America's writers, having basked in more uncritical praise and popularity, reacted negatively to her judgments, but Margaret determined to record them, even if (or perhaps particularly if) they conflicted with majority opinion.

During the period of her editorship the Brook Farm community was founded in nearby Roxbury and most of her circle gave some acknowledgment to the venture. Though never a member, Margaret often visited and sent the "intractable" Lloyd to school there. She doubted the success of the venture, partly because she knew those involved so well and partly because she was, at that time in her life, committed to the paramount importance of individual, not group effort. Her "conversations" were not particularly well received, but those women who came to see her privately went away much impressed and strengthened in their resolve. In their personal relationships with Margaret, women always found magnetism and support, frequently in the form of money drawn from her small savings or a job coaxed from one of her many acquaintances. Tremendously interested in their problems and the conditions of their lives, she had an empathy and understanding for all, no matter how varied their backgrounds. To each of them she communicated her strong conviction that they could be more and do more than they had dared to hope, and that they should have the courage to fulfill their dreams.

Travelling through the West in 1842 with James Freeman Clarke and his sister, Margaret was typically most impressed by the need for her generation of women to match the grandeur of this new land. The "ladies" of Chicago and Milwaukee repelled her; they had the worst of both worlds: the artificiality and foolishness of women in the East, without their education and culture. Clearly it was time for someone to point out the problems and possibilities for women in 19th-century America. Part of Margaret's contribution appeared in "The Great Lawsuit. Man *versus* Men. Woman *versus* Women," published in *The Dial* in 1843. *Summer on the Great Lakes,* her book on her Western travel appeared a year later; and then, in 1845, as an expansion of her *Dial* piece, came *Woman in the Nineteenth Century,* the book that would make her famous and, in some quarters, notorious.

Like Lucretia Mott, Margaret was more concerned with the nature of women than with any specific right of her sex. She hoped her progressive century would provide the opportunity for woman "as a nature to grow, as an intellect to discern, as a soul to live freely and unimpeded, to enfold such powers as were given to her when we left our common home." The argument that women reformers have neglected their roles as mothers, daughters, and wives to fling themselves into public controversy was an early consideration. Regrettably, she admitted, some women were like that, and some men as well. But progress need not, and should not, be accompanied by neglected duties. Women of achievement constituted "some of the most devoted mothers the world has ever known, whose homes were the abode of every domestic virtue." Thus she demonstrated how women artists, astronomers, and writers put down their work at the call of female duty, and took it up again only when the last domestic chores had been completed. She herself had certainly been a dutiful daughter. She had done all that the oldest girl of the family was required to do by the social norms of her day: took care of the younger children, tutored them, helped with the sewing, found jobs for her brothers and, when financial emergency required it, supported the family through her earnings. When asked once for a definition of Transcendentalism she replied briskly, "For myself I should say that if it is meant that I have an active mind, frequently busy with large topics I hope it is so—If it is meant that I am honored by the friendship of such men as Mr. Emerson, Mr. Ripley, or Mr. Alcott, I hope it is so—But if it is meant that I cherish any opinions which interfere with domestic duties, cheerful courage and judgment in the practical affairs of life, I challenge any or all in the little world which knows me to prove any such deficiency from any acts of mine since I came to woman's estate."

Women could only prove their worth when they were "free, . . . fully to develop the strength and beauty of Woman"; and then "they would never wish to be men, or man-like." They must have legal protection, in order to make the search for self-reliance possible. And in that search they must, once and for all, avoid the help of men. Such a search does not imply single status, Margaret concluded, and she discussed the types of marriage possible under the "new relationships" for women. She proposed an idealized "religious marriage" in which two persons made a "pilgrimage toward a common shrine."

When woman changed herself, her education, her means of earning a living, her marriage and relationship to men, she would also change society. These changes in the role and status of women were bound to occur; they were "the destiny of the land, the inexorable epic law." In the meantime women must not ask but demand their rights. They must speak out—against slavery, for example, or against the war in Texas—and tell men they had gone wrong. In the end, changes would occur because of "the law of right, the law of growth, that speaks in us, and demands the perfection of each being in its kind—apple as apple, Woman as Woman." Such passages disclose Margaret to be a true daughter of her century, sharing its belief in progress and perfection.

Because *Women in the Nineteenth Century* dealt with topics such as virginity and prostitution, which Margaret ought, first, to have known nothing about and, second, to have said nothing about, it was regarded as scandalous and shrill. One response to publication appealed to Margaret. It was an offer to write articles for Horace Greeley's *Tribune* in New York. That city symbolized diversity, dirt, and sin in the public mind, and in choosing to leave the rarefied New England air, she was, at last, taking a step into that wider world which, except in her reading, had been denied her.

Margaret lived with the Greeleys, was exposed to the cultivated eccentricities of that often embattled couple, enjoyed the charms of their children, and worked very hard at exploring the city in order to write about its social, political, and literary life. She annoyed Greeley by her headaches, her tea drinking, her vagueness about deadlines and, most of all, her insistence on gentlemanly courtesies. She had an intense friendship with a young German Jew, James Nathan, but retreated in panic and maidenly modesty when his advances showed a "lower nature" manifesting itself. In 1846 she was offered the chance to travel in Europe with Marcus and Rebecca Spring and to be the *Tribune's* foreign correspondent. Although fearing it was "too late" she borrowed money from an old friend, and left for England.

In England and France she was received warmly as an American author and Emerson's friend. She enjoyed Carlyle though, like many others, preferred his wife, and she found George Sand an admirable person who "bravely acted out her nature." Margaret also made a friend of the Polish revolutionary poet Adam Mickiewicz, who responded to her with the warmth and intimacy that she had sought so often in men and had so often been denied. He understood both her mind and her body. His advice to her, as she continued her journey to Italy, was direct and vigorous. "I tried to make you understand that you should not confine your life to books and reveries. You have pleaded the liberty of woman in a masculine and frank style. Live and act, as you write."

In April 1847, after travelling in the South of Italy, Margaret arrived in Rome. Visiting St. Peter's for vespers, she lost her companions as they explored the vast basilica, and was rescued from her confusion by a young Italian with a polite offer to see her home. Giovanni Angelo Ossoli was a nobleman whose republican sympathies appealed to Margaret and brought her to that sense of fulfillment that had earlier seemed so hopeless. The American spinster awakened to her true nature in sunny Italy has long been a staple of popular fiction. Now it became a reality. Margaret continued her travels to Venice and Switzerland but, upon returning to Rome she and Ossoli met again and became lovers. Soon she was pregnant. Again, a story familiar to generations of gentle readers, with its predictably unhappy ending. Madness or death were the only literary conventions appropriate to the fall of woman.

Some time after their child was born in September 1848, probably within the year, Margaret and Ossoli were married. But the engrossing personal drama was subsumed in the larger drama of the Italian Revolution and in the cause of the Republic. Margaret at last found that "high object" she had once recommended. It was the sort of cause needed to overcome female preoccupation with trivialities. Margaret worked very hard as nurse and as correspondent during the siege of Rome. She wanted her readers to know what the Republic stood for and to shame them into making a similar stand against slavery, an evil even more oppressive than papal authority and more offensive to morality. "My country is at present spoiled by prosperity, stupid with the lust of gain, soiled by crime in its willing perpetuation of slavery, shamed by an unjust war, noble sentiment much forgotten even by individuals, the aims of politicians selfish or petty, the literature frivolous and venal." For the first time in her life she felt completely alive. At long last, she was convinced, she had found her true destiny. But the Republican cause failed, and the moment of exaltation was over.

Margaret and Ossoli had left their son with a nursemaid in the country and, returning to get him, found the boy near death from neglect. After he had recovered, the little family went to Florence as political refugees. This last period of Margaret's life was in many ways her happiest. Each day with her baby seemed a new miracle. "What a difference it makes to come home to a child!" she exclaimed, "how it fills up all the gaps of life, just in the way that is most consoling, most refreshing! Formerly, I used to feel sad at that hour; the day had not been nobly spent, I had not done my duty to myself and others, and I felt so lonely! Now I never feel lonely." Ossoli, too, made her life easier by his gentle, watchful care, protecting her time and energy, and diffusing "such a power and sweetness over every day" that she could not bear to plan for the future. However, she spent time on her major project, a book showing that the Republic was eventually going to triumph in Italy as part of the "epic destiny" of progress that marked the century. The idyllic interlude balancing love and work was exactly what she had longed for, what she had been convinced the fates and her own "difficult" nature would forever deny her.

Meanwhile, her political consciousness was being raised. She now perceived herself as a "radical" and as a convinced "Socialist." The problems of women were susceptible to the same solutions as the problems of countries; a communal kitchen, for instance, was a revolutionary benefit she could heartily endorse. For the first time she saw Christmas being celebrated, that "papist" festival New Englanders ignored, and was touched by the joy and hope it offered.

By spring the pleasure of Christmas had faded and financial necessity dictated that Margaret return home, where she could earn a living and consult with friends about the best way to use her skills. Emerson, far from being absorbed in the Over-Soul was, as Margaret well knew, practical and quite successful, and would have some good ideas. From the moment they decided to leave Italy, Margaret was pursued by evil omens. Ossoli had been told long ago to "beware of death on the sea," and she herself remembered terrors of storms and seasickness.

The voyage began on May 17, 1850 and ended in a wreck off New York's Fire Island on July 19. Margaret, Ossoli and their little boy all perished together. Her death spurred her friends into action; they collected her papers for the publication of her *Memoirs*, an obligatory tribute on the part of the Victorians, but in Margaret's case particularly valuable. They were trying to rehabilitate her memory, to suggest that her last years had indeed been her best and happiest, and that she had died a True Woman. In fact, by her own standards and definition, she had always been true to womanhood, and never more so than when she was most criticized. Her death created an intellectual heroine, whose ideas were dramatized by her life. But as Emerson wrote, though it might have been inevitable, the country needed her living presence perhaps even more than her myth and writings.

*   *   *

Harriet Beecher Stowe was born in Litchfield, Connecticut in 1811, only a year after Margaret Fuller, whom she would outlive by almost a half century. Her father was the eminent preacher, Lyman Beecher, and her mother, Roxana Foote, the first of Lyman's three wives. Roxana died when Harriet, the seventh of their nine children, was four. She was idealized by her widower and prayed to, as a "saint in heaven," by her children. Motherhood, its enduring strength and desperate love, is a major theme of all of Harriet's writing. Her life was rich in incidents that only membership in a large, eccentric family can provide. In its vicissitudes and its triumphs, she was aware of the definition of womanhood and never shirked those duties that properly belonged to women. Her books provided similar fictional patterns of American girls and American mothers all conforming to the pattern of True Womanhood as Harriet had come to know it through her life.

Harriet's childhood was remembered as a happy one, in spite of adjustment to a new stepmother who had trusted to Divine Love as the best deterrent to naughtiness. Her somewhat bossy older sister Catharine was reliable and interested in everything she did, and her younger brother Henry was a constant companion for games and walks. Above all, there was Lyman Beecher, who kept things in constant motion. At dinner he would argue passionately on the "wrong" side so that his children would develop debating skills on the "right" side. There were days when he never got out of bed, prostrate with some terminal illness of his own imagination, and spoke to his children only to bid them tearful farewells. The next day he would be on his feet, ready to shoot rabbits, make cider applesauce, or do the Lord's work.

School, even at Miss Sarah Pierce's Litchfield Academy, was never as interesting as home. At 13 Harriet was sent to Hartford, where Catharine had already established a Female Seminary. She was a fitful student, her Latin studies interrupted by those protracted reveries which she had all her life, and which never failed to madden her family. Reading Sir Walter Scott, the only novelist Lyman allowed his children, was a source of pleasure to her and, like most of her generation, she adored the romantic poetry of Byron. Her first verse drama was written into her school notebook, but Catharine discovered it, and the remaining pages were devoted to notes on Butler's *Analogy of Religion*. Catharine's life, rather romantically, had been blighted when her fiancé, a brilliant young professor of mathematics, drowned. But his journal revealed the most blighting thing of all; he was a doubter and, unless there had been an "instant" conversion at his death (which Lyman personally distrusted), he was, then, damned.

Harriet rejected this harsh interpretation of Christianity in her own conversion, which was a response to her father's sermon text: "Come, then, and trust your soul to this faithful friend." Consciousness of her sins, followed by a conviction of Christ's love, prompted her to respond, "I will."

As a dutiful daughter should, she maintained a lifelong conviction of Divine love as parental. Although some members of her family thought she had gotten off too easily—without the internal struggle that marked those who wrestled with the Devil on the way to salvation—Lyman was satisfied. "Then has a new flower blossomed in the Kingdom this day," he said, as he embraced her.

Her adolescence was less idyllic than her childhood. At fifteen she moaned in her journal, "I wish I could die young and let the remembrance of me and my faults perish in the grave, rather than live, a trouble to everyone." She moped about her work, sought some sign of her destiny, and determined to "cultivate the talents" that Christ had given her. Above all, she waited for the liberation of love. "The desire to be loved forms, I fear, the great motive for all my actions."

In 1832 Lyman Beecher became president of the Lane Theological Seminary and moved his family to Cincinnati. Catharine came along to establish the Western Female Institute, consistent with her theories on female education, and Harriet tagged behind. Both joined the literary society in which young women expressed themselves and, as a result of papers presented there, Harriet's first piece of fiction, "A New England Sketch," was published in 1834. She also wrote a child's geography, but that appeared under Catharine's name.

Cincinnati never "felt like home" to Harriet, which perhaps explains why her "New England Sketch" had such realism and poignancy. While in Amherst for Henry Beecher's graduation, she heard that Eliza Stowe, one of her closest friends in Cincinnati, had died. Her widower, the Professor of Biblical Literature at Lane, was susceptible to consolation by his wife's friend upon her return. Calvin Stowe was bald, fat, and in his 30s, and age would not improve his looks. He was, however, learned and given to jokes, when not felled by hypochondria. He had a peculiar set of phantoms from the spirit world who visited him often, talking, laughing and playing musical instruments. He also had almost total recall of his own New England boyhood, brimming with wonderful characters and anecdotes. On the whole, he was a good deal like Lyman Beecher.

In January, 1836, Harriet became the second Mrs. Calvin Stowe. She determined that the marriage would be spiritually productive for each of them, a "second conversion," in which their love would bring both to Christ. Five children, including twin girls, were born during the first seven years. As Harriet told it, perhaps slightly too often, Calvin was rich in learning but nothing else. As a means of escaping "domestic slavery," she began to write short pieces for the ladies' magazines. A "stout German girl" in the kitchen and her "trusted Anna" in the nursery gave her time to supervise the children's education, read Sir Walter Scott aloud to them, and have three hours free for writing. "If you see my name coming out anywhere," she wrote a friend, "you may be sure of one thing—that I do it for *the pay*. I have determined not to be a mere domestic slave, without even the leisure to excel in my duties."

She made a token protest to Calvin, in which she confessed to doubts about whether her work was consistent with her role as wife and mother. Calvin gave her enthusiastic absolution and benediction: "My dear, you must be a literary woman. It is so written in the book of fate. Make all your calculations accordingly. Get a good stock of health and brush up your mind."

These years were dreary ones, until the move to Bowdoin College in Brunswick, Maine, in 1850. Part-time domestic help never solved all the problems and there were days when Harriet would despair of being "sick of the smell of sour milk and sour meat, and sour everything . . ." She discovered a temporary escape-hatch from domesticity in the water-cure sanitarium in Brattleboro, Vermont. During her visits there, or Calvin's absences, in search of work or health, they bombarded each other with letters. Neither would give up on the value of epistolary advice. She warned Calvin against his weaknesses, and he responded by cheerfully admitting them, including temptations to lust and liquor. Harriet, grateful that the problems of male nature were beyond her comprehension, nonetheless insisted that he "overcome" his faults, including even the ill-health which he found so "comfortable." Calvin retaliated by pointing out the differences in their character and personality which made their lives so trying. He liked his meals on time, his rooms picked up, his clothes mended; she was "unsystematic," untidy, unpunctual and, according to his mother, "extravagant."

The little stories Harriet tossed off in her ransomed hours were often about the problems, more amusing in fiction than real life, of the young housekeeper and mother. She even showed Christian charity by making the fictional mother-in-law the source of good advice and encouragement. But throughout all these years of family crisis there was, particularly in Cincinnati, an undercurrent of national tension in the worsening crisis over slavery. Insulated by domesticity and genteel poverty though they were, even the Stowes felt the coming storm when their hired girl, whom they thought was free, turned out to be a fugitive slave and had to be helped to escape to freedom. Harriet disliked the "ultra" tactics and style of the abolitionists, much as she would react to some of the more advanced womens' rights reformers. Nonetheless, in both cases she saw the essential rightness of their cause. She wrote Calvin of the need for some "intermediate" group: "If not, as light increases, all the excesses of the abolition party will not prevent humane and conscientious men from joining it."

Harriet's sixth child, "My Charley—my beautiful, loving, gladsome baby," was born in 1848 and died in the 1849 cholera epidemic. Later she told Eliza Follen, "It was at his dying bed and at his grave that I learned what a poor slave mother may feel when her child is torn away from her." This identification between the slavery of women and that of the Negro was much favored by reformers. Factually it stands up badly; the difference between freedom and bondage is too great for any analogy to bridge. Women indeed suffered, in the civil constraints and the personal restrictions upon their lives, but white women were not slaves. Yet psychologically it was possible to see parallels between slaves and free women, in the feelings common to both of them—their love of their children and their anguish at their loss. *Uncle Tom's Cabin* was Harriet's response to her conviction that slavery was most cruel and inhuman because it violated family love.

The Fugitive Slave Act passed in 1850, as the Stowes were on their way to Bowdoin. She saw it as the catalyst that spurred her to write her antislavery novel. Speaking in the third person, which was one of her least attractive responses to fame, Harriet said ". . . she heard with consternation Christian and humane people actually recommending the remanding escaped fugitives into slavery, as a duty binding on all good citizens . . . she could only think, *these men and Christians do not know what slavery is;* and from that arose a desire *to exhibit it in a living, dramatic reality.*" The proximate and immediate causes of her writing have been veiled in myth, much of which Harriet herself sponsored, and probably believed. She had a "vision" at the Communion rail of the death of Uncle Tom, and from that beginning constructed the novel. When she was very old, and her mind wandered in and out of reality, she told a visitor who praised her work, "I did not write it. God wrote it. I merely did His dictation."

In 1852 the Stowes moved to Andover, Massachusetts, where they would live for a dozen years. *Uncle Tom's Cabin: Life Among the Lowly* appeared in 1853 and it had a tremendous impact. We are too conditioned to monthly best-sellers to appreciate the force with which it spoke and the enthusiasm of its readers. Memoirs of 19th-century men and women describe how the periodicals in which it first appeared were treasured, worn and tear-stained though the pages were, and how copies of the book passed from hand to hand. Recalling how the book had swept through his own family, Henry James found it "much less a book than a state of vision, of feeling and of consciousness." Perhaps it never created an abolitionist but, for a generation of Americans, it gave tangible, emotional expression to what had been an abstract economic and political issue. Over a score of Southern writers wrote retaliatory novels, but none was successful. The book's anti-slavery message was hardly profound, and its readers, we may believe, were drawn to its characters—caught up in the perversity of Topsy, the New England spinster vigor of Miss Ophelia, the heroism of Eliza and the death of Eva—with abolitionism only a corollary to the apparent realism of their personal struggles. Christian love is the actual theme, the love of Christ for all His creatures and the mirror image of that love, the maternal passion.

Following the success of this first novel, Harriet Beecher Stowe became the most famous woman in America. Lionization, titled admirers, encounters with promient authors, distinguished her trips to Europe in 1853, 1856, and 1859. In the pre-Civil War years she published two more novels, *Dred* and *The Minister's Wooing,* as well as a *Key* to Uncle Tom, giving the sources she might have drawn on, had Divine inspiration not guided her pen. *The Minister's Wooing* (1859) in many ways is the most characteristic work of her life. It was also inspired by personal tragedy, the death by drowning of her oldest son Henry, a student at Dartmouth. For the first time since her conversion Harriet questioned God's goodness. She wrote Catharine that it was as if a malicious voice kept mocking her, "You trusted in God, did you? You believed that He loved you?"

The Minister's Wooing contains the famous passage on "the rungless ladder," which one of her literary biographers sees as the central metaphor of her writing. The Platonic image metaphorically suggests the many kinds of love. "There is a ladder to heaven, whose base God has placed in human affections, tender instincts, symbolic feelings, sacraments of love, through which the soul rises higher and higher, refining as she goes, till she outgrows the human, and changes, as she rises, into the image of the divine." She herself, she believed, could so rise through the human affections of her life, and through meeting the trials of that life with love and dignity. And, in her novels, she gives the same opportunities and experiences, to her central characters. The journey is long, the ascent steep, as she admits about her life and plots, but the end is certain.

Harriet's children, as she told her first biographer, constantly demanded things from her, and "To them in their needs I *must* write *chapters* which would otherwise go into my novel." She supported the family through her writing and, after 1864, that included maintenance of an expensive home in Hartford. Twenty pages a day were her customary output, except of course on Sunday. Describing a series of interruptions she concluded a letter, "and now I am at it again, for nothing but deadly determination enables me ever to write."

In the Civil War that some called "hers" Harriet took a role only through written appeals "To the Women of the Free States of America." "O women of the free states," she exhorted them, "What did your brave mothers do in the time of our revolutionary struggle? Did not *liberty* in those days feel the strong impulses of woman's heart?" When the war started, she could "thank God for mothers that cheer on their sons, for young wives who have said *go* to their husbands, for widows who have given their only sons."

11

Modernization and Traditionalism in Jacksonian Social Reform

HORACE MANN
DOROTHEA L. DIX
ORESTES A. BROWNSON

by Gerald N. Grob
Rutgers University

Between 1820 and 1860 American society appeared moving toward fulfillment of the ideals of its Revolutionary founders. The movement to rid the nation of its archaic and immoral system of slave labor was accompanied by a variety of attempts to eliminate the social injustices that stained the nation's fabric. During these decades the foundations were laid for a universal and free public school system. Institutions were also established for the care of the distressed—orphans, the mentally ill and retarded, and sick and old persons unable to survive without some form of assistance. Correspondingly, demands for equal rights for all persons grew in intensity. Most reformers were firmly convinced that man had the power and ability to create a new environment, one that ultimately would help to shape free and moral human beings capable of realizing their broadest potentialities unrestrained by outmoded and repressive inherited traditions.

In one sense this traditional portrait of nearly four decades of American history as an "era of reform" is accurate. But it also leaves many questions unanswered. What made many Americans receptive to social reform between 1820 and 1860? Where did activists come from and what were their goals? How can the dissatisfaction with existing institutions at this time be explained? What was responsible for the apparent failure to create a more perfect social order? And why did those individuals who were neutral or opposed to rapid institutional change fail to retard or reverse it?

Given these problems, how then can we view 19th-century reform? The answer lies not only in understanding individual social activists and their opponents, but—more importantly—in comprehending the context in which they functioned. For however one interprets the evolution of American society in the 19th century, the nation obviously was undergoing a profound transformation in its institutions and social structure as well as in its economy.

Modernization, of course, is a complex and varied process. It involves a massive increase and widespread diffusion of human knowledge about the physical world as well as a conviction that such knowledge provides man with the means by which to control his environment. Demographically, modernization is characterized by new social patterns, an increase in life expectancy, higher levels of health, greater social and geographical mobility, and a sharp rise in the rate of urbanization. Economically, there is a greater specialization of labor, a shift from subsistence to commercial agriculture, and the dominance of a high level of industrial and technological development. Inherent in modernization is the creation of an urban-industrial society where functions are increasingly performed by formal institutions rather than by such primary groups as the family or small village community. Accordingly, newly established specialized structures perform a variety of functions considered vital to the health and well-being of the citizenry.

Neither Horace Mann nor Dorothea L. Dix—two of the most eminent mid-19th-century activists—would have accepted the characterization of themselves as modernizers. Nor would Orestes A. Brownson—one of the most significant traditionalists of this era—have conceived of himself as an opponent of economic and technological change. More significantly, all three saw themselves simply as devout Christians seeking to implement their faith. In some cases this faith led to social activism; in others it became the reaffirmation of a traditional and hierarchical social order. The modernization of American society, therefore, was accompanied by ideological and philosophical diversity that often mirrored fierce social and intellectual conflict.

After first gaining fame as a psychiatric reformer, Horace Mann eventually emerged as the single most influential figure in American education. As Secretary of the Massachusetts State Board of Education, he helped to found a universal, free, compulsory school system held together by an elaborate bureaucratic structure. Dorothea Dix achieved an international reputation for her crusading efforts to set up institutions for the care and treatment of the mentally ill. She was also active in prison reform and played an important role in organizing nursing care during the Civil War. Both, therefore, contributed to the creation of what subsequently evolved into elaborate organizational structures that assumed responsibilities for functions previously reserved for the family, church, or local community. To put it another way, they were among the indispensable agents of modernization. In a certain sense their careers are best understood in terms of a paradox; though creating the new institutional forms that symbolized the dominance of the modern state, they conceived of their work as furthering a religious imperative and perfecting a traditional, and in most respects a premodern, society. The deeper implications of their achievements would only become apparent after their deaths.

Orestes Brownson, on the other hand, was the most famous convert to Catholicism in mid-19th-century America. Thereafter he spent his career as a critic seeking to return to an authoritarian and hierarchical society governed by eternal religious and moral truths. Rejecting much of the prevailing faith in democracy, he became a powerful foe of the emerging secular order, although in the end he himself was overwhelmed by the massive economic and technological transformations in American society.

By the 1850s Mann, Dix, and Brownson were well known in the United States and abroad. Yet little in their childhood and youth presaged their subsequent eminence. All were children of families of modest means; their roots went far back into the colonial period. Mann was born in 1796, Dix in 1802, and Brownson in 1803, the first two in Massachusetts and the last in Vermont. At that time agriculture and shipping were the dominant economic activities in New England. Boston, the largest town of that region, contained only about 25,000 people in 1800. All three, consequently, grew up in a homogeneous and predominantly rural society that stressed traditional values. The transformation of their world lay in the future, for factories, cities, and a large immigrant population—all of which was part of the modernization process—were not to become characteristic until they reached adulthood.

*   *   *

Horace Mann came from a relatively poor family that lacked formal education and insisted upon the inculcation of habits of industry and moral virtue. His childhood was not especially happy, for his health was frail and the extreme Calvinistic teachings of the Reverend Nathaniel Emmons, the local minister, caused him considerable mental agony. When he was but 12 years old, he repudiated the Calvinistic doctrine, which held that man was incapable of saving himself, a break that was both traumatic and irreversible. "From that day," he later recalled, "I began to construct the theory of Christian ethics and doctrine respecting virtue and vice, rewards and penalties, time and eternity, God and his providence, which, with such modifications as advancing age and a wider vision must impart, I still retain, and out of which my life has flowed." In his later career Mann demonstrated repeatedly that his personal religious belief in individual responsibility was a primary force in his numerous undertakings.

Although Mann possessed considerable intellectual ability, he did not attend school regularly. In 1814, however, he decided to prepare for college. Under the direction of a brilliant though eccentric tutor, he completed a course of study that enabled him to enter the sophomore class at Brown University. Brown was a Baptist institution, but it was preferred by many orthodox Calvinists who disliked Harvard's Unitarian atmosphere. Although some of Brown's undergraduates were religious conservatives, they nevertheless espoused democratic political theories that supported the idea of social change. Mann had a brilliant academic record, graduating with highest honors in 1819. By this time he had already demonstrated his belief in the infinite perfectibility of the human race. The subject of his valedictory graduation oration, "The Gradual Advancement of the Human Species in Dignity and Happiness," was a theme that he would reiterate throughout his career.

Brown regarded Mann so highly that soon after graduation it appointed him a tutor in Latin and Greek. Two years later he left to study law at Judge James Gould's well-known law school in Litchfield, Connecticut. He was admitted to the bar in 1823 and practiced law, first in Dedham and then in Boston, for the next 14 years. Driven by a desire to excel, Mann soon established a lucrative law practice that brought him a growing reputation and financial success. Like other young men with ability and ambition, he turned to politics and in 1827 was elected to the Massachusetts General Court. He gave strong support as a freshman legislator to government promotion of railroads; even then Mann identified technological and industrial progress with human happiness.

*   *   *

Career choices facing young men like Mann were varied, and they could easily occupy different roles as they matured. For Dorothea L. Dix, on the other hand, the world was more confined; society's expectations for young women were considerably more restricted. The overwhelming majority of women were taught to look froward to marriage and motherhood. Such roles were by no means inferior or unimportant, for the family prior to industrialization and modernization had functions that only later would be transferred to other institutions. Yet while marriage and motherhood were the accepted norms, there was always the possibility of breaking with them. Such an act required courage, will, and determination. Indeed, what is surprising about mid-19th-century American women was not that so few exhibited these characteristics, but that so many deliberately sought different horizons.

Dorothea Dix's early years and career offered little evidence that she would ultimately become one of the most influential women of her age. Born in a rural community, she had an unhappy childhood. Her mother seemed incapable of offering affection and her father was often intemperate. Her desire to leave home was so great that at age 12 she travelled alone to Boston to live with her well-to-do grandmother (whether she received permission is not known). The move did not bring contentment; she felt keenly the absence of affection and was unable to develop close relationships with others until relatively late in life.

Having made rapid progress in her own schooling, Dorothea Dix, then only 14 years old, decided to open a school for small children in Worcester, where she was temporarily residing with another relative. By the time she returned to her grandmother's home in 1819, her character had matured. She had become an ambitious young woman of singular forcefulness and determination. Against her grandmother's advice and while continuing to manage the household affairs, she opened another school in Boston. She also came under the influence of William Ellery Channing, the renowned Unitarian minister, and her religious commitment deepened in intensity. During the 1820s she briefly embarked on a literary career, publishing several children's books as well as a volume that embodied the ideals of duty, perfection, and Christian piety. In the succeeding decade she continued a teaching career. But in 1836 Dix suffered a nervous and physical collapse that compelled her to abandon her school. She then went abroad, remaining in England for a year and a half. Fortunately, she was financially independent—a bequest from her grandmother providing an annual income of approximately $3,000, a substantial sum by the standards of that day. In 1837 she returned home, still seeking a career that would permit her to serve society and at the same time fulfill her own ambitions.

*   *   *

Like Dorothea Dix, Orestes A. Brownson had an unsettled childhood. His father died shortly after his birth, and his mother, who struggled for six years to keep the family intact, was finally forced to place him in the home of an older couple. There the young boy became engrossed in theology, a concern that would later dominate his never-ending search for meaning and lead him briefly into the ministry. At the age of 14 Brownson was reunited with his family in upper New York where he briefly studied at a local academy. Forced by circumstances to seek employment, he never again attended a school or college; his education would come from internal ambition and avaricious reading. Meanwhile, his interest in theology grew in intensity. Searching for ultimate truths, he moved from one sect to another. For a time he flirted with Calvinism, but found its pessimism too stark and its notions of justice unacceptable. After briefly teaching in the Midwest, he became a Universalist minister. But Universalism proved no more satisfactory than Calvinism, for it seemed to reject the authority of the Scriptures without providing a definitive substitute. "I am amiable and honest, I have intelligence and even some learning; I have wronged no one, and have helped the needed," he confided to himself. "Yet nobody heeds me, nobody loves me, nobody cares for me." Brownson, at age 26, had still to find contentment or meaning.

*   *   *

Had American society remained relatively stable and traditional, Mann, Dix, and Brownson might never have had the opportunity to transcend their respectable but hardly distinguished careers. Mann might have remained a successful lawyer and political figure, Dix a teacher, and Brownson a spiritual wanderer. But within a short period of time all three were presented with opportunities that grew out of those forces contributing to the modernization of American society. Each would respond in a manner that would have significance not only for contemporaries but for generations yet unborn.

By the 1840s the United States was beginning to experience the rapid industrialization that within half a century would give it a place among the leading world powers. Accompanying it were dramatic demographic changes. One involved the increase not only in the number but the size of urban areas. In 1790 only six cities had more than 8,000 residents; these contained 3.35 percent of the total population. By 1850, 85 such urban areas contained nearly 12.5 percent of the total population. In 1790 not a single city had a population in excess of 50,000, and only two had more than 25,000. By 1850 New York, the largest American city, had considerably in excess of half a million people, while five others had between 100,000 and 250,000 and 20 more ranged in size from 25,000 to 100,000.

Another major demographic shift arose out of the immigration to the United States of large numbers of impoverished Europeans. Between 1830 and 1850, over two and a third million immigrants, of whom nearly a million were from Ireland, landed upon American shores. Although such groups added substantially to the labor force, their arrival presented American society with a series of unresolved dilemmas. Often possessing a different culture, outlook, and religion, they were also poor and tended to concentrate in the burgeoning urban centers, which then had to deal with the social problems arising out of illness, dependency, and acculturation.

The economic, industrial, technological, and demographic changes modernizing mid-19th-century American society posed new challenges. Before 1800 reliance on familial and community traditions and practices made it unnecessary to consider alternative approaches to social and economic problems. The family, local community, and church were regarded as the basic institutions of society. Thus the family was charged with educating and socializing children; schools were simply auxiliary aids designed to support but not replace the family. In cases involving distress and dependency, the local community attempted to maintain the integrity of the family by providing needed assistance. Consequently, the modern concept of social policy—which involves replacing traditional institutions with new public structures or procedures on a regional or national basis—was largely absent for most of the 17th and 18th centuries.

By the 1830s and 1840s Americans were encountering the residual problems that followed in the wake of social and economic change. Periodic unemployment, growing class cleavages, and tensions that accompanied the effort to create a modern labor force, all combined to undermine traditional society. Older modes of alleviating individual and familial distress appeared obsolete. The spontaneous and informal manner in which rural communities handled problems of sickness and dependency, for example, did not operate as efficiently in urban areas, where an extraordinarily high rate of geographical mobility tended to limit informal and traditional means of dealing with distress. Such considerations militated against established approaches and favored more systematic and institutionalized patterns.

The problems arising out of dependency and disease were by no means unique. Familial responsibility for education now seemed inefficient, and fear was widespread that immigrant and working-class families would not be assimilated within the new industrial order. The thrust toward modernization, then, created conditions conducive to the establishment of a universal, free, and compulsory system of education. In building schools, colleges, hospitals, prisons, houses of refuge, asylums —to mention only a few examples—Americans manifested an awareness that existing practices and structures were no longer appropriate to their society. A changing world provided such reformers as Mann, Dix, and Brownson with challenges and opportunities even if they themselves were not completely conscious of the underlying forces that made their own creativity possible.

First indications that Horace Mann's destiny transcended the practice of law came shortly after his election to the Massachusetts legislature. By 1829 he had come to believe that intemperance was the prime cause of crime and poverty. Hostile toward either prohibition or total abstinence, he supported instead a moderate system of licensing to bring drunkenness under some form of social control. Uncommitted to any rigid ideology, he saw nothing wrong in using the power of the state to deal with a problem beyond the control of the individual or the local community. The cause of intemperance did not bring Mann reputation or fame. But his leadership in helping to found a state insane hospital thrust him into a limelight that he would occupy until his death in 1859.

After 1800 a steady movement developed in the United States away from local toward institutional care of the mentally ill. Combining to give rise to the establishment of both general and mental hospitals were demographic changes, a growing sensitivity to social and medical problems, a surge in philanthropy, and an acquaintance with new medical and psychiatric advances in France and England. The first hospitals were products of private philanthropy, although they received public subsidies as well. Almost from the start, they had limited admissions to relatively well-to-do groups capable of paying the high costs of protracted care. Responsibility for dealing with the problems associated with mental disease consequently shifted slowly to public hospitals under state authority. These were supported by funding from both state and local governments.

By the mid-1820s concern over mental illness was on the rise. Investigations by the Boston Prison Discipline Society revealed that mentally ill persons were commonly confined in welfare and penal institutions. Efforts to provide other alternatives were made in the legislature in 1827 and 1828, but not until Mann assumed leadership in 1829, did these succeed. Speaking several times before the legislature, he spelled out the case for public facilities for care and treatment. Justice and mercy required public intervention, he argued. In addition, to provide therapeutic hospitals to cure the insane was more economical than to maintain them in custodial institutions. Above all, the state could no longer evade its moral responsibility for the welfare of these unfortunate persons.

As a result of Mann's efforts, the legislature in 1830 authorized construction of a state lunatic hospital. Located in Worcester, the new hospital opened in 1833. Under the leadership of Dr. Samuel B. Woodward (the first superintendent) and Mann (the leading figure on the board of trustees), the Worcester hospital quickly gained a national reputation and inspired other states to found their own public mental hospitals. By 1860 virtually every state had at least one, and some had more. For better or worse, care of the insane became a public responsibility.

Just as Mann was achieving widespread recognition, personal tragedy altered his career. He married Charlotte Messer, daughter of the President of Brown University, in 1830. Less than two years later she died. For Mann her death resulted in a spiritual crisis that lasted for more than a decade. "Oh, Dearest! Dearest!," wrote Mann in his private journal five years after her death. "How far removed from everything upon earth, how unutterably alone, I dwell in this world. Its beauty is perished. Its music is discord. Its pleasures have become pain, but none of its pains have become pleasures. And will this always be . . . yes. I had rather it would, than that I should ever forget thee, my beloved wife"" The grieving young lawyer began a process of self-reflection. Had he been guilty of excessive ambition? Had the quest for material rewards and fame corrupted his very being? Even his religious faith was called into doubt. Out of this profound personal crisis Mann emerged chastened and more mature. Henceforth he would seek a career that might serve mankind.

In 1837 an opportunity presented itself that would radically alter Mann's career and ultimately make him one of the most influential figures in the history of American education. In that year the Massachusetts legislature debated the disposition of the common school fund (which was used to supplement monies raised by towns for support of public education). Heretofore Mann had not been active in strictly educational causes. Nevertheless, his association with several advocates of public education, coupled with his own inclination to meet social responsibilities, served to involve him. Yet in reality his interest in education did not represent a radical departure from his earlier concern with the mentally ill. If the "calamities and sufferings of men" arose out of either ignorance or disbelief of the laws "impressed upon our being by our Creator," he pondered, might not *the* most fundamental change involve the proper education of human beings in their formative years. Would they not thereby know and follow the natural laws governing mankind? And would they not thus avoid incurring the penalties of misbehavior?

But the legislature, Mann believed, seemed to be composed of men of limited vision, and it rejected appropriation bills for school support. But the session was not a total loss, for Mann and his followers managed to secure enactment of a law establishing a State Board of Education. The new agency would collect and distribute information—the first step toward creating an orderly system for the proper education of children. Composed of non-salaried members, the Board was authorized to employ a paid secretary, a position that Mann agreed to take despite a heavy personal financial sacrifice. For the first time he possessed an institutional base that allowed him to affect the way in which American society socialized and educated its children. Indeed Mann's work as secretary of the Board from 1837 to 1848 would help lay the foundation, for a universal, free, and compulsory system of schools joined together by an elaborate bureaucratic and hierarchical structure.

Embarked upon a new career, Mann proceeded to push for a fundamental restructuring of both the form and substance of education. A changing world, he believed, demanded innovation. The new industrialism and the increasing heterogeneity of the population had fragmented a traditional, stable, and deferential society. Consensus on basic moral values had bound society together in an earlier age. The family provided much of the cohesive force. Parents were responsible for socializing and educating their children as well as inculcating virtue and morality. But Mann thought the family's role and authority had so diminished that it was incapable of performing its indispensable functions. Likewise social and class conflict was apparently undermining the social order, while immigration was bringing to American shores people whose customs, beliefs, and culture were not always consistent with accepted behavioral norms. How, then, could the nation avoid being torn apart by these forces? Could a republican society continue to exist if its citizens lacked both knowledge and virtue? Mann had an answer to these troubling questions. *"The Common School,"* he proclaimed, *"is the greatest discovery ever made by man."* Other institutions had to deal with the consequences of human weakness and imperfectibility. Prisons had to reform the character of criminals; mental hospitals had to cure individuals whose behavior was abnormal. But schools were unique; they would receive children whose characters, minds, and bodies were not yet corrupted by an immoral society. Properly conceived and structured, they could serve as both preventive and antidote; ultimately they would eliminate institutional coercion, since they would develop the moral faculties and inculcate internal restraint. The school would thereby replace family, church and village in molding the character of the child. On the school rested the future well-being of American society, if not of mankind. "In a Republic," Mann proclaimed, "ignorance is a crime."

When Mann began his career, formal education in Massachusetts was decentralized and lacking in clear purpose. Although tax-supported and non-sectarian schools existed in many areas, there was no agreement on matters relating to discipline, curriculum, teacher preparation, attendance, structure, or the basic objectives of schooling. Mann's role was essentially catalytic; he helped to define both the goals of schooling and the structure appropriate to them. For over a decade he was the foremost spokesman for educational innovation, carrying his message not only to his Massachusetts constituency but also to the American people everywhere.

The goal of schooling, Mann argued, was to indoctrinate children in the basic precepts of American morality, religion, and culture. In an age of dynamic technological and economic change, schools would constitute a stabilizing force. They would overcome class barriers, prevent strife, and ensure the dissemination of skills necessary to an increasingly industrialized nation. Mann had no doubts about what constituted morality. In a virtuous society men were frugal, honest, industrious, public spirited, philanthropic, temperate, and hard working. Schools for their part would shore up and maintain the characteristics of an earlier and more homogeneous society. In short, they would reunify a divided nation and provide the basis for widespread material prosperity.

To define the proper goals of education was only half of the job. The other half was to provide a structure capable of realizing these goals in practice. Again Mann turned to institutional solutions. Past difficulties, he argued, had arisen because of the absence of an effective *system*. Required now was the formulation of a plan to systematize and to rationalize schools, thereby guaranteeing the performance of those functions for which they had been established. Political and sectarian considerations, he insisted, should not be permitted to intrude. Isolated from base partisanship and narrow self-interest, schools would be free to instruct the community in its responsibilities.

Tax-supported schools, according to Mann, must be integrated within a cohesive structure. Grading of classes was a first step; examinations given at regular intervals would determine whether students had met basic curriculum requirements. Reading and other text materials would reflect the graded nature of the curriculum as well as embody moral values. All children within stipulated age ranges would be required to attend schools for certain periods. State and local school administrations would be created in order to insure educational uniformity and to make certain that both pupils and teachers were following their prescribed roles. Teachers would be trained as professionals, and school committees would no longer be permitted to employ those lacking proper credentials. Establishment and licensing of normal schools (later teachers' colleges) would ensure the continued growth of education as a profession. Above all, public education would be removed from the hands of well-meaning but misinformed amateurs and become the institutional means by which professionals would fulfill their unique and important mission.

The more Mann threw himself into educational reform, the more he grew intolerant of those who had the audacity to disagree with him. To Mann, the battle over education became a struggle between morality and immorality, between narrow-minded and selfish individuals and those who eschewed self-interest. "You and I and others," he wrote to Henry Barnard, his counterpart in Connecticut, "have to work on it, with embarrassment and obstruction, but when I look afar into the future and see the beautiful and glorious development it shall have in other hands, I find not satisfaction in my toils, merely, but I feel a pride in being stationed at this more honorable post of labour. Let us go on and buffet these waves of opposition with a stout arm and a confiding heart."

Dissenters from Mann's educational philosophy included religious groups which rejected his reduction of religion in the public schools to a common set of largely Protestant beliefs and values. Opposition also came from educators who resisted efforts to standardize their schools, often because it meant their displacement from positions of authority. Working-class groups and ethnic minorities sometimes expressed implicit displeasure with schooling by poor attendance, high dropout rates, and opposition to school expenditures. Nevertheless, Mann's vision proved all but irresistible, and by the late 19th century centralized and bureaucratic school systems characterized American public education.

In 1848 Mann temporarily abandoned the field of education; in that year he was elected to the House of Representatives as an antislavery member of the Whig Party. In Washington he demonstrated the same passion that marked his career as an educational innovator. "My zeal grows and glows to continue the contest of evil," he wrote to a friend in 1856. "I love the good causes more than ever; more than ever I want to fight for them; and the most painful idea connected with death is that I must be at most a looker on and not a participant." Eventually Mann received the Free Soil nomination for the governorship of Massachusetts. His defeat in the 1852 elections occurred at the very moment he was being offered the presidency of the newly-established Antioch College in Ohio, a position he accepted and retained until his death in 1859. But the last decade of his life was anticlimactic; his most enduring contributions had occurred during his tenure as secretary of the Massachusetts State Board of Education.

No doubt Mann would have been surprised at the fruits of his labor. His faith in education reflected an underlying religious commitment; virtue and stability were the end products of a proper education. Although he often spoke about the relation of education to industry, he saw the former as a predominantly religious and moral venture. Nevertheless, he did not minimize the economic rewards of schooling or the potential benefits to industry in the form of a literate work force. Even his support of an educational bureaucracy was designed to implement his basic goals. Yet in the succeeding century the school system he helped to design became one of the enduring symbols of an industrialized and modernized America. Seeking virtue and morality, Mann helped pave the way for the advent of a new and different world.

*   *   *

As with Mann, an unforeseen event embarked Dorothea L. Dix on a new career. Following her return from England in 1837, she seemed to drift aimlessly. Boston's small but influential intellectual community did not attract her. More doer than thinker, a quiet life of contemplation seemed peculiarly inappropriate. But how could a lonely spinster find personal fulfillment and still serve humanity? "Life is not to be expended in vain regrets," she wrote to her closest friend in 1838. "No day, no hour comes but brings in its train work to be performed for some useful end, the suffering to be comforted, the wandering led home, the sinner reclaimed. Oh, how can any fold the hands to rest and say to the spirit, 'Take thine ease for all is well'?" Thus when John T. G. Nichols, a young Harvard Divinity School student, asked her if she knew someone who could teach a Sunday school class to female convicts in the East Cambridge jail in 1841, she herself volunteered. At the jail she was horrified to discover a group of insane persons confined with hardened criminals. Moreover, they had suffered from years of neglect. Deeply touched by what she saw, she was determined to improve and expand institutional facilities for the mentally ill.

Recognizing that an unknown and unmarried woman could accomplish little, Dix turned then to Samuel Gridley Howe and Charles Sumner for advice. Both men agreed that the public conscience needed to be shocked. They recommended a comprehensive personal examination of prison conditions, a task that would take many months of arduous work. Howe also reminded Dix that her health was delicate, but the newly-discovered cause superceded personal considerations. Shortly thereafter she began her first investigation, which took nearly a year and a half. While she was visiting every jail and welfare institution in the state, Howe helped out by preparing several exposés for the press.

In January 1843, Dix finally completed her investigations and presented the findings in her famous "Memorial to the Legislature of Massachusetts," the first of many similar documents. Combining moral outrage and knowledge, it gave a highly detailed picture of conditions at virtually every jail, house of correction, and almshouse in the state. "I come to present the strong claims of suffering humanity," she told the legislators. "I come to place before the Legislature of Massachusetts the condition of the miserable, the desolate, the outcast. I come as the advocate of helpless, forgotten, insane, idiotic men and women; of beings sunk to a condition from which the most unconcerned would start with real horror; of beings wretched in our prisons, and more wretched in our almshouses. And I cannot suppose it needful to employ earnest persuasion, or stubborn argument, in order to arrest and fix attention upon a subject only the more strongly pressing in its claims because it is revolting and disgusting in its details." Insisting that the Commonwealth had a moral, humanitarian, and legal obligation toward the mentally ill, she called on the legislature to fulfill its duty and provide for additional facilities at Worcester's overcrowded state hospital. Persuaded further by Mann, Howe, and others, the lawmakers appropriated the necessary funds.

For the next three decades, Dix tirelessly followed a similar course of action in other states. After arriving in a state, she spent considerable time in surveying actual conditions. Then she presented her findings to the legislature, usually in the form of a lengthy and impassioned memorial. Unconcerned with arousing public opinion, she then turned with unerring political instinct to those leaders with the power to innovate. Indeed, her singular devotion to the cause often resulted in consternation among her friends, some of whom felt that she took unnecessary liberties with the truth. As one hospital superintendent wrote to another: "I see Miss Dix has been over your state & *Memorialized* your legislature. I hope good will result from it—& trust that her experience in this state [New York] may make her more courteous in observing and publishing. In this state I am afraid she did hurt by *coloring* & by not accurately observing. She was often mistaken & this has thrown a doubt over all her statements with many." In this respect Dorothea Dix's personality was similar to that of Horace Mann. Like other innovators, both tended to classify humans and institutions as either good or evil. Those who opposed their efforts did so for selfish and partisan reasons.

Dix's unflagging devotion to the mentally ill gave her a key position in the history of American psychiatry and mental hospitals from the 1840s to the 1870s. Many hospital superintendents owed their positions to her influence, and it became a common practice for younger men to consult with her about their future plans and aspirations. Nor was her position as an arbiter and leader merely titular, for often she was called on to adjudicate or to pass judgment upon internal institutional conflicts. Few of those concerned with the problems of the mentally ill—whatever their views—could afford the luxury of ignoring this remarkable and determined woman.

By the close of her career Dorothea Dix was responsible for founding or enlarging over 30 mental hospitals in the United States and abroad. Although the groundwork had often been prepared by others, her role was to act as a catalyst and to bring the specific project to fruition. In many ways her most important contribution was to stimulate the thrust toward broadening the role of government in providing institutional care and treatment of the mentally ill. Her influence was national and international in scope precisely because she insisted on excluding virtually all extraneous issues (prison reform being one of the few exceptions). She was one of the few New England social reformers who received a warm welcome in the South because she never coupled antislavery with psychiatric innovation.

Dix's work, of course, would have been all but futile without some base of support. Such backing existed, for most states already possessed groups of people committed to the amelioration of distress and to social improvement through the expansion of governmental activities. However one may view 19th-century American society, it is clear that the creation and strengthening of formal institutions represented a dominant trend. Dix's insistence upon institutional care for those mentally ill consequently struck a responsive chord among those who were dedicated to the creation of a new and better society.

Shortly after embarking on her new career, Dix came to the conclusion that a virtual revolution was required in the manner in which resources were allocated for the care and treatment of the insane. At that time public mental hospitals were expected to be self-supporting in their operating expenditures. Income was derived from three sources: families who paid for private patients; local communities, which were responsible for poorer and indigent residents; and states, which paid for foreign-born and indigent patients or else provided a lump sum subsidy (all capital expenditures came from the states). In 1848 Dix next presented a lengthy memorial to Congress requesting legislation that would provide for the distribution of 5,000,000 acres of federal land to the states, the proceeds of which would be used for the support of the indigent insane. For six years she labored arduously to convince Congress that the project was both desirable and important. Success finally seemed to come in 1854 with the passage of legislation setting aside not 5,000,000 but 10,000,000 acres of federal land. The moment was one of triumph and satisfaction. "And as I rejoice quietly and silently," she wrote her closest friend, "I feel it is *The Lord who has made my mountain to stand strong.* . . . As for myself longing now and then for rest and truely, it is pleasant to think of the time when labor will not be associated with pain and weariness." Her victory proved illusory, however, for the act met with a veto from President Franklin Pierce, and Congress was unable to muster sufficient support to override it. For the remainder of the 19th and the early part of the 20th century responsibility for the mentally ill continued to be borne by state and local authorities.

During the Civil War years Dix would abandon for the only time in her career her struggle on behalf of the insane. Immediately upon the outbreak of hostilities she went to Washington and offered her services for the care of sick and wounded soldiers. In April 1861, she was commissioned as the first "Superintendent of United States Army Nurses." Her passion for efficiency and humanity seemed peculiarly suited to the task at hand. Although the Civil War was one of the first of the modern wars in terms of strategy and weapons, its medical care unfortunately was traditional. The result was a staggering number of casualties and fatalities, mostly from wounds and disease (aseptic procedures were still nonexistent). The Medical Bureau of the army was largely a paper organization.

Dix's experience in Washington, however, proved an unhappy one. The struggle between the Medical Bureau and volunteers like her and others associated with the Sanitary Commission inhibited her effectiveness. By October 1863 the conflict was so acute that a reorganization was instituted; it stripped Miss Dix of virtually all her authority over the nurses. Although she remained in Washington until the fall of 1865, her power was all but gone.

Too strong-willed to be discouraged by her wartime experiences, Dix in 1867 resumed her earlier career as the leading protagonist for the mentally ill. Slowly, however, the ravages of age began to take their toll, and in 1881 she finally retired to the state hospital at Trenton, New Jersey, where the trustees had provided her with quarters in appreciation of her services. She remained there until her death in 1887.

*   *   *

Horace Mann and Dorothea Dix were practical activists who promoted institutional solutions for contemporary social problems. Orestes Brownson, on the other hand, was more the thinker. Meaning and significance were of greater importance to him than action; consequently, he was less concerned with institution building than with identifying the ideal foundation upon which any moral and just society must rest. A pilgrim in search of ultimate truths, Brownson moved with startling rapidity from one ideology to another. Beginning his career as a social and economic radical, he ended up as a convert to Catholicism and a critic of modern society.

During the late 1820s and the 1830s, Brownson made his way through a bewildering variety of religious and secular reform movements. The socialist ventures of Robert Owen and Fanny Wright with which he was briefly connected gave him no fulfillment. He was attracted to, and involved with, the workingmen's political parties that grew out of the depression of 1828–29, but concluded that labor was no match for capital. Convinced that society must rest on a bedrock of eternal religious truth, he became a Unitarian minister in 1832 and subsequently occupied pulpits in Walpole, New Hampshire, and Canton, Massachusetts. Slowly but surely he acquired a reputation as one of New England's most outspoken intellectuals and authors.

By this time Brownson had come to the conclusion that life could not be understood solely in terms of logic or rationality; some truths were beyond the reach of the intellect. What humanity required was a new church that embodied eternal religious truths. The Reformation had demonstrated the failure of Catholicism, but Protestantism was less a church than a collection of sects. Although lacking precision, Brownson was seeking a synthesis that would unite his religious overview with worldly concerns and thereby offer a guide to human action based on transcendent principles.

Brownson's concern for philosophical issues did not lead him to ignore contemporary problems, as was shown by his participation in labor politics. The fact that his ministry was located in a Massachusetts community with a working-class population forced him to confront practical concerns rather than intellectual abstractions. Yet Brownson did not respond by seeking an environmental transformation. Instead, he concluded that moral reform must precede social reform. "To effect any real reform," he wrote in 1834, "the individual man must be improved. . . . The reformer's concern is with the individual. That which gives the individual a free mind, a pure heart, and full scope for just and beneficent action, is that which will reform the many. When the majority of any community are fitted for better institutions, for a more advanced state of society, that state will be introduced, and those institutions will be secured." But how could people become wise and virtuous? The answer lay in the abolition of the social inequalities that hampered people, especially working men and women, from receiving the kind of education that would cleanse and purify their souls. But Brownson failed to demonstrate how virtue would follow education should the latter be under the aegis of a still corruptly governed nation.

In 1836 Orestes Brownson moved from Canton to Boston, where he was immediately absorbed into the vibrant life of the nation's foremost intellectual community. Members of Boston's tightly-knit intelligentsia usually maintained cordial personal relationships, if only because they were seeking a common consensus. But Brownson did not fit the typical mold. Strong-willed and determined, he did not hesitate to expose, usually in a blunt and undiplomatic manner, the inadequacies of arguments with which he disagreed. With an occasional exception, he lacked close friends. Acquaintances found him rigid and dogmatic even though respecting and sometimes fearing his intellectual capabilities. "Brownson," noted Ralph Waldo Emerson, "never will stop and listen, neither in conversation, but what is more, not in solitude." Moreover, he manifested these very same qualities in his relations with his wife and children, demanding obedience rather than affection. Rarely did he permit family responsibilities to intrude upon his work.

Although Brownson's reputation among Bostonians was that of a contentious social reformer, he also evinced a strong interest in religion and to this end promoted a vague ecumenical movement intended to create an ideal church. The rationality of Unitarianism, he noted in *New Views of Christianity* (1836), did not take into account the affective side of human nature. His vision of a new church rested on the proposition that man was made in God's image and possessed the power and ability to remake society into the Kingdom of God. Religion and social reform were therefore inseparable; the former was a prerequisite for achievement of the latter.

Brownson's thinking in the mid-1830s was still largely abstract. Although he clearly sympathized with the working class, he had not moved beyond his conviction that inner reform must take precedence. The depression ushered in by the panic of 1837 provided a new perspective, however, and he slowly modified his position. Inner reform was all very well, but how could it aid unemployed and starving people? Using the *Boston Quarterly Review* (which he began in 1838) and later *Brownson's Quarterly Review*, he lashed out against the enemies of the people.

Employing a class analysis, he urged that the alliance between government and business be destroyed and that the former be restored to popular control. States' rights, he added, were the guardian of liberty whereas centralization of authority promoted the power of small propertied groups.

Logic impelled Brownson to move into politics in the late 1830s, and his journal became a staunch supporter of the Democratic Party. In the midst of the presidential election of 1840, he published his widely read essay on "The Laboring Classes." Capitalism, he proclaimed, must be destroyed so that true equality could prevail. "Wages is a cunning device of the devil, for the benefit of tender consciences, who would retain all the advantages of the slave system, without the expense, trouble, and odium of being slave-holders." Explicitly repudiating the necessity of inner or moral reform, Brownson railed against "priests" and the clergy in general. They were "miserable panderers to the prejudices of the age, [and] loud in condemning sins nobody is guilty of, but silent as the grave when it concerns the crying sin of the times. . . . As a body they never preach a truth till there is none but whom it will indict." Destruction of the priesthood and revival of a purified Christianity were but two of the elements in his program. His more practical proposals included a sharp limitation of monopoly and privilege and the abolition of the inheritance of property. These propositions rested on the belief that the personal economic relationships of a bygone era could be restored; he never envisaged a modernized and industrialized America.

But Brownson's program was too radical for the Democratic Party, and it disavowed him. The Whigs attempted to exploit the situation by insisting on identifying him with their opponents. Their presidential candidate, Benjamin Henry Harrison, easily defeated the incumbent Democrat, Martin Van Buren, in the election of 1840. The outcome was altogether disheartening to Brownson. His faith in the people had been ill-founded. So too was his belief in democracy as a political system. Government, he decided, had to rest on an entirely different foundation.

Moving toward a strict constitutionalist position, Brownson urged initially that sharp limitations be placed on government power. Moreover, he became friendly with John C. Calhoun, who had reached a similar conclusion much earlier. While Brownson disliked slavery, he did not boggle at the thought of an anti-business alliance of Southern slaveowners and Northern workers. In a public address he attacked the Northern critique of slavery.

> You of the South consist of freemen and slaves, of gentle and simple and so do we of the North. In both sections we find at bottom the same distinction of classes, though while you have the manliness to avow it, we have the art to disguise it from the careless observer, under the drapery of fine names. You call your slaves by their proper name, and while you impose upon them the duties of slaves, you relieve them from

the cares and burdens of freemen; we call our slaves freemen, and impose upon them the labors and burdens of slavery, while we secure to them none of the advantages of freedom. The only advantage we can claim over you is, that our slaves being of the same race and color with our freemen, are individually less hopelessly slaves than yours. The class is as permanent with us as with you; but individuals of the class may more easily escape from it. . . . But on the other hand, if our slaves are under certain aspects less slaves than yours, our freemen are less free than yours.

But increasingly Brownson turned toward strictly religious questions. The election of 1840 had demonstrated that the people were neither wise nor virtuous; perhaps his faith in them was wrong. His hope of realizing the Kingdom of God on Earth rapidly receded and was replaced by a singular concern with the salvation of men's souls. Disillusioned with the rationality of Unitarianism, he undertook once again a search for metaphysical meaning and truth. Yet, he was unable to abandon completely his class analysis, for he still believed that the "growing industrial feudalism" continued to be the single greatest threat to modern society. But how could this threat be thwarted? Brownson's dilemma was compounded by his new assumption that human nature was utterly corrupt. "With ignorant, depraved men," he wrote in 1844, "can you have a rightly organized society?" Slowly but inexorably he found an answer in the Christian epic of sin and redemption as manifested in the traditions and theology of the Catholic Church. Human reason and rationality were too fallible; they required the aid of divine revelation and the "tradition of the race."

Brownson faced the most important decision of his career. If the Catholic Church was the repository of the one true faith, how could he remain outside its fold? But to most Americans, Catholicism was synonymous with superstition and with a power-hungry and depraved hierarchy. Its strength in the United States lay with the Irish, an ethnic group generally considered to be mired in alcoholism, ignorance, stupidity, and crime. Nevertheless, by mid-1844 Brownson had concluded that there was no alternative between Catholicism and other religions. Since truth lay with Catholicism, his only choice was conversion. In October 1844 he took the final step and joined the Catholic Church. So intense were his feelings that he forced his family to follow him.

Brownson's conversion destroyed whatever credibility he possessed among the Protestant intelligentsia. James Freeman Clarke, the famous Unitarian minister, portrayed him as one who was forever changing his views:

> He has made the most elaborate and plausible plea for eclecticism, and the most elaborate and plausible plea against it. He has said the best things in favor of transcendentalism, and the best things against it. He

has shown that no man can possibly be a Christian, except he is a transcendentalist; and he has also proved that every transcendentalist, whether he knows it or not, is necessarily an infidel. He has satisfactorily shown the truth of socialism, and its necessity in order to bring about a golden age, and he has, by the most convincing arguments, demonstrated that the whole system of socialism is from the pit, and can lead to nothing but anarchy and ruin. . . . He labors now with great ingenuity and extraordinary subtlety to show that there must be an infallible church with its infallible ministry, and that out of this church there can be no salvation. But formerly he labored with equal earnestness to show that there could be no such thing as a church at all, no outward priesthood or ministry.

Given Brownson's personality and temperament, his commitment to Catholicism was total. Three years after his conversion he noted that every Catholic "from the fact that he is a Catholic, has the world and the devil for his enemies." Not surprisingly he turned his immense energies to elevating the spiritual and intellectual standards of his fellow Catholics as well as to proselytizing Protestant America with the true faith. His earlier radicalism was muted; reality simply reflected the wishes of God. The world was but a temporary abode for humanity, for "what matters the inconvenience which we may be required to put up with?" Humanity need not concern itself with political, social, or economic problems; its only concern was salvation.

Between 1844 and 1876 Brownson elaborated his new faith in the light of contemporary problems. He condemned the revolutions of 1848 in Europe and insisted that liberalism was destructive of religion, law, and order. Social questions could be adjudicated only in terms of eternal moral principles. Since obedience to the state meant obedience to God, it followed that the Church had to guide and give sanction to the state. Religion and politics were inseparable, since only the former could legitimatize the latter. Still, Brownson's earlier radicalism was not entirely eradicated. When the balance between liberty and authority was threatened, the Church, he held, should place its moral authority on the side of liberty. Just as he opposed the revolutions of 1848, so did he oppose the rising tide of reaction. The Church, he maintained, had to adjust to the problems of a changing world. This attitude did not enhance Brownson's popularity among his co-religionists, many of whom feared and distrusted him.

During the 1840s and 1850s Brownson occupied a position midway between his youthful radicalism and his later conservatism. The debate over slavery, for example, intensified his concern for law and order. In 1847 he defended slavery by insisting that it did not include dominion over the soul. "[It is] our duty," he remarked on one occasion, "to accept the distinction of classes as a social fact, permanent and indestructible in civilized society." But as the Civil War approached, Brownson grew more resentful of the planters' attempt to rule the nation through their domination of the Democratic Party. When armed conflict erupted in 1861, he rushed to the support of the Union. If the destruction of Southern power required the abolition of slavery, then Lincoln's policy of opposing secession by force was justified. His endorsement of the war regained the friendships of many who had been alienated by his conversion to Catholicism. Conversely, it offended some Catholics who were mostly staunch Democrats and fearful that the war might conclude in emancipation. Brownson became further estranged from many of his co-religionists because of his conciliatory attitude toward Protestantism and his rejection of the temporal authority of the Church.

At the war's end Brownson was growing old and physically infirm. The loss of two of his sons during the conflict contributed to his malaise. The Papacy's turn to the right under Pius IX and its rejection of compromise with modernism left Brownson peculiarly vulnerable. Making his peace with Rome during the final decade of his life, he became a spokesman for orthodoxy and conservatism. He insisted that property was a sacred right, that governments lacked authority to change the established order, that justice and right lay with the aristocracy, and that egalitarianism and disrespect for constituted authority threatened the fabric of society. In an essay on democratic principles written in 1873, he explicitly rejected the doctrine that "the people . . . are the origin and source of all authority and all law, that they are absolutely supreme, and bound by no law or authority that does not emanate from themselves." Politics could not possibly be separated from the moral order, which he defined as "justice, eternal and immutable right" constituted by divine sanction and placed under the authority of the Pope, Christ's vicar on Earth.

By the time of his death in 1876 Brownson had come full circle. Beginning his career as a seeker who espoused liberal if not radical causes, he ultimately despaired of man's ability to change the world according to predetermined goals. By aligning himself with the established order, he explicitly rejected both modernism and contemporary industrial society. Whereas Mann and Dix consciously promoted change by human intervention, Brownson resolutely set himself in opposition by supporting an organic social order with a hierarchy of authority that reached through the Church and ultimately to God. The secular thrust that accompanied modernization, however, proved too strong and Brownson's hopes were overwhelmed by the pace of industrial, technological, and social change.

A supreme individualist, Brownson had few friends and many enemies. His fellow Catholics were often angered by his pronouncements and by his refusal to conform completely and they never overcame their suspicions of him. Nor were Protestants more tolerant of his idiosyncrasies.

Independent to an extreme, Brownson mirrored the transformation of his world. No doubt his irrepressible independence and his isolation from organized and institutional protest contributed to his inability to influence his countrymen. Whatever the reasons, his was a voice in the wilderness, little heeded and soon forgotten by friend and foe alike.

Horace Mann, Dorothea Dix and Orestes Brownson provide a fascinating contrast. The former two were firmly convinced that their institutional solutions to problems could only benefit their countrymen. Their goal was a nation in which virtue and prosperity would be distributed among all citizens, thereby facilitating self-government. They had little doubt about the precise definition of virtue and goodness, which they equated with the behavioral norms of their own social class. They believed that organization was an appropriate means of overcoming the disintegrative forces that threatened the foundations of order and stability. The institutions for which they fought—schools, hospitals, asylums, jails—were the means by which society would progress and confer benefits upon its people. In part their favorable view of formal institutional structures was a reflection of the growing importance of organization in a society that glorified the individual but which was inescapably crossing the threshold into modernization and industrialization. Yet their personal vision of America remained essentially traditional; they saw structural innovation as a means of restoring a premodern social order.

Brownson, pondering the relationship of religion to society, ultimately rejected the belief that human nature was essentially good or that mankind could solve its pressing problems. His concern with abstract analysis—a quality that was even present during the radical phase of his career—removed him from actual involvement, and he remained an intellectual apart from the society in which he lived. When his advice went unheeded, he decided that a corrupt humanity could only act affirmatively with divine guidance. He thoroughly distrusted those secular institution builders like Horace Mann and Dorothea Dix who claimed divine sanction for their activities. Ultimately Brownson found his answer in the Catholic Church, which in his age was identified with the defense of the existing order and opposed to liberalism and modernism.

Curiously enough, neither the fears of Brownson nor the hopes of Mann and Dix were ever fully realized. American society never became fully egalitarian, nor did its political system become a vehicle for social and economic change. If Brownson's fears did not materialize, neither did his dream of a hierarchical social order built on eternal religious truths and divine revelation ever approach reality. Future conservatives might adopt him as one of their patron saints, but to the overwhelming majority of his countrymen he remained an enigma with few redeeming personal qualities.

The results of the efforts of Brownson's counterparts also proved to be quite different from their original objectives. The schools for which Mann fought were intended to turn out virtuous, intelligent, and industrious children; the structures he proposed were designed to facilitate this end. But in practice the American school evolved along very different lines. Future generations would be confronted with a new set of problems: a school system that often appeared rigid and unyielding; a system that was marked by an unresolved tension between professional demands for autonomy and community insistence upon control; a system that educated children with very unequal results.

Much the same was true for mental hospitals. Dix, of course, had conceived of these institutions in therapeutic and remedial terms; from the very beginning they were forced to accept increasing numbers of chronic cases which came to constitute a significant proportion of their resident population, thereby undermining their intended curative functions. Hospitals were supposed to remain small to promote the types of relationships deemed conducive to recovery; instead they grew in size, thereby hastening the transition from a charismatic-type institution to one dominated by administrative concerns. In theory all patients received the same type of care; in practice class, ethnicity, and color played a significant role in determining the nature of care and treatment. Interpreting their role in medical and ameliorative terms, superintendents of institutions were rapidly transformed into administrators who became more and more involved with largely managerial problems. Considerations of order and efficiency overshadowed therapeutic efforts.

*   *   *

The careers of Horace Mann, Dorothea Dix, and Orestes Brownson, then, can be understood in terms of a paradox—one endemic to the human condition. In a rapidly changing world each sought the union of stability and morality. Despite some fundamental differences, their goal was to ensure that traditional values and ideals would continue to dominate the lives of their countrymen. Brownson ended up as a conservative who appeared obsolete in a modernized America. The institutions bequeathed by Mann as well as Dix proved an equally perplexing legacy, for they were rapidly absorbed into a secular and urban-industrial society with an entirely new set of values as well as problems. Beneficent innovations in an earlier day, the schools, hospitals, prisons, and welfare institutions would seem to some 20th-century Americans to require radical surgery if they were not to subvert man's humanity. The legacy of Mann, Dix, and Brownson—like the legacy of all human beings—proved ambiguous and troublesome to future generations.

12

The Abolitionist Controversy:
Men of Blood, Men of God

JAMES GORDON BENNETT
WILLIAM LLOYD GARRISON
JOHN BROWN

by Bertram Wyatt-Brown
Case Western Reserve University

In 1860 Daniel R. Hundley devoted a chapter of his *Social Relations in Our Southern States* to the "swearing, tobacco-chewing, brandy drinking [Southern] Bully" who was "cocked and primed to flog the entire" Yankee breed of "crazy old milk sops!" Southern "short-boys" and tipplers of "bust-head, red-eye, and blue-ruin," the author observed, had Northern counterparts, no less willing to put abolitionists "through a course of sprouts in short order." Hundley was poking fun at an authentic, serious theme in the racial and sectional controversy. Grog-shop ruffians were not the only ones to swagger with "vaporing bravado." William Lloyd Garrison, veteran pacifist and abolitionist, also spoke in similar but more eloquent terms. Caught up in the excitement following John Brown's abortive raid at Harpers Ferry, Garrison rallied a Boston audience: "Give me, as a non-resistant, Bunker Hill, and Lexington, and Concord, rather than the cowardice and servility of a southern plantation." Definitions of manhood involved more than the mere possession of the necessary generative fixtures.

The antebellum cult of virility, a romantic concept in a time of romanticism, had universal appeal. Yet only a handful could ever have met the full ideals of manliness extolled in these years. Quite likely, then, the "Vaporing bravado" and "murderous blamnations" that Hundley satirized

230

may have masked inner doubts. "Cowards prove their courage by their ferocity," John Brown acidly observed, referring to his Southern captors. There is considerable accuracy to his observation. Passionate chest-thumping was highly self-conscious in these decades. Perhaps an inner voice had to be stilled. In 1844, for instance, Sydney Howard Gay, a young abolitionist, surrendered his most intimate self-examinations to his fiancee. "The least reflection," he confessed, "on my manliness or truthfulness makes me shrink and wince like a very chicken." Actually, he was no less stalwart than most contemporaries, though more candid; but the age required assertions of warrior-spirit and "forthright" denunciations of an adversary's "cowardice and servility" from its young men. It is always hard to be reasonable and conciliatory when claims and counter-claims of masculinity and degeneracy become common in public exchange. In times of rapid social, industrial, and political expansion, men sometimes find it necessary to portray themselves in such elemental terms. In their upbringing, ideological commitments, and male identifications, James Gordon Bennett, editor of the New York *Herald,* William Lloyd Garrison, and John Brown exemplified different expressions of a common theme—the meaning of 19th-century American manhood.

*   *   *

Of these three remarkable publicists, James Gordon Bennett was by far the most contradictory in character, combining traditional and innovative styles. Born in Scotland in 1795, Bennett fathered modern journalism. He introduced the financial, sports, theater, and society columns, the Washington bureau, and the foreign-correspondent byline. He also helped establish the Associated Press and wire service. Unlike his old-fashioned rivals in the newspaper industry, Bennett profited from high circulation and cheap newsstand prices. His search for a mass market and his experimental operations for his paper paralleled similar trends in the way Northerners conducted all their affairs. The *Herald* did not exist just to make money; its intent was also to promote "the intellectual happiness of the age." Only "through the medium of a daily newspaper," he claimed, "Conducted on cash principles—(Christ also did business on the cash system)"—could age-old "superstition . . . be crumbled to the Earth," he claimed. No less secular was his defense of urban existence while others gushed about the joys of country living. New York, he boasted, would soon become "the big throbbing heart of the nations," the "New Jerusalem," reigning a thousand years. These convictions and accomplishments implicitly sharpened the distinction between the energetic Yankee and unprogressive Southerner. Such convictions made painful listening to Southerners; yet Bennett was their most influential ally in the alien world of Northern business and bustle.

The paradox is not mysterious. Bennett possessed that ardor for Americanism that so many immigrants have displayed for their adopted land. Perhaps a simple desire for public acceptance prompted, in part, an apology for the South. Sectional parity and racist custom were the twin pillars of the Old Republic; the antislavery cause threatened both. Then, too, it was a matter of proximity. Abolitionists were spreading their "disorganizing" gospel close at hand. Slaveholding "Fire-Eaters," though equally menacing, rumbled in the distance.

Self-interest, identification with proslavery constitutionalism, and a journalist's near-sighted eye for news on the doorstep helped to explain Bennett's rebukes of "amalgamationists," "disunionists," "socialists," and "nigger-worshippers"—the gaggle of epithets that he generally invoked as occasion suggested. But the explanation for such epithets had biographical sources as well. Bennett grew up near the village of Keith, in remote Banffshire, far from the intellectual and economic hubs of Glasgow and Edinburgh. For all his boasting of city life, Bennett retained the prejudices of his youth. Like American Southerners, Scotsmen resented their colonial dependency upon an industrial, urban, and imperious neighbor. Aware that English churchmen had induced Parliament to end West Indian slavery in 1833, Bennett would warn New Yorkers in 1838, 'The abolitionists of England are operating here. *We know the fact*' that "a conspiracy" is underway that "will astonish the whole Union." Such hysteria was partly a result of Scottish enmity toward the ancient foe as well as typical American anglophobia.

Bennett felt such provincial irritations the more keenly because his Catholic parents belonged to a persecuted minority. Despised by Englishmen and Scots Presbyterians alike, the anti-Reformation Catholics had fought at Culloden (1746) for the clans, the True Faith, and Bonnie Prince Charlie, last of the Jacobite Pretenders. Stripped of ancient holdings, dirks, claymores, even war-apparel—the kilt and tartan—the Highland clans disintegrated. "A warrior cannot battle in trousers," young James Bennett heard the oldtimers say. In 1780, the right to wear the male gear was restored. By then some Scotsmen had been domesticated in school, factory, and countinghouse. But the back country nourished the old hostilities. Tales of lost glories and British barbarities still burned deep enough in the rural Scottish mind to help form Bennett's animosities.

The Bennetts themselves lived by a peasant code of hard work and simplicity, one also familiar to Southern farming folk. That free-booters and brigands appeared on the family tree supported special claims to masculinity, Bennett thought. Likewise, he admired Southern whites for being untamed and eager to establish agrarian dynasties. In his opinion, they robustly preserved the old ways—personal and family honor, "the good old orthodox religion," and racial and feminine subservience. Planters, he exclaimed, were the last rampart against anarchistic equalities, "filthy mixings," "the poison of rationalism and German mysticism, spiritualism and all the noxious delusions of the age." Bennett always loved the poetry of Robert Burns and the novels of Sir Walter Scott, both celebrants of the grim folkways and warlike nobility of the Scottish Border. Such romantic fare could also be found on library shelves of a plantation mansion.

Life on the Bennett freehold—even the rituals of the kitchen table— also bore a relation to Southern custom. Only his hard-fisted, formidable father was allowed the right to wash up before dining. A chalk line, drawn on the rough table top, separated the hired hands from the inner family circle. Age, gender, relation to the patriarch and, for the "hinds," occupation and seniority in service, determined the seating arrangements. A Southerner would have recognized such distinctions between those who *belonged* and those who were always on the periphery. In fact, Bennett's early milieu was hardly less agrarian, primitive, and socially rigid than the world of the Southern whites. Orderliness and stability, it was thought, required deferences to a hierarchy designed by God; only zealous "levelers" and abolitionists would dare challenge it.

Bennett had no desire, however, to establish a Southern plantation dynasty, with slaves replacing the "hinds." Indeed, after nine boring months on the staff of a South Carolina paper in 1826, he had fled with relief back to New York City. His rationalizations for the Southern way were mostly nostalgic, sometimes even equivocal; but the vehemence of his attacks on blacks and reformers paradoxically derived from rebellion against the Scottish past as well as allegiance to it.

As a schoolboy in Keith, Bennett had to rely on his wits, not his pinched looks and scrawny, thin-rumped frame. His father, impressed by his 14-year-old son, who excelled at Latin and Greek, sent him to Aberdeen to study for holy orders. Since eldest sons ordinarily inherited family lands, the paternal choice suggested special reasons. The Bennetts were a minority within a minority, being among the handful of Catholic Scots who did not have to slave for English overlords at bare wages. The measure of relative prosperity also shielded them a little from the insults of the hated, dominant Scots Presbyterians. In gratitude, the family felt obliged to surrender its eldest, gifted son to the Holy Church.

Several years' study did not bear the expected fruit. James Bennett could not summon the courage to tell his father, but news of his defection from a godly career and even from Catholic persuasion eventually reached the cottage at Keith. Out of fear and rebellion, Bennett abandoned Scotland forever at age 24, putting an ocean between himself and rejected familial duty. Bennett's life thereafter was a perpetual justification of his claim to independence. Moreover, he had absorbed the heretical opinions of Tom Paine and Lord Byron, both heroes to students during the Napoleonic age, and would argue as much to himself as to the readers of the *Herald,* "Have I not a right to create a belief and a church of my own?" His chief purpose became the fashioning of an alternate credo, one in which abolitionism, a religious dogma, he thought, had no place at all.

Journalism, not religion, served Bennett's need for self-expression. With the zeal of a man running away from himself, he worked an 18-hour day and fashioned a rowdy, secular style of reportage that rivals called "polluted vulgarity"; or, as a later age would term it, "yellow journalism." Crude though it was, such a style reflected a compulsive reaction to the earlier religious authoritarianism in which he had been reared—an anti-religious gospel, as it were. After several years' struggle, Bennett founded the *Herald* in May 1835. An early office, which was on Nassau Street, was a dank basement, an appropriate site, some said, for the "hellish" editor. Above it were the headquarters of the leading religious and benevolent societies of the times. It amused Bennett to have close at hand solemn, stiff-collared pietists, so like the arrogant Presbyterian "blue-noses" familiar to his youth in Keith.

Within a few months Bennett became spokesman for those common-school educated masses that shared his aggrieved iconoclasm, gut patriotism, male imperiousness, and racial insensitivity. Pursuing the widest possible readership, Bennett rejected political affiliations and patronage ties. He wanted to be free to criticize the mighty at will. "An editor," he preached, "must always be with the people, think with them, feel with them, and he need fear nothing. He will be always right, always popular, always free." Bennett's trinity was free expression, popular advocacy, and defiance of moral coerciveness. His political preferences, it followed, were not surprising.

Andrew Jackson, victorious hero of New Orleans, was reincarnated as "the old fighting Borderer of prior centuries, cracking crowns with the fiercest, repaying injury with compound interest; a right sufficient captain of men." Scots-Irish himself, Old Hickory was a duelist, slaveowner, Indian-fighter, horse-race gambler, enemy of effete federal bankers, foe of eastern drawing-room snobs and of abolitionist "incendiaries." Democrats —even Tammany Hall—often enjoyed the *Herald's* irreverent support. So did anyone who gave expression to virile Americanism, which was Bennett's most obsessive theme. If Charles Darwin had not translated the existing doctrine of survival of the fittest into scientific terms, Bennett would still have kept the harsh spirit of a natural order alive.

In line with the theme, the *Herald* defied popular convention by lurid celebrations of sexual and other equally titillating events. Two hundred and fifty "beautiful and apparently accomplished young women," Bennett announced, were busy nightly in the city, while uptown "husbands are leaving their wives—clergymen kissing widows—widows enticing clergymen." In 1836, he shrewdly reported the hatchet-murder of Ellen Jewett, lovely resident of Rosina Townshend's bawdy house. He used personal interviews, verbatim conversations with the accused (a dashing apprentice), the police, and the madam herself. Rivals disdainfully accused him of contaminating public sensibility and exploiting his own sins, like "a vampire returning to a newly found grave yard." Bennett retorted that he was a respectable bachelor, too shy for such goings-on. (In his mid-40s, he married a Brooklyn piano teacher, but the *Herald* remained his sole obsession.) As a young gallant, the editor confessed, he had once visited a Nova Scotia brothel. But the girls told his companion, "Never bring that homely scoundrel to our house"; he "gives us the ague." Such self-deprecation went far to increase the loyalty of his subscribers.

The desperate search for fame and personal justification resulted in nine separate scuffles with those scandalized by his columns. James Watson Webb, hot-tempered editor of the *Morning Courier and Enquirer*, assaulted Bennett on Wall Street for accusing him of criminal stock fraud. He "cut a slash in my head one and a half inches in length," Bennett gleefully reported. "The fellow, no doubt, wanted to let out the never-failing supply of good humor and wit . . . and appropriate the contents to supply the emptiness of his own thick skull." Circulation rose dramatically. The stooped Scotsman thrived on making himself the news of the hour and boasted that "neither Webb nor any other man can intimidate me. I will never succumb." One is reminded of Garrison's belligerence; "I am in earnest—I will not equivocate—I will not excuse—I will not retreat a single inch—AND I WILL BE HEARD."

Bennett's editorial position on abolitionism was certainly predictable, one that brought together menacing ideas—clerical manipulation, feminine encroachments upon male prerogatives, and threats of black insurgency, in the form of sexual lust for white women and of slaughter of white males. Bennett did not invent such slanders, but he expanded their scope, relating prejudices to the valid complaints of ordinary Americans beset by a changing and unfamiliar world. Proslavery and racist attitudes were part of the noisy rhythm of Northern life. The *Herald* columns included attacks upon politicians who used racist "sentimentalities" for their own greedy purposes, bankers who knew "the art of rifling the poor" and cheating "the mechanics," fee-grabbing lawyers, do-gooders "who look after everybody's business but their own," and Wall Street brokers, artists of "fraud and deception." Then, too, there were the professors at New York's "colleges, all poor and proud, except Columbia which is rich and lazy, educating only 100 students, yet complaining of hard work." Equally appealing to *Herald* readers were diatribes against the "rogues" in, but mostly out of, state prison. Fearful of rising taxes, New Yorkers chaffed at the "chiselers" on state bounty—the "paupers in the poor house," exclaimed Bennett, and the rest who were "heading there as fast as intemperance and indolence can carry them." Like the workers in New York's dockyards and factories, Bennett fumed about wealthy misers who cut workers' pay so that their sons, the city's "500 dandies," could strut about until they closed "their career with a pistol or a glass of laudanum," the popular drug addiction of the age.

Bennett was more or less singular in his attacks upon "wheedling judges" and other figures in New York's refined and established circles. His imagery fed the appetite of the city-dweller who thought himself a victim of pound-of-flesh bosses, swell-heads, banks, business houses, tax collectors, and parasitic politicians. Then there were the dreamy radicals, "white-coated philosophers," revival deacons with their array of Sunday schools and tract dispensing volunteers—and they, too, preyed upon the ordinary urbanite, and they, too, were targets of Bennett's shafts.

Bennett also portrayed himself as a victim, but one willing to give as much as he got. His readers, as letters to the editor testified, were convinced that he was generous to his friends and to workers, gallant toward women (the deserving ones), godly as only a man free of formal church ties could be, forthright toward his adversaries, moral and respectable, and sound on national and local issues. In a way Bennett was, though he was also misanthropic (refusing even a social glass of wine), virtually friendless, with a bad stomach and a glum, rather cross-eyed expression. The fact that respectable citizens thought him "too pitchy to touch," as a friend of Abraham Lincoln's once exclaimed, only enhanced his reputation among ordinary readers. Many Southerners and Westerners also admired him. To the public at least, he was the kind of fellow a bricklayer thought he would want for a friend.

Antebellum Americans, like many today, clothed themselves and their fears with easily grasped stereotypes that made sense of the incomprehensible and eased their feelings of doubt and insecurity. The result was not consciously nasty, though it could be, particularly during the numerous anti-abolitionist riots of the 1830s in New York City and elsewhere. Bennett served a popular function. He articulated the disenchantments and bawdy preoccupations of the voiceless. At the same time, Bennett himself felt compelled to cry out against self-guilt. There remained a personal connection between his attacks upon abolitionism and the world he had left behind in Scotland.

Three years after the *Herald's* birth, James Bennett returned to Banffshire for a visit to his widowed mother's home. On the afternoon of his reunion at Keith, Bennett read the last letters from Cosmo, his younger brother, dead from causes Bennett attributed to the austerities of seminary living. He burst out in tears of anger and grief, raging about the house in what his relatives thought was a near-demented state. Bennett said nothing about Cosmo's futile clerical sacrifice upon the family altar, the role that he himself had so long ago escaped. But he swore an oath: "For the negligence that led to his death, my holy mother, the Church, must

suffer some, and by my hands! See if she don't!" After a 23 year absence
he abruptly left the old homestead the very next morning.

New York's Catholic bishops were not the only emissaries of God to
feel Bennett's wrath. He arraigned those clergymen who made special
appeal to the Almighty and the public in an evangelistic or dogmatic
way. "A more corrupt, infidel, foolish, ignorant, witless, lazy, degenerate
and rotten race of clergy," he said, "has not existed since the time of
Caiaphus and Ananias, the high priests and high scoundrels of Judea."
Bennett returned to the Old Testament prophets for the origins of the
unmanly spirit of the clergy. "I don't think much of Moses," Bennett
declared. "A man who would take 40 years to get a party of young women
through the desert is only a loafer . . . Moses himself . . . was the first
white man who married a Negro woman, and thus gave a sanction to
amalgamation and abolition."

Bennett was aware that most Northern clergymen feared abolitionism
as much as he deplored it. He applauded whenever the churches and
benevolent societies prevented the passage of antislavery resolutions,
but, like the equally vehement Garrisonians, he believed clerical motives
were not holy or forthright. In 1860 the *Herald* editorialized, "The abolitionists may demand that the Gospels shall be altered so as to make
out our Saviour a Garrisonian," yet "only one thing prevents the societies
from splitting with the Almighty Nigger, and that is the Almighty Dollar."

Like many of the *Herald*'s subscribers, Bennett feared that middle-
class pieties would feminize the nation. They would snatch the convivial
tankard from the honest toiler, close down dance halls and theaters, shut
up the Post Offices and railroad depots on Sundays, encourage blacks "to
seek white mates," and bring on a return to the theocratic tyrannies of
puritan New England. Ancient social and gender rankings would disappear along with "the purity of anglo-saxon blood." All these policies
threatened the traditional image of the male as master of his own destiny,
arbiter of his own morals and sexual habits, protector of his own de-
pendents, whether within the family or outside it on the plantation.
Bennett dwelt almost obsessively upon the modern breed "of unsexed
females," abolitionist products of "finishing" schools, where indeed they
"are 'finished,' as we once heard John Randolph say in the House of
Representatives, 'finished, Mr. Speaker, yes, sir, finished for all useful
purposes.'" But if antislavery women wore breeches, as he claimed, they
consorted with men in "petticoats—vent your mawkishness on that!" In
Bennett's opinion, Wendell Phillips and Garrison, like their clerical
cousins in "white cravats," fought from behind the whalebone and cotton
padding of their female allies, even though their doctrines were "boldly
outrageous" and "madly fanatical." This double accusation of cowardice
and satanism explained in part the passions that prompted a near-riot
at the Broadway Tabernacle in 1850, the symbolism that surrounded

John Brown, and the outbreak of war itself in 1861. But first the Garrisonian counter-style requires explanation.

*   *   *

In many respects, William Lloyd Garrison represented the very antithesis of those values that Bennett and the anti-abolitionists espoused. Where the *Herald* editor glorified the male characteristics that he claimed to embody, Garrison rejoiced in following the standard of the Golden Rule. "If pride, ambition, and every sinful propensity, have been slain within me," Garrison modestly confided, "if love, joy, peace, long-suffering, gentleness, goodness, faith, meekness, temperance, 'the fruit of the Spirit,' dwell in me, it is solely 'by the grace of God.'" Garrison admitted that if he had not already "nailed natural vanity and love and human praise to the cross of Christ, such things would be likely to puff" him "up." Both Garrison and Bennett were egocentrics par excellence. Each thought himself and his mission extraordinary, almost superhuman.

Bennett drew his definition of manliness partially out of his Scottish heritage; Garrison's source was the hardy puritanism of old and New England. One of his heroes was "the martyred patriot of England—the great Algernon Sydney," a Puritan nobleman executed in the 1683 uprising against Charles II. There was always a trace of Cromwellian iron in Garrison's exhortations, and his speeches echoed the Biblical phrases of New England's ministers. Though we must bear "the vicious slanders of worldly men," Garrison intoned, "Deliver us from a boastful, vainglorious, self-confident spirit: but oh! what strength in Christian faith! what triumph in Christian endurance! Let us use, then, the dialect of Christian conquerors!" The Prince of Peace apparently carried a sword, though Garrison insisted that it was always sheathed.

"Muscular Christianity" of this kind was highly popular in the 19th century, culminating in the kind of male body building that Teddy Roosevelt celebrated. Despite his unique religious and reform beliefs, the role of strenuous Christian Achiever did not originate with Garrison; he merely applied the idea to anti-slavery and other issues. Consistent with this role, Garrison identified bluntness with manly duty. "In all my writings I have used strong, indignant, vehement language, direct, pointed scorching reproof," he wrote in 1830, shortly after release from a Baltimore jail for libeling a slave-trading New Englander. "Many have censured me for my severity—but thank God! none have stigmatized me with lukewarmness. 'Passion is reason—transport, temper—here.'" Typical of the polarized view of sexual roles in this day, Garrison struck out in a manner reminiscent of Bennett himself: "Men of natural softness and timidity, of a sincere and effeminate virtue, will be apt to look on these bolder, hardier spirits" of the antislavery crusade "as violent, perturbed and uncharitable." But the cause of "God's oppressed," he continued, required the services of those brave souls eager "*to move and shake nations*," even at their own peril.

Defining the male role in terms of Christian sacrifice, selflessness, and boisterous exposure of wrongdoing, Garrison found the Southern system as demonic as Bennett pronounced it wholesome. Slavery, he insisted, made men—both master and slave—into beasts because unbounded, absolute power recognized no moral or even institutional check. Slavery, in Garrisonian opinion, encouraged the animal appetites and weakened capacities to control temptation. The Victorian moralist, however, thought that the Christian ideal of life demanded self-discipline in mind, body, and action. The age, then, stressed bodily restraints of a very inhibiting sort; but, oddly enough, permitted the most self-worshipping boastings. Teetotalism, sexual abstemiousness, cold-water bathing, rejection of "stimulants" like tea, coffee, sometimes meat, all were considered to be a means to physical purity. Garrison, like most other root-and-branch moralists, opposed "the dreadful vice of masturbation," a pleasure that supposedly led thousands of young people to insanity, physical decay, and moral ruin. On this issue, he was quite unlike Bennett, whose cure would have been a visit to Rosina Townshend's. Abolitionists like Garrison, however, thundered against such "sinks of pollution." However much "licentiousness pervades the whole land," Garrison claimed, "the 16 slave states constitute one vast brothel." Therefore, abolitionism was an effort "to save a million of the gentler sex from pollution, field labor, and the lash. *It is to put an end to an impure and disgraceful amalgamation.*" The sexual imagery used in the Garrisonian attack was almost as graphic as Bennett's smirky apologies, but Garrison was deeply serious and theoretically if not actually correct about the Freudian implications of Southern racial attitudes.

Although early background never explains the whole man, Garrison's determination to be the purest foot-soldier in Christ's faithful army may have been in part a reaction to his father. Born in 1805, ten years after Bennett, he barely knew Abijah Garrison before being separated from him. A genial ne'er-do-well who drifted aimlessly about New England's grog-shops with fellow sailors, Abijah left household duties entirely in the hands of his ill-matched and pious wife. When Garrison was six, Abijah abandoned the family in Newburyport, Massachusetts, and settled in Maine with another woman. Humiliated, forced to take menial jobs, "Fanny" Garrison raised her children as best she could. The eldest boy, James, took to the sea and to the bottle in unhappy imitation of the departed Abijah. James died of chronic alcoholism in 1842. Imbued with a sense of special destiny that his worrisome mother imparted, William Lloyd apprenticed as a printer. Unlike Bennett, however, he realized that this occupation was a conventional vehicle from which to preach Federalist orthodoxy and, later, racial salvation. Bennett had deliberately rejected the priestly function. Garrison embraced it gladly.

Yet the youthful editor, like Bennett, used journalism to express rebellious feelings. The antislavery cause was, of course, a worthy and inspiring enterprise; and Garrison's contribution to it was both imaginative and effective. Nevertheless, he too wished to create a church and a set of beliefs of his own. Such a goal was common enough in the Jacksonian era. Individual approaches to personal and common problems multiplied, reflecting the social tensions and romantic feelings that accompanied commercial and political change. Perhaps Garrison found the answer in perfectionism—loyalty to the only legitimate government— the government of Christ; conceivably it was a means to fame in contrast to his father's obscurity and fall from respectability. In any case, he defied social norms and institutions by advocating radical policies that only a handful of followers could admire. Churches, he thought, chained the conscience to outworn Sabbatarian regulations and sectional timidities. Government masked an underlying military coercion that only total separation of North and South could begin to alter. Political parties corrupted even the antislavery officeholder. The pure of heart, Garrison asserted, ought not to vote simply because to do so was the expedient thing; expediency was a pernicious tactic. Claiming allegiance to the moral government of Christ, Garrison insisted that racial brotherhood would arrive with the millennial coming. Meanwhile, he arraigned the slightest deviation from righteousness. His policy, which included feminine liberation, made the purity of abolitionism obnoxious to the average citizen. To be sure, it also advertised both Garrison and his cause.

In some respects, few journalists were more traditional than the *Liberator's* editor. No memorable innovations arose from its dreary columns. Not without reason, Bennett disliked the "one-idea" papers of which Garrison's was merely another struggling sheet. These efforts, he said, became "after a time, terrible bores, even to the people whose convictions they express." But Garrison was a modern agitator, perhaps the first and the best—not a truly professional journalist like Bennett. In that respect, he displayed an ingenious parasitism. With only occasional flashes of wit and stunning phrase, the *Liberator* thrived on the publicity that Bennett and other opponents provided—with their ridicule of Garrisonian "moonshine." Garrison did not initiate the violence that gave meaning and public influence to the cause of racial freedom. Consequently, there was always a latent provocation in his non-resistant rhetoric. But in emotional intensity, the moral antislavery rebukes of William Lloyd Garrison and the hot-tempered bellicosity of James Gordon Bennett were quite alike.

The annual convention of the Garrisonian American Anti-Slavery Society in May 1850, at New York's Broadway Tabernacle, juxtaposed all the themes of racism and equality, fear and hope, manliness and cowardice. The sessions coincided with an intense Congressional dispute over slavery, and a civil conflict over the territorial spoils of the Mexican War seemed likely. Only later in the fall, after President Zachary Taylor's timely death, did sectional negotiation postpone the conflict. But the scenes in the cavernous, overcrowded revivalist tabernacle prefigured events of a decade later.

For some days prior to the antislavery assembly, Bennett urged *Herald* readers to demonstrate the city's loyalty to the "Glorious Union" between North and South. These "besotted zealots," he cried, are "very much excited about the wrongs of their colored brethren and sisters. They mix with them, fraternizing, slobbering over each other, speaking, praying, singing, blaspheming, and cursing the Constitution." Aware of earlier mob reactions to the Garrisonians, Bennett specifically cautioned that passions be restrained. Otherwise, the abolitionists could claim to be "martyrs to their false patriotism, false pride, and sincere folly." Warming to the task, Bennett continued, "Never in the time of the French Revolution was there more malevolence and unblushing wickedness avowed than by this same Garrison."

Among the 6,000 attending the sessions were Captain Isaiah Rynders and a large contingent of Tammany "b'hoys" who represented Bennett's views from their gallery seats. Recently ousted by the Whigs from his post of U.S. Customs weigher, Rynders held power through his Democratic ward gangs of "Calithumpians" and "Rip Raps" as well as his ownership of the Empire Club gambling casino. Individuals actually may conform to the most exaggerated caricature. So it was with Rynders, a florid-faced, beefy, half-German, half-Irish ex-boatmen—the perfect symbol of the hard-headed anti-abolitionist. Garrison was the first speaker. Answering Bennett's editorial charge of fomenting "blasphemous atheism," he attacked the iniquities of the American church system. "The slaves believe in a Jesus that strikes off chains," he exclaimed. But for whites "Jesus has become obsolete." In fact, "Jesus is the most respectable person in the United States.... Jesus sits in the President's chair." Uncomprehending the gang in the balcony rumbled ominously. "Zachary Taylor," Garrison drove on, "sits there which is the same thing, for he believes in Jesus. He believes in war, and the Jesus that gave the Mexicans hell."

At that point, Rynders shook a fist and shouted: "I will not allow you to assail the President of the United States. You shan't do it!" Rynders then swung down to the stage on a gaslight standard and headed for the podium. "Have some respect for the ladies," cried an abolitionist from the floor. Rynders parried, "I have always respected the ladies, but I doubt very much whether white women who cohabit with the woolly-headed negro, are entitled to any respect from a white man." Somehow, Garrison restored order and scored the "cowards" who hid "behind the safe and popular side of slavery" and had "no fight in them" for anything but "political preferments." When he had finished, Rynders demanded that his side be given the floor.

"Professor" Robert Grant, with a dirty bandage wrapped around one hand, then stepped up at Rynders' command. His lecture, like his clothing, was a shabby affair that "scientifically" linked Negroes with the primates of the jungle. Horace Greeley's *Tribune,* Bennett's reform-minded competitor, wryly observed that "if anybody present was proved the nephew of a rather dull ourang outang, it was Professor Robert Grant; if anybody the first cousin of a very vicious monkey, it was Capt. Isaiah Rynders."

The abolitionists could not have found a more emphatic refutation than in the argument of their next speaker—Frederick Douglass, the brilliant and light-skinned former slave. He replied, "I cannot follow his argument. I will assist him, however. I offer myself for your examination. Am I a man?" Thunderous applause gave the instant response. But Captain Rynders countered: "You are only half a nigger." In mock deference, Douglass cuttingly replied, "Then I am half-brother to Captain Rynders!" Even Bennett's *Herald* conceded that Douglass' subsequent address was the best of the day. Douglass and another equally impressive black orator, had insured that the rowdies could not halt the momentum of the meeting.

That evening the two forces again confronted each other in a smaller hall, this time with greater expectation of a bloody outcome. Stephen S. Foster, a fiery Garrisonian, almost immediately accused the Rynders "working men" of being mere tools in a plot hatched by Bennett and fearful city merchants. But Foster was wrong. The ward-heelers and butcher-boys were not pawns of upper-class interests: they vented their genuine frustrations against a middle-class group of moralists with cultural and religious assumptions that they themselves could never easily accept. To them abolitionists were a sinister and alien force ready to impose religious and racial tyrannies.

The next reform speaker served as an easy target for the hooters in the gallery. Charles Calistus Burleigh, another reform editor, wore his fiery red hair in long ringlets to the shoulders; he also had a beard to match. Even Garrison was unhappily aware that, for all his gifts, Burleigh subjected himself "to the unjust suspicion that he was a weak and eccentric individual." As Burleigh strode toward the platform, someone shouted to Garrison: "Say, Judge, tell us whether that is a man or a woman"; and another: "Why don't Douglass shave that tall Christ and make a wig for him?" The guffaws grew so loud that Burleigh could not be heard.

Meanwhile, Rynders commissioned another Tammany hack to replace the ineffectual "Professor." Thomas Moore, a policeman recently discharged for being drunk in a "house of ill fame," took command. His resolution accurately reflected working-class feelings: "Resolved, That this meeting will not countenance fanatical agitation whose aims are the overthrow of the churches, a reign of anarchy, a division of interests, the supremacy of a hypocritical atheism, a general amalgamation, and a dissolution of the Union." What these "humanity-mongers" ought to do, Moore continued, was to investigate "the progress of degradation among Negroes of the North, and the increasing inequality and poverty of the free whites and blacks of New York." One might argue that the authors, James Bennett among them, included the blacks in this protest against grinding urban conditions as an indication of raceless proletarian solidarity. But their actual object was to contrast the allegedly dreamy abstractions of reform idealism with a more visceral spirit—that paradoxical, mindless notion that there are some good "niggers," so long as they kept their place.

Crowd feelings were growing dangerously overheated. What almost triggered a general melee, however, was not slavery and antislavery as such, but rather the issue of virility. Burleigh tried to regain the attention of this restless crowd and finally cried out in desperation, "You are a God-abandoned people! O, misguided men! You know not what you do!" "Boo, hoo, oo-oo!" yelled the "b'hoys" in high falsetto, waving their handkerchiefs and flapping their wrists. At once, Garrison, outraged, moved Burleigh aside: "There is not a man among you. If you are men of intellect, come up here on this platform. Pick out your man, if you have a man among you who dares to say 'boo to a goose,' which I very much doubt. You have not the manliness to say you are friends of slavery." At least Southerners, Garrison shouted, "have the courage for that." Wendell Phillips then denounced the "cringing wretches" of the North who were doing the South's bidding like slaves themselves. No set of "sacrilegious scoundrels," no "hireling band of Southern aristocracy," no "purlieus of Park Row," Phillips cried, "shall drive us hence. We are able to protect ourselves, and we shall do so." In fact, where better to die "than here—here on this platform—martyrs alike to Freedom and Liberty?" Scuffling broke out on the floor. The ladies present headed for the aisles. Anticipating the worst, Garrison hastily called for adjournment. The Rynders gang replied, "Oh, oh! come, Judge, no more gassing; let up on us, we have given you a good show." Three cheers went up for the *Herald* and its editor.

Just then Sheriff Carnley and a band of police arrived to protect the Library Society's hall and disperse the crowd. Meanwhile, the Hutchinson Family Singers in the gallery struck up an antislavery tune to soothe the throng. Captain Rynders shouted up to the songsters, "You long-haired abolitionists, if you don't stop singing, I'll come up there and bring you down." Pushed along by Carnley's men, the wool-hat boys left with the others. The hymn-singing, the police, and the rough good humor of the workingmen had averted a general riot. One of the last to leave the scene, Rynders was overheard to complain that contrary to the libels of the *Tribune,* he did *not* count apes among his forebears.

Garrison had no doubt that Bennett was the real instigator of the most heated antislavery convention in a number of years: "For all that transpired, that was brutal, profane, indecent, outrageous . . . the miscreant editor of that polluted journal is to be held directly responsible." Although Bennett exhibited a murderous spirit "unsurpassed in the annals of assassination," Garrison claimed, "we freely forgive this abandoned man for all the evil he has sought to inflict upon us; for we cherish no other feelings toward him than those of the deepest compassion." Considering Garrison's version of forgiveness, revenge itself might have been a milder balm. Bennett pointed out that, despite Garrison's disavowal of human government, the Boston editor was demanding that New York officials indict him for inciting a riot. For his part, Garrison saw no contradiction. After all, he maintained, Bennett was "the employer, the principal—Rynders and his gang were only his tools, and are scarcely to be held accountable for their insane behavior." Summing up abolitionist philosophy, Garrison argued that the Society would continue to "procure the abolition of slavery by peaceful agencies, in a voluntary manner, through conviction and repentance on the part of all who are guilty of upholding it, whether in the North or at the South." Carnal weapons were not a solution, he said. Antislavery stalwarts used only spiritual ones for "the pulling down of the strongholds of American slavery."

From 1831 to 1859, the abolitionist crusade, splintered and faction-ridden though it was, remained more or less faithful to the non-violent posture that Garrison insistently preached. The policy was based on a fallacy traditional to American reform; namely, the idea that with proper guidance from enlightened (middle-class) leadership the masses would respond to rational argument. Even slaveholders were expected to rally, as Garrison phrased it from the Bible, to "the foolishness of preaching." To the abolitionist, slavery was a *problem,* like drinking, dueling, cruelty to small animals, and prostitution. For these sins there was the simple remedy of personal repentance, backed by appropriate laws that reflected thousands of individual acts of contrition.

Anti-abolitionists like Bennett and most Southern whites considered slavery a *condition,* not a problem. Race subordination was like poverty, war, government, bloodlines, and hierarchies of individual talent—that is, it was part of the natural order of things. Such matters could be adjusted for better or worse, but the condition itself was immutable and divinely sanctioned. Neither party was totally accurate. Abolitionists were deluded in thinking that the elimination of the problem, "the peculiar institution," would bring on a racial millennium. Bennett's error had a sounder historical foundation, but he romantically overestimated the durability of slavery and ignored the drift toward free-labor capitalism.

Curiously, however, the misperceptions of both parties hastened a revolutionary transformation that could scarcely satisfy either group. Garrisonians had to believe in the efficacy of individual conversion, since the mass of the citizenry—where power resided—was normally phlegmatic and self-concerned. Yet the tactics of "moral suasion," which aimed at antislavery recruitment, had struck another target—confrontation. Abolitionists stirred the blood, not the heart. Garrisonian pacifism, like the offer of forgiveness, provoked indignation. However, without the fulminations of Bennett and others like him, Garrison, Phillips, and Douglass could never have staged so effective a drama that contrasted manly righteousness against ignorance and venality. Each protagonist fed the bellicosity of the other. Gradually, the indifferent and casual observer was being forced to take a stand. But the task of escalating these issues of race and masculinity to the threshold of war itself fell to a former shepherd and insurrectionist.

*   *   *

Shortly after news arrived that John Brown, two of his sons, and most of the fellow conspirators had been captured or killed at Harpers Ferry, Bennett sent a special reporter to Charlestown, Virginia. The *Herald's* coverage was by far the most vivid, detailed, and stirring of any newspaper reporting up to that time. Through it Bennett inadvertently contributed enormously to the polarization of sectional feelings and actually to the dignity of the anti-slavery cause. For the *Herald* as well as other papers in competitive imitation projected the image of Brown as a divine, consecrated man of God *and* blood. "I hold that the golden rule, 'Do unto others as you would that others should do unto you,' applies to all who would help others to gain their liberty," Brown informed the *Herald's* readers. Unlettered though he was, Brown—no less than Bennett and Garrison—showed a masterly grasp of publicity. As Henry Thoreau, one of his most ardent admirers exclaimed, "No theatrical manager could have arranged things so wisely to give effect to his behavior and words."

John Brown's rise to his remarkable prominence involved a strange personal history, which included a growing self-awareness of godly manhood. In a letter of 1857, Brown related a moving account of his inner feelings as child and adult. Written in the third person, as if composed by someone seeking a special detachment, it described how his father, a stern, old-fashioned Edwardsean Calvinist moved the family from rural Connecticut to the Indian-infested Ohio frontier. Born in 1800, Brown was then five years of age, just old enough to feel the tensions of resettlement. When he was eight, Brown lost his mother, and his father promptly married a teenage girl, 20 years his junior. John Brown recalled that he "never adopted" his step-mother "in feeling," but continued to pine after his own mother for years. As the letter revealed, the boy channelled his nervous affections into the possession of pets and toys, particularly "a Yellow marble . . . but at last he lost it beyound [sic] recovery. It took years to heal the wound; & I think at times he cried about it." Finding little love at home, he was compelled to place faith in things that, like his real mother, slipped away too quickly. Since abandoned children often blame themselves for their misfortunes, Brown himself may have thought that God (as well as his grim father) had punished him for misdeeds by depriving him of his mother.

At school, Brown recorded, he was so unhappy and distracted that he "learned nothing of Grammer [sic]" and little arithmetic. Schoolmates thought him a bully *"excessively* fond of the hardest & roughest plays." Dreaming of eventual successes that would silence those whom he could not impress, Brown spent lonely hours at home where he was captive to such self-isolating fantasies. Moreover, he tended to lie compulsively, a habit, he confessed, that was "very bad & foolish" and practiced "to screen himself from blame," since he could not suffer to be reproached. Authority generally provoked Brown's anger unless paternally identified—whether on Earth or in heaven—and praise from older residents, he admitted, filled him with "self-conceit." Outwardly, however, he came to manhood singularly devoted to the visible and publicly approved virtues of hard work, neatness, and practical realities.

Later events did not alter Brown's private convictions of future omnipotence and present distress. Two marriages, the steady accumulation of children (20 by these wives), and many jobs brought more sorrow than pleasure. One baby, for instance, died when two older children plunged the infant in a bath of scalding water. Or witness Brown's business affairs, mostly sheep-raising and tanning, in which he demonstrated a romantic impulsiveness that led inevitably to debts and disputes. Brown took solace by worshipping not a forgiving God, but rather the crucified, atoning victim of human depravity.

When John Brown's eldest son had engaged in some naughty escapades, the father listed them—a "fearful toting up of *debits,*" John Brown, Jr., recalled—in a moral ledgerbook. And then, rather than continue punishment, John Brown stripped off his own shirt and ordered his son to lay on with the remaining two-thirds of the "account." Throughout the ordeal, he cried out, strike "harder, harder, harder!" until the horrified boy could see the blood oozing down his back. The lesson presumably was modelled after the atonement of Christ on the Cross and would be later repeated by Brown himself on the Charlestown gallows. Religion, punishment, countinghouse bankruptcy, paternal anguish, a masochistic pleasure in the pain of receiving the blows for whatever sins he himself felt guilty—all combine to shape the life of John Brown, a charismatic leader beset by feelings he could not otherwise express. But like most religious zealots—and Brown was essentially that—he somehow managed to utilize even his inmost fears and hopes creatively, and by a peculiar alchemy transformed them into a conquering spiritual power.

Brown, it should be noted, was also the model of the dedicated puritan, replete with rather conventional sentiments: "Diligence is the mother of good luck," "God helps those who help themselves," were among his favorite aphorisms. One of the sources of his loathing for the South, not surprisingly, derived from this Puritanism. Vices of idleness, self-indulgent drunkenness, profanity, wild disorder, sexual profligacy, mean-spirited mastery over the souls of others—these crimes against God and morality were identified with "the *foul and loathsome* embrace of the *old rotten whore*, slavery." Temperamental difficulties could hardly explain Brown's genuine sympathies for the blacks.

Brown had little reason to be proud of his accomplishments until going to Kansas in the mid-1850s. There, with his sons, he discovered a godly, revolutionary calling—the struggle for freedom on the borders of slavery. "Transfixed . . . in a kind of trance," Brown watched his guerilla band hack at the fallen bodies of allegedly proslavery farmers near Pottawatomie Creek.

There may have been a psychological basis for the Kansas violence and for Brown's extravagant scheme of arming slaves with the arsenal guns at Harpers Ferry. For him, the enterprise represented atonement for past disappointment and self-thwarted ambitions, as well as an investment in immortality. Writing to his wife after the effort had failed, he declared, "I have been whiped [sic] as the saying is but I am sure that I can recover all the *lost capital* occasioned by that disaster; by only hanging a few moments by the neck, & I feel quite determined to make the utmost possible out of a defeat." (Italics the author's.) At last, the mission for which he confidently believed God had summoned him was fulfilled.

The bloody border chieftain of the Kansas plains and the benign, radiantly calm Christian martyr of the Charlestown prison combined the tense duality of Brown's character. From capture to the scaffold steps, Brown looked forward with "all joy," as he said, to the moment when hated authority meted out punishment and opened the avenue to personal vindication and black liberation. Almost to the end of the raid, Brown could have escaped to Virginia's hill country. His intention, though not wholly conscious, was instead the performance of a religious, testamentary act of sacrifice. It ended all past confusions and made him feel whole and purposeful in a way denied to most men.

Brown's appeal to many of his contemporaries in the North is not terribly perplexing. He evoked adulation because his actions seemingly cut through the Gordian knot of moral vexations. Yearning for saintly heroes in an age of vulgar preoccupations, money-exchange ethics, and moral complacencies, New England luminaries like Theodore Parker, Thomas Wentworth Higginson, Ralph Waldo Emerson, and Henry Thoreau perceived Brown as the ultimate expression of romantic Christianity and 19th-century manliness. Brown's deeds gave the lie to those who thought Yankee abolitionists generally soulless, calculating and money-conscious. Garrison's hot words, after all, were only words. Brown translated them into bold action. "Walter Scott would have delighted" to depict John Brown, Emerson proclaimed. "All gentlemen, of course, are on his side," though not "people of scented hair and perfumed handkerchiefs, but men of gentle blood and generosity. For what is the oath of gentle blood and knighthood? What but to protect the weak and lowly against the strong oppressor?" As Francis Lieber, a prominent Columbia professor, scornfully observed, "Brown died like a man," while "Virginia fretted like a woman."

Even James Gordon Bennett came to recognize that abolitionists possessed the courage that he admired, though not in a cause that ever gained his approval. Remarking upon the contrasting timidity of some Republican leaders after the Harpers Ferry raid, Bennett mused, "Truly there is as much difference between the manly heart and the politician's gizzard, as physically between the massive form of the Abolitionist and the insignificant figure" of a political time-server. "Would not a Southern gentleman respect the former far more than the latter?" Bennett cared nothing for racial freedom—no more so than did hundreds of thousands of other Northern citizens. Nevertheless, he recognized manly acts, even in a "crazy scoundrel" like John Brown. He also acknowledged loyalty to the Northern clan. Complaining bitterly about abolition "mischief" and canting "Black Republicanism," Bennett nonetheless would remain loyal to the Union in 1861. It was a fitting conclusion since Bennett had done so much to test antislavery mettle and publicize the crusade.

The American ideal of manhood was only a myth. Yet it gave meaning to life itself and helped to mobilize armies on both sides of the Potomac. In an effort to deny cowardice, thousands went to their death. Furthermore, this cult of manliness demonstrated that events of history are sometimes determined less by actual circumstances than by the perceptions of them. In these antebellum years, tragedy and inspiration, prejudice and progress, delusion and reason, fear of emasculation and hope of glory conspired together, producing results for which later generations could be soberly grateful.

13

The Peculiar Institution: Defended, Accommodated, and Attacked

JOHN C. CALHOUN
HENRY CLAY
ANGELINA GRIMKÉ

by Charles M. Wiltse
Dartmouth College

After the Missouri Compromise of 1820, the elimination of slavery, the South's "peculiar institution," became the major goal of American reform, while its defense formed the hard core of the nation's conservatism. The northern challenge to Missouri's admission as a slave state forced the South to come to grips with both its conscience and its future. Many of the framers of the Constitution, including slaveholders like James Madison, had assumed that the institution, without renewal, would be progressively diffused and would eventually disappear. The Constitution's provision prohibiting the Congress from halting the foreign slave trade prior to 1808 was only a gesture, for it had already been stopped by the states. In 1790 there were some 750,000 slaves out of a population of approximately four million. Over the next three decades, the proportion of slaves to total population remained relatively unchanged —a little more than 18 percent. However the production of cotton, which came to absorb the bulk of slave labor, increased from 3,000 bales in 1790 to 335,000 bales in 1820.

By the latter date cotton planters, to a man, had convinced themselves that their staple could not be grown and prepared for market without slave labor. If Congress could abolish slavery in Missouri, it could end it anywhere, given the requisite majorities in both houses. Missouri was admitted with slavery but only by a compromise that brought Maine simultaneously into the Union as a free state. The Senate thus remained evenly divided, but to the South, already numerically weaker than the North, equality in the upper house at best afforded shaky ground on which to rest the future of its way of life. Thereafter, the specter of slavery was present in every debate that implied to any degree the supremacy of the federal government over the states. Slaveholders came to oppose all legislation pertaining to internal improvements, the tariff, and a national bank, lest such measures unintentionally concede an excess of power to the federal government.

In the North the great religious revival of the 1830s both fed upon and nourished a growing antislavery mood. Though the defense of slavery was also grounded in Scripture, its immediacy derived from the tariff and the falling price of cotton. Southern planters were absolutely convinced that the one was the cause of the other. With equal obstinacy they believed that the power to override the states by imposing a distasteful tariff might one day be invoked to alter their slave labor system. This possibility, which achieved nightmarish proportions after the slave revolt of 1822, gave a do-or-die impetus to the fight against the tariff as well as to the developing intellectual defense of slavery.

The South's most refined constitutional and intellectual argument came from its most able political theoretician, John C. Calhoun. The South Carolinian's tightly reasoned arguments were countered by a well-organized and vocal abolitionist movement that preferred to rest its case on morality rather than legal hair-splitting. Angelina Grimké has been chosen here as the representative of the antislavery crusade not only because of the importance of her role but because, like Calhoun, she was a South Carolinian. Somewhere between these two extremes were great numbers of Americans, Northerners and Southerners alike, who were prepared to accept whatever the national verdict might be so long as it was indeed national. Henry Clay, whose name is associated with three great North-South compromises, fell into this intermediate group.

*   *   *

No figure in American history has been more controversial than John Caldwell Calhoun, the gaunt, emaciated Senator from South Carolina, the very personification of the antebellum South. He has been variously called a pure-hearted patriot and a traitor to his country, a man of "enlarged and liberal views" and the "philosopher of reaction." By accident of birth and residence, the acknowledged spokesman for a minority interest that came under intensified attack during his lifetime, he spoke for this interest in a period of growing sectional hostility. From an ingenious interpreter of the economy of cotton, he became the "Sentinel of the South" and finally the section's foremost apologist for slavery. Calhoun did not devise the concept of slavery as a "positive good," but he gave it a currency no other man of his time could have done. He himself was a man of strong moral convictions. While he could not defend, nor even accept, an immoral institution, he could and did so rationalize Negro slavery that it became in his hands not evil but good, a blessing to bondsman and master alike!

The Calhouns were only 50 years from Ulster when John Caldwell was born in 1782 in Abbeville District, South Carolina, high in the Appalachian foothills. His family had migrated there in stages from Lancaster, Pennsylvania, by way of the Valley of Virginia. John's early education was meager, but his capacity to learn seemed without limit. He studied a few scattered months at a fly-by-night field school taught by an itinerant teacher and for two years at the academy run by his brother-in-law, Moses Waddel, near Appling, Georgia. Then in 1802 at the age of 20, he enrolled with the junior class at Yale College where his primary interest almost inevitably was history and politics. In New Haven he witnessed at first hand the full bitterness of the Federalist opposition that culminated in the separatist threats of the Essex Junto. He had time to ponder New England's reaction to the Louisiana purchase, which seemed to open the way for more slave states. And he saw political rivalry in neighboring New York State end in the fatal duel between Aaron Burr and Alexander Hamilton. For a few months after his graduation from Yale in 1804, he read law in Charleston; then in the summer of 1805 he entered Judge Tapping Reeve's famous law school at Litchfield, Connecticut.

In the summer of 1807 young Calhoun was back in South Carolina completing his legal training in his native Abbeville. It was there he heard the electrifying news that the American frigate *Chesapeake* had been fired upon by a British warship outside Hampton Roads and forced to strike her colors. Ever since the Revolution Great Britain, in fact, had been interfering with American commerce and kidnapping American sailors for her own navy, but protest hitherto had not survived diplomacy. This time it was different. For a brief time a sense of outrage united the country as it had never been before. Had President Jefferson called for war at that moment the American people would have followed; but his answer was to impose an embargo, and the wound festered. Especially indignant apparently were those who had been born since the Declaration of Independence. One of these birthright Americans, Calhoun prepared resolutions and made his first political speech. In the fall of 1808, he was elected to the South Carolina legislature and two years later to Congress. His personal future was secured at about the same time by his marriage to a cousin, Floride Bonneau Calhoun, who brought him not only a modest fortune but also entree into the tidewater aristocracy.

Thereafter Calhoun's rise was mercurial. In November 1811 he took his seat in the House of Representatives where he quickly identified himself with the War Hawks, mostly new and youthful Congressmen who were hot for war with Britain since the *Chesapeake* affair. Although Kentucky's Henry Clay was making his first appearance in the House, he was the acknowledged leader of this group, which succeeded in electing him Speaker. In turn, Clay took care of them through his committee appointments. Calhoun served on the Foreign Relations Committee; he became its chairman in time to draft the report calling for war with Great Britain. Working with and through Secretary of State James Monroe, the War Hawks, in effect, forced hostilities on a reluctant President Madison.

Calhoun's vigorous nationalism in support of the War of 1812 and of the measures for economic renovation that followed, won him the post of Secretary of War in the cabinet of Madison's successor, James Monroe. There he quickly demonstrated great administrative skill and a capacity for leadership of the first order. By the end of 1821, Calhoun's announcement that he was a candidate for President surprised no one, and except for his youth it seemed not unreasonable. Who then could have foreseen that in ten years time this same ardent and popular nationalist from South Carolina would be asking the cotton growing states to ignore an act of Congress and defy the authority of the national government?

Calhoun's bid for the presidency in 1824 soon proved to be bad politics, for it brought him into immediate conflict with rivals whose claims were based on longer if not more distinguished public service. Moreover, the United States was in the midst of the Era of Good Feelings, the second and last time in American history when there were no political parties—only factions among Jefferson's Republicans. Secretary of State John Quincy Adams felt that his office made him the natural heir; Secretary of the Treasury William H. Crawford was the inheritor of the old but still active Virginia–New York political alliance; Henry Clay certainly had a claim based on distinguished service as Speaker and as one of the peace commissioners who negotiated the Treaty of Ghent ending the War of 1812. He would be an ideal man to break the "Cabinet Succession" and to give the growing West a President. But Andrew Jackson, the popular hero who had won the only decisive victory of the war, was soon to be the front runner. Against any of these Calhoun had little chance, and he soon withdrew, to become the successful candidate for the vice presidency. When the 1824 presidential election was thrown into the House of Representatives because no candidate had a majority in the electoral college, he bent over backward to avoid indicating a preference. As the fourth man, Clay had been eliminated, and ill-feeling developed between Calhoun and Crawford. But both Adams and Jackson had backed Calhoun for Vice President, and he had won with a clear majority. He could not now take sides, or so he believed.

Ultimately the House chose Adams, but within a year Calhoun joined the opposition that was rallying around Jackson and calling itself the Democracy. Calhoun's new political stance was directly related to the tariff issue. As a member of Congress, he had voted for the tariff of 1816, which was designed to protect war-born American industry from ruinous foreign competition. The tariff of 1824, which doubled the 1816 duties, was another matter. The predominantly agricultural southern states exchanged their staples, especially cotton, for manufactured goods. England was both their market and their supplier. Southern planters reasoned, not illogically, that the value of cotton sold must be equivalent to the value of manufactures bought. It followed that every tariff-fostered increase in the price of manufactured goods, to the extent that it reduced imports, would be accompanied by a decline in the price of cotton. The 1824 tariff passed by a narrow margin with southern members united in opposition. As they foresaw, the price of cotton dropped sharply.

Cause and effect or not, no cotton planter would believe otherwise. Henry Clay, the foremost advocate of the tariff, was the presumed successor to Adams, whereas Jackson was himself a cotton planter whose interest would be served by keeping the duties down. More important, the administration did not question the federal government's power to impose a tariff; but to a mind like that of Calhoun, preternaturally acute through generations of living with bondsmen, the same power in the hands of a northern majority might one day be used to emancipate the slaves. Calhoun remembered all too well the Missouri Compromise debates, which had forced the South to affirm for the first time that slavery was a permanent institution. Many Southerners, and particularly South Carolinians, believed the antislavery argument publicly advanced in these debates had inspired the Denmark Vesey rebellion of 1822. Though quickly crushed, it had frightened the South into tightening slave codes and moving toward greater repression. By 1825 Southerners were convinced that tariffs, internal improvements, and anything that tended to increase the power of the federal government were a threat to slavery.

Cotton prices continued to fall, and from the cotton states came rumblings, first of discontent, then of rebellion. Those from Calhoun's own South Carolina resounded the loudest of all. When Congress passed the tariff of 1828—called the "Tariff of Abominations" by its opponents—Calhoun assumed the role of polemicist, preparing the case not only against the tariff itself but also against a system that permitted tariffs to be enacted. In his *South Carolina Exposition and Protest*, published by the state legislature in December 1828, he outlined a defense against the uncontrolled power of the numerical majority. In a brilliant analysis anticipating that of Karl Marx in the *Communist Manifesto* 20 years later, Calhoun demonstrated how capitalism would sharply divide society into owners and operatives. Wealth, he reasoned, would concentrate in the hands of the former, while labor eventually would be reduced to a subsistence level. This condition could be avoided by giving each major interest group a veto upon the will of the numerical majority. Since each of the states was dominated by a major interest, they would perform this role. As matters stood, the manufacturing interest controlled the numerical majority, but by acting through the states, the agricultural interest might interpose to arrest legislation to its detriment. Details of the exposition would be refined later, but here in embryo was the doctrine of nullification. According to Calhoun, the tariff was unconstitutional because its action did not apply equally to all of the states. Consequently any state adversely affected could declare the tariff null and void within its own borders. Calhoun, it should be emphasized, premised this elaborate political procedure on the United States Constitution, which he interpreted as a compact among sovereign states. While delegating certain specified functions to a general government, he had the states retain their individual sovereignties, which they could exert as they saw fit.

Calhoun did not actually invoke the nullification doctrine. He let it dangle for all to see. In particular, it was a warning to Andrew Jackson, who had just won the presidency from Adams. Calhoun had been re-elected vice president, but he wanted Jackson to understand that the South had supported both of them in expectation of tariff reform.

Jackson's first year in office passed with no move in that direction. Nor was there any in his second year. Cotton prices continued to fall, and Calhoun's restless young followers threatened to invoke his doctrine with or without his leadership. He held them off for the time being, but events conspired to force his hand. David Walker's militant *Appeal to the Coloured Citizens of the World*, appearing in the fall of 1829 and calling on slaves to strike for their freedom, violently if necessary, had brought near panic to the South. Once again slave codes were tightened and vigilance intensified. Nor was Southern equilibrium fully restored when the long simmering anti-slavery opposition burst into flaming rhetoric with the appearance of William Lloyd Garrison's *Liberator* in January 1831. And then in the following August came Nat Turner's rebellion, which frightened slaveholders into a common fellowship of fear. In January 1832 the Virginia Legislature debated emancipation, and by the razor-thin margin of a single vote defeated Jefferson's old plan for gradual emancipation. The tariff of 1832, which the South considered no better than its predecessor, was enacted in mid-summer, and in November Jackson was triumphantly re-elected, this time with Martin Van Buren of New York as his running mate.

No longer able to restrain the South Carolina dissidents, Calhoun placed himself at their head and implemented the theoretical remedy of the exposition. Late in November 1832 a special state convention chosen on the issue of nullification declared unconstitutional the tariffs of 1828 and 1832 and enjoined their enforcement within South Carolina.

Senator Robert Y. Hayne was then chosen Governor and Calhoun elected to his vacant Senate seat. He resigned the vice presidency and proceeded to Washington where for 15 stormy years he represented the Palmetto State in particular and the South in general as the great champion of states rights and as the most vocal apologist for slavery. The tariff issue was compromised and the Ordinance of Nullification consequently was withdrawn. But at the same time Jackson had also shown that given sufficient provocation, the federal government could and would use force to uphold the law.

And the law just might be the abolition of slavery! So Calhoun set himself to guard against that frightening contingency under whatever guise it might appear. Thereafter he fought every act that might extend the power of the federal government, either directly or by implication. Because the South was already a hopeless minority, Calhoun sought to curb majority power by identifying a political balance that would parallel the existing balance of interests. If each major interest group might veto legislation it considered harmful, the South could not only block tariff measures but also defeat any future move to emancipate the slaves. By a skillful exercise of dialectic, Calhoun would have shorn the federal government of its sovereignty, supplanting it by a consensus of pressure blocs.

Though Calhoun's course over the next decade remained single minded and undeviating, his response to the panic of 1837 struck a popular note. He was instrumental in establishing the treasury as a substitute for the now defunct Bank of the United States. After the comic opera presidential election of 1840, his hopes rose once more and he began to see himself as John Tyler's successor. He resigned his Senate seat early in 1843 to avoid taking any positions that would be unpopular nationally. Although his lieutenants did a yeoman job, Calhoun's cause was again hopeless, and he withdrew before the nominating convention began its deliberations. Almost immediately he was recalled to public life, this time as Secretary of State in Tyler's cabinet. The annexation of Texas was his special mission. Always a man to say what he thought, Calhoun literally destroyed his chances for the presidential nomination by making a vigorous proslavery argument justifying annexation. He did this in an official despatch to the British minister. In the end Calhoun succeeded in bringing about annexation, but the aftermath was to be a war with Mexico, which he strongly opposed. In still one more of his political maneuvers, Calhoun returned to the Senate in time to denounce the conflict, to help frame the 1846 tariff, which abandoned the principle of protection, and to debate the question of the status of slavery in the territory acquired from Mexico as a result of the conflict.

The territorial issue forced the Compromise of 1850. An all-Southern convention had already been summoned to meet in Nashville in June.

Southerners were all too aware that exclusion of slavery from California and New Mexico would foreshadow massive anti-slavery majorities in both houses of Congress. In that event, few doubted that secession of the Southern states from the union would be proposed at Nashville. But California, her population swollen by gold fever, had opted to exclude slavery and had Senators and Representatives present when Congress met in December 1849. They brought with them a free state constitution for approval. The broad compromise offered by Henry Clay was rejected by Calhoun, who saw no further hope of maintaining parity between North and South, even in the Senate. He had less than a month to live. While Calhoun sat in his seat, too feeble to address his fellow legislators, Senator James Mason of Virginia read his last speech for him on March 4, 1850. Still bent upon the protection of slavery, Calhoun demanded that a sectional veto be added to the Constitution, even if it meant creating a dual presidency.

Who really knows for sure what goes on in the mind of another? Calhoun certainly loved the union and would not willingly have seen it destroyed. Yet he thought it worth preserving only if it dispensed what he considered to be equal justice to all its members. For the South dependence on the ballot alone would never suffice; it could always be outvoted by the free states. Calhoun's most important legacy was his reasoned defense of minority interests, through a species of functional federalism he called the "concurrent majority." The doctrine had worked in the case of the tariff. But as a defense of slavery it did not and could not work, for in the long run morality cannot be compromised. Although the concurrent voice of the slave interest died away with the muffling of the guns at Appomattox, interest groups, in one form or another and for better or for worse, still manage to veto the will of the numerical majority.

* * *

Henry Clay and John C. Calhoun were cut out of different kinds of political cloth. Calhoun was the disembodied intellect, driven by some inner compulsion to analyze the political activities that went on around him. From his analysis he produced sweeping theories for universal application. For his part, Clay was never happier than when he was at the very center of the political stage. He was far more concerned with political process than with abstractions or with far-reaching theories about the nature of government. The Kentuckian was the complete politician, not in the machine sense that described Martin Van Buren, but in the more primary role of organizer, doer, and leader. He had magnetism, charm, wit; he had a restraining sense of values; and he had a superb measure of what we today would call "horse sense."

When Henry Clay first erupted upon the national scene, he was already past master of the art of managing men. Though still in his early 30s, there seemed to be no height that was unattainable. Clay himself assessed his prospects with complete confidence. But as the bitter sectional struggle began to draw the lines ever more tightly, Clay found himself caught in the middle. Calhoun was unequivocally the symbol and spokesman of the slaveholding South, as Daniel Webster of Massachusetts was of the industrial and commercial North. Clay, the self-appointed spokesman for the West, was torn both ways. In the border state of Kentucky he lived, and loved, the life of a Southern gentleman. His home, "Ashland," near Lexington, was a plantation of more than 500 acres with some 50 slaves, and there he dispensed lavish hospitality. But the crop that Ashland produced was not the cotton that required free trade for a profit; it was hemp that needed ample protection from foreign competition. Moreover, Clay lived not on the Atlantic slope, where broad and deep rivers carried commerce effortlessly to the sea, but beyond the mountains where nature required the aid of man by way of canals, locks, and highways. Far removed from the East's financial centers, banknotes (which constituted the only currency aside from unmanageable gold and silver) had a way of declining in value as they circulated farther from the issuing institutions. Only the federal government could, in fact, guarantee a stable medium of exchange. Soon Clay's "American System," defined as a central bank, a protective tariff, and government-financed internal improvements, was openly at war with the interest of those whose prosperity was pegged to the economy of cotton. Just as Calhoun's mature life was devoted to the defense of slavery and the South, so time and again did Clay give his energy and political skill to compromising sectional hostilities.

Born near Richmond, Virginia, April 12, 1777, Henry Clay was the seventh of nine children, with seven more to come by his mother's second marriage. His formal schooling was minimal, but the times themselves were an education. Heroes of the Revolution walked the Virginia earth to be seen and heard by an eager and ambitious lad. When Clay's family moved to Kentucky in 1792, the 15-year-old Henry remained in Richmond as a deputy clerk of the High Court of Chancery. Chancellor George Wythe, who soon became Clay's mentor, was the venerable teacher of law to an earlier generation that included Jefferson, Marshall, and Monroe. Late in 1797, young Henry Clay set out to join his family in Kentucky. He carried in his pocket a Virginia license to practice, a smattering of learning in his head, and the deep conviction of a Jeffersonian Republican in his heart.

In the Blue Grass State politics became Clay's life. Though he was a successful lawyer from the start of his career, the law never meant more to him than a way of earning a living and a stepping stone to political advancement. Marriage to Lucretia Hart in 1799 brought him both social prestige and a modest property. Within five years he was in the lower house of the state legislature and later became its Speaker. In 1806, he was chosen to fill out two months of an unexpired term in the United States Senate, although he had still not reached the required age of 30 when the term expired. He was back in the Senate again for a few months in 1810, but preferred election to the House of Representatives, where he sat with Calhoun and other young War Hawks in November 1811. A little older and more experienced in the legislative art than most of the others, Clay was their choice for Speaker and he skillfully used that office to generate war with Great Britain. The story of that bungling conflict need not be recounted here, save to say that when peace talks reached the negotiating stage, Clay was named by President Madison one of the United States Commissioners to meet with British representatives at Ghent in Belgium. There he was teamed with tough-minded, suspicious, puritanical but immensely able John Quincy Adams, then Minister to Russia, and the former Secretary of the Treasury, Albert Gallatin, who had been one of the pillars of the Republican party from its origin. Gallatin's fabled tact was to be sorely tested as peacemaker between Adams and Clay. Two other members of the delegation, Federalist Senator James A. Bayard of Delaware, and Jonathan Russell, Minister to Sweden, played secondary roles in the negotiations.

No two characters could have been more unlike than Adams and Clay. Short and rotund, Adams was the complete scholar. He was up before dawn and already working at his books and papers, when the tall, lanky Clay would be returning from a night of card playing and good fellowship. Even their goals for the negotiations were unlike; Clay was determined that Great Britain be excluded from the Mississippi River, while Adams was equally adamant about preserving American rights in the North Atlantic fisheries. Each, so it sometimes seemed to their fellows, was willing to sacrifice the other's interest to achieve his own. A generally satisfactory treaty nevertheless resulted, and Clay then joined Adams and Gallatin in a separate mission to London to negotiate a commercial treaty.

Broadened by his European experience, Clay was back in the House when Congress met in December 1815. He was again chosen Speaker. Powerfully aided by Calhoun and others of the old War Hawks, he now sought to heal old wounds with a program of national development that would encourage industrial growth, supply internal transportation, and through a national bank provide the uniform and stable currency so necessary for commerce. The system was left incomplete by President Madison's veto of the internal improvement bill on his last day in office, but New York pointed the way for the states to take up the slack by its financing of the Erie Canal without federal assistance. A new age was at hand. Subsequently the United States would direct its energies toward economic self-sufficiency and internalize its political conflicts. The old

Federalist party of Alexander Hamilton and John Adams offered only token opposition to James Monroe in 1816 and did not again contest a national election.

With new goals, new parties, and new men to lead the nation, who deserved better of his countrymen than Henry Clay? Ambition for the presidency was deep-rooted in the popular Kentuckian, and he cared not who knew it. But circumstances, some of them of his own making, were beginning to work against him. Arrogant and proud he was, and sensitive where his "honor" was concerned. He was also quick to see any threat to his ambition. Monroe, for instance, had offered him the secretaryship of the War Department before it went to Calhoun, but Clay thought he deserved to be Secretary of State, a position from which Jefferson, Madison and then Monroe himself had been catapulted into the White House. He turned it down, and then from his vantage point in the House began a desultory war upon Administration measures. When Andrew Jackson, the military hero of the battle of New Orleans, moved into Florida in pursuit of a band of Seminoles and in the process hanged two Englishmen and seized a Spanish fort, it was Clay who invoked the specter of military dictatorship and denounced the general's action. He did this partly to embarrass Monroe's administration, but also because Jackson was beginning to loom as a formidable Western rival.

When Missouri applied for admission to the union with a pro-slavery constitution, Clay upheld its right to do so, and at the same time he supported the compromise that forbade slavery elsewhere north of 36°30′. A second Missouri Compromise, which explained away a clause in the state constitution excluding free blacks, was of Clay's devising. His middle-of-the-road attitude toward slavery was clear both in 1820 and thereafter. He had no strong moral scruples for or against it. In his first years in Kentucky he had advocated gradual emancipation and would return to this position near the end of this career. He was one of the prime movers in establishing the American Colonization Society, which came into being January 1, 1817, and was its first vice president. Conceivably he was willing to accept almost any expedient that aimed at sectional harmony. And there was something to be said for Clay's position, for it made possible the compromises by which alone the nation survived its first three quarters of a century.

Clay withdrew from Congress in 1821 to rebuild his personal fortune; perhaps he also wanted to think about his future. He was back in Washington however, when the 18th Congress convened in December 1823, and was again chosen Speaker. Now an avowed candidate for the presidency, he was pitted against Jackson who had recently eliminated Calhoun, against John Quincy Adams, and against William H. Crawford, who would receive the endorsement of a thinly attended party caucus. Clay's platform was unchanged from the early post-war years. He cham-

pioned and forced through the House the protective tariff of 1824; he
continued to uphold the hard-pressed Bank of the United States, which
had been badly mismanaged; and he voted at every opportunity for the
internal improvements that Madison had pronounced unconstitutional.
Despite his personal popularity, his qualifications, and his charisma, Clay
was badly beaten. Since no candidate had a majority of the electoral vote,
the House of Representatives had to choose from among the three highest
candidates. Clay was the fourth man and therefore was eliminated. When
the balloting came, Clay's followers voted for Adams, who won out over
Jackson despite the General's greater popular support. When the Kentuckian accepted the position of Secretary of State in Adams' cabinet, the
Jackson managers understandably cried out "Corrupt Bargain."

Over the next four years Clay worked to forge a party from the ill-
assorted groups that for one reason or another backed the administration
or opposed the Jacksonians: Old Federalists, pro-tariff Republicans from
the West, free soil men, and slavery advocates who wanted land reforms
or feared Andrew Jackson. Unwisely, Clay chose to make an issue out of
United States attendance at a Panama conference of Latin American
states. True, he had supported Latin American independence before
Adams and Monroe were ready to recognize it, but joining in this nascent
pan-Americanism was something altogether different. As a slaveholder,
Clay should have foreseen the reaction of the South when it was publicized that Haiti, product of a successful slave rebellion, would be represented at the conference. After a bitter fight, a byproduct of which was
a bloodless duel between Clay and John Randolph of Roanoke, the
Senate confirmed the delegates. But thereafter the administration did not
win another contest with Congress. Adams was easily beaten for reelection
in 1828 and the Age of Jackson began.

For the next two years Clay was out of public life, although his presence was very much felt behind the scenes. With a view to his own
election in 1832, he continued to rebuild the National Republican party,
soon to be called the Whigs. Jackson's veto of the Maysville Road bill
gave him a peg on which to hang his opposition. The 65-mile strip of
narrow, steep, and often muddy road connecting Maysville, Kentucky,
on the Ohio River with Lexington was a link in the network that by 1830
not only joined the eastern seaboard with the western outposts (Ft. Smith,
Arkansas, Ft. Leavenworth, Kansas, and Ft. Snelling, Minnesota) but also
the Great Lakes cities with the Gulf. When Jackson denied federal funds
to improve the Maysville Road, Clay saw an opportunity to uphold
internal improvements, always popular in the West, against an administration that appeared to oppose all of those great elements of national
progress including the tariff and the Bank of the United States.

Clay returned to public life late in 1831 when he took his seat in the
United States Senate; his friend John J. Crittenden had withdrawn in his

favor. A few days later a National Republican party convention nominated him by acclamation. At this juncture Clay persuaded Nicholas Biddle, president of the Bank, to apply at once for recharter. This action was highly premature since the institution had still four years to go on its existing charter. Clay reasoned that Jackson would alienate a portion of his following if he signed such a bill and another portion if he vetoed it. Clay was also instrumental in the passage of a new tariff law that the South found no less objectionable than the existing one. Here he ignored Calhoun's warning and the rebellious mood of the cotton states.

Neither Clay's protectionist bid to the manufacturing states nor Jackson's ringing veto of the Bank recharter bill helped the National Republican candidate. Clay suffered a worse defeat than had Adams four years earlier. But it was only South Carolina's nullification of the 1828 and 1832 tariffs that finally convinced him that the cotton states would not accept protection—or the extension of the federal government's authority. When Congress reconvened, Clay quietly worked out the details of the 1833 compromise tariff bill that would abandon the principle of protection and reduce duties to the revenue level of 1816 over a ten-year period. With the support of Calhoun, John Tyler, and other nullifiers the measure was passed; but so was the Force Bill, authorizing the President to collect the tariff by force if need be.

Clay had once more made peace, and for another half dozen years he and Calhoun worked in harmony. And when Jackson removed the public deposits from the Bank of the United States, the Whig party was born in opposition. Clay's Whigs and Calhoun's Nullifiers combined to censure the President, but they failed to defeat his handpicked successor, Martin Van Buren, in the election of 1836. The strategy was wrong. Clay, who surely deserved something from his party, was passed over as the Whigs put up multiple candidates in hopes of throwing the election into the House of Representatives where they held a majority. But with the Jackson machine behind him, Van Buren beat them all—Daniel Webster, Hugh Lawson White of Tennessee, and William Henry Harrison of Ohio, one of the few American generals who had won a battle in the war of 1812. Harrison's showing was unexpectedly strong, so the Whig convention in 1840 again passed over Clay and named the old general as its candidate for the Presidency and John Tyler of Virginia, a Calhoun Nullifier, for vice president. The Whigs offered no program—had there been one Tyler could not have been on the ticket—but none was needed. The unlucky Van Buren had been engulfed by the Panic of 1837 and simply to defeat him was program enough.

Harrison won easily, and then to the surprise of Whig stalwarts, he named not Clay but Webster as his Secretary of State. As a result Clay sought to control the administration from his dominant position in the Senate. When Harrison died after one month in office, Clay began to put pressure on his successor, John Tyler. In the end he succeeded, for though the unsympathetic Tyler vetoed one Whig measure after another, no Clay man would serve in his Cabinet. Even Webster found it expedient to withdraw midway in the term.

Slavery was now back in the forefront of public consciousness. In an ill-conceived effort to suppress abolition literature, the post office denied the mails to "incendiary publications," while the House of Representatives passed a "gag rule," tabling all anti-slavery petitions without reading or reference to committee. Feeling over both of these actions was still running high in the free states when Tyler undertook to annex Texas, which permitted slavery. It was then that Webster withdrew, to be succeeded after an interval by Calhoun. Clay, meanwhile, was nominated by the Whigs as their candidate in the 1844 presidential election. But before Texas was finally annexed, he was defeated by another slaveholder, James K. Polk of Tennessee. New York state accounted for Polk's victory. There the antislavery Liberty Party, contesting its second election, had taken away a sufficient number of Whig votes from Clay to swing the state to Polk.

The nation's antislavery forces were now entering on to the political scene. They had been given great impetus by the annexation of Texas and the war with Mexico that was the inevitable aftermath. The prospect of extending slavery into the new lands acquired from Mexico triggered unprecedented nation-wide protest. It prompted a new Free Soil party, which for the first time gave a solid political base for the anti-slavery movement. And it boded ill for the waning political fortunes of Henry Clay whom the Whigs once more passed by in choosing their candidate in 1848. Ironically, the Whig candidate, the "war hero" General Zachary Taylor, a Louisiana slaveholder, won the election. Henry Clay's chances of being elected to the presidency were now gone.

After 1848, the extension or restriction of slavery in the territories overshadowed all other political issues. The discovery of gold in California swelled the population of that territory and made some action by Congress imperative. But feeling between slave and free states ran so high that no action seemed possible. In this crisis—and crisis it truly was —the Kentucky legislature once more sent Henry Clay, aging but still magnetic, back to the Senate; he had plans for a compromise already in his mind. These included California's admission to the Union as a free state and the establishment of territorial governments without mention of slavery for the rest of the Mexican cession. Texas was to surrender all claims to parts of New Mexico, and in return the Federal government would assume the state's public debt. The hated slave trade was to be ended in the District of Columbia, but slavery itself was not to be abolished there without the consent of Maryland and Virginia. There would be a new and more drastic fugitive slave law, and Congress was to renounce any power to regulate the interstate slave trade. Calhoun and Taylor were dead, Millard Fillmore was president, and Webster was back as Secretary of State before Clay's Compromise proposals finally passed in August.

But pass they did, with only trivial modifications. It was Clay's last great effort to make peace between North and South, whose diverging needs and aspirations he understood so well. And for a decade more it worked, although the Fugitive Slave Law proved exceedingly ill advised. Henry Clay of Kentucky, the great pacificator, died in the summer of 1852 with the Union he loved still intact. The nation had always withheld from him its highest honor, but it was he who largely gave it the reprieve that ultimately allowed it to survive.

*   *   *

The Grimkés were a South Carolina Huguenot family, like the Bonneaus to which Calhoun's wife belonged; and like the Bonneaus they were fully integrated into the slaveholding culture of the state. John Faucheraud Grimké was educated to the law in England, but returned to his native Charleston in time to fight in the American Revolution. He served as a delegate at the Constitutional Convention in Philadelphia and approved its results. Already a judge at that time, he would be the state's Chief Justice in the last 20 years of his life. The family lived in Charleston but like so many others whose occupation condemned them to the swampy low country, they had a plantation retreat in the highlands reserved for those times when Charleston became unhealthy. Judge Grimké was wealthy, conservative, aristocratic, Episcopalian, a considerable slaveholder, and allied by blood, marriage, or interest with most of the other conservative slaveholding families. His wife was an aunt of Robert Barnwell Rhett, a staunch Calhoun supporter and one of the earliest of the Southern "fireaters."

A more unlikely family to produce two militant abolitionists can hardly be imagined. Worse still, the pair were women who had to prove their right to speak before they would be heard! Driven by a fanatical loathing of slavery, which they themselves had seen in all its horrors, the Grimké sisters, Angelina and Sarah, became the first female agents of the American Anti-Slavery Society as well as pioneer propagandists for women's rights. Angelina was the younger and more gifted of the two though hardly more courageous than her sister. Their impact upon the major reform movements of their time was immense. They could talk to and about the South, because they were not only Southerners, but "ladies." In the North their abilities, their breeding, and their dedication opened doors for them almost at will. Neither Sarah or Angelina was by any stretch of the imagination physically attractive, judging from their photographs; they ill fit the stereotype of the delicate Dixie belle. Their faces had character, to be sure, but certainly not beauty. It took an abolitionist zealot to make a bride of Angelina, while Sarah was never to wed.

Angelina Grimké was born in Charleston in 1805, the last of 14 children. Her sister Sarah, 13 years old and already a lonely, questing child, by her own request stood godmother to her new sister to whom she remained deeply devoted in an almost parental relationship through life. Sarah was early aware of the moral problem posed by slavery. The subject was not discussed and literature on it was not available in the South but this sensitive girl, upon entering womanhood, found ample cause for dissatisfaction in her own observations of the system. How could men and women of the highest social standing beat helpless slaves for trivial reasons and then conduct family prayers and appear as pillars of the church? Still unprepared to speak, she saw her own question answered when Angelina fainted one day in school at the sight of the whip's bloody marks on the legs of a black child.

The turning point came in 1819 when Sarah was a 27-year-old spinster. Frustrated in an attempt to study law, she was increasingly critical of the society in which she lived. Judge Grimké, seriously ill, decided to visit the celebrated Dr. Physick in Philadelphia and chose Sarah to be his only companion. His case was already hopeless. Within a few weeks the judge died quietly in the comparative exile of the unfamiliar New Jersey coast. Her filial duties performed, Sarah stayed on for two months with a Quaker family whom she had met in Philadelphia. She returned to Charleston with more critical eyes to see the brutal side of slavery as she never had before. For a time she attended a Quaker meeting in Charleston, something not easy for a Grimké to do, but she was dissatisfied with the equivocation of the Southern Friends on slavery. Needing a more positive condemnation, she left early in 1821 for Philadelphia, never again to return to the South except for brief visits.

Angelina, meanwhile, was substantially retracing the ground her sister had already traveled, but with a more decisive personality and a nature that was activist to the core. Disillusioned with the Episcopal Church because its members would not acknowledge the existence of sin in slavery, she left it to join the Presbyterians, who had a new and promising minister. Soon she was teaching a Sunday school class and conducting a monthly interfaith prayer meeting. She beseeched the minister to explain why professing Christians apparently saw no wrong in enslaving other Christians. While conceding the moral wrong of slavery, he had no answers save prayer and patience, and these were not enough for the likes of Angelina Grimké. After a visit from Sarah, whose new simplicity she greatly admired, she too tried the Charleston Quaker meeting, now reduced to two old men who disliked each other. She rebuked them and for her trouble was told to mind her own business.

Angelina spent the next summer with her sister in Philadelphia, where she saw and heard nothing to change her feelings. At 23, however, she was not yet ready for exile, preferring instead to reform the Charleston Quakers and her own family. Both efforts met with stout resistance, and she acknowledged her failure. The final indignity came when she was formally expelled from the Presbyterian Church, which she had already left. Her avenues at home were closing fast. Late in 1829 she joined Sarah in Philadelphia, this time for good. Angelina's dilemma was based entirely on her abhorrence of slavery. Of South Carolina's opposition to the tariff, of the doctrine of nullification fresh from Calhoun's hands, of the crisis in cotton, she was uncaring. And certainly she must have been aware of political issues, for the best of the anti-nullification pamphlets was written by her brother Thomas. Her world had narrowed, but it was of an intensity that even Philadelphia could not long endure.

The Grimké sisters found the City of Brotherly Love almost as repressive as Charleston. The Quakers formed a tight organization of their own, and one could join only after months or years of probation. The liberal Quakers, the Hicksites, outnumbered the orthodox, but were given no doctrinal concessions on that account. Women were to be quiet and demure, which did not include speaking out in meetings, nor challenging the authority of the elders on the question of slavery. Sarah talked until bluntly told to hold her tongue. Angelina sought, but was denied, permission to attend Catherine Beecher's school in Hartford.

The momentous political events of 1831, 1832, and 1833 seemingly passed the sisters by. They were aware of the appearance of the *Liberator,* with its unrestrained attacks on the hated institution, but they were still too close to their own genteel upbringing to approve Garrison's tactics. They read, of course, about Nat Turner's rebellion in Virginia. And they were surely aware of the organization of the American Anti-Slavery Society late in 1833, since it took place in Philadelphia. The new society turned the anti-slavery cause from colonization to immediate emancipation; it insisted on education for the blacks and an end to race prejudice.

The sisters would not have been welcome in the AASS had they been ready to go so far, for they were mere women and this was man's work. But they were moving closer. And 1834 was a critical year. Race riots erupted in New York and Philadelphia. John Greenleaf Whittier and Samuel May were stoned in Ralph Waldo Emerson's home town, Concord, Massachusetts. Prudence Crandall's valiant but losing battle to maintain a school for Negro girls in Connecticut was widely publicized. And most importantly for the Grimké sisters, although they were not yet aware of it, Theodore Weld, by his eloquence, leadership, and dedication, converted the students of Lane Theological Seminary in Cincinnati from colonization and gradualism to immediate abolition of slavery. Lane's president, Lyman Beecher, did not agree and the rebels moved to Oberlin. Theodore Weld emerged from these developments as the acknowledged leader of the Western antislavery forces.

Events were now moving with great rapidity for the sisters. The year 1835 saw more race and anti-abolition riots, including one in Charleston where a mob broke into the post office and publicly burned large quantities of abolitionist literature. Angelina took the plunge, joining a Female Abolitionist Society. About the same time William Lloyd Garrison, in the *Liberator*, denounced the widespread disorders and appealed to his fellow Bostonians to give a fair hearing to a visiting English abolitionist, George Thompson. Though Angelina had never met Garrison, she wrote him a personal letter of commendation; for the first time she took a stand in favor of immediate emancipation. Without asking permission, Garrison published the letter, with suitable introductory remarks. Her Quaker friends condemned her action and Sarah was horrified, but Angelina Grimké had crossed her personal Rubicon.

Now identified irrevocably with the radical abolitionism, Angelina moved surely and decisively toward full participation in the movement. It came in 1836 with the publication of her *Appeal to the Christian Women of the South*. The concept was brilliant and the execution flawless. "It is because I feel a deep and tender interest in your present and eternal welfare that I am willing thus publicly to address you," she began. "Some of you have known me as a relative, and some have felt bound to me in Christian sympathy . . . It is because you have known me that I write thus unto you." She then went back to the book of Genesis and proceeded through the Bible to show that the Hebrew slavery, so often cited by Southern polemicists as sanction for their own peculiar institution, was in fact not slavery at all but a form of compensated servitude. She quoted the Southern slave codes most effectively to emphasize the difference. In her hands the Bible became one long antislavery tract. "Can we love a man as we love *ourselves if we do and continue to do* unto him, what we would not wish anyone to do to us?" The very language of the pamphlet, rich in analogy and illustration, was itself almost Biblical and gave the tract a form of sanctity for those to whom it was addressed.

After establishing the case against slavery in many and varied ways, Angelina addressed herself directly to the timidity, the hesitancy, the long repression she knew to be in the character of her female readers. What can you, as a woman, do?, she asked. Read; pray; speak; and finally act. And for sanction she again turned to the pages of Scripture, where time and again, from Miriam to Pilate's wife, she found women leading and speaking out for justice.

The *Appeal* quickly proved to be one of the most influential pieces of abolition writing. Shortly after its appearance the Grimké sisters left Philadelphia to settle in New York. There in November 1836 they attended an "Agents' Convention" of the American Anti-Slavery Society. It was not a convention in any legitimate sense, but a training school for those who were to go out as antislavery missionaries. The Grimkés were the only women in a consecrated group that included Garrison, Arthur and Lewis Tappan, and Theodore Dwight Weld who directed the training program. Weld quickly recognized Angelina's special talents and gave her personal training as a speaker. He recognized other qualities as well, for the two were married a little over a year later.

Angelina first began speaking against slavery under the auspices of the New York Female Anti-Slavery Society, but she was not content to lecture only to women. So great had her reputation become that the problem almost solved itself, for wherever she spoke men came to hear her. In May 1837 she followed her successful *Appeal* to the Southern ladies with another address to "The Women of the Nominally Free States." In June the sisters, escorted by Garrison, visited John Quincy Adams at his home in Quincy. The ex-President, now a congressman, was in the thick of his fight against the House of Representatives "gag rule." Wise in the ways of politics, Adams knew that he could win his case only by tying it to the constitutional right of petition. The sisters, however, thought he was temporizing on the great moral issue.

Meanwhile, Catharine Beecher, the formidable eldest daughter of Reverend Lyman Beecher, had published an answer to Angelina's *Appeal*. Entitled "An Essay on Slavery and Abolition with Reference to the Duty of American Females," it took a harshly antifeminist view. The Beecher pamphlet played into the hands of those who resented participation of the Grimké sisters in the antislavery movement simply because they were women. Angelina answered in a series of "Letters to Catharine Beecher," while Sarah wrote "Letters on the Equality of the Sexes" for the New England *Spectator*. Next followed a "Pastoral Letter of the General Association of Massachusetts to the Congregational Churches under their care" and another from the Andover Theological Seminary, both denouncing Garrison's tactics as well as the appearance of women on the lecture platform.

By this time the Grimké sisters were among America's most famous women—or most notorious, according to the point of view. In February 1838 they spoke by invitation before the Massachusetts Legislature and were an unqualified success. In six months time 40,000 people heard them in New England, where the antislavery message found an increasing number of sympathizers.

After Angelina's marriage to Theodore Weld in May 1838, the period of feverish activity came to an end. There were many reasons. The day after the wedding, for instance, the Welds took part in the dedication of "Pennsylvania Hall" in Philadelphia. The Hall had been built by reformers to provide an auditorium and headquarters for several antislavery organizations. The following day as the newlyweds were attending sessions of the Anti-Slavery Convention of American Women, a mob had gathered outside the hall. Twice they broke in, but were ejected. Rocks were crashing through the windows when Angelina spoke, unperturbed, eloquent, incisive. "What is a mob?" she asked, as glass fell on the floor at her feet. "What would the breaking of every window be? Any evidence that we are wrong, or that slavery is a good and wholesome institution? What if that mob should now burst in upon us, break up our meeting and commit violence on our persons—would this be anything compared with what the slaves endure?" Before the night was done Pennsylvania Hall was burned to the ground along with all of the precious records and documents it housed. The incident occurred with the apparent sanction of the city's mayor, the police, and the fire department.

It was Angelina's last major speech for many years. The duties of homemaker were new and arduous to her; they absorbed all of her energy despite the much needed assistance she would receive from Sarah, who lived with the Welds. Her health suffered from experimental dieting, and there were three children to raise. Despite their household activities, the sisters collaborated with Weld on a lengthy pamphlet called *American Slavery as It Is* (1839). Consisting of hundreds of personal statements by eyewitnesses to the cruelties of slavery—the sisters, needless to say, contributed their own recollections—the book was by far the most powerful and most effective piece of antislavery literature before *Uncle Tom's Cabin*. "No one, who has not been an *integral part* of a slaveholding community," declared Sarah's narrative, "can have any idea of its abominations." 100,000 copies of the pamphlet were sold in the first year. Thereafter the sisters helped Weld with his own publications, but they themselves kept out of the limelight.

The times indeed were changing and so was the focus of the anti-slavery cause. In 1840 the movement entered its political phase with the organization of the Liberty Party. Though the party candidate James G. Birney, a converted Alabama planter, polled less than one percent of the popular vote, the start had been made. Eight years later the Liberty Party merged with the Free Soil Party, and in 1856 their political heirs, the Republicans, carried the anti-slavery fight to the seats of power.

*   *   *

From the Missouri Compromise to the Civil War itself the controversy over slavery was never far from the mainstream of American history. Whatever the immediate issue might be—tariff, public lands, transportation, banking, manufacturing, territorial expansion—the "slave question" quickly became an abrasive factor in the discussion. By the middle 1830s the South, guided, led, and ultimately propelled by Calhoun, took the position that her peculiar institution was beyond criticism or even comment, lest the slaves overhear and become restive. The prospect of slave rebellion was a constant nightmare that invoked ever more repressive measures. Southern fears were fanned by the endless torrent of antislavery literature produced by dedicated reformers like the Grimké sisters, but all attempts to suppress it had an opposite effect, arousing not abolitionists alone, but those who came to the defense of the constitutional right of free speech. Between the extremes of pro- and anti-slavery advocates was the great body of Americans who wanted only to go about the business of living. To them, any reasonable middle ground, any workable compromise such as Clay proposed, would have been acceptable. Indeed, the Compromise of 1850 was favorably received by a popular majority, but it gave to neither extreme all that it desired and consequently renewed the sectional conflict. *Uncle Tom's Cabin* in 1852 went far to solidify Northern sentiment against slavery, while the Kansas-Nebraska Act and the Dred Scott decision removed the last national barriers to the extension of the hated institution. The three approaches to slavery—protection, compromise, and abolition—met head-on in the election of 1860, where the nation made its choice.

14

Different Drums:
The Civil War Era

JEFFERSON DAVIS
ABRAHAM LINCOLN
HORACE GREELEY

by Emory M. Thomas
University of Georgia

"If a man does not keep pace with his companions, perhaps it is because
he hears a different drummer. Let him step to the music which he hears,
however measured or far away."

When Henry David Thoreau wrote these lines, he expressed more
than an ethical ideal; he also described an American reality. Americans
during the first half of the 19th century marched to a variety of "different drummers," and indeed they often seemed to try to keep pace
with several beats at the same time. By mid-century, however, American
drumbeats were fewer in number and harsher in tone. Finally the words
"drum" and "marching" lost their metaphorical quality and became lit-
teral realities amid the cataclysm of Civil War.

Reduced to the simplest of terms, the American Civil War was about
"different drums"—the noisy extensions of conflicting life styles in the
United States. For some time in the North and South, ways of living and
looking at the world differed. As Americans, both Northerners and
Southerners could and did compromise about specific, real issues before
1860; for two generations these Americans had compromised on slavery,
tariffs, foreign policy, and more. Yet divergent life styles became incompatible, and then mutually exclusive. They became so because

270

Northerners and Southerners sanctified their respective ways of life and raised their interests and institutions to the level of ideologies. Divergent lifestyles, interests, and institutions may have been subject to compromise and coexistence; ideologies were not. These ideologies were not material, but moral expressions, and righteousness was not likely to compromise with evil.

The "drum" metaphor is significant here. Just as a drumbeat is more than the sum of its component physical parts—wood, hide, and steel— so also were the sectional ideologies of the antebellum North and South more than the sum of their component interests and circumstances. Just as rhythm and cadence have a transcendent quality distinct from drum and drummer, so did the world views, belief systems, or any other synonyms for ideology have real, separate identity beyond the lives and life styles from which they sprang. So it was that in 1861 the United States was really two nations. Then for four bloody years Americans were in fact two nationalities. In 1865 the United States united once more by force of arms at the cost of 600,000 lives; the "American way" prevailed by right of conquest. Such was the reality and power of "different drums."

Obviously metaphors and generalities can only go so far in explaining the experience of the American Civil War. To amplify these general statements and to understand this very human experience, we must look more closely at some of the humans involved in it. To understand the "drums," we need to become acquainted with some of the "drummers."

Abraham Lincoln, Jefferson Davis, and Horace Greeley were not exactly "average" Americans of the mid-19th century. Lincoln and Davis led their respective nations in wartime, and Greeley was perhaps the most influential newspaper editor in American history. Nor were these men always the most rabid proponents of their respective ideologies. Lincoln, Davis, and Greeley did, however, interact with their times and circumstances in such a way as both to reflect and shape their age. And all three faced, in one way or another, the fundamental issues involved in the Civil War experience.

Lincoln, Davis, and Greeley were part of the ideological conflict that conditioned the era. In time each had to deal responsibly with the question of secession. Davis had to choose his national identity—Southern or American; Lincoln and Greeley had to elect between peaceful secession or union by force. Once the fighting began the three men faced the tasks of defining their respective war aims and in so doing they refined and redefined their ideological positions. Finally each of the three had to set a price for peace, to decide whether any or all of their war aims were worth continuing the bloodshed to total victory or defeat. Because they were strong men in high places, each one dealt with these common questions independently and individually. For this very reason the responses of Lincoln, Davis, and Greeley to the issues raised by ideology, secession, war aims, and peace hopes were crucial, and are significant. And because their responses were identifiably human, these men were and are fascinating.

*   *   *

By the time he was 16 years old, Jefferson Davis already disliked "Yankees." Born into modest circumstances in Kentucky in 1808, Davis spent most of his youth in Mississippi. His father who fought in the Revolution never quite made the transition from "farmer" to "planter"; however Davis' older brother Joseph made a great deal of money very quickly and assumed a place in Mississippi's planter aristocracy. Joseph took charge of his younger brother's schooling and support after their father died in 1824. Jefferson Davis returned to his native Kentucky to attend Transylvania University in Lexington and then with Joseph's aid secured an appointment to West Point. There, for the first time, Davis encountered "Yankees" in any significant numbers. After his first few months at West Point he wrote brother Joseph that his Northern contemporaries were "not such as I formed an acquaintance with on my arrival . . . nor are they such associates as I would at present select." Then Davis informed his brother and patron, ". . . As you have never been connected with them, you cannot know how pittiful they generally are."

Chief among the shortcomings of his Northern brethren, to Davis' way of thinking, was their ability to subsist on the meagre allowance paid them as cadets. Davis indeed took a certain backhanded pride in asking his brother for "Cash" (with a capital "C") to sustain him in the style of a Southern gentleman. Already in the young cadet's mind, to be a "Yankee" was to be narrowly frugal and shrewdly Puritanical. In contrast Davis perceived himself and his Southern kinsmen to be genial, openhanded men of the world, practitioners of the good life. As it happened, much of Davis' experience in later life reinforced his youthful perceptions.

Davis received his lieutenant's commission from West Point in 1828, and although he fought in the Black Hawk War (1830–31), he found little more than boredom in the garrison duty that characterized a peacetime army. Accordingly in 1835 he resigned from the army and embarked upon a career as a Mississippi planter. That same year Davis married Sarah Knox Taylor, daughter of Zachery Taylor, much against her father's will. The couple had hardly settled on their new plantation, carved out of Joseph Davis' lands just below Vicksburg, when Sarah Davis died. The young widower chose to express his grief by losing himself in work and study, and spent the next several years in what might appear to have been limbo. Actually he worked long and hard on his plantation "Brierfield," and cultivated his Democratic neighbors. Thus in 1845, when Davis married again and went to Congress, he had labored ten years to become an "overnight" success.

His second wife was Varina Howell whose family had a well-respected Natchez name and not much else. Varina herself was a strong-willed woman who made fast friends and firm enemies with equal facility. Both Davises enjoyed Washington and its Southern Democrats during their initial stay in the capital. When the Mexican War broke out, Congressman Davis resigned his seat and accepted command of the "Mississippi Rifles." Colonel Davis served briefly but gloriously in the war under his ex-father-in-law General Zachery Taylor. They had already reconciled the difficulties that had caused Taylor's disapproval of his late daughter's marriage, and the battle of Buena Vista brought generous praise from Taylor and a disabling wound in Davis' foot.

Davis returned to Mississippi in 1847 a wounded hero, and promptly won election to the United States Senate. After fighting the good Southern fight during the debates over the Compromise of 1850, Senator Davis again resigned from a national office and sought the Mississippi governorship in 1851. At this point and throughout the turbulent 1850s, he played the role of a militant Southern moderate. He took his intellectual cue from John C. Calhoun and pursued sectional interests within a national orientation. Like Calhoun, he threatened secession as a last resort and constantly demanded that the Northern majority prove its good faith toward the South by making appropriate concessions concerning slavery, expansion, tariffs, and such. Davis, however, was not among the ranks of the Southern "fire-eaters" who despaired of union with anyone and crusaded for a Southern republic.

Ex-Senator Davis lost the Mississippi gubernatorial race to Henry S. Foote in 1851 but soon found political place as Franklin Pierce's Secretary of War. He was an extremely capable Secretary, perhaps the most efficient since Calhoun over three decades before. Although from New Hampshire, Pierce listened closely to his Southern advisors, and in the front ranks of these was Jefferson Davis.

In 1856 Davis ran once more for the Senate and served there until his state seceded in January 1861. Again he championed Southern interests in the Senate; for example in 1859 he led the movement to reopen the international slave trade. Yet Davis left the Union reluctantly. At the conclusion of his farewell speech to the Senate, he reportedly broke down and wept. Still, he concluded, he was more Southern than American and followed Mississippi into disunion. His decision was, at the same time, momentous, dramatic, and natural.

By 1861 Davis had done most, if not all, of those things to which Southerners aspired. He had lived well, served conspicuously, and his contacts with people and place had been primal and meaningful. He had grown up "Southern"; that is, he read the same books literate Southerners read and he thought the same thoughts. By his own achievement and with generous aid from his brother he became a planter aristocrat. As a member of the master class, he could afford to be patronizing toward his slaves and his less successful neighbors. But he felt no guilt over holding slaves; he accepted the South's "peculiar institution" and strove to be a humane master. Indeed, one of Davis' closest lifelong friends was James Pemberton, his body servant since youth and plantation manager in later years.

Davis and his milieu aspired to be comfortable, simple, and open. At base were relationships among familiar people and between men and nature, the high degree of personalism which one scholar termed the persistance of a "folk culture." Whatever nagging contradictions lingered in the reality of the Southern world, Davis and his fellow Southerners believed they had in fact lived out their aspirations. In this Southern version of the "best of all possible worlds," planter aristocrats worked hard, played hard, and served their social inferiors, black and white, faithfully. Black people, Davis and most Southerners believed, were racially inferior and so were best off as slaves. Moreover, Southern non-planter whites deferred to their social and economic superiors out of habit, short range self-interest, and simple neighborliness. These things and more Davis believed. In some cases he believed half-truths, in others lies; but his convictions were supported by his experience. And by the time of the secession crisis these convictions had become articles of faith.

Davis left the Union because he was certain that his world was in peril. Other men had actually initiated the break; Davis took no active part in the secession movement until after South Carolina had acted. Nevertheless he was convinced that the South had the right as well as provocation enough to separate. The Yankee was the villain; and Davis described his activity in 1850 as "the steady advance of a self-sustaining power to the goal of unlimited supremacy." The South, as he saw it, was in the position of the American colonies in 1776, and he was responding to tyranny in much the same way his father had done in joining the Continental Army. Two clauses in Davis' first major address to the Confederate Congress on April 29, 1861, summarized his feelings about the secession crisis. "We feel," he said, "that our cause is just and holy"; and a bit later he added, "All we ask is to be let alone." The Southern lifestyle had become a "cause," a "just and holy" one, and for its sake Davis and his fellow Southerners had chosen to separate.

Jefferson Davis was at home, in "Brierfield," pruning his roses and hoping for a military command, when the messenger arrived to tell him he had been unanimously elected Provisional President of the Confederacy. Varina his wife remembered the scene—Davis' face fell; she despaired that a member of the family had died. Yet he could not refuse the honor. Being President of a rebel nation at war was no easy task.

The experience ultimately tested him and his ideological preconceptions much more than anyone could imagine in 1861.

Davis seemed a quite logical choice for President when the Montgomery convention of delegates from seceded states gathered. The Mississippian had worn Calhoun's mantle as Southern rights champion in the Senate; he had military experience at both the executive and field levels; he was no radical, and for a people in search of national respectability at home and abroad, moderation was mandatory. Also Davis *looked* like a president, and Americans have selected chief executives for less cause than that before and since.

His ability and credentials notwithstanding, Davis was a flawed President. Limited as a political personality, he loved and hated too well, and too often chose righteousness at the expense of success. The Confederate President clung to friends when they were clearly political liabilities; he nourished quarrels with political leaders and generals and fed needless dissension by so doing. Davis had difficulty in delegating authority and thus worked so hard at inconsequential matters that his health faltered. Understandably a sick President was hardly capable of that political congeniality a healthy one sorely lacked. When the administration clashed with state governors such as Joseph E. Brown of Georgia and Zebulon Vance of North Carolina, Davis was perhaps right; but he needed cooperation more than the contrition he seemed to demand. In sum Davis was severely lacking in the skills of political and personal give and take. Still, he gave his all for his section and its cause. Although many of those who shouted assent to his election as President later had second thoughts, Davis served them faithfully and perhaps more wisely than they ever knew.

The Confederacy's war challenged Southerners. They expected physical sacrifice; they did not expect to have to sacrifice the fundamental tenets of their lifestyle to the vain hope of victory. Perhaps Davis' greatest achievement as President was his rare insight into the nature of the war and his willingness to calculate its cost. The one, great, overriding Confederate war aim was independence—"all we ask is to be let alone." Most Confederates recognized this, but most Confederates also clung to the vain hope that independence could be bought cheap. Davis was never so sanguine. He foresaw a long, costly struggle. He perceived the necessity of the undermanned, outgunned Confederacy to fight a defensive war. And he realized that a Southern victory might come only at the expense of some Southern "sacred cows." The situation was paradoxical. Confederates sought independence to preserve their cherished way of life; but to have independence they had to win; and to win the South had to surrender some portion of its way of life.

When Davis and other Southern leaders thought realistically about war, they had to confront some very unpleasant facts. Euphoria might sustain the Confederacy's war effort for the short run; but if the Union persevered as Davis believed it would, a states' rights confederation would be ill-equipped to respond to the need for centralized direction of a national effort., The South was overwhelmingly rural and agricultural, and however much Southerners disdained "Yankees" with their manufacturing, the South entered an industrial war with little or no industry. The irony was cruel. Confederates struck for independence to sustain a states' rights polity and an agrarian economy, yet to achieve it they had to pursue the politics of nationalism and place economic emphasis upon industrialization.

These realities Davis, perhaps more than any other Confederate, understood. Consequently, his administration did several highly "unsouthern" things. Less than a year after the War Office was turning away volunteers because their numbers were greater than the government's capacity to arm and equip them, the Confederate Congress enacted the first draft law ever imposed in North America. Already the President had acted subtly and skillfully to transform the Confederate army from the traditional American amalgram of state militia units into a national force. With the blessing of his Congress, Davis suspended the writ of habeas corpus and invoked martial law in some areas of the Confederacy. Under the sanction of law military commanders could and did impress private property for the use of the army. The Confederacy also levied an income tax and tax-in-kind (ten percent of the gross) on agricultural commodities. It took over all blockade running in 1864 and thus managed the South's foreign trade. Its War Department took an active part in the economy by controlling draft exemptions for laborers, transportation priorities, and raw materials allocations. The draft, impressment, martial law, stern taxation, and economic regulation were novel measures in the South. To Davis' credit he recognized their necessity; unfortunately he was ill-equipped in temperament and political skill to make these actions palatable to Southerners.

The Confederacy had an equally profound impact upon Southern economy. Under Davis' leadership it developed sufficient industry to conduct its industrial war. Such a "crash" program did not of course turn the South into an industrial giant overnight. Still, the Confederacy was essentially self-sufficient in terms of war industry by 1863.

Ultimately the needs of war demanded that the Confederacy sacrifice still more of that way of life it was supposedly defending. War challenged and eventually altered Southern mores to a large degree. For example, when Varina Davis played the role of "first lady" and gave gay luncheons instead of visiting hospitals, she reaped bitter criticism for doing the very things Southern "belles" were supposed to do in antebellum times.

Finally in the fall of 1864 Davis confronted what many Confederates believed was the extreme challenge; he embarked upon a scheme to emancipate Southern slaves and employ them as soldiers. Here the Confederate President employed rare tact and political skill. He began by asking for an appropriation from Congress to purchase 40,000 black men for noncombatant use by the army. Such requests were normal; the details of the bill, though, were indeed unusual. Davis proposed a "radical alteration in Southern law and custom" by suggesting that the laborers be freed in exchange for their loyal service. Congress gave him the appropriation, but denied any hint of emancipation. As things happened the 40,000 laborers bill was Davis' "trial balloon"; next the administration proposed to arm and free the slaves. Congress and the Confederate people debated the measure during the winter of 1864–65 while the nation's military fortunes went from hopeless to non-existent. The issue was all too plain. Arming the slaves was the last, best hope of Southern victory; but arming the slaves also meant the end of the antebellum way of life. Finally Congress passed the administration measure in March 1865. The lawmakers shrank from emancipation, but Davis virtually wrote black freedom into the regulations implementing the act. And even earlier, in December 1864, the President had sent an emissary to Britain and France to offer emancipation in exchange for recognition. The mission was desperate and fruitless, but it served as an index of how far he would go for the sake of independence.

Davis' emancipation and arm-the-slaves proposals came too little, too late. The Confederacy was beyond military redemption by March 1865. Still Davis showed himself willing to make the sacrifice. He had abandoned slavery along with many another tenet of the Southern creed for the sake of independence. As most of his countrymen came to terms with their fate and prepared to live with defeat and reunion, Davis renewed his devotion to the "cause." He spoke of a "new phase" of the war—guerrilla warfare—and assured Confederates that independence was theirs so long as they willed it and resisted conquest.

At this juncture Davis the creative realist lost touch with reality. Southerners may have been willing to give up the major tenets of their way of life for the sake of independence. But finally they had to ask "independence for what?" When they answered, they were manifestly unwilling to commit themselves to guerrilla warfare. Partisans may have kept the "cause" alive a while longer, but they would have had to surrender their ties to people and place. As guerrilla nomads they might indeed have had to conduct reprisals against their own people. The fundamental attachment to people and place, "folk culture," was the one feature of Southernism they proved unwilling to abandon. Davis, however, did not understand. As he fled in the wake of multiple military disasters during the spring of 1865, he tried to exhort his people to renewed resistance. He failed. In the end Davis was captured wearing his wife's shawl and was sent to prison.

When at length the Confederate President left his prison cell, he never quite understood what had gone wrong. Davis had the bad fortune to live long after his "cause" collapsed. During these years he sought justification; he renewed old quarrels with some of his generals, and he spun the old theories about states' rights that Robert Lee's surrender had rendered moot. When Davis defended his world view as war leader of a rebel nation, he proved a flawed politician but a creative statesman. When the ex-President tried to justify a cause already lost, he was in many eyes truly as "pitiful" as those Yankee cadets he had despised so many years before.

*   *   *

President-elect Abraham Lincoln made the long journey in 1861 from Springfield, Illinois, to Washington, D.C., in triumph and trepidation. At every stop along the route people wanted to see Lincoln, most to cheer him, a few perhaps to kill him. Everyone wanted to know Lincoln's opinion of the secession crisis and his prediction about the possibility of civil war. On one occasion in New York City he responded to the inevitable questions by telling a story.

As a young lawyer, Lincoln recalled, he used to ride the judicial circuit in southern Illinois. Once during a rainy spell he and some companions found most of the streams along their way swollen far beyond their normal size. As they crossed these streams with mounting difficulty, the party became concerned about the Fox River, which lay ahead and promised to be even more turbulent than the creeks behind them. Night came on, and the men stopped at a tavern. There by chance was the local Methodist presiding elder who traveled about the region extensively. Lincoln and his colleagues were eager to learn from this man about their prospects of fording the Fox. To their questions the elder replied "O yes, I know all about the Fox River. I have crossed it often and understand it well; but I have one fixed rule with regard to the Fox River, I never cross it till I reach it."

Lincoln enjoyed telling stories. Many were ribald; most were humorous; and some were profound. Often, as in the case of the Fox River story, Lincoln told stories as parables to illustrate, or perhaps obscure, his point of view. Sometimes, though, Lincoln's tales told more about Lincoln himself than they did about their supposed topic or lesson.

Like the elder in his story, Lincoln was a profound pragmatist. He crossed rivers when he had to, in what seemed to him the most effective manner available. In fact it may be that this very quality, this down-to-earth, human approach to the crises that beset him, has been the thing that has most endeared Lincoln to generations of his countrymen. Americans can identify with the image of a practical man wrestling one-at-a time with great problems even more than with the genius of his solutions to those problems.

There is high irony, then, in the fact that Lincoln, the model of pragmatic statesmen, did more to express and refine the ideology of the North than did any of his doctrinaire contemporaries. From the time of its founding in 1854 the Republican Party was the practical political expression of the Northern world view. And from the time of his nomination to the presidency in 1860, Lincoln was the ultimate expression of the Republican Party. Upon Lincoln fell the burden of translating principles into action. His measure of greatness among American presidents rests not so much upon the validity of the principles, but upon his translation of them.

As every schoolchild knows, Abraham Lincoln was born in a log cabin in Kentucky. In fact Lincoln and Jefferson Davis were born within 100 miles and about eight months of each other. There the parallels end of course. The Davis family moved south from Kentucky; the Lincolns north into Indiana and then Illinois.

Little distinguished the young Lincoln from other sons of the midwestern frontier. He read more than his fellows and took more interest in the rude and intermittent schooling available to him. He was very tall (6'4"), and quite strong. He enjoyed the tales and rough humor of men. Perhaps Lincoln's best youthful prank involved an attempt to mix the mates of a double wedding when the couples retired for their first night of marriage. Lincoln did most of the same sorts of things as his contemporaries; and some he did a little better than others.

Like Davis, Lincoln in his young manhood served in the Black Hawk War. He saw no action and returned to New Salem, Illinois. For three years he kept store, served as postmaster, dabbled at surveying and "read law." Then in 1836 he hung out his law shingle in Springfield. Lincoln was a rapid success at law and local Whig politics. He worked very hard at both; if it were possible to apply the "work ethic" to politics, Lincoln did so. He was ambitious, true, but more important he believed that he owed himself his best efforts. If these were not sufficient, so be it.

Lincoln enjoyed an easy comradery with men, which made him a Northern counterpart of a "good old boy" and helped him through the rough and tumble of frontier politics. Women, though, were another matter. In 1840 Lincoln became engaged to Mary Todd, a strong-willed, well-born young lady whose social standing intimidated him. He began having second thoughts; he wondered if he truly loved her. He also suffered from attacks of very deep depression, and probably had one of his severe "down" periods at this time. At any rate he broke the engagement. In November 1842, nearly two years after the marriage was originally scheduled, Lincoln finally married Mary Todd.

At the conclusion of ten years of work and maneuver, Lincoln won his party's blessing to run for his district's relatively "safe" Whig seat in Congress. He served as representative from 1846 through 1847 and then returned to Springfield. Although enjoying Washington and national politics, he did little to distinguish himself during his term in the House and resigned to allow another faithful Whig from his district have his "turn." Perhaps, had the sectional issue not assumed crisis proportions that upset the normal order of many things, Lincoln might have ended his political career a one-term Congressman, genial lawyer, and member of the local Whig establishment.

Events, however, moved more swiftly than institutions could adapt during the late 1840s and 1850s. And Lincoln, the moderate Whig, followed the tide. In the wake of Stephen A. Douglas' Kansas-Nebraska Act in 1854, a group composed mainly of Free Soilers and dissident Whigs founded the Republican Party. Although its founders were considered radicals by moderates such as Lincoln, the Party broadened its base to include many segments of the Northern political mind. The Republicans soon swallowed up many Northern Whigs whose old party no longer had a national existence. In 1856 Lincoln took the plunge and joined the Republican campaign to make John C. Frémont president of the United States.

The Republican slogan, "Free soil, free labor, free men," well expressed Lincoln's hopes and his vision. He opposed the expansion of slavery because he considered slavery an evil that might be endured for a time, but could not be permitted to grow. On the contrary, free labor capitalism had to expand; the achievement, work-oriented "American dream" was real and right for Lincoln. He had lived it. Thus, although he was too profound a pragmatist to stand in the front ranks of the idealists and visionary reformers in his Party, he did stand behind them and their motives, if not their methods.

Frémont ran well in 1856 and the Republicans served notice that they were the second instead of the third party. In 1858 Lincoln carried the party banner against Stephen A. Douglas for the Senate. The campaign attracted national attention, at first because Douglas was a national figure and later because of Lincoln's skill and logic during the series of debates in which the candidates engaged. Lincoln lost the election, but won a reputation in the process. By the time Republicans met in Chicago in 1860 to nominate their presidential candidate he was a genuine contender. His managers worked tirelessly and promised much. Lincoln was enough of an unknown political quantity to draw votes away from men such as William H. Seward, Simon Cameron and Salmon P. Chase who had more formidable reputations but also more formidable political enemies. On the third ballot Lincoln caught the front-runner Seward and took the nomination.

In November the Republicans won the election. Their platform attracted support throughout the Northern tier of states. It called for an end to the expansion of slavery, for a protective tariff appealing to business interests, for a homestead law offering free land to western settlers, and for subsidized internal improvements (river dredging, railroad building, and the like). In 1860 the Republican struck the precise balance between ideals and interests to win. In the wake of Lincoln's victory, however, first South Carolina and then six other states of the deep South seceded from the Union. The President-elect faced the most severe crisis in his nation's young life before he even took the oath of office.

Lincoln assumed the "wait and see" posture of his Fox River parable for two reasons. First, he could not act on secession until he was the President, and even then rash action might make the situation worse by driving the border South into the rebel camp. Second, he simply did not believe that the South was serious about disunion; perhaps the planters were committed to a rump confederacy, but not the great mass of common men. When the confrontation came, as eventually it must, Lincoln believed the vast majority in the South would refuse to follow the planter lead. So President-elect Lincoln was silent while Davis and the Southerners formed their Confederacy, and he was cautious following his inauguration on March 4.

For more than a month Lincoln remained cautious. He talked to politicians from the border South. He worked unceasingly to mold his new administration and to satisfy voracious appetites for political place among Republicans. Yet for all his talking and political maneuvering, Lincoln actually did little, and his administration appeared to be in limbo. Republican regulars had believed all along that the neophyte from Illinois would be their "front" man; Lincoln could win the election, then they would run the country. Accordingly on April 1, Secretary of State Seward said plainly that the government had no policy, and it was high time to adopt one. He then proposed to heal the nation's internal wounds by provoking a foreign war. Finally Seward offered himself as the logical man to carry out the bold stroke he had outlined. Lincoln had reached his "Fox River"; he could temporize no longer.

Contrary to appearances the new President did have firm policies in mind upon coming to Washington. In fact, he had three of them. He planned to be his own president; he did not intend to compromise with the Southerners in such a way as to permit the expansion of slavery; and he was determined to preserve the Union no matter what the cost. So he responded tactfully to Seward's tactless memorandum. Gently but firmly he reminded the Secretary of State that he, not Seward, was president. Lincoln then faced the confrontation with the South. He faced it at

Fort Sumter, because there the issue was most clear. If Davis chose to make a stand, he would have to do so by firing the first shot. The Confederates, of course, did fire on Sumter, and Lincoln called for volunteers to "put down combinations in rebellion."

From hindsight it seemed inevitable that Lincoln should respond to the shelling of Fort Sumter by mobilizing for war. But hindsight too often leaves important questions unasked. Why did Lincoln decide to go to war to keep Southerners in the Union against their will? And why did the American people follow his lead and risk their lives for an apparent political abstraction? The answer to these questions is that the Union was not an abstraction in 1861; no more than was the "Southern way of life." The Union was real. It was the essential vehicle through which Americans could achieve their destiny. It was an arena for reform; it was a source of economic strength; it was the world's laboratory for democratic idealism. The Union was prerequisite for the growth of free labor capitalism and the *sine qua non* of American nationalism. Lincoln could never quite believe that the majority of Southerners did not share these beliefs, and so he fought a war of liberation to free these Southerners from their planter oppressors. Others in the North shared Lincoln's motivation, but the Union fought more than a war of liberation. It also fought a war of conquest—to humble the idle aristocrats in the South and to impose the "American way" of righteousness upon a "degenerate" people. Consequently even in the grim aftermath of the Union debacle at Bull Run, the war's first real battle, Lincoln and his countrymen persevered. In the process of persevering for the sake of union, however, Northerners found it necessary to say with greater precision what the Union meant. Lincoln's war aim was union—that never changed—but the war forced the President to refine and expand the definition of union.

During the first year of conflict, union sufficed as a rationale for bloodshed. Furthermore, wars tend to contain a dynamic of their own, which demands that they go to completion. Once blood is spilled, victory becomes an end in itself. By the summer of 1862, however, Northerners needed more than the words "victory" and "union" to justify the effort. Victory seemed possible, but far in the future, and union demanded definition. At this juncture, for these and other reasons, Lincoln determined to add emancipation to his stated definition of union.

Lincoln opposed slavery even though some of his best friends were slaveholders. His solution to the "problem" had been compensated emancipation for whites and colonization (deportation) for blacks. Yet the conduct of the war brought tremendous pressure to bear on the President. Strong-minded men like Charles Summer in Congress and Salmon Chase in the Cabinet argued in favor of immediate emancipation. Generals asked what to do with the human "contraband" captured from the Rebels. And the war was going badly in the summer of 1862—stalemate in the West, defeat in Virginia. Thus Lincoln decided to move on the subject of emancipation. Characteristically he proceeded deliberately and tactfully. He waited for a military victory and on September 22, 1862, announced his intention to free the slaves in rebel-controlled areas. It was, at the same time, a stroke of humanitarianism and political genius. The Emancipation Proclamation did not free a single slave on the day it went into effect, since Confederate Southerners did not recognize the validity of proclamations by "foreign" presidents and loyal unionist slaveholders were excluded from its terms. Still, Lincoln put himself and his government on record for emancipation, and in essence doomed slavery in the United States. He did so without driving border slave states such as Missouri, Kentucky, and Maryland out of the Union. And he did so without destroying the Republican majority in Congress as some of his advisors feared might happen in the 1862 "off-year" elections. Most important, though, Lincoln gave greater meaning to the war for union. Anti-slavery had been a part of that war all along, part of Lincoln's definition of union; but now the President had articulated the fact. He allowed the "war for union" to become a "crusade against slavery" as well.

Naturally the President and his party expended most of their time and energies presiding over the war effort. Yet the administration also took long strides toward making a reality out of its ideological vision for the nation. The clear Republican majority in Congress and the absence from Washington of otherwise-minded Southerners made the task easier. The non-military legislative record of Lincoln's presidency was impressive. Indeed one historian has termed this legislation the "blueprint for modern America."

Beginning in 1861 a series of tariffs were passed that progressively raised duties and set the tone for more political accommodation to industrial capitalism. In 1862 the Republicans fulfilled another campaign pledge by approving the Homestead Act. The law promised free land for those who would settle on it, but also offered public land for sale at $1.25 per acre. This latter provision opened the door to speculators who "settled" on the best plots and resold them at $15 an acre. The National Banking Act of 1863 outlawed state bank script and effectively standardized union currency. In 1864 Congress passed the Contract Labor Law, which permitted employers to bring in draft-exempt workers from abroad. Such legislation, together with lucrative war contracts, aided the American business community substantially. Taken as a whole the actions of Lincoln's administration well served the American transition from a preindustrial to an industrial state. The President himself was probably no "tool" of moneyed interests; his legislative record was the natural, sophisticated extension of his personal commitment to hard work, thrift, and such capitalist virtues. But "tool" or not, the results were the same. The business of the country was very much in the process of becoming business.

When asked, Lincoln ever maintained that his sole war aim was preservation of the Union. At the height of the agitation over emancipation, during the summer of 1862, the President went so far as to write an open letter to Horace Greeley in which he said, "my paramount object in this struggle *is* to save the Union, and is *not* either to save or to destroy slavery. If I could save the Union without freeing *any* slaves I would do it, and if I could save it by freeing *all* the slaves I would do it; and if I could save it by freeing some and leaving others alone I would also do that." Lincoln meant these words and to the disgust of many of his contemporaries was no doctrinaire reformer. But as the war dragged on he expanded his definition of union until it became synonymous with the interests and ideals of the Northern world view. The President thus became the pragmatic agent of American ideology. The Union that Lincoln insisted his enemies rejoin would not be the same Union they had left.

However much Lincoln eschewed reforming zeal, the thrust of his war aims and peace hopes was to remold the South. He still believed that the mass of Southern men were good, hard-working, frontier democrats like himself. He felt that peace and reunion would bring these people to the fore. The process of war, he hoped, would destroy the planter class, and a generous peace would insure the repudiation of planter leadership in the South by the common-man majority. Consequently the president resisted the heavy-handed peace tactics proposed by the radicals in his party. He "pocket-vetoed" the Wade-Davis Bill, which passed Congress in the summer of 1864; it projected a stern reconstruction for the South to be superintended by Congress. Always he insisted upon reunion and assumed that the union he proposed would itself reconstruct the South. At the abortive Hampton Roads peace conference in December 1864, the President insisted upon union, even to the point of holding out some hope of compensation to the Southerners for their emancipated slaves. And once he had the Union all but restored in April 1865, he counselled the commander of his military garrison in Richmond, "If I were in your place, I'd let them up easy—let them up easy."

A few days after his visit to the fallen Confederate capital of Richmond, Lincoln became one of the war's last casualties. His death was not a little ironic, because his countrymen lauded him in death as they never had in life. It spared him from seeing the South frustrate his hopes for reunion and reject the Union he had fashioned. Perhaps though, had the pragmatic idealist Lincoln ever reached the "Fox River" of Reconstruction, he would have made the crossing.

*   *   *

Late in the year 1861, some members of the Lincoln administration made informal overtures to Horace Greeley, editor of the New York

Tribune. If the *Tribune* should consent to become an unofficial "organ" of the government, the newspaper would receive in exchange advance notice of events and decisions occurring in high places. Greeley consented and the President was delighted. Lincoln said of Greeley, "Having him firmly behind me will be as helpful to me as an army of one hundred thousand men." As it happened Greeley did not long remain "firmly behind" Lincoln; nevertheless the President gave ample witness to the influence of this strange little man.

Born in Amherst, New Hampshire, in 1811, Greeley was "Hod" to the friends and neighbors of his youth. The robust sounding nickname was more appropriate to Greeley's parents, however, than to himself. His father and mother were sturdy farming people who enjoyed drink, tobacco, dance, and song. "Hod" Greeley was a shy, priggish prodigy who in time crusaded against most of the things that gave his parents pleasure. Perhaps Greeley associated creature comforts with poverty and hard times because his parents were never prosperous and often poor. The Greeleys lost their farm in the panic of 1819 and moved once to recoup their savings, then again to western Pennsylvania, to begin farming once more. During his family's difficulties Greeley himself retreated to books and shut himself off whenever there were no family chores to perform.

Greeley's most revealing practice during his early teens was that of lecturing girls against wearing corsets. He even devised a test to determine for sure whether his female companion was bound together with stays and strings. He dropped a handkerchief and challenged the young lady to pick it up. Whenever she did so, Greeley changed the subject. His interest in corsets seems purely that, a puritanical fetish; he seemed to care not at all about the contents of these worldly devices.

Greeley did not accompany his family on the move to western Pennsylvania. He had taken a job as an apprentice printer in East Poultney, Vermont, and remained there to learn his trade and earn his keep. While working on the East Poultney *Spectator,* Greeley reinforced his intellectual talents and bent his emotions toward religious pietism, temperance crusades, anti-slavery sentiment, and the Federalist Party. In journalism he had found his element, a vehicle with which to exercise his gifts and vent his moral fervor.

The *Spectator* folded in 1830, and Greeley rejoined his family in Pennsylvania. He did not stay long. A brief stay on his parents' lean, backwoods farm convinced him to leave his kin to their toilsome fate and strike out for New York. He began his journey to the nation's mecca with $25 in his pocket.

After a short term with a job-printing firm, Greeley founded his own family weekly, *The New Yorker.* The periodical enjoyed modest success in spite of its editor's periodic attempts at belle lettres. Greeley realized his limitations, however, and let others contribute stories and poems so that he could devote most of his attention to criticism and comment. The long-time Federalist evidenced his distaste of Jacksonian democracy. He distrusted mobs, labor unions, women's rightists, and abolitionist agitation; predictably he supported the National Bank against the assaults of "King Andrew."

In 1836 Greeley married a young schoolteacher and set up housekeeping in a modest neighborhood. The couple were never very "close" because Greeley could not allow domestic concerns to interfere with his journalistic pursuits and also because the Panic of 1837 so damaged *The New Yorker* that Greeley had to work all the harder to support his family. In 1838 Greeley began "commuting" to Albany where he edited the *Jeffersonian*, a Whig organ of Thurlow Weed, which sought to make William H. Seward Governor of New York. The venture succeeded, and in 1840 Greeley edited another Weed paper, *The Log Cabin*, as an organ of the Whig campaign to elect William Henry Harrison president. Finally in 1841 Greeley began publishing his own paper the New York *Tribune*.

Greeley's mind and heart shone clearly in the pages of the *Tribune*. A man of great enthusiasms; he flirted in turn with utopian socialism, transcendentalism, abolitionism, women's rights, and the temperance movement among others. He changed his mind often (notably on abolitionists and women) and in fact might have justifiably been charged a dilettante and hypocrite. However Greeley did display a fundamental consistency. He was a romantic reformer by nature; never mind if he altered his opinion of specific reforms. During the panic of 1837 he acquired new respect for the plight of the poor and thereafter believed that government ought to do positive good for society's downtrodden instead of merely preventing evil. He was an elitist, armed with moral rectitude, and eager to impose righteousness upon his fellow man. Greeley, in short, was an extreme expression of the idealistic, reforming bent in the Northern mind. And he attracted readers and converts, not only because of the substance of his ideals, but also because of the passionate, vigorous prose with which he expressed them.

Greeley remained a staunch Whig until 1854, when he accepted the Republican alternative to the nationally defunct Whig Party. In the process he split with Weed and Seward, a division that festered ultimately into open political warfare. At the Republican Convention in 1860 Greeley dedicated himself to preventing Seward's nomination and hoped to get the latter's Senate seat for himself. As it happened, Greeley "backed the wrong horse"; he worked for Edward Bates, a conservative, 65-year-old Whig from Missouri. The *Tribune* supported Lincoln once he won the nomination, but Greeley still believed Bates would have been a more prudent choice. He never quite appreciated Lincoln. In truth, he always seemed out of his element in the rough and tumble of practical politics; and Lincoln, to the bookish idealist, seemed the epitome of politics in the raw. Seward's defeat at the Republican Convention and Lincoln's victory in November were cause for rejoicing; but Greeley then fretted more over Weed's and Seward's successes at patronage in the new administration than about Southern secession. Once again he miscalculated; he did not believe the Southerners were serious.

When Greeley did confront the prospect of secession, his response was quite curious, on the surface at least. In the columns of the *Tribune* he bade the South to "go in peace." "Whenever a considerable section of our union shall deliberately resolve to go out, we shall resist all coercive measures designed to keep it in." This editorial, published in November 9, 1860, attracted much attention throughout the country because of its sentiment and its source. In reality, though, Greeley did not mean what he said. He admonished the South to secede, believing she would not do so. In Greeley's mind the Union was "a reality, an entity, a vital force, and not a mere aggregation." Thus secession was not only unconstitutional, but also unthinkable. All that was necessary was to call the South's bluff. Then the "reality" of the Union, which Greeley believed was a universally held concept, would silence the few hot-heads who preached secession. If, however, the South should persist in its folly, Greeley opposed compromise, which "only panders the South's insanity." He was opposed to war, but "we do not capitulate to traitors."

Greeley's stance on secession was characteristic of the man. At first he refused to believe that any sane person would deny the virtue of Union. When the Southerners proved him wrong, he reacted with the fury of a woman scorned, and after the Sumter crisis the *Tribune* was constant in its demand for blood.

Greeley gravitated wildly when defining the ultimate purpose of the war. In 1861 he was belligerent and convinced that the war was about his beloved Union. For a time, then, the *Tribune* served as an administration paper. But by 1862, Greeley could not understand why virtue was not everywhere triumphant, and he despaired of the North's military leadership. "Buell ought to be shot, and Grant ought to be hung," he privately confided; and, in the *Tribune,* he attacked McClellan's "tinsel imitation" of war. Greeley then concluded that the war must be about slavery as well as union. God was on the side of union but wanted it cleansed of the stain of slavery. He began working with Radicals in Congress toward emancipation and on August 20, 1862 published his "Prayer of Twenty Millions" editorial, which demanded that Lincoln "fight slavery with liberty." Although Greeley could not know it, the President had already decided to issue the Emancipation Proclamation and only required a military victory to emancipate from a position of strength instead of weakness. The *Tribune* applauded the Proclamation when it came, but expressed some concern over those slaves in loyal areas who were excluded from its provisions. Still, in Greeley's mind, the union had struck a blow against slavery; victory must be at hand. When victory did not immediately follow emancipation, Greeley once more despaired. He began talking about the "best available peace" and considered restoration of the old union without emancipation. Consequently he alternated between the Rebels and the war itself as the proper object of distaste. For example, after the Confederate victory at Chancellorsville, he lamented, "My God! it is horrible—horrible; and think of it, 130,000 magnificent soldiers so cut to pieces by less than 60,000 half-starved ragamuffins!" But in the wake of the New York draft riots in July 1863, he had second thoughts about the war. The mob remembered his support of the draft, attacked the *Tribune* office twice, and sang songs about hanging "Horace Greeley to a sour apple tree." Mrs. Greeley spent the week of the riots with a keg of gunpowder in the basement of their home. If the mob came she planned to flee into the woods, then ignite the trail of powder leading to the keg, and blow up some of the rioters along with her house.

Greeley's reenlistment in the war effort and rapprochement with the Lincoln administration was short-lived. By 1864 he was again hoping for peace negotiations and opposing the President's renomination. In the summer of 1864 he actually made contact with semi-official Rebel agents in Canada and offered himself as a free-lance peace negotiator. Lincoln wrote that Greeley might pursue peace as long as union and emancipation were understood as absolute conditions. But Greeley went to Niagara to meet the Rebels without mentioning conditions, and the venture was a fiasco. Despite some harsh words about the President's conduct of the "Niagara Conference," Greeley supported Lincoln's re-election. And despite the embarrassment caused him by Greeley's well-meant duplicity, Lincoln welcomed the *Tribune's* help.

In the end victory produced the peace and restored the union for which Greeley crusaded. The editor shared Lincoln's hopes for a generous, speedy restoration. But whatever else Reconstruction was, it was neither generous nor speedy. Greeley clung to his ideals during the postwar years, and they led him down strange paths. He turned on the Republican Radicals and then on the Republicans altogether. Greeley ran for President in 1872 as a Democrat. He *was* true to his ideals. He simply never reconciled his zeal for perfection with the realities of politics and personal interests. Having scoffed at Lincoln's temporizing and pragmatic leadership, Greeley apparently realized Lincoln's greatness only after the assassination and called the martyred President, "the one providential leader, the one indispensable hero" of the war of union. He even had second thoughts about the Rebels. In the name of his own notion of justice, he journeyed to Richmond on May 13, 1867, and signed his name to Jefferson Davis' bail bond. "Hod" Greeley was not a "man of the world" as his youthful nickname tended to imply. Still his ideals and reform enthusiasm stamped him as very much a man of his world. That he was increasingly out of step with the real world as he grew older revealed more about the world than about the indomitable Greeley.

The "real world" eventually overcame each of the "drummers" we have heard. Davis finally lost touch with the reality of the Southern world and ended his life beating a broken drum. Lincoln was a victim of an ideological intensity he scarcely shared but which he molded and effectively led to victory. Having directed the "drummers" he never completed his march. And Greeley just beat essentially the same drum during his whole life—long after his beat was obsolete. Nevertheless in their prime each of these men—Davis, Lincoln, and Greeley—played upon the essential themes of their era. They not only reflected their respective world views; they strove to act them out.

15

Republicans Confront Reconstruction

THADDEUS STEVENS
ALBION TOURGÉE
ROBERT B. ELLIOTT

by Michael Les Benedict
Ohio State University

After the Civil War those who had sustained Northern arms faced the hardest imaginable task: to restore the Union and secure the basic rights of freedom to ex-slaves without permanently depriving ex-Confederates of their privileges as American citizens. Unionists knew the two goals seemed incompatible. Southern whites would undoubtedly resort to the ballot box to subvert the rights of ex-slaves. Yet most Unionists could not bring themselves to sustain permanent suppression of those who had supported the Confederacy. Such a policy would inflict too much damage on the nation's free institutions. Consequently they passed national legislation to protect black Southerners against discriminatory state laws. And in an effort to enable blacks to protect themselves, they enfranchised the freedmen, even though the latter were fresh from slavery and still considered an inferior race by almost every American.

The effort failed. All three of the following men were to some degree victims of that failure.

* * *

Of all the Republicans responsible for the program of Reconstruction that Congress imposed upon the South, white Southerners probably hated

Thaddeus Stevens the most. For them, this stern-visaged lawmaker with his deep-set, almost satanic eyes burning beneath a heavy brow and a power of invective that scattered opponents with its scorn and passion, seemed to embody Northern fanaticism and vengefulness. Understandably, there was rejoicing among white Southerners when he died in 1868 just as most of the Southern states reentered normal relations with the Union. "The prayers of the righteous have at last removed the Congressional curse," one Southern newspaper gloried.

But in Washington, where Stevens' body lay in the Capitol rotunda, thousands of mourners filed by the bier; only Lincoln had received a greater tribute. As if the incredible force of his will outlived his shattered body, he delivered a final lesson to his countrymen: four white and four black pallbearers bore his body to the Capitol; an honor guard of black militiamen stood by it. A week later, he was buried according to his instructions, in a mostly black cemetery in Lancaster, Pennsylvania, where he had lived most of his life. He explained why in the words he directed to be inscribed on his tombstone:

> I repose in this quiet and secluded spot,
> Not from any preference for solitude,
> But . . . that I might illustrate in death
> The principles which I advocated through a long life,
> EQUALITY OF MAN BEFORE HIS CREATOR.

Like so many Northern Republicans, Stevens' family origins lay deep in New England. His parents were Baptists, fierce Calvinists in an age when the traditional New England churches, Congregationalist and Presbyterian, were drifting away from the old dogmas. With other Baptists, they had left Massachusetts and settled in remote northern Vermont, still a frontier wilderness. There Stevens was born in 1792, clubfooted like his older brother, the crippled embodiment of his father's failures as a farmer, surveyor, and, ironically, shoemaker. Ultimately, his father became an alcoholic and deserted the poverty-stricken family.

As if to defy his handicap, the young Stevens worked to develop athletic ability; he became a powerful swimmer and a horseback rider. But he could not join in children's sports, either because of the deformity itself or his embarrassment over it. He suffered a lonely childhood, grew desperately attached to his mother, and found solace in reading. Taunted by other children, he learned to hide his own pain behind a gruff exterior and came to feel the pain of others, especially those who were also discriminated against because they happened to be born different.

From his Calvinist New England heritage Stevens inherited a powerful conviction that human beings, himself included, were essentially bad. He was often oppressed by personal guilt, which he tried to expiate by sudden and unexpected acts of kindness, even towards his enemies. But where there was guilt, he stubbornly maintained there had to be punishment.

Scarred by the experiences of his youth, Stevens found it difficult thereafter to establish close personal attachments with social equals. He doubted the sincerity of warm friendship when it was offered and was quick to suspect treachery from his associates. Unable to exploit social connections for personal advancement, he always imagined that others did so. He scorned them for it. For emotional sustenance, he turned to those not on an equal social plane, whose rejection he need not fear. Even in gruff old age, Stevens was known for his fondness of children; once established as a lawyer, he was uncommonly kind toward fledgling barristers. His generosity to the poor was famous. Uncomfortable with women of his own class, Stevens' best friend, perhaps his mistress, was a witty and attractive black woman, Lydia Smith, who kept house for him during the last 20 years of his life.

His mother's dogged efforts put Stevens through college, where his personal unpopularity prevented his nomination for membership in Phi Beta Kappa. Admitted to the bar a few years after his graduation, he opened a law office in Gettysburg, Pennsylvania, and soon established a reputation as a formidable opponent in a trial: witty, sarcastic, razor-sharp in his logic. He concentrated singlemindedly upon making money, as if to compensate for the poverty of his youth. Soon he was the richest man in Gettysburg. Unable to win love, he could still command respect.

Stevens' political interests were generated by the rise of the anti-Masonic movement in the mid-1820s. Many Americans were suspicious of Masonic secrecy, hostile to its aristocratic social pretension, and alienated by the Masons' religiously liberal, freethinking tradition. When a renegade New York Mason disappeared after threatening to expose the order's secrets, the public outcry made anti-Masonism a potent political force. The movement had a powerful appeal for Stevens, who was convinced that others conspired for their own advancement in such cabals, from which he seemed always to be excluded. Elected to the state legislature in 1833, he became the leading anti-Masonic lawmaker. In the statehouse he showed inflexible hostility toward those opposing him, a willingness to bully and cajole allies, and dogged adherence to a policy once it was established. But when anti-Masons allied with other opponents of Andrew Jackson's Democratic Party in the loosely organized Whig Party, Stevens was excluded from its leadership. Still, he remained a power to be reckoned with.

Stevens always feared that small groups of aristocrats were plotting to secure inordinate political power. Such men, he worried, could manipulate the ignorant and the poor, those without intellectual or economic independence. They might be especially successful among the foreign-born, who did not hold his own strong commitment to republican liberty. Stevens shared with New England expatriates a distrust of the distinctly non-Yankee habits of foreign immigrants and migrating Southerners.

These sentiments led Stevens to resist Jacksonian Democratic pressure to eliminate the last restrictions on the right of white men to vote. Yet they also made him Pennsylvania's leading champion of free public education. If ignorance, poverty, and foreign ideas were dangerous to American society, a free system of education was its salvation. Stevens played an important role in establishing such a system in the state in 1834 and then almost single-handedly defeated Democratic efforts to repeal it in 1835.

Again, like many Americans with New England roots, Stevens disliked slavery well before it became a burning issue. Raised in a culture that made a virtue of hard work, he resented those who lived off the labor of others. And his feelings were strengthened by his personal identification with those who suffered because of accidents of birth and by his passionate hatred of "aristocracy."

Stevens began to make his antislavery feelings known in the years following his great victory for public education. But no politician taking such a position could be acceptable to the Whig party leadership, which sought to maintain party unity between Northerners and Southerners. By 1840 Stevens seemed to have arrived at a political dead-end. Retiring from politics, he rebuilt his law practice and personal wealth.

When the slavery issue erupted in the late 1840s, it was inevitable that a man of Stevens' temperament and political ambition would play a leading role. His acid tongue and bellicose approach were precisely what his neighbors wanted in 1848, and they elected him to Congress as the most outspoken antislavery candidate. Stevens served until 1852, when his assaults on Democrats and pro-slavery Whigs alike made him seem too radical to a constituency now worried that the Union might not survive the sectional controversy. But in 1858, with resurgent Northern hostility towards slavery, he was returned to Congress again, where he served through the 1861 secession crisis, firmly resisting compromise efforts that he regarded as Southern blackmail. Unaffected by the prevailing uncertainty, Stevens was like a reassuring rock of confidence in stormy seas.

When secession in 1861 left the new anti-slavery Republican party in control of Congress, Stevens became chairman of the extraordinarily influential Ways and Means Committee. This position was usually held by the Congressional leader of his party, and Stevens was ideally fitted for the role. With his power of invective and readiness to impose discipline on Republican deviants, he was the perfect "enforcer" of party decisions. He rarely made policy. That was done in Congressional committees or caucuses, where he shared influence with other leaders. But once policy was established, he held the party whip, and few Republicans dared to challenge him.

Stevens vigorously supported a tough Civil War policy. The slave South represented everything that he had always loathed: a plantation aristocracy, whose power derived in part from its ability to dupe poor and ignorant whites into supporting a system built on the oppression of those who happened to have been born black. These aristocrats, he was convinced, had conspired to control the Union for years before 1861 and then to destroy it when that control was lost. He and other Republicans called it "the slave power conspiracy."

According to Stevens, the only way to restore the Union securely was to destroy this social system. So while Republican conservatives, such as President Lincoln, were at first willing to reconstitute the Union without major changes, Stevens from the beginning demanded an end to slavery and stringent reconstruction policies. After the Confederates surrendered in 1865, President Lincoln's successor, Andrew Johnson, was willing to reintegrate the secessionist states into the Union with only slavery abolished. Many Republicans agreed. The Southern states, they argued, might return to the Union once they guaranteed ex-slaves basic civil rights. Others demanded that black men also be given the right to vote so that they could protect their own interests. But Stevens and a few others wanted much more.

Stevens believed that equal rights, including the right to vote, would not in themselves mean much. He had never had much faith in the ability of poor people to use the ballot wisely. They would always be duped by aristocratic conspirators if they were not made intellectually and economically independent. Stevens, then, went well beyond equal rights and equal suffrage; he wanted to confiscate the lands of the larger Southern planters and distribute them to poor blacks and whites. He also endorsed nationally supervised free public school systems in the South. But most of all, he urged delay in reintegrating the Southern states back into the Union. As land redistribution and education would bring de facto equality, black and white Southerners could "practice" real democracy by electing territorial governments under congressional supervision. Others might think this policy too harsh, but Stevens believed that guilt called for punishment. Let others call for mercy. He wanted justice, especially when it alone could exterminate the evil social system that had led to secession.

Stevens served on the joint congressional committee that devised Reconstruction policy but could not persuade its members to follow him. In 1866 President Johnson joined Democrats in demanding that the Southern states be restored immediately, under the control of ex-Confederates and without any guarantees that the basic human rights of ex-slaves would be protected. Most Republican leaders feared that if they sought more than equal protection of the laws for the ex-slaves, Johnson and his Democratic allies might well succeed in their objectives. Consequently, the Reconstruction committee made this proposition the centerpiece of the Fourteenth Amendment. Important sections guaranteed the rights of American citizens to all, regardless of color, and disqualified Confederate leaders from holding office. If the Southern states ratified the amendment, most Republican leaders made it clear that they would recognize their restoration to the Union. But radical Republicans were dissatisfied, and Stevens used all his power to keep them in line. Any divisions, he warned radicals, would play into the hands of the President and the Democrats. His bitterest invective was reserved for those Republican Congressmen who wavered in their opposition to Johnson, and ultimately few did, owing to Stevens. His threats were effective, they knew, because he spoke for their constituents. But to white Southerners, he was the arch-fiend, the despot who single-handedly drove his party to what they considered extreme measures.

By 1867 every Southern state but Tennessee refused to ratify the Fourteenth Amendment. Moderate and conservative Republicans were willing to let matters drift until ratification, but, radicals argued, such stubbornness proved that Southerners had not repented for their treason. They insisted upon a more forceful policy. In the bitter struggle that ensued, Stevens desperately sought to impose his will on his recalcitrant colleagues. Finally both sides were forced to compromise. Under the Reconstruction Act of 1867, Southerners were put under military government until they framed new state constitutions that would permit black men to vote and guarantee equality before the law, and until they ratified the Fourteenth Amendment. But radicals had to give up on land reform, a long period of probation for the South, and federally-mandated public education systems.

White Southerners thought Republicans were deliberately destroying their section in revenge for secession and particularly damned Stevens for his efforts. But, like other radicals, Stevens lamented that Republicans had not gone far enough. Without land, without education, without political experience, Southern blacks could not defend themselves against hostile white neighbors. They were being thrown upon their own meager resources. Republicans "said to the colored man, . . . 'Root, hog, or die,' " a radical Republican in the South wrote later. "It was cheap patriotism, cheap philanthropy, cheap success!"

Stevens did not live to see these fears realized. In 1867 his health was failing; the struggle over Reconstruction of that year was the penultimate one for him. The final battle came in 1868 when the House of Representatives impeached Johnson for breaking the Tenure of Office Act when trying to obstruct enforcement of the Reconstruction Act. Too weak physically to do much to persuade senators that they should convict the President, he watched helplessly as political considerations and tactical mistakes undermined the shaky Congressional case for impeachment. He was deeply depressed in the months before death and disconsolately confessed to a friend, "My life has been a failure." Stevens knew the Republican Reconstruction program would not succeed; and he foresaw the injustice that failure would bring. Despite the successes of his own life, he shared to the end the pain of those who, like him, had been born different.

*　　*　　*

It was Albion Winegar Tourgée who complained that Republicans had taken the easy way out in Reconstruction, that it was "cheap philanthropy, cheap success." Though not asserting as much until the late 1870s, he held these sentiments back in 1867 as an ambitious young northern migrant to North Carolina. Tourgée was a "Carpetbagger," the demeaning label that white Southern opponents applied to Northerners who became Republican activists in the South.

Tourgée, born in 1838, was 46 years younger than Stevens but his background was similar in many ways. His parents were New Englanders who also had rejected that region's dominant churches. They had joined their neighbors who flooded the Western Reserve in northeastern Ohio. And here Tourgée's father realized his life's dream of establishing a prosperous farm.

Stevens lost his father at an early age; Tourgée lost his mother. Until he was six, when Tourgée Sr. remarried, the latter bestowed on him the warmth and affection that normally came from both parents. For the next ten years, however, the jealous boy warred with his stepmother, a situation made worse by the arrival of a stepsister. He rejected parental discipline and would maintain a lifelong resistance to all authority.

Young Tourgée was physically unafraid to the point of recklessness and had a series of accidents, the worst of which left him blind in one eye. But unlike Stevens' experience, Tourgée's infirmity made him something of a hero to his friends. Stevens, moreover, had clung desperately to his mother for love; Tourgée turned to his peers for respect and affection, winning it by bravado and a willingness to lead in any adventure.

This quality of Tourgée's was reinforced by the intensely romantic spirit of the age in which he grew up. Tourgée read voraciously, the medieval romances of Sir Walter Scott being his favorite books. From an early age he too wanted to write. In both high school and at the University of Rochester, he concentrated on the personal and the emotional—while ignoring such worldly distractions as politics.

The excitement of the antislavery struggle finally grasped him in 1860, especially when his college president banned political demonstrations. The rebellious Tourgée promptly organized a Republican club, whose members threatened to leave the college en masse; they forced the school to back down. When war broke out a few months later, Tourgée and his friends immediately volunteered. They wanted to be dashing cavalry men; instead they were assigned to the infantry.

Tourgée's military career combined success and failure. He rose to lieutenant on the strength of his bravery—he was wounded three times—but he could achieve no higher rank because of his chronic inability to obey the orders of his superiors. Weakened by injuries and frustrated, he resigned from the service in 1863, married, and prepared to become a lawyer and to settle down.

But Tourgée was an impatient and ambitious young man. When peace was restored in 1865, he was convinced the South offered opportunities for social and economic success. The section was destitute. Plantations were wrecked. Money and brains were needed to help rebuild the economy, and to replace slavery with a new social system. Such a mission appealed to the romantic in Tourgée. Years later, he named the carpetbagger hero of a semi-autobiographical novel Comfort Servosse, because the twin desires for material comfort and service to the nation had motivated him.

Tourgée moved to western North Carolina in 1865, bringing along his wife, her family, and two business partners. Together they invested $4500, a considerable sum in those days, in a plantation nursery and a law firm. Although white Southerners always charged that Carpetbaggers had come to the South destitute and bent on plunder, Tourgée's case was, in fact, more typical. The Northern immigrant usually carried money, idealism, and personal ambition, all packed together like the clothes in his carpetbag.

At first Tourgée attended to business, but politics soon interfered. Having grown increasingly sympathetic to the plight of the slaves during the war, he was now determined to treat black employees fairly. This attitude led to arguments with his partners. Worse, it also made him popular with the former slaves and prompted suspicion among native whites. Then, too, he came to admire the substantial minority of western North Carolinians who remained loyal to the Union throughout the war and had suffered for it at the hands of their Confederate neighbors. He was dismayed by President Johnson's willingness to turn control of the state back to the ex-Confederates, who were still treating these Southern Unionists as traitors. By 1866 he was cooperating with the Unionists in efforts to overturn presidential policy. He published a newspaper which, with Tourgée's characteristic boldness, attacked the political enemy.

Tourgée hoped that Congress would enact something similar to the policy Stevens proposed. Like Stevens, he did not think that enfranchising black men would enable them to protect their interests if it were not accompanied by other measures. "Hunger is more potent than patriotism," he warned, and the economic power of the old Confederate leaders would surely overcome the political power Congress was trying to give to former slaves to protect themselves. Nonetheless, when Congress rejected such counsel and enacted the Reconstruction Act, Tourgée joined with other Northern immigrants, Southern Unionists, and the newly enfranchised blacks to organize a Republican party in the state.

Tourgée's deepening political involvement contributed to his financial ruin. Influential white neighbors refused to do business with him. He himself neglected business affairs. Finally, his partners sold out to him, but failed to disclose some heavy debts they had incurred. Creditors then forced Tourgée to the wall. The nursery failed; the newspaper was sold; the debts mounted. Politics became even more important to him. He needed political office to survive financially.

Coming from the North, with a New England–Western Reserve background, Tourgée was more willing than Southern Unionists to espouse the cause of North Carolina blacks. Most of the state's Republican leaders hoped to gain power by combining enough white votes with those of the newly enfranchised blacks, who could be counted on to support the party of Lincoln. They urged a program of reform that would appeal to the white small farmers of the central and western hill country. Included in it were taxes on property rather than a fixed per capita tax on each citizen, state help for economic development of the interior, and laws to protect homesteads from being foreclosed for debt. At the same time, these Republican strategists feared that too much pro-Negro legislation would alienate whites.

William B. Holden was the leader of the new party. He had been identified with similar proposals even before the war began. But he had also been strongly pro-slavery, had persecuted Unionists, and had helped precipitate North Carolina secession. Many Unionists could not forgive him, and some, including Tourgée, did not trust him. Tourgée was especially critical of Holden's reluctance to press for more legislation to benefit ex-slaves or to allow them to be nominated for office on the Republican ticket. His outspokenness on these issues made him popular with the black men who constituted the bulk of the Republican rank-and-file. To the chagrin of his more conservative Republican competitors, he became the leader of the local party organization.

Despite Tourgée's constant criticism of Republican state leaders, they co-operated with him. He played a prominent role in the 1868 constitutional convention, which attempted to bring North Carolina into line with the requirements of Reconstruction law. He also emerged as the convention's leading reformer and one of its most influential members. Indeed, he was largely responsible for the resulting constitution, the most progressive in North Carolina's history.

At first, the Republican program seemed to work. Republicans swept the 1868 elections. Holden won the governorship. Tourgée was elected a state judge, and also was named to a commission to revise the state legal code. A powerful figure in the party and partaking of political patronage, Tourgée was again making his way.

Tourgée's differences with the Republican leadership were inconsequential compared to those with their Conservative (Democratic Party) political opponents. Southern Conservatives were convinced that equal civil and political rights for blacks meant social, economic, and political disaster. They shared the conviction of Stevens and Tourgée that unless men were economically and intellectually independent, they could not be politically independent. But they drew a different conclusion about what the consequences would be. Conservatives gloomily predicted that unscrupulous whites would dupe former slaves into supporting them politically in exchange for impossible promises to improve their lot at the expense of whites. They constantly urged the new black voters to support "honest" Conservative candidates. When blacks ignored their appeals and elected Republicans, the Conservatives were confirmed in their forebodings. They bitterly attacked black suffrage and urged whites to unite against "Negro domination." Such tactics proved effective in offsetting Republican appeals to the white small farmers.

Men like Tourgée were not idealists to Southern Conservatives. They were not looked on as ordinary politicians, but as scoundrels who never could have obtained public office on merit or on issues; they appealed to the worst instincts of ex-slaves who were too ignorant to know better. Any benefits they incurred through legislation, such as financial help for railroads that they owned or payment for construction of public buildings, amounted to thievery. Conservatives considered the taxes they were forced to pay to Republican governments to be no more than extortion.

Conservatives, of course, were denying to blacks what they guaranteed to white constituents: the right to vote for people who first and foremost promised to look after their interests. But being convinced that blacks were incapable of judging what their interests were, they failed to see the lack of logic in their position.

Realizing that they could not win at the ballot box, Conservatives turned to violence to overthrow the Republican-led state governments. By 1868 independently organized guerilla groups had spread across much of the South. They terrorized black leaders and intimidated white Republicans, seeking thereby to destroy their ability to organize for election campaigns. They also took revenge on individuals for private grievances and tried to force blacks to adopt subservient attitudes despite their supposed equality.

By 1870 these organizations, now generally known as the Ku Klux Klan, became active in North Carolina. There they virtually served as an arm of the Conservative party and sought to gain control of the state legislature by the fall elections. Concentrating on Tourgée's judicial district, they murdered several of his political associates and threatened his own life.

Republicans across the South were at first paralyzed by the violence. Upon asking for national help, they were told that Reconstruction was over and that they must handle the problem themselves. Tourgée urged Holden to hire detectives to ferret out Klan leaders and bring them to trial before his court. But the governor was convinced that Tourgée would be assassinated and that the jurors would either be intimidated into acquitting the defendants or would sympathize with them. Against Tourgée's advice he decided to declare martial law and hold suspected Klansmen temporarily without trial. As Tourgée expected, the result was a wave of protest in North Carolina and criticism even from Northern Republicans. Klan violence subsided, but Holden's tactics united North Carolina whites against him. That, combined with Klan violence, led to a Democratic electoral victory. The new Conservative state legislature promptly impeached and convicted Holden. As a result the Republican party passed into the control of more cautious leaders.

Tourgée's political career was also gravely affected by the Conservative resurgence. He lost influence inside the party and was stripped of his judicial position in the Conservative landslide of 1874. He then turned to writing. In 1874, he published his first novel, *Toinette,* about a love affair between a white Southerner and his beautiful mulatto slave which could not survive the impact of emancipation. For the next four years he practiced law, tried to rebuild his political career, and continued to write fiction. By 1878 it became clear he could not advance economically or professionally in North Carolina; his views were too unpopular with the now dominant Conservative white leadership. In 1879, after living in North Carolina 14 years, he left for New York, still combative but recognizing defeat. In the same year he published his most famous novel, *A Fool's Errand, By One of the Fools.* A great success in its time, it described the life and work of Comfort Servosse, a Carpetbagger who had hoped to make his mark in a changed South.

*   *   *

We know far more about the early lives of Thaddeus Stevens and Albion Tourgée than that of Robert B. Elliott. A capable and ambitious black man, Elliott lived almost invisibly on the fringe of society before the Civil War. During the conflict and in the postbellum years, many Northerners and nearly all Southern whites insisted that blacks were markedly inferior and consequently should be denied equal legal and political rights. To counter such arguments, antislavery activists were quick to draw attention to those blacks who disproved the stereotype. Young Elliott recognized this, and claimed for himself a glamorous background that magnified his obvious capabilities.

His English accent, Elliott claimed, was the result of a British upbringing. He had been educated at Eton, he asserted, and had studied law with a distinguished English jurist. None of this was true. But Elliott was so talented that no one questioned his account and it made him, a man whose race normally would have put him on the bottom rung of American society, socially acceptable to many of those at the top, especially in the North. Moreover, it prompted even greater respect among fellow blacks than he would have otherwise had.

No one knows Elliott's true background. His English accent apparently was real; his knowledge was certainly broad. He may have been a Boston newspaper typesetter in the 1850s. We don't know.

Physically, Elliott was striking. He was a handsome and charismatic man. Well educated and well read, he was also an excellent speaker. Indeed, he rivalled the great black leader Frederick Douglass, probably the finest orator of his day. Although Elliott shared the typical American hope for a life of respectability and material comfort, practically all avenues of advancement were closed to him. But the new social system augured by Reconstruction seemed to offer a world of possibilities. Black people would need social and political leaders as well as the manifold professional services of talented and educated blacks. So in 1867 Elliott moved to Charleston, South Carolina, a flourishing black social and intellectual center, where he became coeditor of a black newspaper and studied law.

Elliott was quickly swept into politics, and, much like Tourgée in the North Carolina constitutional convention, he played an important role in that of South Carolina in 1868. Afterwards, in the same year, he was elected to the state legislature. Politically ambitious, he consciously promoted his popularity with black South Carolinians, who made up the bulk of the state Republican Party's rank-and-file. Thus he opposed property or educational limits on the right to vote and supported provisions guaranteeing blacks equal access to government services and public facilities such as streetcars, railroads, hotels, theaters, and restaurants.

Inevitably, the aspirations of Elliott and black politicians like him led to conflict with white leaders of South Carolina's Republican Party, many of whom were racists. Although more sympathetic to black claims for justice than Conservative leaders, they could not bring themselves to associate with the former slaves as equals. Like North Carolina conservative Republicans, they hoped to win white support. Too much pro-black legislation, and especially the nomination of blacks to high office, was sure to alienate the white voters they wanted to attract.

As a result, black leaders like Elliott had to stay in the background, even though they organized and delivered the black votes necessary to elect white Republicans. Typically, Elliott was made assistant adjutant general of the state militia, where he did nearly all the work while his white superior collected a fat salary as well as the graft.

Corruption, one of the biggest problems of post-Civil War America, was worst in the South, owing to a lack of respect for the law in that section. Since most Southern whites believed that Republican officials were mere demagogues elected by ignorant ex-slaves, they were sure their interests would never be promoted by the ordinary political process. Given such circumstances, they believed there was justification in trying to influence the state government through bribery of its officers. Such temptation proved too much for many white Republican leaders, such as Elliott's superior, Adjutant General Franklin J. Moses, who in fact *was* a scoundrel.

But more than bribery was involved. For all groups in the South, law had become the vehicle for enforcing the power of those who governed, rather than a means of enforcing justice. Southern Unionists, on the one hand, had seen how the Confederates had suppressed dissent before and during the Civil War. Ex-Confederates, on the other, thought Republicans were using the law to oppress them. Blacks, of course, had the most bitter memories of all. During Reconstruction each side believed, with justification, that whoever got control of the state would use legal institutions to promote its own interests at the expense of the losers. Given the ambience, even essentially honest men, like Elliott, succumbed to the temptation to use their positions for personal gain. Desperate to live in the style identified as "respectable," Elliott borrowed money from those who sought influence. He knew of and tolerated outright bribes to lawmakers, though they all insisted that their votes weren't motivated by such payments (much as legislators today deny that campaign contributions and lecture fees from special interests determine their votes).

Black leaders quickly grew restless under white Republican domination. They demanded that white Republicans offer something more—lucrative and prestigious political positions—especially since white Conservatives, desperate to regain power, were now also wooing blacks. Those who agreed won black support and, with it, control of the Republican party, and in 1870 a black man was nominated and elected lieutenant governor. Three of four members of the Republican state executive committee were blacks, including the state party chairman. Three black leaders, among them Robert Elliott, were sent to Congress.

In Congress Elliott's abilities won national attention, and by 1872 he held a secure place in South Carolina's Republican leadership. In that year he chaired the state party convention that gave his ally and former boss, Franklin Moses, the gubernatorial nomination.

Two years later, however, scandals over Republican corruption began to undermine the South Carolina party. Northern Republicans were critical, and Republican President Ulysses S. Grant hinted that support might be given to a new Reform coalition of conservative Republicans and Conservatives. Both worried and sensing a political opportunity, Elliott became an important spokesman for reform in the party, linking the issue to his own low-key campaign for the Republican gubernatorial nomination.

Elliott did not get the nomination. Instead panicky Republicans turned to Daniel H. Chamberlain, an able Massachusetts native, who like Elliott had established a reputation for probity after participating only briefly in a few shady operations. However, Chamberlain's idea of how to increase Republican support alienated most black leaders. As governor, he openly courted Conservatives, vetoing Republican legislative proposals and selecting few blacks for government positions (although Frank Cardoza, the black state treasurer, was his closest political ally and a personal friend). This effort to court and conciliate South Carolina whites not only threatened the personal ambitions of black politicians but also presaged a deemphasis upon the Republican commitment to racial justice.

As newly appointed speaker of the state House of Representatives, Elliott led the black opposition to Chamberlain. Cooperating with such discredited whites as Moses, he worked to impeach Cardoza and to force the election of Chamberlain's party opponents to important local offices. This confrontation almost wrecked South Carolina's Republican organization. By 1876 Chamberlain expected to gain complete control of the party and run for reelection as a Republican without Conservative opposition, or to run as an Independent Republican with Conservative support if regular Republicans refused to back him. But Chamberlain had not taken sufficient account of divisions among Conservatives. Many of them, especially in closely contested counties, wanted a "Straight-Out" Conservative nomination. If Conservatives did not nominate an opponent to Chamberlain, they feared that apathetic whites would not vote, thereby costing them local elections in their home counties. Those Conservatives who favored cooperation with the governor argued that a Conservative nominee could not win because there were more black than white voters in South Carolina; but these "Straight-Outs" pointed to Alabama and Mississippi, where violence had helped Conservatives win elections in 1874 and 1875.

To promote their cause, Straight-Outers engineered a race riot in the town of Hamburg. The "Hamburg Massacre," in which whites wantonly murdered captured blacks, destroyed Chamberlain's plans. Straight-Outers went on the offensive in the Conservative party, appealing to white racial pride. Those Conservatives cooperating with Chamberlain did not dare denounce the murders and simply repeated the Straight-Out lies about what happened. In the aftermath of Hamburg, Conservatives, repudiating Chamberlain, nominated Confederate General Wade Hampton for governor. In response to the Conservative threat, Republicans reunited behind Chamberlain, who in turn accepted Elliott as a candidate for Attorney General.

Conservatives ran a double-edged campaign in 1876. Hampton himself promised to protect the rights of ex-slaves and apparently believed that he had won the backing of many of them. But the Straight-Out leadership was breaking up Republican meetings, assaulting Republican leaders, and intimidating black voters. In much of the state they marched in red-shirted uniforms and with rifles in open displays of military force.

Republicans and Conservatives disputed the election returns. Republicans refused to count ballots from those areas where Conservatives had engaged in violence; Conservatives charged Republicans with fraud. Early in 1877 Hampton declared himself governor, won a questionable decision from the state supreme court sustaining his claim, and appointed the red-shirts as state militia to enforce his authority. Chamberlain called on national troops for protection and got them until matters could be straightened out. Meanwhile Conservatives and Republicans met in separate state legislatures.

The outcome depended on the action of the national government, because the Supreme Court had ruled that Congress or the President was to determine which of two competing state governments to recognize, and the President had performed that task on several occasions. Washington itself had been the scene of a bitter dispute over who had won the contested 1876 election, and the Republican candidate, Rutherford B. Hayes, had been declared the victor. South Carolina Republicans expected him to recognize their government. They were all the more certain because Hayes himself was inaugurated only because he had been credited with winning in South Carolina. His votes were based on the same election returns that Chamberlain, Elliott, and the other Republican claimants relied upon. But Hayes refused to sustain them. Instead, he announced he would withdraw federal troops and recognize whomever emerged the winner in the aftermath. The Republicans, lacking local armed forces to match Hampton's, had no choice but to give up the fight.

For Elliott, collapse of the Republican government in South Carolina was a personal as well as political disaster. Politics had been his life. It had brought him respect and financial rewards. With blacks again relegated to a subordinate position, subject to economic exploitation and unable to achieve financial independence, there was no way for Elliott to achieve similar success in another line of work. The minor patronage appointment he did get from the federal government in 1879 could not sustain him. His law firm foundered. He lost his beautiful Victorian home, went further into debt, and in 1882 was deprived of his government job. Completely adrift, Elliott eked out a living defending petty criminals before the New Orleans police courts. He died in 1884. Only a little over 40 years old at the time, he was as much a victim of Reconstruction as the black men killed in the Hamburg Massacre.

* * *

The end of Republican rule in North Carolina and South Carolina was typical of the whole South. By 1877 not a single Republican government was left. Blacks were rendered politically powerless first by fraud and violence, and then in the 1890s and 1900s by disfranchisement. Shortly thereafter, white Southerners set up a complex system of government-enforced discrimination against blacks. It was to keep them permanently powerless and exploited—until Civil Rights activism began to change conditions almost a century later.

At first many Northerners sympathized with the blacks. But by 1900 they too endorsed racial discrimination. Not all of them, to be sure. Not Albion Tourgée. He never changed his mind. Upon returning to the North, he championed racial equality in his books, lectures, and law practice. He died in 1905, near the nadir of post-Civil War American race relations. But his life, like that of Stevens, bore testimony that black leaders and sympathetic whites could work together to secure the fruits of emancipation—racial justice for all Americans.